AF571824

The Great National Project

A HISTORY OF THE CHESAPEAKE AND OHIO CANAL

By
WALTER S. SANDERLIN

EASTERN NATIONAL
FORT WASHINGTON, PENNSYLVANIA

Eastern National, Fort Washington, Pennsylvania 19034
Published by Eastern National, 2005
Eastern National provides quality educational products and services to the visitors to America's national parks and other public trusts.
ISBN 1-59091-049-4

Originally published: Baltimore: Johns Hopkins Press, 1946. (The Johns Hopkins University studies in historical and political science; ser. 64, no. 1)

Cover image: *Closing of Lock Gates on the C & O Canal*, Watercolor over Graphite on Watercolor Paper by John Louis Wellington, ca. late 1910s. Image used with permission from The Maryland Historical Society, Baltimore, Maryland.

To

W. M. G.

PREFACE

It is curious that in the unending quest for research topics and thesis subjects the history of the canal era in the United States has been so largely neglected in American historiography. Certainly no one will deny that river improvements and artificial waterways played an important role in the westward expansion and economic growth of the country in the early national period. The fortunes and misfortunes connected with the construction and operation of canals provide, moreover, a colorful episode in the social history of the nation in the nineteenth century. In spite of the obvious significance of the early waterways and the potential wealth of materials contained in their chronicles, surprisingly few volumes have been written about the canal era in American history. Individual canals have been almost entirely ignored—save for a few short articles tucked away almost apologetically in the journals of local historical societies.

As a consequence of this widespread apathy toward the history of waterways, the subject has suffered a kind of enforced oblivion. The lack of publicity for the canals has resulted in an indifference on the part of more general writers to the real significance of these improvements in the social and economic history of the country. This neglect by trained historians has left the story of the canals to the less skilled treatment of antiquarians and the reminiscences of aged natives. The subject has thus been reduced to the level of romantic nostalgia, even as most of the waterways themselves are now, in truth, merely relics. It is only necessary to point to the sharp contrast in the voluminous and comprehensive treatment of the railroad age and of individual railroads to bring home the unimportant position which the canals and canal era have held in the estimate of American historians.

The purpose of the present volume is to fill in a part of this gap by tracing the history of one of the major canal projects proposed in the early nineteenth century for the connection of East and West. Although the Chesapeake and Ohio Canal was never completed to the Ohio River and therefore never became a major east-west route, the story of this project does merit investigation. In its time this canal was something of a symbol in the campaign for improved communications with the West. Furthermore, the experiences of the Chesapeake and Ohio closely paralleled in many ways the trials and triumphs of the other waterways, especially the Erie and the Pennsylvania canals. The history of the improvment of the Potomac route, in which the canal is but one phase, has also interesting ramifications of a political and biographical nature. Finally there is in existence an almost complete file of the private records of the river improvement and canal companies which was available for this study without any restrictions. It is hoped, incidentally, that the publication of the present volume may help to redirect the attention of historians to the American canal era and encourage further investigations along the lines of this work.

The adequate treatment of the subject requires both an analytical study and a social history. The absence of earlier detailed accounts has indicated that the former should be met first. The limitations of space and the dictates of form have also necessitated the subordination of much of the social history of the waterway to the historical analysis of the canal's place in American life. Perhaps a more popular account of life along the old ditch will be possible at a later date.

The history of the Chesapeake and Ohio Canal grew out of a doctoral dissertation at the University of Maryland. It was made possible by the assistance of many persons in universities, libraries, and other institutions, and of the inhabitants of the valley communities along the line of the canal. It is possible to mention only a few of those who aided in the collection of materials and in the preparation of the manuscript, but the greatful appreciation of the writer is extended to all. The recognition of their willing cooperation and valuable assistance, however, in no way makes them responsible for the expressions of opinion or for any errors of fact which may appear in this study. Not is it intended to imply that the individuals named have always agreed with the author in his conclusions or in his handling of the subject.

An immeasurable debt is owed to Professor Wesley M. Gewehr who has been for the past decade a never-failing source of enlightenment, encouragement, and assistance. Dr. Gewehr and the other members of the Department of History at the University of Maryland, Dr. Frank Freidel and Dr. Kenneth Stampp in particular, read and discussed early drafts of the study and made many valuable suggestions for its improvement.

Professors Sidney Painter and Charles Barker of the Johns Hopkins University also read the entire manuscript and offered many helpful criticisms concerning the handling of the subject. Dr. Painter has generously extended the facilities of the "Studies" for the publication of the monograph. Miss Lilly Lavarello, of the Johns Hopkins University Department of History, provided invaluable assistance in preparing and reading proofs.

Among the members of the staffs of the several libraries and institutions who did so much to forward the work of research, the author wishes to express his thanks to Dr. Herman Kahn and Miss Margareth Jorgensen of the National Archives, to Miss Mary McColligan and Mrs. Margaret L. Beck of the Department of the Interior, to Mr. Edward Oswald, Clerk of the Circuit Court for Washington County, and to the author's father, Dr. George B. Sanderlin, of the Library of Congress.

Finally, he cannot express too highly his appreciation to his family for their patience and assistance during the past few years and to his colleagues and students whose interest and cooperation during the years of research and writing helped to smooth his path.

W. S.

Washington, Pennsylvania
1946

TABLE OF CONTENTS

Chapter I

THE PROBLEM AND ITS SETTING

The history of the Potomac River as a channel for trade falls logically into two major periods. In the first of these, primarily the seventeenth and eighteenth centuries, that section of the river below the fall line was the center of activity. Beginning in the eighteenth century, the rise of the new West brought the part of the stream above tidewater into prominence. After the emergence of the upper valley as a source of provisions and a market for Eastern goods, local entrepreneurs turned their attention to the problem of utilizing the advantages of the Potomac as a channel for the new trade. At first they were content for the most part to supplement and improve river navigation. In the nineteenth century, however, they turned to permanent, artificial means of transportation and communication. The climax of these later efforts was the inauguration of the Chesapeake and Ohio Canal and the Baltimore and Ohio Railroad in 1828. A brief summary of the settlement and growth of the Chesapeake Bay region will provide the necessary introduction to the study of the attempts to establish the Potomac as a major trade route to the West.

The Chesapeake Bay and its tributaries form one of the deeper penetrations of the Atlantic Ocean along the eastern coast of North America. In addition, nature has endowed the bay region with a central location, a temperate climate, and many miles of navigable waters more or less protected from the violence of the open sea. The area was thus well situated for the settlement and exploitation of its lands by European peoples in the seventeenth century. It is not surprising then that it became one of the earliest sites of English colonization on the mainland and a center for the expansion of British dominion in the New World. Other natural harbors along the Atlantic coast—Massachusetts Bay, the lower Hudson River, Delaware Bay and River, and the tidewater inlets of the southern colonies performed similar functions in their own regions.

The first permanent English settlement on the continent of

North America was made in 1607 at Jamestown on the banks of the James River, a tributary of the Chesapeake Bay. As soon as the security of this outpost was effected, other stockades sprang up on the James and neighboring streams in the Commonwealth of Virginia. The grant to Lord Baltimore of a tract of land north of the Potomac River was followed by settlements in the upper bay area, in the new colony of Maryland. The first site occupied under the auspices of the new proprietors was St. Mary's, on the Potomac, in 1634. Additional migrations from England and from Virginia soon began to fill up southern Maryland and to extend the settled area northward on both sides of the bay.

As the colonies spread out along the fringes of the Chesapeake and its tributaries an extensive trade with the mother country sprang up. The character of the land and the climate, the inclination of the settlers, the influence of British mercantile policy fostered the development of an agricultural economy in the colonies. The agrarian way of life and the extensive navigability of the bay and the rivers in turn tended to discourage the rise of a major port such as Philadelphia and New York. Instead, the entire area became a vast harbor with small landings scattered along the shores.

In the course of colonial expansion, the rivers emptying into the bay emerged as the principal arteries of trade. One of the largest and longest of these streams is the Potomac, which winds its way in an easterly direction between Maryland and Virginia for over two hundred miles above tidewater, and for over one hundred miles from the fall line to the bay. Settlements were made on both sides of the Potomac early in the seventeenth century. On the north bank, the Maryland colony spread westward along the river in the decades following the establishment of St. Mary's. On the opposite shore, the peninsula between the Potomac and the Rappahannock rivers which had been granted to Lord Hopton and his associates in 1649,[1] filled up gradually as it was divided and subdivided among the owners, their friends, and their successors. The entire valley soon took on the familiar pattern of large plantations, each

[1] Samuel M. Wilson, *The Ohio Company of Virginia, 1748-1798* (Lexington, Kentucky, 1926), p. 5. The peninsula was known as the Northern Neck (of Virginia).

with its own boat landing, which had characterized the bay colonies since the establishment of tobacco as the staple crop early in the seventeenth century.

Throughout the colonial period the Potomac continued to perform its function as a channel for the commerce between the plantations and the Old World. In this role, however, it was merely one of the many tidal estuaries of the bay, and it was by no means the most important. The character of the trade on its waters was largely determined by the nature of the local economy. Tobacco was the principal item shipped from the colonies in exchange for slaves, manufactures, spices, and other commodities needed by the plantations.

This type of commerce continued on the lower river long after that part of the stream above tidewater had become important. The decline of the tobacco plantations, which accompanied the exhaustion of the soil in the latter eighteenth and early nineteenth centuries, caused only a slight modification in the trade. Tidewater planters turned to the cultivation of wheat and corn, but they still required regular shipments of manufactures and the other necessities of an agrarian life. In fact, the eventual decline of commerce on the lower river was not so much the result of the passing of the tobacco plantations as it was the consequence of the rapid changes in transportation. The increasing size of the ships, the establishment of regular commercial routes and ports of call, and the rise of new trade relationships combined to make frequent stops at individual plantations more difficult and less economical. At the same time the improvement of roads and land transportation, and the growth of markets in the cities established at the fall line turned the attention of the planters inland.

In the meantime the area of settlement had spread westward. After the early colonists had taken up the more desirable lands in the tidewater region, all that remained there was the relatively inaccessible land farther back from the rivers. The dependence of the first settlers in the New World on the streams as a means of transportation and communication directed the course of expansion up the river valleys rather than away from the water. Thus the settled area soon stretched inland as far as the fall line. Finally the wave of migration moved beyond the tidewater region westward to the first range of mountains, still following the course of the rivers. The extension of the colonies into the Piedmont area brought into prominence the question of river improvements in order to eliminate the obstacle of the falls. It also promoted the establishment of cities near the head of tidewater to provide transfer facilities for the trade on the upper rivers.

Nor did the westward tide of migration stop at the first range of mountains. At the same time that the expansion of these early settlements was taking place, other colonists were penetrating the passes and valleys beyond. Beginning in Pennsylvania and extending in a southwesterly direction through Maryland and Virginia, the Appalachian mountain region is divided into two distinct ridges. The eastern range, commonly called the Blue Ridge Mountains, is relatively lower and narrower than the massive western range, the Allegheny Mountains. As such, it represented a much less formidable barrier to migration. Several passes and rivers penetrate the Blue Ridge providing direct access to the rich Cumberland and Shenandoah valleys beyond. Down these valleys spread many newcomers, filling up the fertile farmlands they found there. The gradual removal of the Indian threat by means of wars, treaties, and purchases facilitated this westward migration.

The fur trade provided another motive, besides the ever-present land-hunger of the colonists, for this extension of settlement into the valleys and mountains of the Appalachian region. The interest of Virginia and Pennsylvania trappers first turned to the Indian trade of the transmontane region in the eighteenth century. After 1744 it rapidly increased. The Treaty of Lancaster in that year marked the starting point of a general interest among English entrepreneurs in the Western trade. By this treaty the colonists came to a definite understanding with the Indians in regard to participation in the fur trade of a region extending as far west as the Ohio River. By the Treaty of Logstown, in 1748, these rights were extended to include the area from the forks of the Ohio to the Mississippi.[2]

For routes of trade, communication, and migration the early pioneers depended for the most part on the rivers and trails which penetrated the first range of mountains. In New York,

[2] Kenneth P. Bailey, *The Ohio Company of Virginia and the Westward Movement, 1748-1792* (Glendale, California, 1939), pp. 103, 106-107.

the Hudson and Mohawk valleys were the main route to the new West. In Pennsylvania, the Juniata River and Forbes Road provided the easiest access to the Western territories. To the south the Potomac, the James, and the South Carolina trails served settlers and trappers alike. Each one had its advantages and disadvantages. The central routes, in Pennsylvania and the Chesapeake Bay colonies, were shorter and served a greater number of settlers. On the other hand, the extreme northern and southern paths, in New York and South Carolina, had topographical advantages arising from their location at either end of the Appalachian Mountains.

Under the influence of the growing fur trade and Western settlements, the position of the Potomac as a commercial channel changed. For a while, the new role of the river in the Western trade supplemented its older function as a tributary of the bay. Eventuall, it surpassed the tidewater commerce in importance. The intercourse with the West which brought the upper stretch of the valley into prominence also introduced new articles of trade. Furs from the mountains passed down to the coast for transshipment to European ports; and wheat, corn, wood, livestock, and building materials began to find their way to the markets in the cities at the fall line. In return, textiles, firearms, hardware, and trinkets moved upstream to the settlers and the Indian traders. To facilitate this traffic, new towns sprang up at strategic points along the river, such as Harpers Ferry, at the junction of the Potomac and the Shenandoah, and later Wills Town (Fort Cumberland), at the mouth of Wills Creek.

The growth of the transmontane trade eventually focused all attention on the development of the Potomac as an effective route to the West. The Indian trade, the frontier settlements, the Ohio trade, and the Cumberland and West Virginia coal fields were sources of continuing interest to Eastern promoters, reviving periodically agitation for the improvement of the Potomac route. But the problem remained the same—how to establish a cheap, dependable means of transportation via the Potomac valley. It was to find an effective solution to this problem that the various projects for internal improvements in the valley were advanced.

The Potomac had many advantages which argued for its primacy among the major competitors for the Western trade.

Its greatest superiority lay in the fact that it was the shortest possible route between tidewater in the East and the head of navigation on the western waters. The distance from Washington to Pittsburgh via Wills Creek is 341 miles, while from Philadelphia to Pittsburgh the most convenient route was 394 miles, and from the Lakes to the Hudson at Albany was 362 miles.[3] The Potomac possessed an important strategic advantage in its central location (in terms of the original thirteen colonies) and in its termination in the East at the ultimate seat of the national government. It also had powerful support in its contention for primacy. In the colonial days it was backed by perhaps the most powerful and influential English colony on the mainland of North America—Virginia. In the national era it might, because of its location, expect equally strong support from the federal government.

To offset these marked advantages there were important natural obstacles to the successful establishment of the Potomac's supremacy. The possibilities of establishing an all-water route via the narrow, winding, and often precipitous river are clearly limited. In addition, the volume of water in the stream above the fall line is subject to great fluctuation because of the heavy run-off during the spring and autumn rains and the frequently severe drought conditions prevailing during the summer months. Finally, the height of the land mass between the Potomac and the southern branches of the Ohio presents a major obstacle for both land and water routes to the West. The most advantageous route, via Wills Creek, requires the attainment of an elevation of at least 1,900 feet.[4] This compares unfavorably with the 500-foot rise required for the route through New York State.[5]

[3] *Report of the Committee on Roads and Canals*, January 30, 1827, 19th Cong., 2d sess., House of Representatives, Report No. 90, Appendix 15, pp. 80-81; Seymour Dunbar, *History of Travel in America* (4 vols. in 1, New York, 1937), p. 799. The distances given are those for the Chesapeake and Ohio Canal, the Erie Canal, and the Pennsylvania Main Line of Public Works. If the Schuylkill Navigation is used instead of the Philadelphia-Columbia Railroad, the Pennsylvania route is much longer.

[4] See the map in the Appendix.

[5] Dunbar, p. 799. A comparison of the lockage required on the Erie Canal and the Chesapeake and Ohio Canal shows clearly the great obstacles which the mountain barrier presented to the success of the Potomac route. Even with a four-mile tunnel on the summit level far below the crest of the mountains,

In addition to these natural disadvantages, there were serious obstacles arising from the political and economic nature of the Potomac route. The river did not lie wholly within the limits of one state. On the contrary, the success of the central route required the cooperation of at least three states and the federal government (for the District of Columbia). Interstate rivalries and the reluctance of Congress to sponsor works of internal improvement in the early years of the national era contributed greatly to the failure of the attempt to establish the Potomac route. Because of the predominantly agricultural character of the region local fluid capital was too limited to finance adequately the proposed improvement. It was certainly insufficient to construct the three competing works which Maryland and Virginia undertook.[6]

Notwithstanding these obstacles which seemed to foreshadow the ultimate failure of any project to establish the Potomac route, there were no less than five major efforts to develop and improve the means of transportation in the upper valley. The first of these was by the Ohio Company (1749-1798), which established the route and blazed the trails over the mountains to the headwaters of the Youghiogheny and the Monongahela rivers. The second, by the Potomac Company (1784-1828), attempted to render the river travel cheaper and more dependable by a system of improvements including canals around the major falls and excavations in the bed of the stream. The third effort was the federally sponsored National Road, which began improvements at Cumberland in 1811, near the western end of the river, and extended them over the mountains to the Ohio at Wheeling, which it reached by 1817.[7] The fourth project was by the Chesapeake and Ohio Canal Company (1825-1828-1938), which substituted a permanent artificial canal for the system of river improvements constructed by the Potomac Company. The last organized effort was by the Balti-

the Chesapeake and Ohio required 3,258 feet of lockage, while the Erie called for only 688 feet. *Report of the Committee on Roads and Canals*, January 30, 1827, pp. 80-81.

[6] That is, the James River improvements and the James River and Kanawha Canal, the Potomac Company and the Chesapeake and Ohio Canal, and the Baltimore and Ohio Railroad.

[7] Archer B. Hulbert, *The Cumberland Road* ("Historic Highways of America," Vol. X, Cleveland, 1904), p. 54; Dunbar, p. 692.

more and Ohio Railroad Company (1827 to date) which sought to build an effective, all-weather, all-land transportation line by means of an artificial road of rails.

Although the full history of the attempt to establish the Potomac route to the West has not been written, there are volumes on most aspects of the subject. Kenneth Bailey, Samuel Wilson, and Herbert Leyland have studied the history of the Ohio Company.[8] John Pickell, Mrs. Cora Bacon-Foster, and Rear Admiral Homer R. Stanford have written accounts of the Potomac Company.[9] Thomas Searight and Archer B. Hulbert have published books on the National Pike.[10] George Washington Ward has a monograph on the origins of the Chesapeake and Ohio Canal project in the Johns Hopkins "Studies." [11] And Edward Hungerford has written the standard history of the Baltimore and Ohio, although it should be supplemented by Milton Reizenstein's able account in the "Studies" of the economic aspects of the early history of that railroad.[12]

Our intention in the following pages is to fill in the remain-

[8] Bailey, *The Ohio Company of Virginia and the Westward Movement, 1748-1792*; Samuel M. Wilson, *The Ohio Campany of Virginia, 1748-1798* (Lexington, Ky., 1926); Herbert T. Leyland, *The Ohio Company, A Colonial Corporation* (Cincinnati, 1921).

[9] John Pickell, *A New Chapter in the Early Life of Washington* (New York, 1856); Mrs. Cora Bacon-Foster, "Early Chapters in the Development of the Potomac Route to the West," *Proceedings of the Columbia Historical Society*, XV (1911); and Homer R. Stanford, "The Historic Potomac," a carbon copy of the manuscript of a speech delivered before the Newcomen Society, in National Capital Parks, File 1460 (Chesapeake and Ohio Canal), Section 1 (Department of Interior, Washington, D. C.). Although both the latter papers were later printed separately, Washington, 1912, and Princeton, 1940, respectively, the page references following are to the sources first mentioned.

[10] Hulbert, *The Cumberland Road*; Thomas Searight, *The Old Pike* (Uniontown, Pennsylvania, 1894).

[11] George Washington Ward, *The Early Development of the Chesapeake and Ohio Canal Project*, "Johns Hopkins University Studies in Historical and Political Science," Series XVII (1899), Nos. 9, 10, 11 (Baltimore, 1899). The following page citations, however, are to the original manuscript thesis deposited in the Johns Hopkins University Library. Brackets have been omitted from the page references although the thesis itself is not paged. The numbering adopted runs consecutively from the first page of the Introduction which has been taken as page one.

[12] Edward Hungerford, *The Story of the Baltimore and Ohio Railroad* (2 vols., New York, 1928); Milton Reizenstein, *The Economic History of the Baltimore and Ohio Railroad, 1827-1853*, "Johns Hopkins University Studies in Historical and Political Science," Series XV (1897), Nos. 7 and 8 (Baltimore, 1897).

ing gap by unfolding the history of the Chesapeake and Ohio Canal. In tracing the construction and operation of this project, we shall be especially concerned with five aspects of the story: (1) the canal as the culmination of the attempts to establish an all-water route to the West; (2) the construction of the waterway as a case study in the problems of canal-building; (3) the role of the Chesapeake and Ohio in the development of Maryland as an indication of the relations generally between the states and works of internal improvements; (4) the fortunes and misfortunes of the canal in terms of the larger economic and social movements in the country as a whole; and (5) the influence of the old ditch on the development of the Potomac valley.

Chapter II

PREDECESSORS OF THE CANAL

The first organized attempt to utilize the Potomac as a trade route to the West was by the Ohio Company.[1] This enterprise was established in 1749 to exploit the growing fur trade with the Indians and to share in the development of the rich valleys of the mountain region. It made considerable headway prior to the French and Indian War in spite of the competition of French and Pennsylvania trappers and their established routes of trade. After 1763, however, the fortunes of the Ohio Company declined in the face of renewed colonial competition and loss of royal favor. By the end of the American Revolution the company had ceased to be an important factor in the development of the Potomac route.

In the year in which the Ohio Company received its charter, the Board of Trade of England licensed no fewer than three enterprises to engage in the Western trade and in land activities.[2] One of these, the Loyal Company, had received its grant in 1745, but waited until 1749 for its charter. The second, the Ohio Company, obtained official approval in 1748 and was chartered in 1749. The third, an offshoot of the latter, was a patent issued to John Hanbury, a London capitalist, who was also connected with the second. Of the three the most significant and the most active was the Ohio Company.

This company included in its membership " some of the most opulent and respectable inhabitants of the colonies of Virginia

[1] The bibliography on the Ohio Company of Virginia is not very extensive. The three outstanding studies already mentioned (see above, p. 20, n. 8) should be supplemented by the following accounts of the leading persons associated with the enterprise: *Journal of Christopher Gist* (Pittsburgh, 1893); Albert T. Volwiler, *George Croghan and the Westward Movement* (Cleveland, 1926); Kenneth P. Bailey, *Thomas Cresap, Maryland Frontiersman* (Boston, 1944); Louis K. Koontz, *Robert Dinwiddie, his Career in American Colonial Government and Westward Expansion* (Glendale, California, 1941); and Nathaniel W. Stephenson and Hilary Dunn, *George Washington* (2 vols., New York, 1940), especially I, 35-67. Parts of Mrs. Bacon-Foster's study and Rear Admiral Stanford's paper also relate the history of the Ohio Company.

[2] Bailey, *The Ohio Company*, pp. 28-29, 66-67. This monograph will be cited hereafter as Bailey.

and Maryland."[3] To a surprising extent they were holders of the comparatively recent grants in the Northern Neck. Foremost among them were Thomas Cresap; George Fairfax; Robert Dinwiddie; Lawrence, Augustine, and George Washington; John, George, James, and John Francis Mercer; Thomas Lee; Richard Lee; and George Mason.[4] It is interesting to note that the Washingtons, the Mercers, and the Masons, three of the leading families of the Northern Neck, later produced the founders and directors of the Potomac Company and the Chesapeake and Ohio Canal Company. Thus there was a distinct personal continuity in the early history of the attempt to improve the Potomac route.

The activities of the Ohio Company were spread over a large part of what was then western Virginia, including sections of present-day Kentucky, West Virginia, and southwestern Pennsylvania.[5] Its greatest efforts were concentrated in the region of the Monongahela and Youghiogheny valleys, an area then in dispute between Virginia and Pennsylvania.[6] French and Pennsylvania trappers had been active in this region for some time, but comparatively few traders from the Chesapeake Bay colonies had been fully aware of the value of the fur trade and of the Potomac route. Foremost among those who had actively entered into the trade from Maryland and Virginia were the intrepid Thomas Cresap and Thomas Lee.[7] The early representatives of the bay colonies traded as individuals in the manner of their rivals.[8]

The Ohio Company now organized the activities of these trappers and entered into competition with the Pennsylvanians. Although the latter used every possible device to discredit the newcomers, the company, with the greater resources of an organized enterprise, began to make headway. The efforts of

[3] *Report of the Committee on Roads and Canals on the Chesapeake and Ohio Canal*, April 17, 1834, 23d Cong., 1st sess., House of Representatives, Report No. 414, p. 1.

[4] Bailey, pp. 35-36.

[5] Wilson, pp. 30 ff., emphasizes the activities of the company in the extreme western part of Virginia (present-day Kentucky and West Virginia). Bailey, on the other hand, concentrates exclusively upon its experiences in the upper Potomac region and in the lands of southwestern Pennsylvania.

[6] Bailey, pp. 116-122.

[7] Bacon-Foster, pp. 96-101; Stanford, p. 1.

[8] Bailey, p. 17.

the Pennsylvania traders to turn the Indians against the company representatives failed. Their arguments that the Ohio Company, which was by its charter both a land and a trading enterprise, was a threat to the security of the Indians proved ineffective.[9] On the other hand, the company succeeded in buying the services of some of the better Pennsylvania trappers, including George Croghan and William Trent.[10]

In addition to its trading privileges, the Ohio Company obtained rights of settlement in the disputed area. It promptly secured a large tract of land which it intended to sell to prospective settlers.[11] It also conducted land surveys for purposes of trade and settlement which contributed much to a better knowledge of the Potomac valley and the land between the Potomac and the Ohio. George Washington participated in a surveying mission for the company in 1749, and may have reached the mouth of Wills Creek.[12] In 1750 and 1751, Christopher Gist went up the river to Wills Creek, overland to the Monongahela, and down that stream to the Ohio. He continued along the latter as far as the falls of the river near the site of present-day Louisville, and then returned. In 1751 and 1752, he made another trip up the Potomac, concentrating this time, by request, on the more accessible region to the east of the Ohio.[13]

Under Lawrence Washington's guidance, in 1752, the company made a determined effort to induce immigrants to settle on its lands. In that year Christopher Gist and the Indian chief Half King signed a treaty at Logstown, permitting colonists to occupy the territory southeast of the Ohio River.[14] At the same time, Washington sought to interest a group of Pennsylvania Germans in settling on the newly acquired tract. The

[9] *Ibid.*, p. 111.

[10] *Ibid.*, pp. 71, 154. See also Volwiler, especially pp. 41-54. Volwiler stresses the independence of Croghan as a trader.

[11] *Report of the Committee on Roads and Canals*, April 17, 1834, p. 1. Some of the land purchased by the company for its sites was already in the possession of its own members; for example, Lord Fairfax owned the site of Wills Town. Bailey, p. 73.

[12] Stephenson and Dunn, I, 41; Bailey, p. 70. Washington also made other surveying trips after 1752, but not under a commission from the Ohio Company. Pickell, pp. 17-19 (1753-1754), 24-25 (1770, 1772, 1774), and 35-37 (1784).

[13] Bailey, pp. 88-96, 97-100. See also the *Journals of Christopher Gist.*

[14] Stanford, p. 3.

latter insisted that as part of the bargain they be relieved of the onerous duty of contributing to the established church. Washington died, however, before any agreement could be reached.[15] As its part, the Virginia Assembly passed three acts to facilitate the settlement of its western lands.[16] In 1752, it relieved its frontier inhabitants of the obligation to pay taxes. In 1754, it appropriated £10,000 for the expenses of providing military protection on its western borders. In 1766, it approved a grant of £200 for the improvement of the Braddock Road. Despite this encouragement, the Ohio Company apparently made no other sustained attempt, after the failure of Washington's scheme, to fulfill the requirements of its charter to settle colonists in the area.

Because trade was the primary reason for its organization, the company concentrated mainly on that part of its business. It established a regular route for the commerce to and from its western posts via the Potomac valley. The eastern terminus of the trail was Belhaven (Alexandria), on the Virginia side of the river just below the fall line. From there the goods were carried overland in wagons to the phantom town of Philae, about eighteen miles up the river at the upper end of Great Falls.[17] In this way the two most serious obstacles to the navigation of the Potomac, Little Falls and Great Falls, were avoided. From Philae the traders used the river to the mouth of Wills Creek, which was at that time, as it was later, considered the upper limit of satisfactory navigation on the Potomac. At Wills Creek the company built a storehouse and fort in 1749, and changed the name of the site from Wills Town to Charlotteburg, and later to Fort Cumberland.[18]

[15] Bailey, p. 80.

[16] Stanford, p. 4.

[17] Bacon-Foster, p. 101. The town of Philae never really developed. See also *Report of the Committee on Roads and Canals*, April 17, 1834, p. 2. As a general rule, the modern spelling and names of towns, rivers, and places will be used: Potomac, Catoctin, Antietam, Hagerstown, Pittsburgh, Youghiogheny, and Conogocheague, instead of the numerous early forms such as Patowmack, Kitoctin, Anti Eatum, Hagarstown or Elizabeth Town, etc. The most common contemporary spelling will be used for personal names, however. This procedure seems best to satisfy the desire for accuracy, consistency, and easy identification.

[18] *Report of the Committee on Roads and Canals*, April 17, 1834, pp. 1-2; Stanford, pp. 2-4; Bailey, pp. 76-78.

From this point the earliest route led over the mountains to the three forks of the Youghiogheny, a spot known for obvious reasons as Turkey Foot.[19] The trappers laid out a second warehouse and town just below the junction of the Youghiogheny and the Monongahela, at the mouth of Chartier Creek, near the site of present-day McKeesport.[20] In 1752, Nemacolin, an Indian scout in the company's service, blazed a new trail from Wills Creek to the Monongahela at the mouth of Red Stone Creek. Here, on the banks of the river near the site of modern Brownsville, the traders built another storehouse, first called the Hangard (or Hangyard), later Red Stone Old Fort, and later still Monongahela.[21] It was Nemacolin's path which General Braddock enlarged to a wagon road on his ill-fated campaign against Fort Duquesne.[22] It was later followed by the National Pike and currently by the National Old Trails Highway.

By 1756, the fortunes of the Ohio Company had reached their zenith. The French and Indian War from 1755 to 1763 brought widespread destruction to the company's property and trade in the West. After the war, the removal of the French threat to the British position in America led to a decline in official support for the company from the English government. As long as England needed aid against the French in America it was inclined to look with favor upon the Ohio Company. Now the relationship between the government and the company was reversed.[23] The company had also lost many of its more aggressive leaders through death and the many reorganizations it had undergone At the same time other enterprises rose to challenge its position. The latter years of the company, from 1764 to 1792, were filled with numerous futile petitions to the crown and many legal quarrels with new rivals.[24]

The decline of the Ohio Company after the French and Indian War was not accompanied by a general lapse of interest

[19] Bailey, p. 153.

[20] Stanford, p. 3.

[21] Bailey, pp. 153-154: The French destroyed Red Stone Old Fort in 1754. The city of Brownsville was established on the site in 1785. Wilson, p. 20; Stanford, pp. 3-4.

[22] Stanford, p. 3; see also *Report of the Committee on Roads and Canals*, April 17, 1834, p. 2.

[23] Bailey, pp. 11-12.

[24] *Ibid.*, pp. 253-259, 269.

in the West or in the Potomac route. In fact the opposite is nearer the truth. The loss of favor by the company, the growth of a speculative spirit in the colonies, and the focusing of attention on a relatively safer West gave rise to many schemes to exploit the region.[25] A similar increase of interest in the improvement of the Potomac River had occurred in the pre-Revolutionary years. No less than three attempts were made to improve the navigation of that river. In the 1760's, the Johnson brothers of Frederick, Maryland, proposed to form a company for that object.[26] In 1772, George Washington, who had discouraged the Johnsons' scheme, secured a charter from Virginia for a company to achieve the same goal. Maryland failed to confirm the act, and the second effort failed.[27] Also in 1772, John Ballendine advertised a scheme for opening the river which had the support of powerful interests in the colonies and in England. His plans for canals and channel improvements were widely publicized in London in 1773.[28] However, the combined efforts of the Ohio Company, Thomas Walpole, Samuel Wharton, Benjamin Franklin, and others in behalf of the proposal were of no avail.[29] Thus, on the eve of the Revolu-

[25] The Ohio Company encountered the competition of such Pennsylvania-sponsored land enterprises as the Vandalia scheme (1756 ff.), the Indiana project (1768 ff.), and the revival of the Vandalia proposals by the Walpole Company in the late sixties. The latter organization, under the guidance of Samuel Wharton, secured a grant from England and made overtures to the agent of the Ohio Company, George Mercer, Jr., for a merger of the two enterprises, but failed to convert the leaders of that undertaking in the colonies. Bailey, pp. 237-238, 260-262, 269; Bacon-Foster, p. 115. See also, George E. Lewis, *The Indiana Company, 1763-1798. A Study in Eighteenth Century Frontier Land Speculation and Business Venture* (Glendale, California, 1941).

[26] Bacon-Foster, pp. 110-111.

[27] *Ibid.*, pp. 111-114; the letter is reprinted in full. See also Washington to Boucher, May 4, 1772, John C. Fitzpatrick, ed., *Writings of George Washington* (37 vols., Washington, D. C., 1931-1944), III, 81; Stephenson and Dunn, I, 304; Pickell, pp. 30-31; Stanford, p. 5; Bacon-Foster, pp. 116-117; and Hugh Taggart, "Old Georgetown," *Proceedings of the Columbia Historical Society*, XI (1907), 176-177.

[28] Copies of these estimates and proposals are filed among the Potomac Company records in the National Archives (Washington, D. C.). They are printed in the *Report of the Committee on Roads and Canals*, January 30, 1827, Appendix 2, pp. 23-28. See also Bacon-Foster, pp. 117-123.

[29] *Report of the Committee on Roads and Canals*, April 17, 1834, p. 2. Bacon-Foster, pp. 118-119. Franklin assured the Lords Commissioners of Trade that Alexandria was the best and cheapest seaport for the Ohio trade.

tion, plans for the improvement of the Potomac were still without success.

Despite the rapid decline of the enterprise after the French and Indian War, the activities of the Ohio Company were significant in the history of the Potomac valley and of the colonies as a whole. It has been pointed out that the organization was itself a transitional step between the old proprietary companies engaged primarily in trade and the new speculative enterprises interested in the purchase and sale of western lands as well.[30] The operations of the company also helped to focus the attention of the East on the inland empire. Although the latter consequence of the company's activities was not restricted merely to the Chesapeake Bay region, the Potomac did get off to a good start in its competition with the other routes for the Western trade. The same families which were active in the Ohio Company's affairs subsequently produced the men, George Washington, John Mason, and Charles F. Mercer, who promoted and directed the fortunes of the later companies which sought to establish the Potomac as a major artery to the Ohio valley. On the other hand, the experience of this undertaking gave an early indication of two obstacles to the success of the Potomac Company and the Chesapeake and Ohio Canal Company: the threat of effective competition from the Pennsylvania route, and the danger of internal weakness resulting from the conflicting interests and influence of local politics in company affairs. Thus the Ohio Company both provided the basis for the development of the Potomac and indicated two of the most serious threats to its success.

The place of the dormant Ohio Company in the exploitation of the Potomac route after the Revolution was taken by the Potomac Company.[31] This enterprise, organized in 1785, promoted a series of river improvements designed to extend the effective navigation of the Potomac to the highest possible point, thus bringing the West within easy reach of the Eastern merchants. After pushing the major part of its work to com-

[30] Bailey, p. 285.

[31] The bibliography of secondary works on the Potomac Company is as limited as it is for the Ohio Company. Of the three studies mentioned above (see p. 20, n. 9) Mrs. Bacon-Foster's is by all odds the best. Pickell's volume is sound as far as it relates the history of the company. Rear Admiral Stanford's paper is based largely on Mrs. Bacon-Foster's work.

pletion by 1802, the company succumbed to the pressure of financial and physical difficulties and followed the Ohio Company into inactivity and failure.

The Potomac Company was chartered by the Assemblies of Maryland and Virginia in 1784-1785 as a result of the revival of interest in the development of the Potomac route.[82] The conclusion of the Revolutionary War had permitted merchants, adventurers, and a few far-seeing statesmen to turn their attention once more to the lure of the West. The Treaty of Paris ending the successful struggle for independence had confirmed the claims of the seaboard colonies to western lands, at least as far as the Mississippi River. Indirectly it reaffirmed the rights of individuals and companies in this region under grants from the former colonies. In effect, the peace treaty transferred the whole question of special privileges in the area from England to the state legislatures where they would be subject to the pressures of local politics. There was nothing to hinder the operation of these influences, which would affect the future development of the entire West. This fact is an important key to the history of internal improvements generally, and the development of the Potomac route in particular, in the early national period.

According to the terms of its charter, the purpose of the Potomac Company was the opening of the Potomac River to the highest point of permanent navigation. The minimum goal was Fort Cumberland, at which point a connection would be made with the improved Braddock Road, providing access to the rapidly filling lands tapped by the Ohio and its tributaries. The efforts of the Potomac Company were later imitated by New York, Pennsylvania, and southern Virginia, each of which sought to develop or improve its own highway. Unlike some of these competitors, the Potomac route was neither a new proposal nor a product of local state pride. It had already served the Ohio Company traders for almost forty years, and

[82] Act of the General Assembly of Virginia, passed October, 1784; Act of the General Assembly of Maryland, passed November Session, 1784. Texts of these acts are available in several pamphlets prepared by the Chesapeake and Ohio Canal Company, and in *Documents Relating to the Chesapeake and Ohio Canal,* July 11, 1840, 26th Cong., 1st sess., Senate, Document No. 610, pp. 76-85, 101-110.

during the Revolution it had been one of the three major paths leading into the trans-Allegheny West.[33]

The successful launching of the company was primarily the result of one man's efforts and influence. George Washington had long been interested in the improvement of the Potomac, and was completely convinced of the practicability and superiority of the route it provided. Indeed it has been said with considerable justification that the project had become almost an obsession, second only perhaps to his interest in the future of the Union.[34] Before the war, Augustine and Lawrence Washington had been actively associated with the Ohio Company. George Washington himself had made several inspection trips to the West and was speculating in lands on the Monongahela.[35] After his glorious role in the Revolution, his influence in national affairs and particularly in Virginia and Maryland reached its zenith. Nothing these two states could do for him seemed too much. When Washington asserted his belief in the great possibilities of the Potomac route, Virginia legislators promptly passed an act incorporating the Potomac Company and subscribing to one hundred and twenty shares of its capital stock, fifty of which were placed in the hero's name.[36] When Mary-

[33] Bacon-Foster, pp. 123-124.

[34] Alexander Lane, "Government Acquires Historic Canal—to Become National Park," MS, National Capital Parks, File 1460 (Chesapeake and Ohio Canal), Section 2. "Some students of General Washington's life feel that his long belief in the feasibility of connecting the Monongahela and the Potomac hovered closely to an obsession. Private letters as well as existing public records tend to confirm this." See also Clark, "Historical and Other Notes on the Chesapeake and Ohio Canal," a typewritten report dated March 12, 1930, in Informational Material in *re* Chesapeake and Ohio Canal, Records of the Rock Creek and Potomac Parkway Commission, Department of Interior Archives (National Archives, Washington, D. C.); and Stephenson and Dunn, II, 207-209, 211-212.

[35] Pickell, pp. 17-19 (1753-1754), 24-25 (1770, 1772, 1774), 35-37 (1784); Stephenson and Dunn, II, 191-192.

[36] Washington to Benjamin Harrison, Governor of Virginia, cited in Pickell, pp. 38-39; Stanford, p. 6; Act of Virginia, passed October, 1784, *Documents Relating to the Chesapeake and Ohio Canal*, July 11, 1840, pp. 85-86. Washington declined the gift and requested that the shares subscribed in his name be assigned to some public purpose such as the establishment of a national university. (Washington to the Governor of Virginia, Pickell, pp. 63-64, and Stephenson and Dunn, II, 202.) Virginia acceded to his request by an act passed in October, 1786, directing the shares to be assigned to such public object as Washington should designate. (*Documents Relating to the Chesa-*

land, torn by internal dissension, hesitated to pass an act confirming the Virginia law, a visit from George Washington swept the Assembly off its feet. Maryland affirmed the charter and subscribed to fifty shares in the new company.[37]

The enterprise was formally organized in May, 1785, with George Washington as its president.[38] It immediately embarked on an energetic though cautious program to complete the improvement of the river within the five years permitted by its charter. The intention was to deepen the channel and cut canals around the falls to permit the passage of boats capable of carrying fifty barrels of flour in the driest seasons. That it was still endeavoring to accomplish its purpose in 1820 is evidence of the nature of the region and the imperfect knowledge of it in 1785, rather than the result of an indifferent attitude on the part of the directors.

From the very beginning the company encountered obstacles which made the progress of its work much more difficult than had been anticipated and which closely foreshadowed those later experienced by the Chesapeake and Ohio Canal Company. For this reason it is worthwhile to examine briefly the nature of these problems and the solutions which the Potomac Company sought to apply.

Some of the difficulties, such as politics, competent supervision, labor, etc., were always present. Local politics have

peake and Ohio Canal, July 11, 1840, pp. 86-87.) On the alacrity and unanimity with which the Assembly followed the General's advice, see Pickell, p. 42.

[37] Stephenson and Dunn, II, 197, 211; Bacon-Foster, p. 133; Pickell, pp. 43-46; Act of the General Assembly of Maryland, November Session, 1784; *Documents Relating to the Chesapeake and Ohio Canal*, July 11, 1840, pp. 101-110. See also the letter from Madison to Jefferson, January 9, 1785, Worthington C. Ford, ed., *Writings of Washington* (14 vols., New York, 1889-1893), X, 415n-418n. The meeting between the Virginia and Maryland Commissioners began a series of conferences which culminated in the Philadelphia convention to amend the Articles of Confederation, in which the new federal Constitution was written. Bacon-Foster, p. 142.

[38] Proceedings of the Stockholders of the Potomac Company (May 17, 1785), Letter Book A, p. 1. The minutes of the early meetings of the stockholders are recorded in a volume entitled "Letter Book A." The annual meetings were held in August, and will be cited as Annual Meeting (year). Special meetings of the stockholders sometimes occurred; they will be cited as Special Meeting (date). These proceedings as well as the Annual Reports, correspondence, Proceedings of President and Directors, etc., are all in manuscript form and are deposited in the Department of Interior Archives (National Archives, Washington, D. C.).

already been mentioned in connection with the acts incorporating the company.[39] They continued to influence its affairs throughout its existence. In Virginia, the proponents of the James River improvement hindered aid from that state. On the other side, the city of Baltimore looked askance at Maryland's support of a scheme which would benefit the rival ports of Georgetown and Alexandria.

Another constant problem was the acquisition of the services of a skilled engineer to superintend the construction and operation of the works. An appeal published in Baltimore and Philadelphia newspapers failed to bring a satisfactory response, and local talent of doubtful quality was tried.[40] James Rumsey, an inventor, who had fascinated Washington with an experimental steamboat in 1784, was the first incumbent.[41] In 1786, he resigned in a quarrel with his assistant, Richardson Stewart, and the latter succeeded him. Then followed in rapid order: James Smith in 1788, Captain Christopher Myers in 1796, Leonard Harbaugh in 1797, Thomas Leoffler in 1798, and Harbaugh again in 1802.[42] Fortunately, George Gilpin, one of the directors, had some ability as an engineer.[43]

The appeal for laborers was equally unsuccessful. There were simply not enough hands in the predominantly agricultural region of the Potomac valley to supply the large requirements of the project. Advertisements published in Philadelphia, Baltimore, and Alexandria newspapers produced unsatisfactory

[39] See above p. 31, n. 37, and also Washington to Jefferson, March 29, 1784. Ford, X, 375-380 (quoted in part in Stephenson and Dunn, II, 531-532, p. 200, n. 23).

[40] Proceedings of the President and Directors of the Potomac Company, Journal A, p. 4 (July 1, 1785) (MS, National Archives, Washington, D. C.). This source will be cited as Proceedings of Directors.

[41] *Ibid.*, A, 5 (July 14, 1785); Stephenson and Dunn, II, 206; Bacon-Foster, p. 134. Washington was a passenger on a later trial run, March 14, 1786, Stanford, p. 6.

[42] Proceedings of Directors, A, 20-27 (October 2 and 3, 1786), 33 (June 2, 1788), 66-67 (January 4, 1796), 100-102 (May 2, 1797), 134-135 (June 6, 1798), 239 (May 26, 1802).

[43] Gilpin made a survey of the entire river and frequently acted as a supervisor. Annual Meeting (1790), Letter Book A[15]; (1792), [20]. See also *Report of the Committee of the District of Columbia to whom were Referred Sundry Memorials from the Inhabitants of Pennsylvania, Maryland, and Virginia, Praying the Aid of the Federal Government towards the Improvement of the Navigation of the river Potomac*, May 3, 1822, 17th Cong., 1st sess., House of Representatives, Report No. 111, pp. 14-17.

results.[44] Whenever the company undertook any large-scale construction, the labor problem had to be solved first. When the work began to lag for lack of sufficient force, the company became desperate. It experimented in turn with the use of indentured servants from ships in Philadelphia and Baltimore,[45] and with Negro slaves from the neighboring countryside.[46] The indentured servants, often called the Blue Boys and the Red Boys according to their ships, proved as unruly as the free laborers had been. The company unsuccessfully tried various ways to control them and prevent desertions, usually involving the shaving of heads and eyebrows. The Irish servants were said to be especially troublesome.[47] Although the use of Negro slaves also had its drawbacks, it was continued for some time, for lack of any other way to secure labor. As late as 1811, the directors authorized the superintendent to hire workers, offering them "as high wages as are given by others, or even more."[48] The problem of obtaining food for the hands at a reasonable cost was solved by contracting with enterprising farmers in the valley to supply the meat, flour, and spirits at a fixed charge per ration.[49] In the matter of labor supply, wages, and the cost of provisions, the Potomac Company's experiences were a valuable lesson for the Chesapeake and Ohio Canal Company. The latter thought the solution lay in contracting with others for the work of construction instead of undertaking

[44] Proceedings of Directors, A, 2-3 (May 31, 1785). The daily rations included: 1 lb. of salt pork, 1¼ lb. of salt beef, or 1½ lb. of fresh beef or mutton, 1½ lb. of flour or bread, and three gills of rum. *Ibid.*, p. 6 (July 14, 1785).

[45] *Ibid.*, p. 10 (September 9, 1785), 11-12 (September 26, 1784), 85-86 (October 5, 1796); Bacon-Foster, p. 162.

[46] Proceedings of Directors, A, 14 [12] (October 18, 1785), 42 (November 5, 1792), 66 (December 22, 1795), 207-208 (December 17, 1800); Thomas Johnson to Washington, September, 1785, Bacon-Foster, p. 161; also 163, 176; Stanford, p. 10.

[47] Proceedings of Directors, A, 10 (September 9, 1785); Bacon-Foster, pp. 161-163; Stanford, p. 10. Mrs. Bacon-Foster reprints several notices from local newspapers reporting runaways, for example, Maryland *Chronicle*, February 22, June 21, July 10, 1786; Alexandria *Gazette*, January 1, 1786.

[48] President and Directors to Josias Thompson, July 24, 1811, Directors' Journal B, 101. (The correspondence cited is all in manuscript form in the National Archives unless otherwise noted.)

[49] Proceedings of Directors, A, 15-16 (February 1 and 2, 1786), 76 (May 6, 1796), 335 (August 28, 1805).

the task itself as had its predecessor. It soon learned that the labor problem was not to be solved so simply.

In addition to these three major problems there were many lesser ones which were irregular in occurrence and usually of short duration. The latter included unexpected obstacles to construction, for example, the discovery of solid rock in the excavations at Great Falls and the obstruction of navigation by many large boulders in the river bed. Other hindrances to navigation—floods and droughts—threatened to defeat the purposes of the enterprise. Above all, shortly after work began the company encountered financial difficulties which soon overshadowed all its other troubles.

The construction of the Potomac Company's improvements falls readily into three major periods. Between 1785 and 1802, the work progressed most rapidly. The company concentrated mainly on digging canals around the falls of the Potomac. From 1802 to 1816, financial considerations were more important. The limited resources at the disposal of the directors permitted only minor excavations to clear out the bed of the main river and to improve the larger branches. After 1816, the affairs of the company became more or less stagnant, and attention shifted to other projects for the improvement of the Potomac route.

The company began its work with all the enthusiasm of a new enterprise in which high and confident hopes were embodied. It commenced operations on all five of the major falls in the Potomac which were to be passed by canals. Of course, this did not lessen the acuteness of the labor shortage. Nevertheless, by 1792 the three canals around the uppermost rapids, House's, Payne's (Shenandoah), and Seneca Falls, had been completed.[50] At Little Falls and Great Falls, the only ones which required locks, the work was much more difficult. The construction of the canal around the former moved along about as rapidly as the supply of labor permitted. The lock pits were dug and wooden locks erected on the Maryland side of the river in a hasty and impermanent fashion. In this manner the work was finished in 1795.[51] The directors resolved to locate

[50] Annual Report of the President and Directors (1792), Letter Book A [19]. Cited hereafter as Annual Report (Year).

[51] Annual Report (1794), Letter Book A [26]; (1798), A [32].

the canal and locks at Great Falls on the Virginia side of the stream. This proved to be an unfortunate decision, for after operations were well advanced the engineer discovered that the eastern end of the canal would have to be cut through solid rock.[52] Besides being an engineering task of no mean proportions, it required the employment of a large number of skilled laborers and consequently heavy expenditures.[53]

After the company had exhausted almost all its financial resources, the completion of the works at Great Falls was subordinated to the more immediate problem of securing the $40,000 which, according to the best estimates, was needed to finish the locks. The directors resolved not to resume operations until sufficient funds were available to insure the completion of the locks at Great Falls, but they were unable to obtain loans in sums sufficient to warrant renewing construction.[54] In order to provide the means to meet the ordinary expenses of the enterprise and to begin accumulating the $40,000 the directors applied to the Assemblies of Maryland and Virginia for permission to collect tolls on produce using the river, as if the locks at Great Falls were already finished. To justify the adoption of this irregular procedure, the company agreed to transport the goods around the rapids by wagon at its own expense and to deliver them at an inclined plane near the lower end of the falls. Under this arrangement the states granted the permission requested.[55] The tolls collected, however, were far below the amount needed to begin new operations at Great Falls. The directors used the receipts from tolls to employ work gangs in the bed of the river removing obstacles to navigation above and below the rapids.

By 1799, company affairs seemed to have come to a standstill, and the company itself was on the verge of failure. At this critical point, the state of Maryland stepped in and

[52] *Ibid.* (1796), A [36]; Bacon-Foster, pp. 156, 185-186. The annual reports after 1796 are entered in proper chronological sequence among the proceedings of the directors.

[53] Annual Report (1798), Directors' Journal A, 128.

[54] Annual Meeting (1797), Directors' Journal A, 113; (1798), 143-144.

[55] Report of the Directors to a Special Meeting (February 8, 1798), Directors' Journal A, 128; Act of the Maryland Assembly, November Session, 1797, *Documents Relating to the Chesapeake and Ohio Canal*, July 11, 1840, pp. 117-118.

breathed new life into the enterprise by an additional subscription to one hundred shares of capital stock at £130 per share.[56] The Board of Directors promptly ordered the resumption of work on the locks at Great Falls. In 1802, the canal was completed, and the immediate objective of the Potomac Company reached.[57] The Potomac River was now navigable for approximately two hundred and twenty miles, from the mouth of Savage River to tidewater.[58]

After the completion of the locks at Great Falls, the company concentrated on the improvement of navigation in the river bed and on the major branches. The problem of clearing a safe channel in the river bed itself, of sufficient depth to permit the passage of boats capable of carrying fifty barrels of flour in the driest seasons, remained unsolved. Therefore, the terms of the charter had not been fully complied with. Under these circumstances, the directors confidently undertook the deceptive task before them. Two work gangs, varying in size from twenty to thirty men each, were kept constantly employed in the river when the water was low enough to permit operations. At other times, for the sake of economy, they were used to quarry stone for the new locks at Little Falls to replace the wooden ones.[59]

The completion of the major work at Great Falls permitted the company to turn some of its attention to the improvement of the principal branches of the Potomac. There had already been several proposals to begin the work on the largest tributary, the Shenandoah River, during the earlier period. Without funds even to complete the locks and canals on the main river the directors had done nothing at that time.[60] After 1802,

[56] Special Meeting (December 10, 1799), Directors' Journal A, 168. See also *Documents Relating to the Chesapeake and Ohio Canal*, July 11, 1840, p. 116.

[57] Annual Report (1802), Directors' Journal A, 246. The locks were a real engineering feat; they were described in European engineering journals. Bacon-Foster, p. 156.

[58] John Mason to the Secretary of the Treasury, January 20, 1808, Directors' Journal B, 26. The Potomac was navigable for 218 miles, 350 yards, including canals, above tidewater.

[59] Proceedings of Directors, A, 258 (June 20, 1803); Annual Report (1802), Directors' Journal A, 249-250; (1803), A, 268.

[60] Annual Meeting (1792), Letter Book A [20]; Annual Report (1795), Letter Book A [33]; (1796), A [37-38]; (1797), Directors' Journal A, 111-112.

the directors undertook the heavy part of the projected improvements on the Shenandoah. In this endeavor, as in the development of the other branches of the Potomac, the company was assisted by limited local support. As the first step, in September, 1803, the Board ordered the necessary surveys and land condemnations to be made.[61] The major obstacles to the navigation of the Shenandoah were five falls near the junction with the Potomac. These were eventually passed by canals and locks.[62] The work was then reduced to clearing the bed of the river, as it was in the Potomac. By 1808, John Mason, then a director of the company, was able to report that the Shenandoah had been rendered navigable for a distance of two hundred miles, via the South Fork.[63] Like the improvements on the Potomac, those on the Shenandoah left much to be desired.

In the meantime, the Board also sought to improve other branches on the main river. It considered at one time or another, the Cacapon and the South Branch in Virginia, and the Monocacy, the Antietam, and the Conogocheague on the Maryland side. Limited resources and often total absence of local support prevented the development of all these projects. The Monocacy and the Conogocheague eventually were opened for forty and fifteen miles respectively, and some work was done on the Antietam.[64]

On the whole, the attempt to improve the branches of the Potomac was more harmful than helpful. It exhausted the company's resources without contributing measurable returns. Furthermore, it diverted the directors' attention from the pri-

[61] Proceedings of Directors, A, 271-272 (September 14, 15, October 8, 1803); Annual Report (1804), Directors' Journal A, 302.

[62] Annual Report (1806), Directors' Journal A, 355-356; (1807), Directors' Journal B, 7-8; John Mason to the Secretary of the Treasury, January 20, 1808, Directors' Journal B, 22-23.

[63] John Mason to the Secretary of the Treasury, January 20, 1808, Directors' Journal B, 26. Farmers on the North Fork later offered to advance labor and capital to improve it, but nothing was done. Proceedings of Directors, B, 151-153 (November 8, 1812).

[64] Mason to the Secretary of the Treasury, January 20, 1808, Directors' Journal B, 26; Mason to Bernard Peyton, Secretary of the Virginia Board of Public Works, December 9, 1817, Directors' Journal B, 342; Proceedings of Directors, B, 116-117 (December 17, 1811), 207 (March 2, 1814); Annual Report (1812), Directors' Journal B, 140; (1813), B, 176-177; (1814), B, 220.

mary purpose of the enterprise, that is, the improvement of the Potomac as a route to the West. By 1816, the company was concentrating almost exclusively on the exploitation of the Potomac valley and especially on the Shenandoah trade. In line with this changing emphasis, the directors restricted the gangs working in the bed of the Potomac to that stretch of the river below Harpers Ferry and in the Shenandoah to the section of the stream between Harpers Ferry and the forks of the river.

The company left no stone unturned in its desperate efforts to raise sufficient funds to complete the projected improvement of the Potomac. It borrowed heavily from local banks, and it repeatedly petitioned the Assemblies of Maryland and Virginia for further aid. The appeals to Maryland were successful, for in 1814 the state again came to the rescue with a loan.[65] The company also took advantage of an act of the Maryland Assembly which had been passed at its own request, permitting lotteries.[66]

The business of the lottery, which occupied much of the attention of the directors between 1810 and 1818, provides an interesting interlude in the history of the Potomac Company. The lottery never did prove very popular, and the tickets sold slowly despite incentives to the agents in the form of commissions and bounties.[67] Many of the sales that were eventually effected were made on credit, payable within thirty days after the drawing. Nevertheless the drawing began, and fortunately it went favorably to the company's interest in the early stages. The first-class drawing netted $15,134.41. The second-class lottery proved disastrous, however, and the company lost $14,648.38.[68] The third-class lottery was never drawn. Thus the whole lottery raised only $486.03, instead of the $300,000 anticipated. It consumed the greater part of eight years and involved the company in long and costly litigation. The lottery

[65] Proceedings of Directors, B, 200-203 (February 16, 1814).

[66] *Ibid.*, p. 65 (March 6, 1810); Bacon-Foster, p. 200.

[67] William Hartshorne, Treasurer, to Charles Lewis, July 1, 1811, Letter Book C [32]. A quarter cask of Madeira was given as an award for services in connection with the sale of lottery tickets.

[68] Proceedings of Directors, B, 361 (May 16, 1818). For a detailed account of the drawing, see the "Running Book" of the lottery, containing dates of drawings, numbers drawn, and prizes awarded, in the records of the Potomac Company.

was apparently the final blow to the Potomac Company's hopes. Its failure brought to an end sustained efforts by the directors to improve Potomac navigation.

The course of company fortunes in the middle years of its existence left its immediate aims and future policy indefinite. In the beginning of the final period, this uncertainty increased. The creation of a Board of Public Works by the Virginia Assembly in 1816, which ushered in this final period, was a much more serious threat to the company's welfare. The lottery was just drawing to its dismal close, and the work in progress was limited to the replacement of the old locks at Little Falls, which was completed in 1818.[69] Projects for competing works in the Potomac valley, financial difficulties, and the failure to complete the improvement of the Potomac River cast a heavy shadow over company affairs in the years from 1816 to 1828. On the whole, the last period was one of stagnation, or more accurately, somnolence, from which the company roused only to resist attacks upon its vested rights in the Potomac valley.

Except for sporadic efforts to keep existing canals and locks in repair, work on the main river came to an end. The efforts to open the navigation of the branches were already at a complete standstill. The Potomac Company had surrendered all rights to the improvement of the Shenandoah to the New Shenandoah Company which had been formed by local interests in 1815.[70] Although it had spent over $729,000 on the improvement of the Potomac by 1822,[71] the company still had not fulfilled the charter stipulation requiring the establishment of permanent navigation for boats capable of carrying fifty barrels of flour.

The financial condition of the Potomac Company deteriorated rapidly after the failure of the lottery. Debts continued to increase, until the annual profit from the operation of the works was not sufficient to pay the interest due. By 1822, these debts

[69] Annual Report (1818), Directors' Journal B, 367. The repair and replacement of the locks had taken five years and cost $64,176.17. (*Ibid.*, p. 377, Table No. 5.) In the meantime, the old locks had finally caved in, July 11, 1817. (*Ibid.*, [1817], Directors' Journal B, 322-323.)

[70] Proceedings of Directors, B, 233-236 (June 24, 1815); 243-246 (October 31, 1815).

[71] John Mason to the Virginia Commissioners, December 20, 1822, Directors' Journal C, 4. The amount expended on construction was $729,387.29.

amounted to over $175,000.[72] Thus the company was stripped of all means to continue the work on the river, and at the same time, its dismal financial condition discouraged any new investments by public or private interests. In this way two blows were struck against its future hopes and prospects. Together they proved fatal.

The trade on the Potomac in the latter years of the eighteenth and early years of the nineteenth centuries was largely agricultural in character. Corn, wheat, flour, livestock, whisky, and meat were the principal articles passing through the Potomac Company's works on the upper river.[73] Traffic was primarily seasonal in nature, fluctuating with the local harvests, and with the volume of water in the stream. Commerce all but disappeared during the summer droughts, and then suddenly assumed sizable proportions as the fall rains swelled the river and the crops were harvested. The amount of trade increased irregularly during the first quarter of the nineteenth century. The actual quantity passing through the locks at Great Falls varied according to the size of the harvest, the expansion of the settled area, and the rise of competing routes to the markets.

Life along the river was casual, if not leisurely. There were few regular boatmen, most of the crops being brought to market by the farmers and their sons. The rafts and boats reflected the impermanence of the trade. Most craft were makeshift floats designed hastily and cheaply for the trip to the market. Their size was determined by the size of the harvest or of the Potomac Company locks and canals. On reaching Georgetown they were broken up and sold for firewood. The few that were intended for more than one trip were long and narrow, designed for easy maneuverability and for the arduous trip upstream against the current.[74]

The trip to market was an experience for all who essayed it. The swift current of the river, the treacherous rapids and whirlpools, and the lurking rocks tested the ability of the most

[72] *Ibid.* The debts of the company totaled $175,886.59.

[73] See Appendix, Table III.

[74] One of these boats was discovered near Romney, West Virginia, in 1930. It was hand-hewn from a single poplar tree, and was 30 feet long and 3 feet wide, with a draft of 10 inches. (Washington *Sunday Star*, July 30, 1930; Washington *Evening Star*, October 6, 1931.) By 1812, the boats were said to be 75 feet long and 5 feet wide, with a draft of 18 inches.

skilled navigator. The crude chutes of the Potomac Company around the major falls were another test of the dexterity of the boatmen, and the numerous illegal fish pots and mill dams added to the dangers of the trip. If the boat survived the journey (and many did not), the boatman sold his produce, broke up his craft or sold it too, purchased his stores for the coming season, and trudged back home with his helper. If the boat was regularly engaged in trade on the river, the captain collected his return cargo and undertook the difficult trip upstream with the help of stout ropes, long poles, and strong crewmen.

The works of the Potomac Company encompassed relatively a small part of the river journey. The main centers of its business were at Great Falls and Little Falls. There the keepers tended their locks, collected the tolls, and farmed or fished in their spare time.[75] These employees and the farmers along the river were the only constant elements in the trip. Boats, boatmen, travelers, even the river and the woods sometimes changed but the lock tenders and the farmers remained. They performed the same functions in the river trade that their counterparts in the canal era did—as sources for news and gossip, the objects of vituperation and jest, and, for the lock-keepers at least, as the representatives and protectors of the company's interests.

The experiences of the Potomac Company have essentially a twofold significance in the history of the development of the Potomac route. The general contribution of the company's efforts is the relation between its achievements and the economic and commercial progress of the valley. The specific interest in the story of the company lies in the lessons which its experiences provided for the promoters of the Chesapeake and Ohio Canal project. These will be noted later, in the account of the origins of that proposal. The chief concern here is the general position of the Potomac Company in the history of the valley.

In the beginning of the national era, the upper Potomac valley was just emerging from the frontier fur-trade era into the agri-

[75] See petition of Captain George Pointer, September 5, 1829, in Letters Received, Records of the Chesapeake and Ohio Canal Company (National Archives, Washington, D. C.). Captain Pointer, an ex-boatman and keeper of the Little Falls locks, reminisced at some length about his early life on the river.

cultural stage of development. A description of the state of Maryland in 1784 gives a good indication of the economy of the valley:

> Maryland, then, had no incorporated towns from which commerce was conducted — but Annapolis — quite remote from the Potomac. Washington, then called Dudington, was not even a village; Baltimore, an inconsiderable town, was not incorporated for twelve years afterwards; the settlements of Frederick and Montgomery [counties] were purely agricultural, remote from towns, and in a helpless state of dependency; in Washington and Allegany [counties] the wolf roamed, and the Indian was only kept at bay by the guns of Fort Cumberland.[76]

The Potomac Company sought successfully to encourage the agricultural potentialities of the Potomac watershed. On the other hand, it indirectly resisted even limited industrial activity through its control of the use of water from the river.[77] The company considered its primary function to be that of providing a cheap means of transportation to and from a rich and newly settled region. As such it reserved all the water in the river for the purposes of navigation. Existing mill dams and fish pots were swept aside where they interfered with free passage in the river.[78] Technically the directors were correct in this decision, for subsequent experience showed that with all these precautions there was still not enough water to provide permanent navigation in the bed of the river. Economically they were hobbling their own future by restricting the valley to an agricultural economy. In the second period, this same policy was carried to the branches of the Potomac, with the same retarding results.[79] At the end of the middle period, the economic horizons of the company had become so limited that efforts to improve the river were concentrated on the lower Potomac and Shenandoah valleys.[80] The upper Potomac was abandoned as beyond further improvement.

After 1816, a change occurred in the directors' attitude toward

[76] *A Letter from J. J. Speed to the Representatives of Maryland in the Congress of the United States on the Subject of the Canal* (Baltimore, 1844), p. 8.

[77] Proceedings of Directors, B, 114 (December 3, 1811). The Board rejected an application for a forge on the river below Harpers Ferry.

[78] Proceedings of Directors, A, 348 (May 29, 1806). See also the petition of Captain George Pointer, September 5, 1829.

[79] Proceedings of Directors, B, 43 (July 2, 1808), 62-63 (October 21, 1809).

[80] Annual Report (1811), Directors' Journal B, 104.

the economy of the valley. They slowly abandoned their opposition to the use of water power for manufacturing purposes. It is only possible to speculate concerning the reasons for the change, for the discussions preceding the adoption of the resolution announcing the new policy have not been preserved. The decision may have been merely an indication of the economic coming-of-age of the company similar to that which in the national arena saw the passage of the tariff of 1816. Perhaps the need for money influenced the Board. Apparently the hostility of the Georgetown millers and founders was in some way appeased. Regardless of motive, the company became interested in the industrial development of the valley after the War of 1812 and began to encourage the establishment of mills, etc.[81] It entered into negotiations with John K. Smith for the sale of factory sites at Little Falls, but a protracted disagreement concerning the rights and privileges of each party in the projected development prevented the new policy from becoming effective on a large scale.[82]

The second interest of the Potomac Company, the development of trade with the West, also underwent several changes of fortune during the existence of the company. In the earliest days, the West was just beyond the first range of mountains, easily accessible to river traffic. The technological improvements of the boats had not yet reached the point at which the relatively shallow Potomac would be at a disadvantage. By all measures, water transportation was still much cheaper than transportation in wagon over rough, unimproved roads. By 1802, the beginning of the middle period, the West was beginning to move beyond the immediate reaches of the Potomac valley. Perhaps this was a factor in the company's concentration on the valley itself, and the neglect of the river as a route to the West. The War of 1812 marked another turning point in the interest of the Potomac Company in the Western trade.

[81] Proceedings of Directors, B, 225-226 (December 15, 1814), 358-359 (May 16, 1818).

[82] Annual Report (1816), Directors' Journal B, 257-258; John K. Smith to President and Directors, December 3, 1816, Annual Meeting (December 3, 1816), B, 273-276; Annual Meeting (December 3, 1816), B, 276-279. See also the extensive correspondence beginning on November 15, 1819, *ibid.*, pp. 394 ff. The dispute lasted into the early years of the Chesapeake and Ohio Canal Company.

At the time that the West was fading beyond the company's horizons, the war demonstrated the need for safe interior communications with the Ohio and Mississippi valleys.

The period following the war saw the rise of the West as an economic factor in the nation, which may partly explain the rediscovery of it by the East. The old Potomac Company was unable to perform a leading role in this new era, and the Potomac route lost valuable ground in the race for Western trade. Capitalists and merchants of Maryland, Virginia, and the District of Columbia became keenly aware of this, and sought, unsuccessfully at first, to establish new companies to undertake the work of reopening the Potomac route. By 1822, these efforts were beginning to show the first indications of success despite the opposition of the existing company. But by 1822, the Erie Canal was almost completed and plans for the Pennsylvania main line of public works were well advanced. Thus a new competitor and an old one were ahead of the Potomac route, over terrain that was geographically more favorable. The advantages of the established Potomac channel were rapidly being overcome.

In 1822, the Potomac Company was to have six more years of life. By that time, however, its significance was mostly historical. Its primary influence was that of the retarding deadhand of an outmoded vested interest. For the story of the continued efforts to develop the Potomac route, we must turn to the activities underway outside the company, to projects for a new enterprise to complete the unfinished work of the old.

Chapter III

THE CANAL PROJECT

(1822-1828)

The decline of the Potomac Company coincided with the dawn of the canal era in the United States. The age of simple river improvements had passed. In the nineteenth century attention turned to the feasibility of building permanent, artificial canals as an effective means of transportation. Canals combined the cheapness of water travel with the reliability of an artificial waterway and the ease of a level, stillwater route. Early efforts to enlist the support of the federal government for the various canal projects failed, and the states turned to their own resources.[1] The commencement of the Erie Canal by New York State in 1817 marks the beginning of the active phase of the canal era. Pennsylvania followed with its main line of public works in 1826 as competition for the newly completed Erie Canal.[2] Ohio and the western states were also participating in the canal-building race. Nor did Maryland and Virginia lag far behind the others in planning a canal to the West via the Potomac.

Promoters of schemes to replace the Potomac Company were able to draw five valuable lessons from the experiences of that enterprise. Thus they might avoid the pitfalls of the earlier undertaking while striving to attain the fruits of success which eluded it. The first and most obvious lesson was the need of adequate financial support for a renewed undertaking. A second vitally necessary preliminary would be the successful integration of the interests of Virginia, Maryland, and the federal government (for the District of Columbia) in the new endeavor. The new company might expect to encounter engineering problems arising from the rocky, narrow, and winding nature of the valley and the question of an adequate supply of water for navigation. There was also every reason to anticipate further trouble in securing cheap, skilled labor of all

[1] Ward, p. 36.

[2] Dunbar, pp. 788-789.

kinds. Finally, the new company, like the old, would eventually have to provide for technological improvements, that is, to solve the problem of obsolescence. Inability to meet any one of these problems might easily spell failure for the enterprise. Yet, as clear as the lessons must have been, the Chesapeake and Ohio Canal Company never completely solved any of the difficulties.

On the other hand, the experiences of the Potomac Company justified expectations of a fair return if the goal of river improvement could be attained. In the first place, despite the relative somnolence of the company in regard to Western commerce after 1802, the river remained by virtue of the activities of the Ohio Company and the Potomac Company an established route of trade and communication to and from the West. Thus it had the very real advantage of early favor and reputation. Geographically, the Potomac was the shortest route between East and West. In addition it served the seat of the national government as well as the Chesapeake Bay states. The river also promised to be profitable to investors. At times in its existence the annual profits of the Potomac Company exceeded 6 per cent of its invested capital.[3] At first these sums had been turned back into the work of improvement. Later they were applied to the payment of interest on loans contracted to continue the excavation of the river bed. If the Potomac could be placed in a reasonably permanent state of improvement, it would seemingly produce a fair return on the capital invested. If a through route to the Ohio valley could be opened and the trade of the Cumberland coal banks also tapped, it seemed logical to assume that a much larger revenue would be forthcoming. In short, the large sum required to build a canal all the way to Pittsburgh might still be assured of a reasonable return. In one respect the experience of the Potomac Company proved misleading. It had had very little difficulty with nature, except in the normal periods of drought. Only one great freshet, in 1810, gave any reason to anticipate trouble on that score. Even then the company's works had held up well.

Several factors indicated that the first step in the realization

[3] Petition to the Virginia Assembly, December, 1816, Proceedings of Directors, B, 284. Total trade and revenues remained high and even improved after 1816. *Report of the Committee of the District of Columbia*, May 3, 1822, Appendix B, p. 12.

of the projected improvement of the Potomac would be to secure the support of the federal government. In this way, the large sums of capital needed would be assured (both from public and from private sources), and the submergence of local interests to the national theme would be emphasized. Promoters of the project, therefore, renewed the campaign to convert the general government to a program of internal improvements.

The interest of the federal government in a national system of internal improvements had survived and indeed increased during the ascendancy of Jeffersonian ideals. The history of this interest has already been adequately treated in another work;[4] therefore it is only necessary here to give a brief sketch of it and to refer to the earlier study for a more detailed account. The crux of the whole problem during the administrations of Jefferson, Madison, and Monroe was the constitutional question involved. Did the federal government have the power to use public money for a national system of internal improvements without regard to the states? If this was permissible, did the government have the power to exercise control over those improvements after they were completed? The struggle over the answer to these two questions raged throughout the period. Albert Gallatin's report, in 1808, was itself an outgrowth of many years of discussion which preceded it.[5] In it the Secretary of the Treasury proposed an integrated system of internal improvements supported by the federal government. Despite the failure of Congress to adopt the Gallatin plan, the fight continued over proposals to aid the construction of tidewater canals and to build a national road across the mountains.[6] The latter was eventually built with federal funds but was turned over to the states for control.

Toward the end of President Monroe's term in office, it seemed that progress was finally being made in the campaign to win the support of Congress and the administration. It is impossible to say positively what arguments were decisive in bringing about the change in attitude, but all of the following were advanced at one time or another. The disposal of surplus revenue, one of the earliest, appeared even before the Gallatin

[4] Ward, see especially Chapter II, pp. 14-39.

[5] *Ibid.*, pp. 23 ff.

[6] *Ibid.*, pp. 20-22, 31-33.

report, and was used again in the discussion in the twenties.[7] The military necessity plea was a favorite theme as early as 1803. Of course, after the experiences of the War of 1812, it became a much more popular point.[8] The claim that certain projects were national in scope, beyond either the means or the local interests of the several states, also may have borne weight.[9] The filling up of the West after the War of 1812 made it both a political force in Congress and an economically attractive market for the Eastern merchants in the postwar period. The support of these interests, especially in the Clay-Adams wing of the Republican party, should not be discounted. The growing popularity of the American System among the electorate was referred to indirectly by President Monroe as a reason for his shifting ground.[10] Finally, the glittering assembly at the first Chesapeake and Ohio Canal Convention, held in the Capitol itself, apparently made an impression on the President as an indication of the course of popular opinion.[11]

Regardless of the reasons advanced or assumed, President Monroe took a fairly strong stand in favor of national aid to internal improvement companies in his annual message to Congress in 1823.[12] His constitutional scruples were satisfied by the belief that the government could assist improvement projects if the operation of these works was turned over to the states

[7] *Ibid.*, pp. 20-21; *Report of the Committee on Roads and Canals*, January 30, 1827, pp. 5-6.

[8] Ward, pp. 15-16; *Report of the Committee on Roads and Canals*, January 30, 1827, p. 9. See also *Report of the Committee of the District of Columbia*, May 3, 1822, p. 5.

[9] Ward, p. 19; *Report of the Committee on Roads and Canals*, January 30, 1827, p. 9; *Report of the Committee of the District of Columbia*, May 3, 1822, pp. 2-3.

[10] James D. Richardson, ed., *A Compilation of the Messages and Papers of the Presidents* (10 vols., Washington, 1896), II, 216. The President also mentioned the military necessity argument and the union plea. See also *Report of the Committee on Roads and Canals*, January 30, 1827, Appendix 3, "Extract from the President's Message to Congress . . . (December 3, 1822 [1823])," p. 36.

[11] Richardson, II, 216; *Report of the Committee on Roads and Canals*, January 30, 1827, Appendix 3, p. 36. See also, Answer of the Chesapeake and Ohio Canal Company, Chesapeake and Ohio Canal Company *vs.* Baltimore and Ohio Railroad Company, *Maryland Reports*, 4 Gill and Johnson 24.

[12] Richardson, II, 216; *Report of the Committee on Roads and Canals*, January 30, 1827, Appendix 3, p. 36. He asserted his belief in the power of Congress to make appropriations for internal improvements if the control of the improvement companies remained in the states.

or to private companies after completion. Although real participation by the general government in internal improvement projects had to await the inauguration of John Quincy Adams, the President's message was a sort of a go-ahead signal, and much groundwork was done in the later years of his regime. On the last day of his administration, President Monroe signed an act of Congress confirming the charter of the Chesapeake and Ohio Canal Company.[13]

While friends of internal improvements and of the Potomac river route were trying to conciliate the strict constructionists in Congress and to secure the aid of the general government, others were active in the several states. In Virginia, between 1812 and 1823, there were at least three separate efforts to charter companies to construct canals along the banks of the Potomac River. The earliest attempt, 1812, called for a canal from Seneca to Hunting Creek. The second project, in 1816, a modification of the first, proposed to construct an artificial waterway from Seneca all the way to Alexandria.[14] Both provoked the vigorous opposition of the Potomac Company. In combatting the second proposal the old company enlisted the services of Charles F. Mercer, later President of the Chesapeake and Ohio Canal Company, to help defeat the act of incorporation in the Virginia Assembly.[15] The primary interest in these early projects for this study lies in the plan to abandon river improvements for an independent canal, and in the rivalry manifested between Georgetown and Alexandria merchants. The early proposals also provided a measure of the intention and ability of the Potomac Company to resist encroachments on its vested interests.

The creation of the Virginia Board of Public Works in 1816 was a much more significant event.[16] It coincided with the

[13] Act of Congress, approved March 3, 1825, *Documents relating to the Chesapeake and Ohio Canal*, July 11, 1840, p. 13.

[14] Proceedings of Directors, B, 158 (December 29, 1812), 267-268 (November 13, 1816).

[15] Mason to C. F. Mercer, December 16, 1816, Directors' Journal B, 303-308.

[16] *Report of the Committee on Roads and Canals*, January 30, 1827, Appendix 12, "Report of the Committee of the House of Delegates of Virginia, December 28, 1815," p. 60; Ward, pp. 12, 36. This report was the basis of the act creating the Virginia Board of Public Works and the Virginia system of internal improvements.

general revival of interest in canals and internal improvements in the North Atlantic states, and it marked the end of piecemeal attempts to modify the Potomac navigation. The Board immediately set about to bring some order into the state's system of internal improvements. During the course of its study of existing projects, it inquired into the works constructed by the Potomac Company and the current state of that enterprise.[17] The discovery that despite the expenditure of large sums the company had failed to fulfill the requirements of its charter led to a more searching investigation of the whole undertaking.

All parties to the company's charter participated in the examination which followed. Seeing the trend of public opinion and fearful of its vested rights, the Potomac Company formally requested a survey of its works.[18] The state of Virginia authorized the Board of Public Works to conduct the inspection and to include a survey of the land between the Potomac and the southern branches of the Ohio for a possible connection of the two rivers. Thomas Moore, the engineer of the Board, made two examinations in 1820 and 1822.[19] At the invitation of Virginia, the state of Maryland also sent an engineer, Isaac Briggs, to accompany Moore on his second trip. After the untimely death of Moore during the second surveying expedition, Briggs completed the study under special authorization from the state of Virginia.[20] Moore's report on the findings of the first inspection confirmed the opinion that a connection between the Potomac and the Ohio was entirely practicable, and estimated the cost of a canal along the Potomac to be about $1,100,000.[21] In the second report, Briggs estimated the cost

[17] Proceedings of Directors, B, 340 (December 8, 1817); Peyton to President and Directors, November 8, 1817, Mason to Peyton, December 8, 1817, *ibid.*, pp. 342-350.

[18] Annual Meeting (1819), Directors' Journal B, 382; Answer of the Chesapeake and Ohio Canal Company, 4 Gill and Johnson 19.

[19] Ward, pp. 40-41, 44-45; Annual Meeting (1820), Directors' Journal B, 440-441; Answer of the Chesapeake and Ohio Canal Company, 4 Gill and Johnson 19-20.

[20] Ward, pp. 42-45.

[21] Report of the Engineer of Virginia in *re* a Canal to the Ohio, Potomac Company Correspondence, 1820 (also printed in *Report of the Committee on Roads and Canals*, January 30, 1827, Appendix 3, pp. 33 ff.). The estimated cost was $1,114,300.

of the canal, 30 feet wide at the surface, 3 feet deep, and 20 feet wide at the bottom, to be about $1,574,000.[22]

The next question to arise was, how should this improvement be put into effect? A choice of two alternatives was indicated: an additional subscription to the Potomac Company, or the creation of a new company to take over the rights and privileges of the old one. The officials of the existing company obviously expected the former course to be adopted, and they argued for it throughout the discussion. Ultimately, however, it was decided to create a new enterprise, designated as the Potomac Canal Company to indicate its purpose and to distinguish it from the older organization. The Virginia Assembly passed an act of incorporation, February 22, 1823.[23] The act did not require the consent of Congress, but did stipulate that it must be confirmed by the state of Maryland to become operative. In Maryland, it encountered the opposition of local interests, especially because of the large pecuniary contribution which the state was expected to make to the capital of the new company. The Baltimore merchants in particular could not see what benefits they would receive from the project which would favor their competitors on the Potomac. The bill failed to pass the Maryland legislature, and, lacking the consent required, the Virginia act became inoperative.[24] Thus ended in failure the third and last attempt by Virginia and Maryland to effect a real improvement of the Potomac without federal support.

Nevertheless real progress had been made by 1823 in the effort to reopen the river as a route for Western trade. The interest of the District cities and the states of Maryland and Virginia had turned again to the Potomac.[25] In Congress, the

[22] Ward, p. 46. The report, May 3, 1822, is printed in part in *Report of the Committee on Roads and Canals*, January 30, 1827, Appendix 3, p. 35.

[23] Annual Report (1823), Directors' Journal C, 14-15.

[24] Answer of the Chesapeake and Ohio Canal Company, 4 Gill and Johnson 21-22; *Report of the Committee on Roads and Canals*, April 17, 1834, p. 4. Maryland was to subscribe $500,000, one-third of the total capital. The bill to charter the company and subscribe to its capital was so amended in the Maryland legislature that friends of the undertaking lost all interest in its passage, and even suspended efforts to secure a subscription from the Virginia Assembly.

[25] General excitement was manifested in the states concerned. Annual Report (1823), Directors' Journal C, 15. The District cities were also active in the agitation for the incorporation of the Potomac Canal Company. They deputed

friends of internal improvements were beginning to make headway in their campaign for federal support. The government seemed to be ready to undertake a general program of aid to public works. It was in this atmosphere that the first Chesapeake and Ohio Canal Convention met in Washington, on November 5, 1823.

The convention assembled at the call of a meeting of the citizens of Loudon County, Virginia.[26] This earlier gathering had been held to discuss the state of proposals for the improvement of the river after the Potomac Canal Company project proved abortive, and to expand the scope of the project to include a canal all the way to the Ohio. It requested similar meetings in other counties to support the citizens of Loudon in their appeal for a general convention.[27] In response to this plea many counties in Virginia, Maryland, and Pennsylvania, including all through which the proposed canal would pass, chose delegates to the conference.[28] In addition to these representatives there were members from the District cities and several unofficial guests from Ohio. Among those present were: Albert Gallatin of Pennsylvania; Bushrod C. Washington, Richard E. Byrd, and Charles F. Mercer of Virginia; Frisby Tilghman, George Peter, Joseph Kent, Thomas Kennedy, and George C. Washington of Maryland; and Francis Scott Key,

"agents to solicit and advance the plan with the two legislatures." Answer of the Chesapeake and Ohio Canal Company, 4 Gill and Johnson, 21. See also the proposals of Abner Lacock, *Great National Project: Proposed connection of the Eastern & Western Waters by a Communication through the Potomac Country* (Washington, 1822), a series of letters reprinted from the Washington *National Intelligencer*, and the *Report of the Committee of the District of Columbia*, May 3, 1822, on the memorials from inhabitants of the District and neighboring states.

[26] *Report of the Committee on Roads and Canals*, April 17, 1834, p. 4. The date of the Loudon County meeting was August 25, 1823. It is interesting to note that the first choice of the promoters for a name for their project was "The Union Canal," a title which was designed to emphasize the national character and importance of the work. Unfortunately, a short canal in Pennsylvania already bore the same name. The convention then chose "The Chesapeake and Ohio Canal" as an alternative.

[27] *Ibid.*, Appendix A, p. 67; Answer of the Chesapeake and Ohio Canal Company, 4 Gill and Johnson 22.

[28] *Report of the Committee on Roads and Canals*, April 17, 1834, Appendix A, "Minutes of the Meeting of Citizens of Prince William County, Virginia," pp. 67-68. This was the first county in Virginia to follow the example of Loudon County.

John Mason, and many others from the District of Columbia.[29] On the whole it must have been an impressive gathering. Governor Joseph Kent, of Maryland, an old and staunch advocate of internal improvements, was the presiding officer of the convention, but Charles F. Mercer, United States Representative from Virginia, exercised the guiding hand as chairman of the all-powerful central committee.

The primary functions of the convention were the organization of public opinion behind the proposed connection between the Potomac and the Ohio and the creation of organizations to give effect to this aroused interest. The physical achievements of the convention were simply the adoption of resolutions urging the connection with the West and the naming of committees to formulate the plans for the canal and to petition Congress and the several states for consent and aid in the project.[30]

The success of the convention can best be measured by the course of events in the years immediately following.[31] In his annual message to Congress in December, 1823, President Monroe referred to the convention's activities and urged Congress to give favorable consideration to the project, if its constitutional scruples would permit. Congress responded by providing $30,000 for a detailed survey of the proposed route by the United States Board of Engineers.[32] Petitions to the several states met with varying receptions. The memorial to Virginia for an act of incorporation was immediately successful. The Assembly of that state passed the necessary law on January

[29] At the second assembling of the convention, Andrew Stewart and Thaddeus Stevens of Pennsylvania, Philip E. Thomas and Joseph W. Patterson (both later associated with the Baltimore and Ohio Railroad) of Baltimore, George Washington Parke Custis of Alexandria County, D. C., and Henry Clay (representing Washington) were also present. Roger B. Taney was chosen as a delegate but did not attend. *Journal of the Chesapeake and Ohio Canal Convention, 1823 and 1826* (Washington, 1827), pp. 1-4. See also the Memorial of the Central Committee, *Report of the Committee on Roads and Canals*, January 2, 1828, 20th Cong., 1st sess., House of Representatives, Report No. 47 (hereafter cited as Memorial of the Central Committee), pp. 7-10, 16-23.

[30] Memorial of the Central Committee, pp. 10-13.

[31] The course of the petitions and their success and failure is reviewed in the *Report of the Committee on Roads and Canals*, January 30, 1827, Appendix 15, "Report of the Central Committee (December, 1826)," pp. 70-72, 75.

[32] Answer of the Chesapeake and Ohio Canal Company, 4 Gill and Johnson 24-25.

27, 1824.[33] On the other hand, the appeal to the state of Maryland for a confirmatory act failed in the same year because of the opposition of Baltimore and the indifference of the counties. By the time the next session of the legislature convened in December, 1824, the campaign to arouse the counties had succeeded, and on January 31, 1825, the Maryland Assembly confirmed the Virginia act of incorporation.[34] The petition to the Pennsylvania legislature failed completely in 1824 and 1825, owing to the opposition of Eastern, particularly Philadelphia, interests.

The U. S. Board of Engineers made a preliminary report on February 14, 1825.[35] In it, the Board concurred in the opinion of the Virginia engineer, Thomas Moore, that the connection between the upper Potomac and the Youghiogheny or Monongahela by an artificial waterway was practicable. The report seemed to assure the ultimate success of the project by removing all remaining doubts as to its practicability. Congress confirmed the act of the Virginia Assembly, chartering the canal company in a measure approved by President Monroe on March 3, 1825.[36] Pennsylvania confirmed the charter, with reservations, early the next year.[37] The company had now hurdled the legal obstacles to its final organization.[38] Friends of the project

[33] Act of the General Assembly of Virginia, *Documents relating to the Chesapeake and Ohio Canal*, July 11, 1840, pp. 1-12.

[34] Act of the General Assembly of Maryland, *ibid.*, pp. 12-13.

[35] *Report of the Committee on Roads and Canals*, January 30, 1827, Appendix 3, "Report of the Central Committee (December, 1826)," p. 76; Answer of the Chesapeake and Ohio Canal Company, 4 Gill and Johnson 25-26. An extract of the report is printed in *Report of the Committee on Roads and Canals*, January 30, 1827, Appendix 3, p. 37.

[36] Act of Congress, *Documents Relating to the Chesapeake and Ohio Canal*, July 11, 1840, p. 13.

[37] Act of Pennsylvania, February 9, 1826, *ibid.*, pp. 31-34. The principal reservations required the canal company to begin the construction of the western section within three years and to use Congressional appropriations equally for both eastern and western sections.

[38] According to the terms of the charter, the Chesapeake and Ohio Canal Company was empowered to accept subscriptions for the purpose of financing the construction of an artificial waterway from tidewater on the Potomac in the District of Columbia to the highest point of permanent navigation on the Ohio at Pittsburgh via the shortest practicable route. The charter stipulated that the eastern section of the canal must be completed before the western section could be started. To enable the company to accomplish its purpose, the act gave it the power to condemn land and hold it in fee simple when used for canal purposes and granted it the right to use the water of the rivers for purposes

promptly plunged into the campaign for public support with renewed vigor and confidence.

On October 23, 1826, however, the Board of Engineers made its full report, which the President transmitted to Congress on December 7, 1826.[39] The report reiterated the belief of the Board that the proposed connection was physically practicable, but estimated the cost of the canal upon the enlarged dimensions required by the federal government at approximately $22,000,000.[40] The revised estimate fell like a thunderbolt on the hopes of the canal supporters. The latter had been thinking in terms of a slightly smaller canal at a cost of between four and five million dollars. They now sent out a call for the reassembling of the convention of 1823, to be held in Washington on December 6, 1826.

The second session of the convention met according to plan and immediately went to work. Its principal task was to dispel the gloom which paralyzed its friends and to reassure prospective supporters. A twofold course was indicated: to discredit the estimate of the U. S. Board of Engineers and to cause a new survey to be made to ascertain the true cost of the work on the enlarged dimensions. The report of the government engineers was exhaustively examined and criticized. Comparisons were made with the actual cost of work done on the New York and

of navigation. Furthermore, the company was to be forever free from taxation. It must, however, complete and put into use at least one hundred miles of canal within five years and must complete the entire project in twelve years. The dimensions of the waterway were to be at least 40 feet wide and 4 feet deep (28 feet wide at the bottom). To permit the officers of the company to carry on their work with the least possible hindrance the use of injunctions to stop work was specifically prohibited. Two important powers which were left in doubt by the charter, the right to raise money by loans based on the pledge of canal property and revenues and the right to sell surplus water from the canal, were added later.

[39] Answer of the Chesapeake and Ohio Canal Company, 4 Gill and Johnson 26; *Report of the Committee on Roads and Canals*, January 30, 1827, Appendix 15, "Report of the Central Committee (December, 1826)," p. 75; *ibid.*, Appendix 15, "Report of the U. S. Board of Internal Improvement," p. 69. The full report is printed in *Message of the President of the United States, transmitting a Report from the Secretary of War with that of the Board of Engineers for Internal Improvement, on the Chesapeake and Ohio Canal*, December 7, 1826, 19th Cong., 2d sess., House of Representatives, Document No. 10.

[40] The detailed estimates were: $8,177,081.05 for the eastern section, $10,028,-122.86 for the middle section, and $4,170,223.78 for the western section, making a total of $22,375,427.69.

Pennsylvania canals. The critics discovered that allowances for labor costs were much too high, as were the estimates for masonry, walling, and excavation.[41] The criticism in part was valid, both on the basis of the experience on other canals and on the ground that the allowances made for many types of work were extravagantly generous. In the meantime, friends of the project in Congress prevailed upon the President to submit the conflicting estimates made by the convention and the Board of Engineers to a review and revision by practical and experienced civil engineers. President Adams agreed and appointed James Geddes and Nathan Roberts. They completed their surveys in 1827 and reported in the same year. They estimated that the canal could be constructed as far as Cumberland for approximately $4,500,000.[42]

Fortified with this estimate and reassured of the inaccuracy of the U. S. engineers' report, the canal protagonists re-entered the fray. Subscription books were opened on October 1, 1827, but the formal organization of the company was delayed until Congress should act.[43] In May, 1828, after a brief but sharp struggle, the friends of the canal project in Congress secured the passage of an act subscribing $1,000,000 of the public funds to the stock of the Chesapeake and Ohio Canal Company. The news of the subscription was received wildly everywhere. The Mayor of Washington hoisted a flag atop City Hall, and cannon saluted the event in Washington and Georgetown. There was a great illumination at Cumberland and a festive banquet at which U. S. Representative Andrew Stewart, one of the original proponents of the project, was the guest of honor. Leesburg, the home of Charles F. Mercer and the seat of Loudon County, Virginia, gave its most famous citizen a banquet. Old Town, Maryland, and Martinsburg, Virginia, were also reported to be highly pleased.[44]

[41] *Report of the Committee on Roads and Canals*, January 30, 1827, Appendix 15, "Report of the Central Committee (December, 1826)," pp. 82-87; *ibid.*, Appendix 13, "Report of a Committee appointed December 6, 1826, to prepare and report a revised estimate," pp. 89-97.

[42] Answer of the Chesapeake and Ohio Company, 4 Gill and Johnson 26-27; a copy of the report is filed among the Chesapeake and Ohio Canal Company records in the National Archives.

[43] Answer of the Chesapeake and Ohio Canal Company, 4 Gill and Johnson 28-29.

[44] Washington *National Intelligencer*, May 27, 1828; John Quincy Adams,

The subscription on the part of the United States fulfilled the condition of an earlier Maryland subscription of $500,000 to the stock of the canal company, and that act now became effective.[45] Congress also permitted the three cities of the District of Columbia to subscribe another $1,500,000 to the company.[46] These sums, together with private investments, insured the successful launching of the long-awaited national project.[47]

The formal organization of the Chesapeake and Ohio Canal Company took place at a meeting of stockholders in Washington, June 20-23, 1828.[48] Upon the nomination of Richard Rush, Secretary of the Treasury and the proxy for the United States, Representative Charles F. Mercer, of Virginia, was chosen the first president of the company which he had labored so long to create. The Board of Directors included: Phineas Janney, an Alexandria banker; Walter Smith, a Georgetown landholder and merchant; Peter Lenox, a merchant, and Dr. Frederick May,

Memoirs, ed. Charles F. Adams (12 vols., Philadelphia, 1874-1877), VIII, 6. See also Wilhelmus B. Bryan, *A History of the National Capital* (2 vols., New York, 1916), II, 111.

[45] Act of the General Assembly of Maryland, passed December Session, 1827, *Documents Relating to the Chesapeake and Ohio Canal*, July 11, 1840, pp. 24-26.

[46] *Report of the Committee on Roads and Canals on the Memorial of Washington, Georgetown and Alexandria to enlarge the powers of the corporate authorities to facilitate payment of subscriptions to the Chesapeake and Ohio stock*, January 30, 1828, 20th Cong., 1st sess., House of Representatives, Report No. 112, pp. 1-2 and appendices. The debts of the District cities were thereby doubled and tripled. The total indebtedness of the towns had been: Washington $361,826, Georgetown $155,149, and Alexandria $277,776. To this was added $1,000,000, $250,000 and $250,000, respectively. Bryan, II, 110-111.

[47] Individual subscriptions amounted to $607,400. Of this, residents of the three District cities contributed: Washington $233,600, Georgetown $229,700, and Alexandria $47,300. Special Report on the Completion of the Canal (February, 1851), Proceedings of Stockholders, D, 403.

[48] Proceedings of a Special Meeting of the Stockholders of the Chesapeake and Ohio Canal Company (June 20, 1828), Journal A, 1-3. Hereafter the regular annual meetings of the stockholders on the first Monday in June will be cited simply as Annual Meeting (year), Proceedings of Stockholders, Journal, pages; special meetings will be similarly designated, with the exception that they will be cited as Special Meeting (dates), etc. If the reference is to a report of the president and directors to a special meeting, the citation will read Report to Special Meeting, etc. Thus: 1st Annual Meeting (1829), Proceedings of Stockholders, A, 40. Special Meeting (September 10, 1828), Proceedings of Stockholders, A, 12. The proceedings of the Directors, and those of the Stockholders, Correspondence, Legal papers, etc., are in manuscript form in the Department of Interior Archives (National Archives, Washington, D. C.).

both of Washington; ex-Governor Joseph Kent, of Maryland; and Representative Andrew Stewart, of Pennsylvania.[49] In this manner the three states which were parties to the charter, the three District cities, and the United States were all represented. The practice of providing representation for each of the interested parties to the charter continued throughout the canal's history, though somewhat modified in later years.[50] The first Board was truly distinguished in its membership. Only twice in later years did the canal possess a group of officers as united in purpose, and only once a Board as zealous.[51] The by-laws of the company were drawn up, considered, and finally adopted on July 3, 1828.[52] To fill the principal appointive offices of the company the new Board chose John P. Ingle, of Washington, as Clerk, and Clement Smith, of Georgetown, as Treasurer.

After completing the business of organization, the directors proceeded immediately to the selection of a competent chief engineer to supervise its works. At the first official meeting of the Board, June 23, 1828, Judge Benjamin Wright of New York was named to the post.[53] Judge Wright enjoyed a wide reputation for his ability, and the choice apparently met with general approval. He had been actively associated with the construction of the Erie Canal and was at the time of his appointment the chief engineer of the Chesapeake and Delaware Canal.[54] In choosing as chief engineer a man with experience on the northern canals, the directors adopted a course which they followed

[49] Special Meeting (June 20, 1828), Proceedings of Stockholders, A, 4-6.

[50] The failure to construct the western section resulted in the elimination of Pennsylvania representation on the Board. The increased holdings by Maryland ultimately led to the control of the Board by that state. Thereafter the composition of the Board was usually: president and four directors from Maryland, one director from Virginia, and one director from the District cities.

[51] The other Boards that were outstanding were that under James M. Coale, from 1843 to 1847, and that under Arthur P. Gorman, from 1872 to 1882. The former was probably as united and zealous as the first Board. The latter was certainly as united and perhaps as zealous, although its enthusiasm tended more to political channels.

[52] Special Meeting (July 3, 1828), Proceedings of Stockholders, A, 7-11.

[53] Proceedings of the President and Directors of the Chesapeake and Ohio Canal Company, Journal A, 2 (June 23, 1828). Hereafter cited as Proceedings of Directors, etc. Inasmuch as there will be no further references to the records of the Potomac Company it will be possible to adopt the same convenient short form of reference that was used for the latter.

[54] Report to Special Meeting (September 10, 1828), Proceedings of Stockholders, A, 16-17.

in completing the staff of engineers. The Board took full advantage of the availability of tested men, experienced in the construction and operation of both foreign and domestic canals.[55]

The canal company paused long enough in the bustle of getting under way to indulge in gala ceremonies marking the formal inauguration of the canal project. Upon the suggestion of the city authorities of Washington, the directors chose the Fourth of July as the appropriate day for the commencement of this national project.[56] To add the crowning touch to the occasion, the Board invited the President of the United States, John Quincy Adams, an old friend of internal improvements and of this canal project, to attend the ceremonies and to turn the first spadeful of earth.

The day dawned bright and sunny,[57] an auspicious omen for the canal. Activities got under way at the early hour that was customary in those days. Many representatives of official Washington and of the foreign delegations were among the dignitaries present at the ceremonies. After breakfasting in Georgetown, the directors and their guests proceeded up the river about five miles in boats especially provided for the occasion. They disembarked at the foot of Little Falls and went directly to the Powder Magazine at the head of the falls where the ceremonies were to take place.

[55] 1st Annual Report of the President and Directors (1829), Proceedings of Stockholders, A, 48. All of the *Annual Reports* (and they will be thus cited hereafter) were printed separately. Wherever copies of those reports have been found, they will be used in preference to the copies written into the Proceedings of Stockholders. The 1st, 3d, 4th, 21st, 22d, and 23d are transcribed in the Proceedings and have been cited therein. The two types of citations to the reports will be: 1st Annual Report (1829), Proceedings of Stockholders, A, 50; and *2d Annual Report* (1830), p. 10.

[56] Proceedings of Directors, A, 5 (June 24, 1828). The use of the Fourth of July for such occasions was a common practice in those years. The Erie Canal, for example, formally began construction on July 4, 1817.

[57] The following account of the inaugural ceremonies is based on the report in the Washington *National Intelligencer*, July 7, 1828, and the diary of John Quincy Adams, published in his *Memoirs*, VIII, 48-50. President Adams gives a faithful account of the episode sagely remarking that he "got through awkwardly, but without gross and palpable failure. . . . The incident that chiefly relieved me was the obstacle of the stump, which met and resisted the spade, and my casting off my coat to overcome the resistance. It struck the eye and fancy of the spectators more than all the flowers of rhetoric in my speech, and diverted their attention from the stammering and hesitation of a deficient memory."

A large crowd had already gathered at the site by the time the official party arrived. At first there was the usual number of short speeches emphasizing the national character of the work. Fortunately for the assembled throng, and perhaps for the speakers, most of those present could not hear what was being said. President Adams then gave his blessing to the undertaking in a short talk. As he finished his benediction, he took the spade and with appropriate words and flourishes went through the motions of breaking the ground. Much to everyone's consternation, the spade struck a root, and the President's effort was foiled. Visibly calm and undaunted, the President tried again, and again the spade failed to bite into the soil. Here indeed seemed to be a bad omen for the canal; but this was the nineteenth century, and all knew there was an explanation for every occurrence and a way where there was a will.

John Quincy Adams laid down the shovel and stripped off his coat. The crowd howled its delight, for though it could not hear the speeches, it could see the pantomime and could guess from the President's actions what had happened. In his un-Presidential but workmanlike attire John Quincy Adams again took up the spade, and with the cheers of encouragement from the spectators ringing in his ears drove it home quickly and firmly. The palisades of the Potomac rocked with the roar of approval from the onlookers. The canal was officially inaugurated. President Adams donned his coat and retired, undoubtedly highly gratified with his success and with his sudden popularity. The members of the official party returned to Georgetown where they partook of a handsome collation and then dispersed to resume the business of the day.

The affair was a huge success, notwithstanding the annoying incident of the spade. It successfully focused public attention on the Chesapeake and Ohio Canal as a national work. In so doing, it overshadowed the inaugural ceremonies of the Baltimore and Ohio Railroad in Baltimore on the same day.

CHAPTER IV

UNPROMISING BEGINNINGS
(1828-1832)

After the delightful interlude of the Fourth of July, the directors turned to the preparations for construction. On August 21, 1828, they formally accepted the Potomac Company's surrender and conveyance of its rights.[1] To avoid any unpleasantness or favoritism in the letting of contracts, they forbade canal officials to be connected in any way, directly or indirectly, with contractors for the work on the line.[2] The company also adopted an official seal commemorating the purposes of the undertaking: the union of Eastern and Western waters and the encouragement of agriculture, industry, and commerce.[3] Having finished with these incidentals, the directors took up the preliminary matters concerning the location and dimensions of the waterway, the selection of a competent staff of engineers, and the existence of an adequate supply of cement. Only after settling these questions could contracts be let and construction begin.

For some time after its election, the Board was occupied with the problems associated with determining the line of the canal. It had adopted almost immediately the route surveyed by the United States Engineers and by Geddes and Roberts along the north bank of the river.[4] Aside from this general decision, however, the exact location of the trunk was left indefinite until the last possible moment. The company hoped in this way to prevent speculation and to keep down land costs as much as possible.[5] The directors divided the entire canal into three parts—eastern, middle (mountain), and western. Inasmuch as the charter required that construction begin in the East, that leg of the canal was subdivided into three parts of 120 sections each. The average section was half a mile in length, and twenty

[1] Proceedings of Directors, A, 43-44 (August 25, 1828).
[2] *Ibid.*, p. 37 (August 9, 1828); p. 114 (November 22, 1828).
[3] *Ibid.*, pp. 63-64 (September 3, 1828).
[4] *Ibid.*, p. 8 (June 26, 1830 [1828]).
[5] 1st Annual Report (1829), Proceedings of Stockholders, A, 41.

sections formed a residency.[6] An injunction which had been obtained by the Baltimore and Ohio Railroad prevented work on the canal above the Point of Rocks.[7] Therefore operations were restricted to the forty-eight miles of the first division below that spot.

The definite organization of the canal line made possible the assignment of engineers. The engineer corps was divided into five grades: chief engineer, board of engineers, resident engineers, assistant engineers, and rodmen. The board of engineers consisted of three members, each of whom also had charge of one division of the eastern section. The engineer in charge of the first division was automatically chief engineer.[8] In making appointments, the Board relied almost exclusively upon the available supply of men experienced on Northern or foreign canals. It made every effort to secure the most competent engineers, paying liberal if not extravagant wages.[9] The board of engineers included, besides Judge Wright, Dr. John Martineau, a close associate whom he had brought down with him from New York, and Nathan S. Roberts, another noted New York engineer, who had made the survey of 1827. The resident engineers in the first division were: Thomas F. Purcell, of Virginia; Daniel Van Slyke, of New York; Wilson M. C. Fairfax, of Virginia; Erastus Hurd, of Massachusetts; and Alfred Cruger, of New York. Among the assistant engineers were: Horman Boye, of Denmark; Charles Ellet, Jr., of Pennsylvania; James Mears, Jr., of New York; Charles Ward and R. G. Bowie, of Maryland; and Charles B. Fisk, of Connecticut.[10]

The principal exception to the selection of experienced Northern engineers was in the choice of rodmen. The directors chose the latter from inexperienced applicants, frequently youths

[6] *Ibid.*, p. 48.

[7] Proceedings of Directors, A, 8 (June 26, 1930 [1828]).

[8] "Rules and Regulations for the Engineer Department," *ibid.*, pp. 108-109 (November 22, 1828).

[9] Report to Special Meeting (September 10, 1828), Proceedings of Stockholders, A, 22.

[10] Proceedings of Directors, A, 114-115 (November 22, 1828); *Documents Relating to the Chesapeake and Ohio Canal*, July 11, 1840, pp. 126-127. The directors complained of the difficulty encountered in obtaining the services of able men because of the advanced season of the year at which the company commenced operations. But they seem to have succeeded fairly well. 1st Annual Report (1829), Proceedings of Stockholders, A, 33.

from the neighborhood who were seeking careers in engineering. Some of the more promising were taken on as apprentices and allowed their board and clothing. Others were appointed strictly on trial and had to pay their own expenses.[11] In this way the canal became a school in practical engineering, a common procedure in the period. The intention of the Board in adopting such a policy was to promote interest in internal improvements in the South and to train a group of engineers from among the Southern youths.[12]

Notwithstanding the careful selection of skilled and tested engineers, the inexperienced directors reserved to themselves the final decision on every question no matter how specialized.[13] In addition, President Mercer frequently participated actively in the discussion of engineering technicalities. Under such conditions, differences of opinion which arose between members of the engineering department were frequently carried over the head of the chief engineer by appeals from aggrieved or ambitious underlings.[14] Only on the too infrequent occasions when Judge Wright adopted a firm attitude did the proper degree of order emerge.[15]

The directors also had to determine the size of the canal before the final location of the line could be made, the estimates drawn up, and the bids called for. The original dimensions of the canal as proposed by the Virginia Board of Public Works had been 30 feet wide and 3 feet deep.[16] The canal convention

[11] Mercer to Bryant, August 27, 1828, Letter Book A, 12; Mercer to Fairfax, December 22, 1828.

[12] 1st Annual Report (1829), Proceedings of Stockholders, A, 48; Mercer to Bryant, August 27, 1829, Letter Book A, 12; Mercer to Roberts, October 4, 1828, *ibid.*, p. 30. It would be interesting to trace the subsequent careers of these rodmen to see how successful the training policy was. It is known that several of the resident and assistant engineers later found positions in the southern and western states.

[13] "Rules and Regulations for the Engineer Department," Proceedings of Directors, A, 107, 109-110 (November 22, 1828).

[14] See, for example, Wright to Mercer, February 9, 1830, and Van Slyke to Mercer, February 27, 1830.

[15] In 1830, Judge Wright flatly vetoed President Mercer's plan to abolish the position of volunteer rodman by making the incumbents all inspectors of masonry, a job for which they were utterly unqualified. Wright to Mercer, February 24, 1830.

[16] Special Report on the Completion of the Canal (February, 1851), Proceedings of Stockholders, D, 318. This valuable summary of the early history

originally considered a waterway 32 feet wide and 4 feet deep, but eventually decided on a width of 40 feet and a depth of 4 feet. This was the minimum size permitted by the charter. For the purposes of the federal government, a larger canal was desired. The U. S. Board of Engineers made its survey on the basis of a canal 48 feet wide and 5 feet deep. The size finally determined upon by the canal board was 60 feet wide at the surface of the water, 6 feet deep, and 48 feet wide at the bottom.[17]

The directors decided to adopt the larger dimensions because of the increased advantages attainable at small additional cost. The greater size would give the canal a cross section of 301 square feet and a prism of 58,862 2/9 cubic yards as compared with 136 square feet and 26,595 5/9 cubic yards on the New York, Pennsylvania, and Ohio canals.[18] It was estimated that the increased prism would reduce water resistance to the equivalent of unimpeded sea navigation. Much of the masonry work, the most expensive part of the construction, would be unaffected by the increase in size. On some sections, the Georgetown level for example, the larger dimensions would pay for themselves through the greater quantity of water power which would be available for sale.[19] To men who were fully convinced of the practicability and certain success of this national project,

of the canal is also printed separately. For convenience it will be cited hereafter simply as Special Report on the Completion of the Canal, page.

[17] 1st Annual Report (1829), Proceedings of Stockholders, A, 40. At first a 5-foot depth would be accepted, but ultimately the full 6 feet would be required. When the canal was extended below Little Falls, it was to be generally 80 feet wide. Where the Little Falls road forced a reduction of the waterway to 70 feet, the depth would be increased to 7 feet. Above Harpers Ferry it was planned to reduce the width of the canal to 50 feet, but final decision on that was reserved for future deliberation. *Ibid.*, p. 45; Report to Special Meeting (September 10, 1828), Proceedings of Stockholders, A, 19; Proceedings of Directors, A, 204 (Apil 22, 1829).

[18] 1st Annual Report (1829), Proceedings of Stockholders, A, 40. The northern canals were generally 40 feet wide and 4 feet deep.

[19] *Ibid.*, pp. 42-43. The latter was not altogether a legitimate argument, for the right to sell water did not belong to the company. There was serious opposition to the grant of the privilege by Maryland citizens, and there was some doubt that the legislature would agree to it. As a matter of fact, the right to sell water would still be in doubt after the necessary legislative grants, for there was a legal dispute on that point pending in the courts. Furthermore, if the Maryland Canal were built as planned, there would be little surplus water available for sale.

who were building for the future, and who were thinking in terms of steamboats on its waters, industries along its banks, and centuries of service ahead, these advantages far outweighed the increased cost of the moment.[20]

Even before the first contracts had been let, an internal rift in the company threatened to develop over the question of the eastern terminus of the waterway. The charter stated simply that the canal should terminate at tidewater of the Potomac in the District of Columbia.[21] The dispute centered around the interpretation of this vague stipulation. The Board understood it to mean the highest point of the tide, at the foot of Little Falls. Accordingly, the inaugural ceremonies had been held near that spot. The representatives of Washington insisted on a location more favorable to their city, preferably on the Eastern Branch. In July, 1828, the Board voted against any extension of the canal below the Little Falls, at least until the westward progress of the work had reached Harpers Ferry. The directors agreed, however, to submit the whole question to a special meeting of the stockholders in September.[22]

At the general meeting the differences were fully aired and a compromise agreement reached. In its official report, the Board ignored the inter-city rivalry involved and stressed the danger to the health of Georgetown from a canal cut through its streets and the heavy property damages which would be encountered.[23] Representatives of Washington maintained, on the other hand, that the canal must terminate where shipping facilities were available, if it was to be of any value. Nothing less than a site in Washington, for example, the mouth of Tiber Creek, from which the city could construct a canal to the Eastern Branch, would be acceptable.[24] Washington was able

[20] See for example *2d Annual Report* (1830), p. 7. "If, in its plan, the Board have erred, it has arisen from their inability to forget, that a work destined to be the great central thoroughfare of so many States, and the firmest bond of their happy union, should be commensurate with its great end, and fulfil the wishes of the Government, Cities, and People, who have impressed upon it this high character." This determination to build a model structure severely handicapped the canal's prospects for ultimate success.

[21] Act of Virginia Assembly, passed January 27, 1824, *Documents Relating to the Chesapeake and Ohio Canal*, July 11, 1840, pp. 1-14.

[22] Proceedings of Directors, A, 29-30 (July 28, 1828), 32 (July 30, 1828).

[23] *Ibid.*, pp. 57-62 (September 3, 1828).

[24] Proceedings of the Corporation of Washington, September 5 and 6, 1828,

to exert tremendous influence in the meeting by threatening to withhold payments on its large subscription to the canal stock, an eventuality which the company was in no position to ignore. The city also enlisted the support of the United States representative, Richard Rush.[25] In the face of this overwhelming pressure, the canal board modified its position. On behalf of the directors, President Mercer recommended the mouth of the Tiber as a compromise between the Little Falls site and the Eastern Branch. The stockholders promptly agreed to the proposed solution.[26]

A final question which had to be answered before estimates could be made with any degree of certainty and construction begun on a large scale concerned the availability of an adequate supply of hydraulic lime for cement. Stone of a suitable quality had been discovered near Shepherdstown, on the Virginia side of the river, early in 1828, and a mill and kiln had been erected to grind and burn the lime.[27] Subsequently, canal officials found a better grade blue stone nearby and adopted it.[28] However, the presence of large deposits of stone in the valley did not insure that sufficient quantities of high-grade cement could be supplied to the contractors to fill their needs. The Potomac Mills were creating a new industry in this region. A period of experimentation was inevitable, as a "whole new science" was being learned the hard way. Unfortunately this experimentation continued during the early years of the construction of the canal, and the lime which the contractors received was not

printed in the Washington *National Intelligencer*, September 10, 1828. The threat was ever present that unless Washington received satisfaction it would make no further payments on its one million dollar subscription to the Chesapeake and Ohio Canal Company. This eventually would have seriously endangered the immediate future of the canal.

[25] Proceedings of Directors, N, 404 (May 8, 1889).

[26] Special Meeting (September 17, 1828), Proceedings of Stockholders, A, 28-29. The main basin of the canal would be at the mouth of Rock Creek, between Georgetown and Washington, but when the latter provided a basin three feet above tide at the mouth of Tiber Creek, the company would extend the canal down to it.

[27] Henry Boteler to Mercer, January 14 and 22, 1828, *Report of the Committee on Roads and Canals*, February 11, 1828, 20th Cong., 1st sess., House of Representatives, Report No. 141, Appendix 4, pp. 38-39.

[28] Leckie to President and Directors, May 11, 1829; Proceedings of Directors, A, 195-196 (April 8, 1829).

always the high quality that was desired.[29] Furthermore, the capacity of the kilns was limited and often insufficient to supply heavy seasonal demands.[30] As a consequence, the masonry work on the canal was frequently delayed.[31]

The directors made every effort to provide an adequate and regular amount of the hydraulic lime at reasonable prices. To expedite the transportation of the lime from the mill to the sites of construction, the company itself hired the boatmen to ship the cement, and purchased large quantities of bags in which to pack it. The boatmen were slow, indifferent, and expensive; and the bags were abused, frequently lost, and on the whole highly unsatisfactory. Canal officials experimented with the shipment of lime, without bags, in specially constructed boats, but the plan was never widely adopted.[32] To fill the gaps in the local supply, the Board imported large quantities of cement from other regions.[33] The problem of an adequate supply of high-grade lime continued to plague the directors throughout the early years of construction.[34]

Notwithstanding these distractions, canal engineers laid out thirty-four sections immediately above Little Falls in July and August, 1828. Within a three-day period toward the end of

[29] McFarland to Ingle, May 29, 1829; McFarland to Leckie, July 23, 1829; Ingle to Boteler and Reynolds, April 22, 1830, Letter Book A, 205.

[30] Leckie to President and Directors, July 22, 1829; Ingle to McFarland, January 8, 1830, Letter Book A, 155. The contractors were so desperately in need of cement that they were going to the river and stopping all boats loaded with lime, no matter for whom they were intended. See also, Mercer to Boteler and Reynolds, May 5, 1830, *ibid.*, 214-215.

[31] Wright to President and Directors, March 23, 1830; Mercer to Boteler and Reynolds, May 5, 1830, Letter Book A, 214-215; Leckie to Cruger and President and Directors, July, 1830.

[32] McFarland to Ingle, October 7, 28, 1829, March 10, 12, 1830; Boteler and Reynolds to Ingle, January 1, 1830; John Strider to President and Directors, April 21, 1830.

[33] Proceedings of Directors, A, 105 (November 15, 1828), 173 (February 28, 1829), 283-284 (June 10, 1829), 287-288 (June 17, 1829, 382 (October 23, 1829); Leckie to President and Directors, July 22, 1829.

[34] In all these efforts the Board dealt directly with the Potomac Mills. The company undertook to supply the cement to the contractors on the line under a separate arrangement. Its unfortunate experience in this practice, together with similar results in the attempt to obtain laborers, soon persuaded the directors to retire completely from the business of construction. Proceedings of Directors, A, 171 (February 21, 1829), 181 (March 17, 1829), 195-196 (April 8, 1829).

August, the Board let contracts for all these sections. A hundred contractors were present and submitted bids; in all 462 proposals were received. Most of the successful bidders had had experience in the construction of canals in New York, Pennsylvania, Connecticut, Ohio, and Canada.[35] New York and Pennsylvania men secured eighteen of the contracts, amounting to $160,000 of a total of $218,000 let. Late in October the directors let fifty more sections of the line, from Seneca to the Point of Rocks, and all the masonry work, locks, aqueducts, culverts, etc. There were 1,308 proposals for these contracts. On December 5, the five miles between Little Falls and Georgetown, and Dams Nos. 1 and 2 (at Little Falls and Seneca Falls, respectively) were let. The remaining lockhouses were put under contract on December 11, 1828.[36]

The successful contractors soon began the work of construction. Every possible contingency seemed to have been anticipated and provided for. In the event that something had been overlooked, the Board issued a flood of letters and circulars advising engineers and contractors alike on all phases of the work.[37] It gave detailed instructions to regulate the building of locks, walls, culverts, and aqueducts. The manner of providing for ferries across the canal, the method of making the basins, and the proper slope of the banks were carefully outlined. Inevitably there was an equally great deluge of instructions from the engineers themselves to their subordinates and to the contractors.[38] This was partly in self-defense and partly

[35] Report to Special Meeting (September 10, 1828), Proceedings of Stockholders, A, 17-18.

[36] Proceedings of Directors, A, 129 (December 11, 1828); 1st Annual Report (1829), Proceedings of Stockholders, A, 33. The work undertaken in the latter months of 1828 included approximately forty-eight miles of excavation, walling, etc., two dams, two aqueducts, sixty culverts, twenty-seven locks, seventeen lockhouses, several basins—one of which was the terminal basin of the canal proper at Rock Creek—and the mole at the mouth of the creek. In all it was a substantial beginning for the enterprise.

[37] Mercer to Fairfax, November 12, December 22, 1828; Mercer to Boye, November 18, 1828; Circular to the Engineers, May 15, 1829.

[38] Report of the Inspector of Masonry [Leckie], December 3, 1828; Wright to Fairfax, December 8, 1828; Roberts to Fairfax, December 26, 1828; Leckie to Purcell, July 3, 1829; Leckie to Fairfax, July 3, 10, 1829; Leckie to Van Slyke, March 4, 1830; Wright to President and Directors, October 2, 1930; Purcell to the President, November 9, 1830.

the result of a tendency to interfere in all phases of construction, in the manner of the directors. There is little wonder that at times the contractors were bewildered and disgusted.

Despite all these precautions and detailed instructions, the progress of the canal was repeatedly disrupted by problems growing out of the actual work. In the main these early trials of the canal project closely foreshadowed the future obstacles to its successful completion. The shortage of laborers was felt as soon as large-scale construction commenced. Land disputes occupied much of the attention of the canal board as local proprietors resisted the efforts of the company to keep costs at a minimum and sought instead to extract the maximum benefit from the loss of their lands. In the end, the company itself became involved in financial difficulties arising from the other troubles and from its own ill-advised enthusiasm. On top of all these distractions, the Board had to contend with a legal controversy growing out of a dispute with the Baltimore and Ohio Railroad Company over the right of way in the Potomac valley and an injunction obtained by the railroad directors prohibiting the construction of the canal above Point of Rocks.

As early as May, 1829, the contractors were in difficulty.[39] Judge Wright later pointed out, "The truth is that *we know* the prices of these contractors are all very low, and that it yet remains doubtful whether they can sustain themselves."[40] He had made this statement *after* a general increase had already been allowed. Even if the bids had been high enough for the prevailing level of wages and prices in 1828, some difficulty would have arisen from the general inflation which followed. In the first year the actual costs of construction were above the estimates of Geddes and Roberts. Payments for lumber, stone, provisions, and labor all exceeded contract figures.[41] The cost of lime alone was 200 and 300 per cent higher than the estimate. Contracts for locks had to be abandoned and relet several

[39] Report of the President, Proceedings of Directors, A, 230-231 (May 27, 1829).

[40] Wright to Mercer, February 9, 1830.

[41] 1st Annual Report (1829), Proceedings of Stockholders, A, 39, 52; Bracket and Wines to President and Directors, January 20, 1829; Kavanaugh and Co. to President and Directors, March 27, 1829; W. W. Fenlon to President and Directors, January 19, 1830; Wright to Mercer, February 21, 1830.

times, and one general increase of 25 per cent was granted.[42] By 1832 rate of wages was almost double that prevailing in 1828.[43]

Other early developments in construction tended to increase costs for contractors. The first excavations above Georgetown revealed gravel and hardpan, totally unexpected from surface indications.[44] The blasting which was necessary because of the rocky nature of the ground resulted in many annoying accidents. For example, the concussion of the explosions and the flying rock damaged several buildings. To reduce the damage from this cause, the Board ordered the use of smaller charges and required that the blasting be covered with brush.[45] The net result of this policy was more delay and increased expenses. The weather was responsible for other costly delays in digging the trunk of the canal. The winter of 1828-1829 was unusually severe, and many contractors who had begun work were forced to suspend operations until spring.[46] The freshets which occurred regularly in the spring and fall often filled the lock pits and parts of the canal trunk, further retarding the work.[47] The high banks on the river side of the canal were a third source of increased costs. The contractors proceeded carefully so as to leave some of the trees standing in order to give the banks greater stability. The company also directed that others be planted along the new walls to help retain the earth.[48]

Contractors resorted to various expedients to avoid disastrous losses. The responsible ones sought redress in petitions for the payment of retained money and for increased allowances. Their pleas often met with the recommendation of the chief

[42] 1st Annual Report (1829), Proceedings of Stockholders, A, 38-39.

[43] 4th Annual Report (1833), Proceedings of Stockholders, A, 221-222.

[44] 1st Annual Report (1829), Proceedings of Stockholders, A, 38; *2d Annual Report* (1830), p. 5.

[45] Proceedings of Directors, B, 87-88 (May 31, 1830), 152 (July 31, 1830), 191 (October 2, 1830), 248 (December 22, 1830), 257 (January 22, 1831), S. B. Balch to President and Directors, August 28, 1830; Purcell to O. H. Dibble, September 4, 1830; W. Wade to Mercer, June 2, 1831.

[46] 1st Annual Report (1829), Proceedings of Stockholders, A, 54.

[47] Holdsworth and Sherwood to President and Directors, September 24, 1829. On the other hand, the steady rains of autumn helped to settle the banks. Van Slyke to President and Directors, January 13, 1831.

[48] Proceedings of Directors, B, 309 (April 29, 1831); John McP. Brien to [President and Directors], February 3, 1835.

engineer and the favorable action of the Board.[49] Others sought to avoid losses by slipshod and fradulent construction.[50] Still others absconded with the monthly payments on the estimates, leaving both laborers and creditors unpaid.[51] On the whole, the quality of work done on the Chesapeake and Ohio canal was said to be about equivalent to the contract prices.[52]

The major problem with which the company had to contend during the actual digging of the canal was the supply of labor. The scarcity of workers and the consequently high rate of wages threatened to upset all the calculations of the contractors. There were few laborers available in the valley itself, and few could be attracted to it because of the reputation of the Potomac for ill health in certain seasons and because of the construction of other public works. The competition between the contractors for workers and the high wages of the harvest season also affected the rate of wages at certain times.[53] By means of special agencies and extensive correspondence, the Board undertook to encourage the migration of workers from all parts of the Union and from various countries of Europe, especially Great Britain, Germany, and the Netherlands.[54] The company

[49] Proceedings of Directors, A, 205 (April 22, 1829); 1st Annual Report (1829), Proceedings of Stockholders, A, 38-39; Wright to Mercer, February 21 (two letters), March 25, 1830. A portion of each payment to the contractors for work done, usually 5 or 10 per cent, was retained by the canal company as protection against the failure of a contractor to finish his job satisfactorily.

[50] Van Slyke to President and Directors, July 21, 1830; Cruger to Mercer, November 18, 1829; McFarland to Ingle, May 25, 1831.

[51] Proceedings of Directors, A, 289 (June 24, 1829); Cruger to Ingle, November 8, 1829; Purcell to Ingle, October 23, 1830.

[52] J. J. Abert, *Report on a Canal to Connect the Chesapeake and Ohio Canal with Baltimore* [April 23, 1838] (Washington, 1874), p. 18. Many contractors were ruined by their experiences on the canal, and few if any prospered from their connection with it. See the speech of William Price, canal director, on the opening of the canal, October 10, 1850, Cumberland *Civilian*, quoted in Special Report on the Completion of the Canal, pp. 390-391.

[53] 1st Annual Report (1829), Proceedings of Stockholders, A, 52; *2d Annual Report* (1803), pp. 5-6.

[54] Mercer to Thomas P. Cope, November 18, 1828, Letter Book A, 40-41; Mercer to James Barbour, November 18, 1828, *ibid.*, p. 42; 1st Annual Report (1829), Proceedings of Stockholders, A, 55. Wages averaged $10 to $12 a month for common labor in November, 1828, and continued to rise to $12 and $13 a month in July, 1829. Mercer to Richards, July 8, 1829, Letter Book, A, 84; Proceedings of Directors, A, 140 (January 7, 1829), 309 (July 15, 1829).

inserted advertisements in English and Irish newspapers offering prospective workers meat three times a day, plenty of bread and vegetables, a reasonable allowance of liquor, and $8, $10, and $12 a month wages. The notices said that ten thousand workers were needed.[55] Friends of the canal in Congress even petitioned for the use of troops in the construction of the proposed tunnel on the mountain section, the most formidable undertaking of the projected connection between the Potomac and the Ohio.[56]

The efforts of the directors to secure a sufficiently large number of workers at low wages led to an interesting but disastrous attempt to revive the system of indentured service which had flourished in the early colonial period. On January 31, 1829, the Board authorized the president to open negotiations with Henry Richards, a Welshman formerly employed on the Erie and the Chesapeake and Delaware canals.[57] Richards was to be the agent of the Chesapeake and Ohio Canal Company in Great Britain and was to secure laborers to work on the line. The Board also continued for a while to negotiate for workers from the British Isles through James Maury, the American consul at Liverpool. In its general instructions to Maury and Richards, the company offered to pay all costs of transportation in return for the indentures of the immigrants for three months. The directors requested that the workers be sent out in time to arrive by late September or the first of October. In this way they would avoid the "sickly" season and yet have three months of good working weather before winter. Quarrymen and stonecutters were most in demand for they were badly needed to stimulate the lagging masonry work. The Board discouraged the enlistment of families and if they came, required them to pay their own way. Furthermore, it provided no accommodations for them on the line.[58]

The detailed instructions to Richards included the following additional stipulations. (1) Upon his arrival in England he

[55] Mercer to James Maury, November 18, 1828, Letter Book A, 39; Daniel Teer to Mercer, January 12, 1829.

[56] *2d Annual Report* (1830), pp. 25-27.

[57] Proceedings of Directors, A, 153 (January 31, 1829), 175 (March 6, 1829); Mercer to Maury, March 7, 1829, Letter Book A, 61.

[58] Mercer to Maury, July 8, 1829, Letter Book A, 83; Mercer to Richards, July 8, 1829, *ibid.*, pp. 84-85. A month was computed at twenty-six working days.

was to cooperate in every way with Maury, the consul. (2) He was to concentrate his efforts on securing the services of English, Welsh, and Scottish laborers accustomed to digging. (3) Common laborers must sign obligations requiring seventy-eight days' labor, while masons were to sign indentures for fifty-four days' service. (4) Any advances beyond the cost of transportation were to be repaid at the rate of $8 a month for common laborers and $16 a month for masons. (5) They were to receive the same subsistence as the other workers, but were to be boarded free of charge. (6) If necessary, Richards was authorized to offer wages as high as $10 a month for common laborers and $20 a month for masons. (7) Finally, the men so transported were to work on the canal for one year after the termination of their indentures at the prevailing rate of wages or at a stipulated rate, whichever the laborer in question desired. No contracts were to be made to extend beyond December 1, 1830.[59]

The mission of Richards on behalf of the canal company came at a most opportune time for the latter's purpose. England was in the midst of an economic and political crisis marked by widespread unemployment, high prices, and suffering and unrest among the working classes. There was also extensive agitation for political reform, especially in the midland and northwestern industrial towns. Under these conditions the Irish, Welsh, and English workers in the mines, mills, and factories were receptive to the terms offered by the Chesapeake and Ohio agent.

Richards began sending the men over in August, 1829. The first group of about three hundred and twenty laborers crossed the ocean in the *Pioneer*, the *Julian*, and the *Boston*. Concerning these immigrants, he wrote:

> I have been very careful to select men of good character, steady and industrious. . . . Some few Irishmen are among them but all these have worked some time in England & amongst Englishmen and are good workmen and peacable [*sic*].
>
> There are a great many Miners and Colliers chiefly in the Boston. The Masons and Quarry Men have been selected from the Quarries Rail Roads and Canals in the different Counties of England and Wales.

---

[59] Instructions to H. B. Richards, *ibid.*, pp. 85-87.

. . . Some few of the men are rather Small and Young—but most of these if you think it is required will Serve for a longer time—

According to your first instructions the men have agreed to work in lieu of their passage—the Stone Cutters and Masons and some Black-smiths & Carpenters for three months the laborers agree to work Four months. . . . The instructions received yesterday . . . authorize me to make the time shorter say 2 months for Masons and 3 months for others. but as I shall be able to engage men on the same terms as before I shall continue to do so leaving it to you to shorten their time after they arrive if you think proper. and this will perhaps be more satisfactory to the men themselves—who will think it a great favor—

I have sent as few women and Children as possible and those only the families of good workmen. I will send no more if I can possibly avoid it.

. . . I have sent with each vessel a careful and trusty man . . . [who will] see the workmen delivered to you.[60]

Another contingent of laborers came over on the *Nimrod*.[61] Although Richards requested further instructions beyond his authority to hire a thousand laborers, the group sent over on the *Shenandoah*, which arrived late in October, were the last.[62]

The trip over was a harrowing affair for all concerned. The overseers who were sent out with each boatload of immigrants were responsible for the safe delivery of the hands assigned to them. They were also charged with the distribution of rations on board ship. On both counts they gained the hatred of the laborers. They differed widely in character: Peter Powell, for example, was a wretched, ignorant, terrified person; George Gill, on the other hand, was proud, arrogant, and utterly dis-dainful of the workers to whom he referred as "clowns," "brutes," and "frauds." [63] The experience of the bosses was quite similar.[64] The daily distribution of the bread and meat always brought tempers to a high pitch. The poor immigrants complained of favoritism, short weight, and inedible provisions.

[60] H. B. Richards to [President and Directors], August 21, 1829.

[61] Boteler and Reynolds to Ingle, November 5, 1829.

[62] Richards to [President and Directors], August 21, 1829; Proceedings of Directors, A, 380 (October 21, 1829); Ingle to Janney, October 26, 1829, Letter Book A, 123-124. Ingle wrote that "176 more plagues" had arrived.

[63] Peter Powell to President and Directors, November 18, 1829; George Gill to President and Directors, November 18, 1829.

[64] The following account is based upon the versions given in P. Powell to President and Directors, November 18, 1829, Gill to President and Directors, November 18, 1829, and R. Jones to President and Directors, November 18, 1829.

They appealed to the ship captains, who invariably washed their hands of the quarrel and often suggested that the men take the matters into their own hands. Although the overseers were subjected to a constant stream of threats and abuse, all of them survived the trip.

The company directed its agents to send the laborers to either Alexandria or Georgetown. The Board feared that if the men landed at another port they "might be decoyed from our service." On their arrival they were assigned to directors Walter Smith at Georgetown and Phineas Janney at Alexandria.[65] The latter paid the marine insurance on them, and completed arrangements for housing, feeding, and superintending them in one large building.[66] They were then placed under the supervision of a Superintendent of Imported Laborers, one of the assistant engineers assigned to that duty, and those among them who were sick received medical attention.[67] Subsequently they were turned over to the contractors and their indentures delivered up to the latter upon proper receipt and upon the assumption of responsibility for the cost of transportation. The contractors called the roll to have the indentures acknowledged by the laborers. If any of them refused they were promptly sent to jail.[68]

The experiences of the contractors with the immigrants varied widely, probably according to the character of the workers and the treatment given them. Those assigned to the Potomac Mills were entirely satisfactory, although the wages paid were below the $10 per month average for the canal.[69] Others along the line were said not to be worth their board.[70] Some of the laborers had real grievances in the treatment they received at the hands of the contractors. Those working for M. S. Wines

[65] Mercer to Maury, July 8, 1829, Letter Book A, 83; Mercer to Richards, July 8, 1829, *ibid.*, p. 89; Richards to [President and Directors], August 21, 1829.

[66] Proceedings of Directors, A, 347 (September 23, 1829), 380 (October 21, 1829); Janney to Ingle, October 23, 1829.

[67] Ingle to Dr. Joshua Riley, October 21, 1829, Letter Book A, 124; Edward Watts to President and Directors, November 4, 1829.

[68] Proceedings of Directors, A, 364 (September 28, 1829); Mercer to Ingle, September 30, 1829. The cost of transportation was fixed at $32 per person.

[69] Boteler and Reynolds to Ingle, November 5, 1829; Ingle to Boteler and Reynolds, November 19, 1829, Letter Book A, 134.

[70] Edward Watts to [Ingle], October 23, 1829.

left him and returned to Washington. They consented to resume work only on certain conditions. They demanded a weather-proof house, a sufficient supply of meat, bread, and other customary provisions, the transportation of their baggage to the section without delay, and the establishment of an account definitely listing the debts for passage and the credits for work done. They agreed to allow the contractor a reasonable amount of time to fulfill the conditions. In return, the company promised that if he failed to do so it would transfer them to another section.[71]

Other dissatisfied workers were not so patient or conscientious. Many simply deserted the line of the canal and disappeared into the neighboring countryside. At first the runaways that were captured and imprisoned were released upon a promise that they would return to the canal.[72] The directors believed at this time that the grievances could be corrected and the men retained. As they continued to abscond the Board began to lose faith in their good intentions.[73] Some of the men fled to the Baltimore and Ohio Railroad and found jobs.[74] Others went to the city of Baltimore where they sought the protection of the law. There the company caught up with them and prosecuted them as runaways and debtors.[75]

The trials proved to be a costly failure. Baltimore was hostile to the claims of the company, and the laborers received sympathetic assistance from lawyers, merchants, and brawlers.[76] The City Court of Baltimore ruled that the agreements between the company and the workers were not of a master-servant character, but were merely contracts for work. The men

[71] Ingle to M. S. Wines, October 3, 1829, Letter Book A, 112-113. These terms were ordered to apply to the entire line of the canal, and the clerk was directed to go up the line and to investigate the complaints so generally made. Proceedings of Directors, A, 367 (October 6, 1829).

[72] Proceedings of Directors, A, 367-368 (October 6, 1829).

[73] The directors were able to compromise the differences between the absconding workers and the contractors in the case of Knapp, Ford and Co. (*Ibid*., pp. 376-377 [October 13, 1829].) But when the laborers continued to run away, the Board ordered more effective steps taken to apprehend them. *Ibid*., p. 379 (October 21, 1829).

[74] *Ibid*., p. 369 (October 7, 1829), quoting a letter from R. Jones; p. 377 (October 13, 1829); R. Jones to President and Directors, October 21, 1829.

[75] William Wirt to Ingle, Baltimore, October 28, 1829, November 4, 1829; Proceedings of Directors, A, 389 (November 7, 1829).

[76] Ingle to Janney, October 26, 1829, Letter Book A, 122-123.

therefore were freed, though subject to damages and costs. The company could still sue for debts. If so, the men could plead bankruptcy and either get off entirely or be sent to jail at the company's expense. In a jury trial there was always the possibility they might argue that the company had first broken the contract by providing "stinking and putrid beef" on the voyage over. With this plea, true or false, no jury in Baltimore would convict them, especially when it might be composed of railroad men looking for workers themselves. In view of this unpromising prospect, the cases were dropped.[77]

The immigrants who remained on the line, servants and freemen alike, suffered greatly from ill-health due to the rigors of acclimatization and the unhealthy atmosphere of the Potomac valley. The sick and destitute workers poured into Georgetown in ever-increasing numbers. As early as October, 1829, they were being picked up off the streets of the town, sick and starving, and carried to the poor house. By that time, 126 had been cared for by the city authorities. The latter complained that these people were not city poor and that the company should look out for its own.[78] The influx increased as winter approached. Some found their way to Washington and to the city poor house there. Private charity took care of still others.[79] The miserable conditions of the laborers and the even more dismal tales of their treatment aroused humanitarians to such violent attacks that the company was obliged to take official notice of the accusations and defend itself.[80]

The use of imported laborers succeeded in momentarily stabil-

[77] Wirt to Ingle, November 6, 1829, Ingle to Wirt, November 7, 1829, Letter Book A, 127; Ingle to Glenn, January 28, 1830, *ibid.*, p. 162.

[78] John Litle, Trustee for the Poor of Georgetown, to President and Directors, October 13, 1829, enclosing the report of John Brigum, Overseer of the Poor, October 10, 1829. The Board appropriated $150 for the care of the sick workers of the city. Proceedings of Directors, A, 380-381 (October 21, 1829). Later it appropriated an additional $117.45 for Georgetown and $267.45 for Washington for the same purposes. *Ibid.*, B, 65 (April 28, 1820). See also Mercer to the Justices of the Circuit Court of the District of Columbia, March, 1829, Letter Book A, 68-69.

[79] John G. Whitwell, Trustee of the Poor of Washington, to Mercer, March 9, 1830, enclosing the report of John McNerhany, Intendant, Washington Asylum; Mercer to Mrs. Susan Decatur, December 13, 1830.

[80] Jo. Gales to Ingle, February 8, 1830; Joseph Lenox and R. G. Herring, Stewards of the Society of the Sons of St. George, Philadelphia, to Ingle, February 17, 1830.

izing and indeed lowering the rate of wages on the canal.[81] The total working force on the line rose from a low of sixteen hundred or two thousand in the sickly season to over thirty-one hundred in November, 1829.[82] In the long run, however, the experiment was a failure, and the difficulty of enforcing the agreements under existing laws led to its suspension. The entanglements in law suits, in poor-house claims, and in unfavorable notoriety more than offset the immediate advantages. In fact, the stabilization of wages and the increase in the working force might have resulted naturally from the suspension of work on the Pennsylvania canals in September, 1829.[83]

Before the lessons of the episode had been learned, the directors resolved upon the purchase of one hundred slaves for the use of the company.[84] In taking this step, as in the case of the indentured servants, the Board was following the example of the Potomac Company, despite the warning of the unfortunate results of the earlier experiments. The directors took no action to carry out this resolution, however, and when a proposal to purchase three hundred and fifty slaves came up before the annual meeting in June, 1830, it was decisively defeated.[85] By that time, the stockholders had had enough of the schemes to provide cheap labor for the contractors.

As construction advanced, the Board continued to have trouble with its working force. The annual sickly season took its toll among the laborers and engineers alike. It also indirectly forced wages up to unexpected levels.[86] The presence of so many men on such an extended line created problems of morale and coordination. To solve these, a new postal route

[81] *2d Annual Report* (1830) pp. 5-6.

[82] Report of the President, Proceedings of Directors, A, 353 (September 25, 1829); Ingle to Thomas Cuthbert, December 12, 1829, Letter Book A, 145-146.

[83] Report of the President, Proceedings of Directors, A, 353-354 (September 25, 1829).

[84] Proceedings of Directors, A, 310 (July 15, 1829).

[85] 2d Annual Meeting (June 12, 1830), *2d Annual Report* (1830), p. 28.

[86] Henry Smith to the Board of Directors, August 2, 1828 [1829]; E. L. Lanham to President and Directors, July 22, 1829; Ingle to Cruger, December 9, 1829; Jared Darrow and Co. to President and Directors, July 22, 1830; Dr. Charles Laub to Walter May, July 7, 1830; McFarland to Ingle, August 28, 1831. See also the Report of the President, Proceedings of Directors, A, 352 (September 25, 1829); *2d Annual Report* (1830), p. 25; and M. F. Harris to Mercer, July 26, 1830.

was established with its own offices scattered along the canal. These offices bore descriptive local names, such as Magazine, Section Eight, Bear Island, Clementon, Seneca Mills, Edward's Ferry, Conrad's Ferry, Mouth of Monocacy, and Catoctin.[87] Contractors had trouble with shopkeepers along the line who maintained grog shops or surreptitiously sold liquor to the men.[88] Furthermore, many of the workers insisted on taking an extended vacation at Christmas time to return to their families.[89]

A third major obstacle encountered in the construction of the canal was the high cost of land. Some of the landholders on the route over which the canal was to pass readily granted the company the title required, or at least rights to the use of the land. Many others obstructed the work and refused to surrender their property voluntarily, in the hope of realizing great profits from forced sales.[90] In the latter instances, condemnation proceedings were resorted to. These became more and more the rule as construction moved up the river and as the speculative fever of the petty farmers rose.

Among those who resisted the condemnation efforts of the company were at least two groups: those who held out for the highest possible price, and those who would not sell at any price. The former included those who resisted the verdict of the juries, called for new trials, and generally tried to secure higher prices by delaying tactics which raised their nuisance value.[91] The second group usually had other motives in the background. Charles Carroll of Carrollton, for example, brushed aside all offers for his lands in the valley. He stressed the

[87] John McLean to Mercer, October 3, 1828; Mercer to the Postmaster-General of the United States, May 29, 1829, Letter Book A, 74-75; A Nelson to Mercer, September 28, 1829; C. K. Gardner to Mercer, September 29, 1829; S. R. Hobbie to Mercer, February 19, 1830. In most cases the contractor on the section was appointed postmaster, on President Mercer's recommendation. Although not very satisfactory, this route remained the only means of regular communication with the canal.

[88] Watts to President and Directors, December 9, 1829. In 1832, Mercer sought to secure the passage of a law by the Maryland Assembly prohibiting the sale of liquor within two or three miles of the canal in Frederick, Washington, and Allegany counties. (Mercer to Ingle, January 23, 1832.) His efforts were in vain, however.

[89] Peter Owens to Board of Directors, December 23, 1829.

[90] E. Hurd to Mercer, January 26, 1829; 1st Annual Report (1829), Proceedings of Stockholders, A, 41-42.

[91] 1st Annual Report (1829), Proceedings of Stockholders, A, 42.

great suffering which his tenants would experience during the actual construction. In return for this hardship to them, there was only the promise of increased land values for him if the canal were ever completed—which he doubted.[92] Charles Carroll was one of the founders of the Baltimore and Ohio Railroad Company, which was at this time locked in a struggle with the canal company for the right of way in the Potomac valley.

The extension of the canal from Little Falls to Rock Creek brought on renewed trouble with proprietors. Here again several motives were usually involved in the resistance of certain landowners. Georgetown merchants were extremely reluctant to see the canal extended below its former terminus, which was favorable to the commercial position of their town. They also disliked giving up what was and would be valuable property in Georgetown. They were not satisfied that what they received then was a fair price in terms of the value the property might have if the town experienced the growth they anticipated. The directors had prophesied that awards for damages would run very high, and this expectation was fully borne out by experience.[93]

A final factor which increased the cost of land was the decision to purchase the strip between the canal and the river. The directors were obsessed with the idea of dispensing with bridges over the canal. They hoped in this way to facilitate the development of steamboats on the waterway. To relieve the company of the necessity of providing access from one piece of land to another where separated by the canal, they took the course of purchasing the segment lying on the river side of the waterway.[94] This was not strictly within the terms of the

[92] Carroll to Mercer, February 26, 1829.

[93] Proceedings of Directors, A, 59 (September 3, 1828); *2d Annual Report* (1830), p. 11. At the same time, the canal became involved in disputes with many of its old friends and supporters in Georgetown, including John Mason, Francis Scott Key, Walter and Clement Smith, and others. Mercer to Justices of the Circuit Court of the District of Columbia, March, 1829, Letter Book A, 68; Proceedings of Directors, A, 167 (February 17, 1829), 182 (March 18, 1829). See also, Chesapeake and Ohio Canal Company *vs.* Key, *U. S. Reports*, 3 Cranch C. C. 599; Chesapeake and Ohio Canal Company *vs.* Mason, *ibid.*, 4 Cranch C. C. 123; and Chesapeake and Ohio Canal Company *vs.* Union Bank (of Georgetown), *ibid.*, 4 Cranch C. C. 75, 5 Cranch C. C. 509.

[94] Mercer to A. Lee, January 17, 1829; Letter Book A, 57; *2d Annual Report* (1830), p. 11.

charter which allowed the condemnation of private property for canal purposes only. However, the line was located so close to the river that the amount of land required was not very great.

The cumulative effect of greater allowances to contractors, increased labor costs, and higher land payments brought the canal company to the end of its financial resources. The company had begun its operations with a subscribed capital of about $3,600,000. Included in this total were subscriptions of the United States for $1,000,000; the city of Washington for $1,000,000; the city of Georgetown for $250,000; the city of Alexandria for $250,000; the state of Maryland for $500,000; and Shepherdstown, Virginia, for $20,000. Subscriptions by private individuals accounted for the remaining $600,000. The total cost of the eastern section had been estimated at $8,000,-000 by the U. S. Board of Engineers and at $4,500,000 by Geddes and Roberts. The canal company chose to rely on the latter estimate. Even so it had begun construction without sufficient funds to insure the completion of the eastern section under the most optimistic estimate.

The Board and the stockholders felt secure nevertheless in beginning work with the available resources. They confidently expected further aid from Congress and from the interested states, especially Virginia which had as yet made no subscription. Supporters of the canal were convinced that the work would prove to be a profitable venture and that further private subscriptions would be encouraged by its success. In terms of conditions in 1828 they were probably justified, if somewhat optimistic, in these expectations. As it happened, the anticipated subscriptions were not forthcoming at this time from either public or private sources. Appeals to Congress proved futile, and a measure before the Virginia Assembly to subscribe $400,000 to the enterprise also failed.[95] The company had to rely upon its existing resources for the prosecution of its work.

From the very beginning the Board encountered difficulties in securing the payment of the calls on the subscribed capital. Maryland insisted on paying part of its share in state bonds.[96]

[95] 1st Annual Report (1829), Proceedings of Stockholders, A, 51.

[96] The directors were persuaded to accept this procedure because the railroad company had already agreed to it and because it was necessary to placate the

The cities of the District of Columbia ran into trouble making payments on their subscriptions. To secure funds to meet the calls on the canal stock, the local authorities appointed Richard Rush, ex-Secretary of the Treasury, to act as the agent of the District cities to negotiate a loan in Europe. After failing in his mission in England, Rush succeeded in obtaining the loan in Holland.[97] The canal company also had the usual trouble with delinquent private stockholders and had to resort to threats and legal suits to obtain satisfaction.[98] By June, 1832, the Board had issued calls for the payment of 60 per cent of the capital stock.[99]

As early as 1829, the company realized that the higher costs would jeopardize the completion of its work. To offset this danger and to increase the subscriptions to the level necessary to finish the canal, the Board constituted Richard Rush the agent of the company to open books in Europe to receive subscriptions up to $6,000,000 for the eastern section and $10,000,000 for the whole canal.[100] As the railroad injunction continued in effect, the expense of a large and high-salaried clerical and engineering staff became a great burden on the company's financial condition. Strict economy and retrenchment became the order of the day. Accordingly the Board released engineers as soon as they found positions elsewhere, reduced salaries, and left vacancies unfilled.[101] While not yet desperate, the

canal's enemies in the state legislature. The company had so little success in selling the bonds that it resorted to hypothecations in order to obtain loans from the local banks. Kent to Mercer, October 4, 1828; C. Smith to Ingle, January 4, 1831; Proceedings of Directors, A, 373 (October 12, 1829), 377-378 (October 17, 1829).

[97] Rush to Mercer, July 15, October 7, November 13, 1829; Mercer to Ingle, December 29, 1829. See also the correspondence between Rush and the corporate authorities of Washington, Georgetown, and Alexandria, and between Rush and the Barings and the Crommelins, in the Manuscripts Division of the Library of Congress (Washington, D. C.). These letters and related materials are filed in two folio cartons entitled "Washington, Georgetown, and Alexandria—Holland Loan."

[98] See, for example, Letters Received, December, 1829, and Proceedings of Directors, B, 291 (March 25, 1831).

[99] W. S. Ringgold to Ingle, June 18, 1832.

[100] 1st Annual Report (1829), Proceedings of Stockholders, A, 50. There were no large subscriptions.

[101] Proceedings of Directors, A, 294 (June 26, 1829), B, 171-173 (August 30, 1830). See also, 1st Annual Report (1829), Proceedings of Stockholders, A, 61-62, and 3d Annual Report (1831), *ibid.*, p. 175.

financial condition of the company was rapidly deteriorating by 1832.

The greatest deterrent to the westward progress of the canal after 1828 was the existence of a series of injunctions prohibiting the extension of the waterway above Point of Rocks. These injunctions were in turn the cause of a long and costly court struggle between the canal company and the railroad company. The question involved in the cases was a dispute over the right of prior location of the respective projects in the Potomac valley. The matter was not fully settled until early in 1832.

The legal controversy between the rival internal improvement projects was the culmination of a clash of interests that had been developing since the early twenties. Baltimore had at first been an active supporter of the canal project, but its enthusiasm began to wane as it became apparent that the canal if built would favor the development of a rival emporium on the banks of the Potomac. Doubts arose as to the practicability of tapping the waterway far enough up the valley to allow Baltimore to share in its trade.[102] Therefore, the merchants of Baltimore sought some other way for their city to compete with the commercial centers of New York and Philadelphia which were fed by the Erie and Pennsylvania canals, respectively. The proposal for a railway originated at a meeting of Baltimore citizens in February, 1827. It was immediately adopted, and the Baltimore and Ohio Railroad Company was subsequently organized.[103] The canal company had been chartered in 1824-1825, but the report of the U. S. Board of Engineers had delayed the organization of the company until 1828. Both companies formally commenced construction on the Fourth of July, 1828.

Both enterprises ultimately chose the Potomac valley as the route of their respective works. The canal company felt secure in its right of prior location which it inherited from its predecessor, the Potomac Company. Consequently, it proceeded in a regular fashion with its operations. The railroad company, on the other hand, sent surveyors ahead to locate its line and secure land waivers, especially in the narrow passes of the val-

[102] A later survey, by William Howard, a U. S. engineer, confirmed these fears.

[103] Answer of the Chesapeake and Ohio Canal Company, 4 Gill and Johnson 32-33. See also the Bill of Complaint, *ibid.*, pp. 7-8, and Edward Hungerford, *The Story of the Baltimore and Ohio Railroad*, I, 29-31.

ley at which a conflict with the canal might be expected.[104] To stop this usurpation of their rights, canal company stockholders secured an injunction, in the Washington County Court, June, 10, 1828, prohibiting the railroad from proceeding beyond the Point of Rocks, the place at which it entered the Potomac valley.[105] The railroad company countered with three injunctions against the canal which it obtained in the Court of Chancery at Annapolis, June 23, 24, and 25.[106] The canal company protested that the conduct of the Baltimore and Ohio was an infringement on the canal's chartered rights and an unfriendly act. It pointed out that it had not opposed the railroad's charter and insisted that the railroad officials had given the impression that their work would avoid the circuitous Potomac route for a more direct northwesterly course to Pittsburgh.[107] The legal question involved was whether the Potomac Company's rights inherited by the Chesapeake and Ohio were still valid or whether the Baltimore and Ohio had acquired them by virtue of its charter from the state of Maryland in 1827 and the first exercise of the rights of location. The real issue, however, was the political one between the city of Baltimore through the state of Maryland and the cities of the District of Columbia[108] —with local politics within Maryland adding to the confusion.

[104] Answer of the Chesapeake and Ohio Canal Company, 4 Gill and Johnson 35-36; 3d Annual Report (1831), Proceedings of Stockholders, A, 166; 1st Annual Report of the Board of Engineers, *2d Annual Report of the Baltimore and Ohio Railroad Company* (1828), Appendix, pp. 3-4.

[105] Answer of the Chesapeake and Ohio Canal Company, 4 Gill and Johnson 36; 1st Annual Report (1829), Proceedings of Stockholders, A, 55; *2d Annual Report* (1830), p. 9; *3d Annual Report of the Baltimore and Ohio Railroad Company* (1829), p. 9.

[106] 4 Gill and Johnson 14-15; Proceedings of Directors, A, 8 (June 26, 1830 [1828]). See also *2d Annual Report* (1830), p. 9.

[107] "Proceedings of the Meeting of Baltimore Citizens," quoted in Answer of the Chesapeake and Ohio Canal Company, 4 Gill and Johnson 32-33. See also *Memorial of the Chesapeake and Ohio Canal Company*, February 23, 1829, 20th Cong., 2d sess., House of Representatives, Document No. 127, p. 3.

[108] See, for example Representative Mitchell's speech, February 28, 1829, quoted in *Niles' Register*, XXXVI, No. 4 (March 21, 1829), 53. The course of the controversy in all its mainfold aspects can be followed best in the uncatalogued series of about thirty letters, apparently taken from the canal company's files for purposes of publication as a continuous narrative of the struggle, recently discovered among the papers concerning the Holland Loan in the Manuscripts Division of the Library of Congress.

In the course of the legal struggle, the Baltimore and Ohio was content to fight a delaying action in the courts, while its influence, and that of the city of Baltimore, had its effect in the General Assembly of Maryland and in Congress. In both instances the petitions of the railroad company met with considerable success. The Maryland legislature became distinctly hostile to the canal company's claims, choosing to look upon the railroad as a purely Maryland project which was deserving of the state's protection and patronage.[109] In Congress the influence of the canal company was checked by the railroad's petition and by the hostility of the Jacksonian Democrats to federally sponsored internal improvements.[110] The railroad insisted that both works be considered experiments until time tested the relative merits of each. This involved both companies in a long discussion of the historical comparisons of railroads and canals in England and the United States. In the meantime, the Baltimore and Ohio was occupied in constructing its road across Maryland to Frederick and then south to the Point of Rocks. Its resources were limited, but it had the very real advantage that its road began operating as quickly as it was finished. The railroad company could afford to wait.

The canal company found itself in the opposite position during the struggle. At first, it too was content to allow the wheels of justice to grind slowly.[111] Then, as the court showed no signs of reaching an early decision, the directors became restless. The company had ample resources to undertake a large part of the work, and it was anxious to take advantage of the satisfactorily low prices for which the first contracts had been let.[112] In addition; the line of the canal above the Seneca feeder was useless until the next feeder was reached at Harpers Ferry,

[109] A. Lee to Mercer, February 15, 1829; Ingle to Mercer, February 2, 1831. On the other hand, it was hotly denied that the state was in any way responsible for the long delay in the case between the railroad and the canal companies. See *A Candid Appeal to the Stockholders of the Chesapeake and Ohio Canal Company* (Washington, 1832).

[110] Proceedings of Directors, B, 78 ff. (May 22, 1830); *Niles' Register*, XXXVIII, No. 3 (March 13, 1830), 62-63.

[111] The canal company did not file its answer to the bill of complaint until May 16, 1829. Answer of the Chesapeake and Ohio Canal Company, 4 Gill and Johnson 16.

[112] Report to Special Meeting (September 10, 1828), Proceedings of Stockholders, A, 21.

twelve miles above Point of Rocks.[113] Above all there was the charter requirement that one hundred miles of the canal must be completed in five years. Eventually the delay itself began to be costly. The large staff of engineers and clerks represented a real burden while construction was so greatly restricted.[114] While the Board was satisfied with the neutrality of Congress in the controversy with the railroad, its position in the Maryland legislature was much more difficult. There was already a considerable amount of hostility to the canal in the Assembly. Furthermore, the company was simultaneously involved with many landholders in western Maryland on several points: land prices, the sale of water power, and the substitution of ferries for bridges across the canal.[115] The canal company could not afford to wait, but it was hardly in a position to press its claims.

Nevertheless the Board did make earnest efforts to come to an early understanding with its adversary. In November, 1828, it proposed to draw up jointly with the railroad company, a case to be submitted to the Chancellor for his early decision.[116] In February, 1829, it expressed an interest in the proposal of a Maryland legislator for joint construction of the works, at least as far as Harpers Ferry.[117] The Baltimore and Ohio hastily proclaimed its desire for an early settlement, but preferred joint construction at least as far as Williamsport. A little later, the directors of the canal, fearing for the charter, agreed to this proposal, but this time the railroad refused and insisted on extending the agreement all the way to Cumberland. This the canal rejected.[118] Finally, when a decision from the Chancellor

[113] *2d Annual Report* (1830), p. 6.

[114] 1st Annual Report (1829), Proceedings of Stockholders, A, 55.

[115] *Memorial of the Chesapeake and Ohio Canal Company*, February 23, 1829, p. 3; A. Lee to Mercer, February 15, 1829; Cruger to Mercer, February 13, 16, 1831.

[116] *2d Annual Report* (1830), p. 8. The railroad rejected this proposal because it said that a case satisfactory to both companies could not be drawn up. *3d Annual Report of the Baltimore and Ohio Railroad Company* (1829), p. 10.

[117] James McCulloh to Mercer, February 7, 1829; Proceedings of Directors, A, 168-170 (February 20, 1829).

[118] Proceedings of Directors, B, 84 (May 22, 1830), 152-153 (July 31, 1830); 3d Annual Report (1831), Proceedings of Stockholders, A, 137; Mercer to President and Directors of the Baltimore and Ohio Railroad Company, November 6, 1830, Letter Book A, 276-277; *4th Annual Report of the Baltimore and Ohio Railroad Company* (1830), p. 5. See also *ibid.*, Appendices C,

seemed to be as far away as ever, the canal board proposed to accept a *pro forma* decree against its claims in order to expedite the inevitable appeal. This too the railroad refused, consistent with its policy of procrastination.[119] The judgment of the general committee of the canal company stockholders in 1829 that the Chesapeake and Ohio Canal was not to blame for the failure of attempts at conciliation seems to be fully borne out by the course of events.[120] The best that can be said for the railroad's attitude is that apparently both companies ultimately hoped to win and to exclude the other.

In the Chancery Court, the case followed the lackadaisical course preferred by the Baltimore and Ohio. The Chancellor decided early in the proceedings that a joint survey of the points of collision, suggested by the railroad's counsel, was an indispensable preliminary to a decision on the *legal* rights of the two companies to prior location.[121] The canal company protested in vain against the expense and delay of another survey of the valley.[122] The railroad company merely waited, quite content to see the commencement of the survey postponed as long as possible. Abandoning hope for a reversal of the order, the canal directors decided to push the survey.[123] By the time the surveying party reached Harpers Ferry, however, the canal board saw that the whole survey would take many months, perhaps the whole time allowed by the charter for the completion of the hundred miles.[124] It thereupon recalled its engineer, and con-

D, E, pp. 135-151. The railroad company later admitted it had acted "under feelings more natural, perhaps, than prudent." *6th Annual Report of the Baltimore and Ohio Railroad Company* (1832), pp. 13-14.

[119] Walter Jones to Ingle, October 10, 1831.

[120] Report of the General Committee, 1st Annual Meeting (1829), Proceedings of Stockholders, A, 64.

[121] Mercer to Roberts, February 24, 1830, Letter Book A, 183-184.

[122] 3d Annual Report (1831), Proceedings of Stockholders, A, 138. It was the fourth survey of the Potomac valley in six years.

[123] The Board named Nathan Roberts to make the joint survey with the railroad engineer but secretly ordered him to make a preliminary survey for the canal company first. Proceedings of Directors, A, 373-374 (October 12, 1829), 378-379 (October 21, 1829). In February, 1830, Mercer repeated the request for an early survey. Mercer to Philip E. Thomas, President of the Baltimore and Ohio Railroad Company, February 15, 1830, Letter Book A, 172.

[124] 3d Annual Report (1831), Proceedings of Stockholders, A, 138.

sidered proceeding with construction. The worst that could happen in such an event would be a quick decision against its claims. This would facilitate the inevitable appeal, an excuse for which it was already seeking.[125] The Chancellor eventually decided that enough ground had been covered (or time consumed) for his purposes and in 1831 reversed his order for the survey. In the September term, 1831, he rendered his decision releasing the railroad from the injunction against it and making those against the canal permanent.[126] In making his decision he took the puzzling position that this was not the proper time to consider the question of prior right. The conduct of the case, the final decision, and the basis of his opinion could not have been very different had the Chancellor been a representative of the railroad's interests.

The canal company now appealed the Chancellor's decision to the Court of Appeals of Maryland, in its December session. The case was immediately set for hearing, despite the continued policy of procrastination followed by the railroad company. One argument used by the latter was that the absence of one of its counsel, Roger B. Taney, recently appointed Secretary of the Treasury, deprived it of a lawyer familiar with the case from the beginning.[127] For a while, the canal company feared the delay might be countenanced, but the court took up the case as planned. Despite the absence of one of its own members, it rendered its decision in January, 1832. By a vote of 3 to 2 it reversed the decision of the Chancellor and confirmed the canal company in its claim to the right of prior location.[128]

[125] Ingle to Roberts, April 22, 1830, Letter Book A, 204; Alexander Magruger [Magruder] to Richard S. Coxe, May 25, 1831. Two other engineers, Cruger and Fairfax, were permitted to continue the survey.

[126] 3d Annual Report (1831), Proceedings of Stockholders, A, 139; Chesapeake and Ohio Canal Company *vs.* Baltimore and Ohio Railroad Company, 4 Gill and Johnson 71.

[127] W. Jones to [Mercer], December 2, 1831; Magruder to Wirt, December 10, 1831; Wirt to Mercer, December 25, 1831. It was later ascertained that Taney's absence was purely voluntary. Mercer to Ingle, January, 1833.

[128] Opinions of the court, 4 Gill and Johnson, 71-164, 164-226. The opinion of the majority adopted the argument of the canal company. *Niles' Register*, XLII, No. 24 (August 11, 1832), 419; Proceedings of Directors, C, 48 (January 7, 1832); Special Meeting (April 28, 1832), Proceedings of Stockholders, A, 196; 4th Annual Report (1832), *ibid.*, p. 200.

The struggle between the Baltimore and Ohio and the Chesapeake and Ohio for first choice of routes in the Potomac valley profited no one. Both the railroad and the canal lost financially and competitively as a result of the delay. Maryland, the Potomac route, and the valley inhabitants also lost several years of trade opportunities. Both Baltimore and the District cities marked time while New York and Philadelphia forged ahead as commercial centers at the eastern end of a rich and growing western trade via improved transportation systems.

Chapter V

MARYLAND ASSUMES CONTROL
(1832-1836)

The successful termination of the Baltimore and Ohio controversy enabled the Chesapeake and Ohio to resume the construction of its waterway. The directors wasted no time in following up their advantage and placing the entire hundred miles under contract. It was now a twofold race: the five years allowed by the charter for the construction of the first hundred miles would expire in 1833, and the exhaustion of the company's immediate financial resources was in the offing. Immediately after receiving the official copy of the decision, the Board ordered contracts to be let on February 23, 1832, for the twelve miles between Point of Rocks and Harpers Ferry.[1] Later, the directors reconsidered their action and authorized the president to make contracts for the two miles immediately above Point of Rocks without the usual public advertisement.[2]

On January 9, 1832, the directors solicited contracts for the canal all the way to Williamsport, but the winter continued so severe that the Board suspended the order for all work above Harpers Ferry. On March 14 and June 2, canal officials let

[1] Proceedings of Directors, C, 48-49 (January 7, 1832).

[2] *Ibid.*, pp. 52-53 (January 14, 1832); Mercer to Cruger and Purcell, January 23, 1832, Letter Book A, 402. The two miles included some of the narrowest of the disputed passes. The unseemly haste in contracting for the canal around the disputed Point of Rocks was sharply criticized as betraying an intention to insure the exclusion of the railroad from the Maryland side of the river. See, for example, *Niles' Register*, XLII, No. 24 (August 11, 1832), 419; *Maryland Senate Journal*, 1832, Appendix, p. 5; *Maryland House Journal*, 1832, pp. 23-24.

It is certainly true that the company acted quickly to occupy the most favorable location for its waterway. In so doing it assumed that the railroad would cross the river at Point of Rocks and proceed up the Virginia shore. It is highly improbable that the Baltimore and Ohio would have behaved at all differently had it won the case. It is, moreover, extremely doubtful that the latter, supported in its position by the state, would have acquiesced in the joint construction of the two works. Under the combined pressure of the railroad company and the state Assembly, the Chesapeake and Ohio did consent to the accommodation of its rival in 1833.

enough of the line above Harpers Ferry to complete (with slackwater navigation at some points) the hundred miles required by the charter.[3] The company took the opportunity to reassert, although not without dissent, that it had sufficient funds to complete the contracts.[4] At the same time, the usual indication of approaching financial difficulties was manifested in the revival of the proposal to substitute slackwater for canal navigation.[5]

The resumption of construction brought a renewal of the grievances of earlier years. Masonry work fell far behind schedule as the problem of rock and cement supplies reappeared.[6] There were more reports of absconding contractors, as in the case of one McEntire, on section 177.[7] Most serious of all, land costs continued high as the canal entered Washington County, near Harpers Ferry. The first land condemned was that of Gerard B. Wager, a bitter opponent of the canal company. The damages awarded were very high, and the verdict provided a discouraging precedent for the Board.[8] The determination of the local landholders to exact full satisfaction was further strengthened by the award in the condemnation of Caspar Wever's land.[9] Even some of the friends of the canal participated in the onslaught that followed.[10] The more impatient proprietors resorted to injunctions to enforce prompt payment of their awards.[11] The local counsel of the company urged the directors to advertise the renewal of negotiations

[3] 4th Annual Report (1832), in Proceedings of Stockholders, A, 204-207.

[4] Proceedings of Directors, C, 65-69 (February 11, 1832); Mercer to Purcell, May 7, 1832, Letter Book A, 439-440; 4th Annual Report (1832), Proceedings of Stockholders, A, 210. Colonel Abert objected.

[5] Proceedings of Directors, C, 71-72 (February 15, 1832).

[6] McFarland to Mercer, November 5, 1832.

[7] Purcell to President and Directors, August 24, 1833.

[8] Crüger to President and Directors, August 3, 1832; Mercer to Ingle, August 8, 1832. The Board had hoped for more favorable settlements in Washington County. Wager's long feud with the company made the verdict even more distasteful.

[9] B. Price to Ingle, August 25, 1832; B. Price to Mercer, November 5, 1832. See also the appeal of the company to set aside the inquisition taken on Wever's land, November 16, 1832, Letters Received. Wever, a friend and official of the railroad, was another enemy of the canal project. Like Wager, he exacted the utmost damages obtainable.

[10] Cruger to President and Directors, August 3, 1832.

[11] B. Price to Ingle, August 25, 1832; Price to Ingle, June 10, 1834.

with Virginia landholders to shift the canal to that side of the river.[12] The Board adopted the suggestion hoping that this announcement might bring about a reduction in the prices of the lands it wanted. Unfortunately for the canal, the notice failed to have any permanent effect.

The Baltimore and Ohio Railroad Company continued in active opposition to its arch rival, refusing to give up the fight after its defeat in the courts. It maintained its agitation in the Maryland legislature, and at the same time it conducted a nuisance campaign in the Potomac valley to hinder the progress of the canal. It sponsored and circulated petitions to compel the canal company to construct docks at Point of Rocks to provide transfer facilities for the Baltimore trade, and to require the canal board to build bridges over its waterway to give the Maryland farmers greater access to the river.[13] It promoted an injunction, ostensibly in the name of local landholders, to force the canal company to protect access to a river ferry near Catoctin.[14] Baltimore and Ohio interests were undoubtedly involved in the extraordinary procedure of Caspar Wever in going all the way to Annapolis to obtain an injunction from an old friend, the Chancellor, to stop the construction of the canal on his land until he was paid in full.[15] Later still, the railroad company revived the agitation for an injunction to protect the public road at Point of Rocks, guaranteeing to pay all costs if the suit failed.[16] Railroad interests were said to have influenced the appointment of Benjamin S. Forrest, an avowed friend of the railroad who was known to be hostile to the canal, as the representative of the state of Maryland's interest in the canal company.[17] Forrest immediately demanded from the canal

[12] W. Price to Ingle, November 8, 1833.

[13] John McNeill to [President and Directors], January 28, 1832.

[14] Cruger to President and Directors, March 21, 1832; Proceedings of Directors, C, 113 (March 24, 1832).

[15] B. Price to Ingle, August 25, 1832; Mercer to R. S. Coxe, September 3, 1832, Letter Book B, 19-20.

[16] B. Price to Ingle, August 25, 1832. The local justice, Judge Shriver, of Frederick, denied the request for an injunction, but it was later issued by a Baltimore judge on the plea of the counsel of the Baltimore and Ohio, Gwynn.

[17] Ingle to Mercer, February 2, 1831; Littleton D. Teackle to Mercer, February 5, 1831. Thus Forrest was in a position to exert pressure on the canal company immediately after the railroad board gave up its efforts to persuade the canal board to permit joint construction.

officials an explanation of their conduct after the court decision, and promptly rejected their replies as "no answer." [18] The purpose of these widely scattered attacks on the canal was to stir up popular feeling in Maryland against the company, to enlist support for the measures which were to be taken to force joint construction, and to gain time for the political pressure that was being built up to have its effect.

On top of renewed construction difficulties, high land costs, and conflicts with the railroad, there was a disastrous cholera epidemic in the Potomac valley in September, 1832, which helped to prevent the completion of the first one hundred miles of the waterway by 1833.

The canal project had been plagued from its inception by the annual "sickly" season in the Potomac valley.[19] The season extended from July until late September and coincided with the drought months in the region. Popular belief soon associated the two and attributed the aches and fevers which developed in these months to the effects of the drought on the river and the atmosphere of the valley. The lowness of the water in the Potomac exposed the river grasses and vast areas of the murky, malodored river bed. With the return of the high water caused by the heavy autumn rains, the river lost the unhealthy miasma which had emanated from it during the

[18] B. S. Forrest and James L. Ranson to President and Directors, June 6, 1832; Cruger to President and Directors, June 15, 1832; Forrest to Ingle, June 16, 1832. Forrest insisted that the canal board had shifted the center line of the waterway away from the river after the court decision, thus making the extension of the railroad all but impossible. Cruger replied that the trunk had been changed but slightly from the location made by Roberts in 1828, and had been moved closer to the river as often as it had been shifted inland. The railroad, in his opinion, was certainly no worse off than before.

[19] *Report of the Committee on Roads and Canals*, April 17, 1834, Appendix U, p. 237. Officials of the Department of Health of the District of Columbia believe that the illnesses described were probably of various origins, coinciding in occurrence. Water-borne diseases such as typhoid and paratyphoid may have been the most prevalent. Insect-borne fevers undoubtedly accounted for many more. Dysentery from several causes and possibly milk-borne diseases seem best to fit the other symptoms described. On top of these were all the other human illnesses which when occurring in the sickly season, were attributed to the river. The occurrence of the water-borne and pest-borne diseases in late August and September coincided with the mosquito season in the Potomac valley and the peak of the warm water period in the stream (at which time water-borne diseases are most potent).

summer. So firmly had these ideas become established in the minds of the inhabitants that there was usually a noticeable slackening of work on the canal during the summer months. Often there was a marked exodus of company officials and contractors as well as laborers.

To offset the threat of the sickly season and to keep the work going in the critical year of 1832, the company resorted to unusual precautions. The safeguards provided were the customary ones, but the attempt to prevent or ameliorate the effects of illness among the workers was unprecedented on this canal. The Board resolved to hire a physician to inspect the workers' shanties from time to time during the months from July to October. He was to report upon their condition, to recommend measures for preserving the health of workers and contractors alike, and to care for the sick. The directors also created the office of Superintendent of Construction to supervise the removal of the sick and provide the necessary hospital stores. In July, they removed the prohibition on the use of spiritous liquors by laborers. In August, the president suggested renting a building to be used as a hospital in case it was needed.[20] By publicizing these measures for the care and prevention of sickness, the company sought to encourage workers and contractors to stay on the job, and perhaps to attract laborers from other works.

Despite all the precautions, the summer of 1832—the first one in which unrestricted construction was possible—proved the most disastrous to the health of the workers. Late in August, Asiatic cholera, which had gradually been spreading south from Montreal,[21] made its appearance on the line near Harpers Ferry. The plague was soon general from the Ferry down to Point of Rocks. Work was suspended on many of the sections, and fear spread rapidly among the workers.[22]

[20] Proceedings of Directors, C, 174-175 (June 23, 1832), 185-186 (July 11, 1832); Mercer to Ingle, August 27, 1832. By this time cholera was nearing the canal.

[21] Thomas J. C. Williams, *History of Washington County* (2 vols., Hagerstown [?] 1906), I, 221. The progress of the cholera may also be traced in the current issues of *Niles' Register*.

[22] Proceedings of Directors, C, 212 (August 31, 1832), 214 (September 8, 1832); Charles M. Rush to President and Directors, August 5, 1833 (reviewing the epidemic of 1832).

If the Board but imagine the panic produced by a mans [*sic*] turning black and dying in twenty four hours in the very room where his comrades are to sleep or to dine they will readily conceive the utility of separating the sick, dying and dead from the living.[23]

The result of the panic was the flight and dispersal of the terrified laborers.

The cholera gradually spread up the river to the west of Harpers Ferry. As it advanced, the same reports of the suspension of work and the panic and flight of the laborers accompanied it. From Shepherdstown the proprietor of the Potomac Mills wrote:

Before this letter reaches Washington, the whole line of canal from the point of rocks to WmsPort [*sic*] will be abandoned by the Contractors and Laborers — The Cholera has appeared amongst them, and has proved fatal in almost every case, There has been upwards of 30 deaths nearly opposite to us since friday last, and the poor Exiles of Erin are flying in every direction . . . it is candidly my opinion, that by the last of this week you will not have a working man on the whole line.[24]

The company's counsel in Frederick described the effects of the plague in similar terms.

They have since been suffering great mortality west of Harpers Ferry, & I fear the work is by this time suspended. The poor creatures, after seeing a few sudden & awful deaths amongst their friends, straggled off in all directions through the country; but for very many of them the panic came too late. They are dying in all parts of Washington County at the distance of 5 to 15 miles from the river. I myself saw numbers of them in carts & on foot making their way towards Pennsylvania.[25]

The scenes of suffering and death caused both anguish and alarm to the inhabitants of the neighborhood. "Humanity is outraged," wrote engineer Purcell,

by some of the scenes presented; men deserted by their friends or comrades, have been left to die in the fields, the highways, or in the neighboring barns & stables: in some instances, as I have been told; when the disease has attacked them; the invalid has been enticed from the shandee [shanty] & left to die under the shade of some tree.

Excited by the sufferings of the miserable victims of this disease; the citizens of this place [Sharpsburg] have ministered to their wants, and

[23] Mercer to Ingle, September 3, 1832.
[24] Boteler to Ingle, September 4, 1832.
[25] B. Price to Ingle, September 5, 1832.

sought to sooth their dying moments; but unfortunately for the cause of humanity, nearly every person who has been with the dead bodies or has assisted in burying them have paid the forfeit with their lives: and now it is scarsely [*sic*] possible to get the dead buried.[26]

The company immediately adopted measures to care for the sick and to calm the panic. It is doubtful, however, whether the steps taken shortened the duration of the epidemic or softened the force of its blow. Upon the president's recommendation, the directors authorized the establishment of two hospitals on the line.[27] Meanwhile General Mercer made an effort to lease an abandoned mill owned by Caspar Wever, to be used as a hospital. The terms offered were so exorbitant and repulsive that they did not receive consideration.[28] The hospitals, if such they may be called, were finally established in some cabins rented near Harpers Ferry and in a large shanty at section 112 west of Harpers Ferry. Another was contemplated at Point of Rocks. These temporary quarters left much to be desired, but the permanent hospital at Harpers Ferry was not established until late in September.[29] Even then the accommodations were probably not very elaborate, for as late as August 27, 1832, the president thought that it would only be necessary to purchase

some hundred feet of plank for bunks and some blankets and sacks for straw and as few and as cheap articles for the Hospital as possible and place it in the charge of a physician of this place [Harpers Ferry] after engaging one or two nurses to attend the sick. . . .[30]

The method by which the hospital was supported was a form of group insurance. Each of the workers contributed 25

[26] Purcell to President and Directors, September 11, 1832. See also W. Price to [Ingle], September 18, 1832.

[27] Mercer to Ingle, September 3, 1832; Proceedings of Directors, C, 212 (August 31, 1832), 214-215 (September 8, 1832). The cost of hospitals was fixed at $500.

[28] Mercer to Ingle, August 27, 1832; Mercer to Wever, September 11, 1832, Letter Book B, 21; Wever to Mercer, September 13, 1832; Mercer to W. Smith, September 24, 1832. Wever's terms were $350 a year (double the rate when the long-vacant mill was last rented), plus all damages awarded by Samuel Claggett and Edward Garrett upon examination after the mill was relinquished.

[29] Mercer to W. Smith, September 24, 1832; Rush to President and Directors, August 5, 1833.

[30] Mercer to Ingle, August 27, 1832.

cents a month for the doctor's fees and for the upkeep of the hospital.[31] This system had worked successfully before on the James River Canal,[32] but it was a novelty on the Chesapeake and Ohio. As might be imagined, it worked only as long as the fear of sickness was sufficiently great to cause the men to consent to the deduction from their wages. With the coming of winter and the disappearance of the cholera, the workers refused to countenance further deductions, and the program fell through.[33] The following spring the affairs of the hospital were brought to a close and the equipment sold.[34]

But the harm had been done. As a result of the many hindrances to construction the cost of the work had risen sharply, and the westward progress of the canal had all but halted. Attempts to secure loans from private banks in New York, Philadelphia, and Washington, or further aid from the interested states proved fruitless.[35] In fact, the city of Washington was about to suspend payments on its original subscription.[36] The Board prepared to stop all work above Harpers Ferry when Washington defaulted.[37] So limited were the company's resources that not even the twelve miles from the Point of Rocks to Harpers Ferry were completed during 1832. Consequently the company found itself facing almost insurmountable financial and legal problems at the end of the year.

The only course open for the canal company was to petition for an extension of its charter and at the same time seek further large-scale aid. The sources of legal and financial relief for the canal were the states of Pennsylvania, Virginia, and Maryland, and the Congress of the United States. In no instance were the prospects encouraging. Pennsylvania had shown

[31] Mercer to Ingle, September 3, 1832; Mercer to W. Smith, September 24, 1832; Rush to President and Directors, August 5, 1833.

[32] Mercer to Ingle, September 3, 1832.

[33] Rush to President and Directors, August 5, 1833.

[34] Proceedings of Directors, C, 263 (January 5, 1833); J. Gore to Ingle, April 6, 1833.

[35] Proceedings of Directors, C, 174 (June 23, 1832); 240, 243-244 (November 23, 1832); Mercer to Ingle, October 8, 25 (two letters), 26, 31, 1832.

[36] Proceedings of Directors, C, 236-237 (November 17, 1832), 290 (November 23, 1832). Notices arrived simultaneously from the Mayor of Washington notifying the company of the city's inability to meet the twenty-ninth installment and from the Secretary of the Treasury refusing to make further payments for the United States until the District cities caught up with their payments.

[37] *Ibid.*, p. 290 (November 23, 1832).

initial interest only in the western section of the canal, and was now completing its own system of public works. Virginia had failed to make any subscription to the Chesapeake and Ohio, and was also engaged in constructing its own canal from the James River to the Kanawha. Neither of these two states would be likely to provide the necessary funds to allow the canal company to continue large-scale operations.

The position of the canal company in Maryland was perhaps even more precarious. The Maryland legislature was so decidedly hostile to the canal's petitions that the possibility of receiving further aid from that state seemed small indeed. The Baltimore and Ohio, still smarting under its defeat in the courts, was active in the state and in the Assembly seeking assistance in its struggle with the canal. As early as January 28, 1832, the railroad company had revived the proposal for joint construction of canal and railroad which it had rejected while the legal controversy was still undecided.[38] When the canal showed no signs of accommodating the railroad above Point of Rocks, except on its own terms,[39] the railroad directors turned to the legislature where they had been so successful in pleading their case.

The legislature responded with a memorial to the canal company requesting joint construction as a favor to the state. The petition urged the accommodation of the railroad as far as Harpers Ferry, on the condition that the Baltimore and Ohio would pay all extra costs that the simultaneous progress of the two works would require.[40] The Chesapeake and Ohio countered with a proposal that the railroad and canal companies combine their resources and complete the canal to Cumberland, receiving any dividends declared on a pro-rata basis. The railroad then would be free to go on its way and would also have the right to fill in the gap between Cumberland and Point of Rocks, if it wished.[41]

[38] *Ibid.*, pp. 58-60 (January 28, 1832); Mercer to Ingle, January 28, 1832.

[39] Mercer to Ingle, January 28, 1832; Proceedings of Directors, C, 60 (January 28, 1832), 101-103 (March 10 and 14, 1832), 214 (September 8, 1832).

[40] *Proceedings of Directors*, C, 108 (March 17, 1832); Special Meeting (April, 1832), Proceedings of Stockholders, A, 196-197.

[41] 4th Annual Meeting (1832), Proceedings of Stockholders, A, 244-247; *6th Annual Report of the Baltimore and Ohio Railroad Company* (1832), pp. 16-17.

The state agent, Benjamin S. Forrest, a constant and dutiful friend of the railroad, then made a modified proposal. It was designed to meet the objections of the canal company to the reduced dimensions which the state's plan required of the waterway (while maintaining the railroad at its full width). He offered, on behalf of the Baltimore and Ohio, to construct the canal to its full dimensions, guarantee repairs for five years, pay all extra costs, and finish the work by December 1, 1833. The canal company objected to the length of time required for the completion of the twelve-mile stretch, whereupon the railroad agreed to complete the section by the time the canal was ready to introduce water from the feeder next above Harpers Ferry.[42]

The Chesapeake and Ohio then had to admit the real basis of its opposition to joint construction, that is, the fear of competition. It reasoned that there was not enough trade in the valley to warrant the construction of both works at this time. Nor would the Board be true to its responsibilities to the stockholders if it thus endangered the return on their investment. Instead, the company reiterated its own proposals: the union of the two for the construction of the canal to Cumberland, the crossing of the river by the railroad at Point of Rocks, or—a new scheme—the construction of the railroad on the river side of the canal. The latter, a form of joint construction, was quickly rejected by the Baltimore and Ohio which, aside from technical difficulties, wished no part of the heavy repair costs the river hazards would involve or the economic disadvantages arising from the interposition of a rival transportation agency between it and the countryside.[43]

The "obstinate" course of the canal company caused a clamor in the state which had been markedly absent during the

[42] *Memorial of the Baltimore and Ohio Railroad Company*, February 18, 1833, 22d Cong., 2d sess., House of Representatives, Document No. 113, p. 3.

[43] 4th Annual Meeting (August 4, 1832), Proceedings of Stockholders, A, 253-260, especially pp. 258-259. The Baltimore and Ohio had adopted a similar position regarding the profitableness of two internal improvement projects in the Potomac valley during the long controversy over the right of way. See, for example, P. E. Thomas to Joseph Kent and Walter Smith, January 19, 1830 (Papers concerning the Holland Loan, Manuscripts Division, Library of Congress).

three and one-half years of railroad opposition.[44] The Governor officially called the attention of the Assembly to the "defiance" of the legislature's request to allow both works to continue. He suggested that the state might force the canal to accommodate the railroad by withholding further aid.[45] A Senate committee responded with a stinging and frankly prejudiced report recommending the refusal of an extension of the charter. The committee stated that they regarded the railroad "as decidedly and unqualifiedly a Maryland work; while they do not regard the canal in this light." [46]

The early months of 1833 saw an intensification of the railroad's campaign on all fronts. Its cause was brought before Congress both directly and indirectly. In January, 1833, President Mercer wrote of the extreme pressure upon him in the House of Representatives in behalf of the railroad's proposals.[47] Henry Clay was among the members of Congress urging a settlement. In February, the railroad company petitioned the Congress to deny the financial relief sought by the District cities. The memorial asserted that such assistance would indirectly help the Chesapeake and Ohio Canal Company and enable it to persist in its obstinate and defiant course. The corporate authorities of Washington replied with an anguished protest against the unwarranted interference in the relations between the general government and the federal district.[48] At the same time, Baltimore opinion was being marshalled for the struggle, and the local newspapers added their shrill voices to the general hysteria.[49]

The last source of aid still available for the canal company was Congress. As long as the Board could expect help from that quarter it could largely ignore the indifference or hostility

[44] *Memorial of the Baltimore and Ohio Railroad Company*, February 18, 1833, p. 4.

[45] *Ibid.*; *Maryland House Journal*, 1832, pp. 23-24.

[46] *Maryland Senate Journal*, 1832, Appendix I, p. 4.

[47] Mercer to Ingle [January 22, 1833].

[48] *Memorial of the Baltimore and Ohio Railroad Company*, February 18, 1833, p. 9. *Memorial of the Citizens of Washington Counter to the Memorial of the Baltimore and Ohio Railroad Company*, February 22, 1833, 22d Cong., 2d sess., House of Representatives, Document No. 117, pp. 1-7, but especially pp. 1-4.

[49] Mercer to Ingle [January 22, 1833]. Mercer cited the "selfish clamor of the Baltimore press" as evidence of the increased tempo of the campaign against the canal.

of the several states. The prospects of assistance from the federal government, however, were slight after the victory of the Jacksonian party in 1828. The early record of the administration clearly indicated its hostility toward national support for internal improvements in general and for the Chesapeake and Ohio in particular. In December, 1828, Jacksonians in Congress introduced a joint resolution against further aid to the Cumberland Road and opposing federal ownership of stock in private internal improvement companies.[50] In June, 1829, the new regime failed to send a representative to the annual meeting of the stockholders of the canal company.[51] On March 1, 1830, a Congressional committee on internal improvements recommended that no further aid be granted to the project until the relative value of canals and railroads was proved by trial.[52] In 1832, the administration reversed its former policy of ignoring canal company meetings and actively interfered in company affairs, seeking to replace General Mercer by a president of its own choosing.[53] Meanwhile Congress refused to accede to any of the directors' petitions for further aid.

Failing to secure relief from the federal government, the canal board belatedly sought to make peace with Maryland. A subscription by Virginia for $250,000 was too small and too encumbered with stipulations concerning its use to provide any real assistance.[54] Therefore, in February, 1833, even before the bill providing for the Virginia subscription passed, the directors agreed to submit to the stockholders any compromise of its differences with the state and the railroad which the Maryland Assembly might suggest, compatible with the com-

[50] *Joint Resolution for the Care and Preservation of the Cumberland Road, and of other Roads made or to be made by the Federal Government within the different States*, December 8, 1828, 20th Cong., 2d sess., Senate, Document No. 6.

[51] Mercer to Ingle, September 1, 1829.

[52] *Report of the Committee on Internal Improvement, to which were referred Sundry Petitions, Praying for an Appropriation to the Chesapeake and Ohio Canal Company, to be expended on the Western side of the Mountains*, March 8, 1830, 21st Cong., 1st sess., House of Representatives, Report No. 280, p. 1. This coincided with the position taken by the Baltimore and Ohio.

[53] Boteler to Mercer, July 28, 1832.

[54] Proceedings of Directors, C, 282-283 (February 6, 1833). The Board agreed to apply $80,000 of the amount subscribed to the construction of locks from the canal to the river. See Report of the Completion of the Canal, p. 336.

pany's interests.[55] In March, the legislature proposed an arrangement in which all three parties would participate, the state, the canal, and the railroad.[56] In return for permission to construct its tracks from Point of Rocks to Harpers Ferry, the railroad company was to subscribe to 2,500 shares of canal stock. This subscription covered the costs of extending the railway to Harpers Ferry on the dimensions and location specified in the act. The canal company undertook the actual construction of both works through the difficult passes at which they came together. As its part, the legislature offered to pass two acts, long the subject of dispute between it and the canal, when the railroad reached the Ferry. These gave the canal board permission to sell surplus water and to begin the western section before completing the eastern part of its work.

The directors hastened to call a special meeting of the stockholders to make sure that the onus of refusing the compromise would not fall on them.[57] The committee which reported on the act for the general meeting recommended the rejection of the compromise.[58] However, this appears to have been merely a statement for the record; the company was in no position and in no mood to resist further. On May 9, 1833, after the railroad signified its consent to some preliminary conditions designed by the canal company to protect its rights, the Chesapeake and Ohio formally accepted the Maryland act.[59]

[55] Proceedings of Directors, C, 282-283 (February 6, 1833).

[56] *Ibid.*, p. 312 (April 2, 1833); Mercer to Ingle, March 31, 1833; *Laws and Resolutions Relating to the Chesapeake and Ohio Canal* (Washington, 1855), pp. 42-48. See also *5th Annual Report* (1833), Appendix, p. 20.

[57] Mercer to Ingle, March 31, 1833; Proceedings of Directors, C, 312 (April 12, 1833).

[58] Special Meeting (May 9, 1833), Proceedings of Stockholders, A, 268-269.

[59] *Ibid.*, pp. 270-274. The Baltimore and Ohio agreed to subscribe $266,000 to the stock of the canal company in return for the grading of four and one-tenth miles of roadbed at the narrow passes between Point of Rocks and Harpers Ferry. Proceedings of Directors, C, 341-342 (May 7, 1833). Hungerford gives a completely erroneous interpretation of the event in his *Story of the Baltimore and Ohio Railroad*, I, 141. "The obligatory subscription of the Baltimore and Ohio to 2500 of its shares—which in the end virtually amounted to a purchase of the canal—" At the time of this "purchase" for 2,500 shares, there were almost 40,000 shares of canal stock outstanding, of which 25,000—the controlling interest—were held by the United States and the District cities. In 1836 and 1839 the additional subscription by the state of Maryland of 30,000 and 13,750 shares respectively secured control of the canal for the state. The

The acceptance of the compromise did not mark the end of trouble between the railroad and the canal, but there did ensue a brief period of unusual amity. The railroad even revived talk of abandoning its road to the West in favor of a line down the Shenandoah valley.[60]

After the compromise of 1833, the legal shadow on the canal's future faded into the background, but the financial problem remained. The company turned for aid first to Congress and then to the states of Maryland and Virginia. In an effort to win the favor of the national administration, it consented in 1833 to the replacement of its president, Charles F. Mercer, by ex-Secretary of War John Eaton, a friend of Andrew Jackson and a principal in the Peggy Eaton affair.[61] Fortified by this important accession, the canal board memorialized Congress for a further subscription.[62] Notwithstanding the influence of the new president, Congress refused further aid to the project. The appeal to Virginia was also unsuccessful, but the Maryland Assembly voted an additional subscription of $125,000 in March, 1834.[63]

By the end of 1834, the financial condition of the company

latter retained control of the stock until after the turn of the century. By that time, the Baltimore and Ohio was in control of the operation of the canal through its ownership of the bonds of 1844. The affairs of the company were being managed by the trustees of 1844 under the direction of the court. In 1905, the state sold its stock in the canal company to the Vice-President of the Western Maryland Railway Company, F. S. Landstreet. During the latter's financial difficulties in 1907 and the years following, the stock of the canal company was turned over to the Continental Trust Company. From there it was transferred to the Baltimore and Ohio. See below, Chapters VII and XII.

[60] *5th Annual Report* (1833), pp. 9, 15. This was not a new idea, for it had been suggested back in 1831 during the legal controversy. A. Lee to Mercer, January 13, 1831. It seemed to be a routine proposal used by the railroad to lull the canal into a sense of security and to demonstrate to the Assembly the railroad's selfless efforts to accommodate its adversary. There is no evidence that the railroad seriously considered the project at this time.

[61] 5th Annual Meeting (1833), Proceedings of Stockholders, A, 313; *Niles' Register*, XLIV, No. 17 (June 22, 1833), 270-271. The vote was 5054 to 3430; 1798 votes of Maryland and Georgetown were lost because of a division among the proxies. If cast for Mercer, as had been expected, they would have been sufficient to elect him.

[62] 5th Annual Meeting (December 9, 1833), Proceedings of Stockholders, A, 320-321; Eaton to W. Price, January 3, 1834, Letter Book B, 184; *6th Annual Report* (1834), p. 4.

[63] Report on the Completion of the Canal, p. 336.

was again desperate, and once more the directors sought aid from Congress and the states. It was supported in its petitions by the internal improvement convention which met in Baltimore in December, 1834. The meeting assembled at the call of an earlier gathering in Allegany County in October, 1834, at which friends of the waterway in Western Maryland had urged further assistance for the project.[64] Representatives of Maryland, Virginia, Pennsylvania, Ohio, and District cities were in attendance at Baltimore.[65]

The intentions of the convention were clearly manifested in the selection of George C. Washington, third president of the canal company, as chairman. They could also be seen in the adoption of resolutions and the appointment of committees.[66] Charles F. Mercer, an ex-president of the canal, reported for the principal committee named to ascertain the probable cost of completing the canal. The report stated that $2,000,000 would be required to finish the eastern section, making the total cost of that part of the canal, $6,500,000. This figure was based on an estimate by Alfred Cruger of the probable cost of the twenty-seven miles between Dam No. 5, above Williamsport, and Dam No. 6 at Cacapon, above Hancock. The entire canal, to the Ohio, was expected to cost $14,500,000 under the revised estimates.[67] Subsequently, Representative Mercer brought up the subject of substituting a railroad for the proposed tunnel through the mountains. He pointed out that if the railroad were used at all it would have to extend over the entire middle section, because the water supply for the eastern slope had to be drawn through the tunnel from the west.[68] Another report to the convention reviewed in glowing terms the probable trade and revenue of the completed canal.[69] Reassured by the factual surveys and enthused over the future prospects of profits, the

[64] *Jounal of the Internal Improvement Convention* (Baltimore, 1835), pp. 3-7.

[65] *Ibid.*, pp. 7-10. The choice of the monumental city as the site of the convention is significant as an indication of the shifting basis of support for the canal and of the fact that Baltimore had been temporarily mollified by the compromise of 1833. Maryland was about to assume the sole responsibility for completing the work.

[66] *Ibid.*, pp. 11-16.

[67] *Ibid.*, pp. 59, 63.

[68] Loammi Baldwin to Mercer, December 28, 1834, *ibid.*, pp. 63-64.

[69] *Ibid.*, pp. 45 ff.

convention adopted memorials to be presented to Congress and the state legislatures for further aid.[70] It then adjourned to press the petitions.

Once again the first efforts were made to obtain the assistance of the United States. Despite the favorable recommendation of the committee on roads and canals, Congress again refused to grant the aid requested. After that the friends of the canal despaired of direct appropriations and confined their efforts to obtaining $500,000 from the dividend of the Bank of the United States. In return for this sum the company offered perpetual release from tolls for government business on the waterway. Even this proposal failed to pass the Senate.[71] The United States had indeed renounced all interest in the project.

The failure of Congress to assume the role which had been expected of it in the direction and support of the Chesapeake and Ohio placed the future of the work in the hands of the District cities and the interested states. The former were financially embarrassed and incapable of rendering further aid, and the latter, except Maryland, were no longer interested. Friends of the canal in the Virginia Assembly introduced a bill to guarantee a loan of $500,000 for the canal company in return for a mortgage of canal property to the state. This was the best that they felt they could push through the Assembly. After a checkered career of debate, rejection, reconsideration and passage in the lower house, the proposal met final defeat in the Senate. It lost by only one vote when called up during the absence of several known friends of the project.[72] The canal was thus forced to rely solely upon the support of the state of Maryland.

The company brought great weight to bear on the Maryland legislature to pass a bill to loan the entire $2,000,000 required to complete the eastern section. The memorial of the politically impressive Internal Improvement Convention

[70] *Ibid.*, pp. 12-14, 15-16. The memorials to Congress, Baltimore, and Virginia are printed on pp. 27-34, 35-36 and 37-40, respectively.

[71] Washington to Colston, January 31, 1835, Letter Book B, 401; Report to Special Meeting (April 22, 1835), Proceedings of Stockholders, A, 365-366, 370.

[72] *Niles' Register*, XLVIII, No. 1 (March 7, 1835), 2; No. 2 (March 14, 1835), 18.

played its part, assisted by the new president of the canal company, George C. Washington, who was personally active at Annapolis. The influence of certain members of the Assembly was also a factor in the ultimate success of the agitation.[73] President Washington concentrated all his efforts on the Maryland bill, expressing little hope of obtaining any aid from Congress or from Virginia.[74] The Maryland Assembly eventually passed the act authorizing the loan, with members from Baltimore and the Eastern Shore supporting it as well as the pro-canal delegates from the western counties.[75] One argument which apparently had a great effect in winning support for the measure was that the future revenues of the canal would provide sizable financial returns to the state later on.[76] Moreover, the delegates were said to fear the consequence of mortgaging the canal to Virginia for only \$500,000—a sum clearly inadequate to complete it to Cumberland.[77] The act provided for the payment of \$600,000 on June 20, 1835, \$200,000 on October 1, 1835, \$200,000 on January 1, 1836, and four quarterly installments of \$250,000 each on the first of April, July, and October, 1836, and January, 1837. The stockholders formally accepted the loan and authorized the mortgage at a special meeting in April, 1835.[78]

Unlike its disastrous experiences later on, the company obtained without much effort the money for the bonds issued to pay the loan. Financial conditions here and abroad were favor-

[73] Proceedings of Directors, E, 83-84 (June 29, 1836), 165 (November 9, 1836). Joseph Merrick was paid \$3,000 for his services at Annapolis during the winter of 1834-1835.

[74] Washington to Ingle, March 1, 1835. Even while the Maryland loan was still in doubt, President Washington accepted the defeat of the Virginia proposal philosophically. It was just as well that the latter lost, he wrote, for the company could not accept both acts (each of which required a mortgage of canal property). In this way the directors were saved the embarrassment of refusing proffered assistance. Washington to Colston, March 10, 1835, Letter Book B, 427-428.

[75] Proceedings of Directors, D, 265 (March 20, 1835); Washington to Ingle, March 1, 1835; A. Stewart to Ingle, March 6, 1835; Alexander Nesbit to Washington, April 8, 1835.

[76] Washington to Ingle, March 1, 1835. It was proposed to give to the counties for educational purposes all receipts over the amount necessary to provide a sinking fund to redeem the debt.

[77] Ingle to Barnard, March 6, 1835.

[78] Proceedings of Directors, D, 283 (April 15, 1835); Special Meeting April 22, 1835), Proceedings of Stockholders, A, 376-377.

able to the disposal of the state bonds (the form Maryland aid invariably took) at a premium. The directors offered them as a block to avoid speculation on future sales, and accepted the bid of a Baltimore house to take the bonds at a premium of $16.40 per $100.[79] General satisfaction was expressed that the state loaned the money instead of forcing the company to seek the funds from foreign capitalists. Maryland was interested in the project and could be counted upon to deal fairly with the canal company. In fact, by foregoing dividends as a one-sixth stockholder to permit repayment of the loan, the state would be repaying her own loan to that extent![80]

With the proceeds from the first installment of the loan, the canal company liquidated its entire debt of over a half million dollars and resumed the construction of its waterway.[81] The continued high cost of land and labor during the inflationary cycle of the thirties, and increased construction difficulties soon forced the actual cost of the canal far above the estimates which were the basis of the two million dollar loan. In 1834, the engineer, Alfred Cruger, had allowed $663,676 for the construction of the twenty-seven miles between Dam No. 5 and Cacapon. Engineer Charles Fisk revised this figure in June, 1835, on the basis of work actually done, raising it to $1,022,534. In June, 1836, another revision raised the cost to about four times the original estimate, $2,427,497.[82] As a result of these developments, the resources of the company were woefully inadequate for the job. Curtailment of operations began as early as January, 1836. In that month the Board suspended the letting of contracts and the condemnation of land above Cacapon.[83]

[79] Robert White to Washington, April 11, 1835; George Mackubin, Treasurer of the Western Shore of Maryland, to Washington, June 5, 1835.

[80] Special Meeting (April 22, 1835), Proceedings of Stockholders, A, 371.

[81] Washington to Treasurer of the Western Shore, June 4, 1835, Letter Book C, 26; *Report of the Committee to Investigate the Chesapeake and Ohio Canal Company* (Annapolis, 1836), p. 4. Washington said the debt was between $400,000 and $500,000; the report said $559,771.05. The canal scrip was also retired. See, for example, Proceedings of Directors, D, 408 (September 30, 1835). The clerk of the company paid out upwards of $400,000 before sunset of the day the initial payment of $600,000 was received. Ingle to Bender June 22, 1835, Letter Book C, 34.

[82] *8th Annual Report* (1836), pp. 3-4.

[83] Ingle to Bender, January 9, 16, 1836, Letter Book C, 187, 196; Bender to Ingle, January 19, 1836.

Again the company petitioned the District cities, Virginia, and Maryland for further aid. The District cities, however, were in no position to offer assistance. Indeed they were bankrupt, and were saved from foreclosure only by the assumption of their debts by the federal government in May, 1836.[84] A petition to the Virginia Assembly produced a bill for an additional subscription from that state. After a promising course in the early stages, the proposal met defeat through parliamentary maneuvering by its rival, the James River improvement project.[85]

In Maryland, there was widespread support for the canal company's appeal for assistance. The announcement of the curtailment in January, 1836, caused consternation among the long-suffering but impatient citizens of western Maryland.[86] The popularity of the waterway had grown as it advanced westward and became an increasingly important factor in the local welfare. Town meetings, like that at Cumberland, passed resolutions urging the legislature to grant further aid.[87] Then, too, the Baltimore and Ohio Railroad was in need of further assistance at this time. Finally, an internal improvements fever was sweeping the state with projects for several local railroads and canals.[88]

Nevertheless there was strong opposition in the Assembly to large appropriations for public works. The legislature conducted another investigation of canal affairs to ascertain whether the two million dollar loan had been misused. It decided that the company had erred in judgment but not in design in adopt-

[84] Proceedings of Directors, E, 66 (May 27, 1836).

[85] Friends of the latter secured a vote on their measure first and with the assistance of the Potomac interests were successful. They then left the chamber, and the Chesapeake and Ohio bill which came up for a vote next was defeated. John Sherrard to R. H. Henderson, March 19, 1836.

[86] The effect of the work stoppage on business at Cumberland was immediate. It "caused a very considerable panic in Cumberland. Two hours after the arrival of the news, the price of produce came down at least 10 per cent. Business still continues to be dull, our principal streets presenting an unusual barrenness; the merchant is idle; the mechanic slow in the transaction of his business; the specualtor is cut to the quick. . . ." *Niles' Register*, XLIX, No. 25 (February 20, 1836), 426.

[87] William H. Lowdermilk, *History of Cumberland* (Washington, 1878), pp. 338-339.

[88] Special Report on the Completion of the Canal, pp. 340 ff.

ing the estimate of Cruger and the report of the Internal Improvement Convention. Concerning the alleged misappropriation of funds, the committee report agreed that the company had to discharge the greater part of its $559,771.05 debt before it could comply with the legal conditions of the loan.[89] The report closed with an admonition to the Assembly to put an end to all doubts and provide for the completion of the state's program of public works. Another committee urged a large internal improvement program as an aid to state finances in the future.[90] Notwithstanding these recommendations and the activity of many friends of the railroad and canal companies, the bill providing eight millions for these projects failed to pass the House of Delegates by one vote, 35 to 34, March 31, 1836. The Assembly then adjourned until May 4, when a special session would take up the proposal after the citizens of Maryland had had an opportunity to discuss it.[91]

The friends of internal improvements, merchants, capitalists, and others, stirred up the local populace to a fever pitch. The agitation came to a climax with a monster rally in Baltimore on May 2, which met at the call of an earlier town meeting in the same city. Representatives of the whole state and friends from Pennsylvania and Virginia attended.[92] The meeting adopted resolutions urging the state to complete the public works. To this end, Maryland should secure control of the Chesapeake and Ohio, bring its trade to Baltimore by means of the Maryland Canal, permit the extension of the Baltimore

[89] *Report of the Committee to Investigate the Chesapeake and Ohio Canal Company*, pp. 3-4. The company was accused of misappropriating $879,000 of the $2,000,000—applying it to past debts and to repairs and improvements, rather than the completion of the eastern section.

[90] "Report of the Committee on Ways and Means of the House of Delegates, on the Subject of the Finances and Internal Improvements," March 9, 1836, *A Short History of the Public Debt of Maryland* (Baltimore, 1844), Appendix, Document K, pp. 52-62.

[91] *A Short History of the Public Debt of Maryland*, pp. 18, 21. The Board paid Joseph Merrick $10,000 for his services in 1836, 1837, and 1838, Proceedings of Directors, E, 406 (May 9, 1838). McCulloh was content to accept only his expenses. David Ridgely also received payment for his services. Ridgely to Washington, June 4, 1836.

[92] "Journal of the Internal Improvement Convention (Baltimore, May 2, 1836)," *A Short History of the Public Debt of Maryland*, pp. 23-25. See also the "Address of the City of Baltimore to the People of Maryland, April 12, 1836," *ibid.*, Appendix, pp. 68-72.

and Ohio to the West through Maryland, and encourage the development of local railroads in other parts of the state.[93] After this tremendous outburst of enthusiasm, the friends of internal improvements turned to Annapolis to await the new session with impatience and confidence.

The special session met in May, 1836, to consider the present condition of state finances and public works, and the subjects were duly referred to the joint committee on internal improvements. The majority of the committee reported unfavorably on an omnibus bill in a penetrating review of the whole question. It criticized the haste and lack of adequate information which characterized the preparation of the measure. There had been no surveys made for the Baltimore and Ohio Railroad and no accurate data presented upon which to estimate the probable cost of the work. The members could see no reason for extending the canal if its terminus was to remain in the District of Columbia. Yet despite assurances that it would be brought to Baltimore, there had been no surveys or estimates of the probable cost of a branch canal upon which to base an appropriation.[94] It was difficult to see the reason for extending both canal and railroad if one were more advantageous than the other, making it inevitable that one of the works should become a liability. Similar criticisms were applied to the proposed Eastern Shore Railroad. Above all, the exhausted condition of the state treasury would not permit large expenditures for public works.[95] The minority rejected the defeatist, do-nothing policy of the majority report and urged the passage of the Eight Million Dollar bill as a logical culmination of the state's efforts to secure a share of the Western trade and as a measure to provide for the future stability of state finances.[96]

The Assembly, undaunted by the warning of the majority report, adopted the views of the minority. The House of Delegates passed the internal improvements bill, June 3, 1836,

[93] "Journal of the Internal Improvement Convention," *ibid.*, pp. 27-30.

[94] "Majority Report of the Joint Committee of Both Branches of the Legislature, appointed to Investigate the Subject of Internal Improvement," *A Short History of the Public Debt of Maryland*, pp. 33-34, 38.

[95] *Ibid.*, pp. 34-38.

[96] *A Short History of the Public Debt of Maryland*, p. 39. Merrick made the report for the minority.

by a vote of 48 to 39, and the Senate passed it shortly thereafter, 11 to 2.[97] The act provided for the subscription of $8,000,000 to various internal improvement companies: $3,000,000 each to the Chesapeake and Ohio and the Baltimore and Ohio; $1,000,000 to the Baltimore and Susquehanna Railroad; $500,000 to the Maryland Canal Company (for a branch canal to Baltimore); and $250,000 each to the Annapolis and Elkridge Railroad and the Eastern Shore Railroad.[98] Before any payments would be made on the two major subscriptions, the Maryland Canal Company must be organized with sufficient funds to insure the construction of its work.[99] The Baltimore and Ohio was released from the prohibition against extending its line in Maryland beyond Harpers Ferry before 1840. As usual, the subscriptions took the form of state bonds.

Carrying out the provisions of the act was a relatively simple matter. The Chesapeake and Ohio and the Baltimore and Ohio came to an agreement over the settlement of any disputes that might arise between the two companies.[100] The canal stockholders accepted the act, July 28, 1836, the same day that the arrangement with the railroad was consummated.[101] Promoters of the cross-cut canal project went through the process of obtaining subscriptions from Baltimore citizens and organizing the company. The fact of organization was duly certified by the Treasurer of the Western Shore, although the two earlier surveys had shown the only practicable route to lie through the District, a route specifically forbidden by the omnibus act.[102] The subscriptions to the Baltimore and Ohio and the Chesapeake and Ohio were then released from the legal restrictions of the act.

In the face of the increasing cost of construction, the financial

[97] *Ibid.*, pp. 40-41.

[98] *Laws and Resolutions Relating to the Chesapeake and Ohio Canal Company*, pp. 55-63. Payments to the Chesapeake and Ohio were to be made in three equal annual installments. *8th Annual Report* (1836), p. 6.

[99] Report of the General Committee, 8th Annual Meeting (1836), Proceedings of Stockholders, B, 260.

[100] Washington to Joseph Patterson, July 7, 1836, Letter Book C, 351-353; 8th Annual Meeting (July 28, 1836), Proceedings of Stockholders, B, 40-43.

[101] 8th Annual Meeting (July 28, 1836), Proceedings of Stockholders, B, 49.

[102] *A Short History of the Public Debt of Maryland*, pp. 44-46; Special Report on the Completion of the Canal, pp. 346-348; 8th Annual Meeting (July 18, 1836), Proceedings of Stockholders, B, 26.

support and control of the canal company finally shifted to the state of Maryland. One after another of the principal promoters of the project had retired from active responsibility for its completion. The national administration, hostile to federal support of internal improvement companies, had renounced its interest in the fulfillment of "the great national project." The District cities had involuntarily given up their holdings because of their own financial insolvency. Virginia and Pennsylvania had been diverted from contributing their share by the construction of competing projects wholly within their respective states. Only Maryland, already burdened with the expense of the Baltimore and Ohio Railroad, was willing to furnish the necessary additional assistance to allow the work to continue. The subscription of $125,000 in 1834, the loan of $2,000,000 in 1835, and the purchase of $3,000,000 of canal stock in 1836, gave the state control of the company and a mortgage on its property. This domination of canal affairs was further strengthened by a subscription of $1,375,000 in 1839. The future of the waterway was thus inseparably intertwined with the destiny of the state.

CHAPTER VI

A DECADE OF CONSTRUCTION

(1833-1842)

With the continuing financial support of the state of Maryland, construction proceeded fairly regularly, if somewhat slowly. The joint construction of the canal and the railroad between Point of Rocks and Harpers Ferry, which had been undertaken in 1833, was completed in 1834.[1] In the same year the section of the waterway from the Ferry to Dam No. 4, below Williamsport, was finished and opened to trade.[2] At this point the canal had been completed for eighty-six miles. By using the slackwater backed up by Dam No. 4, boats could now reach Williamsport. As far as it had been constructed the Chesapeake and Ohio was without equal—the Erie Canal was likened to a mill race in comparison.[3]

Upon receipt of the first installment of the two-million-dollar loan, work on the canal was resumed with increased vigor. The company ordered the route from Cacapon to Cumberland to be surveyed for the final location of the line preparatory to putting this last stretch of the eastern section under contract.[4] The Board appointed one of its members, George Bender, to fill the new office of Commissioner which it created to provide effective supervision of the construction.[5] The work had moved so far westward that it was no longer possible for the directors, meeting in Washington, to maintain adequate control of operations. The Commissioner had authority over the lesser officials, the acquisition of land, the use of the company property, and the re-letting of abandoned contracts. On the other hand, the Board reserved to itself the first letting of contracts and the right of review of all the Commissioner's acts.

[1] *Niles' Register*, XLVI, No. 8 (April 19, 1834), 119.

[2] *6th Annual Report* (1834), p. 4.

[3] Fredericksburg *Arena*, October 6, 1835, quoted in *Niles' Register*, XLIX, No. 8 (October 24, 1835), 127.

[4] Proceedings of Directors, D, 342 (June 17, 1835).

[5] *Ibid.*, pp. 294-301 (April 29, 1835).

The extension of the canal from Cacapon to Cumberland brought up a new series of problems. The actual task of surveying the line of the canal was a problem in itself and was carried on under many difficulties.[6] The party was slow in getting underway,[7] it had difficulty in securing necessary supplies and accommodations for its trip,[8] it encountered the worst sickly season in ten years in the upper valley,[9] and it was marked by a series of clashes between company engineers.[10] The two major questions above Cacapon in addition to the definite location of the line concerned the site of the dam at the mouth of the South Branch, and the level to be adopted for the canal at Cumberland. After considering several locations for the dam (No. 7) the Board decided simply to omit it entirely.[11] The discussion over the route of the waterway at Cumberland was long and heated. The directors were at first inclined to pass the canal behind the town to Wills Creek, the shortest line to the West.[12] Upon receiving the protest of the local citizens and an offer of the city to waive all claims to property damages, the directors reconsidered their plans and

[6] *Ibid.*, p. 311 (May 25, 1835).

[7] *Ibid.*, pp. 328-329 (June 10, 1835). The Board censured Purcell, the engineer in charge of the survey, for the delay which was largely the result of the low wages it offered to rodmen, axe-men, etc.

[8] Bender to Ingle, August 1, 1835. Only the most miserable accommodations were available and then only at "the most extravagant prices, & hardly at any price." The party frequently had to build its own makeshift quarters.

[9] Fisk to Bender, August 17, 1835.

[10] See Letters Received, July-December, 1835, and Purcell to Washington, January 12, 1836. At times the differences between the two engineers were slight and not too frequent. On occasions, however, they became serious. See, for example, their joint report of December 18, 1835. Purcell finally resigned in March, 1836. Purcell to President and Directors, March 4, 1836; Proceedings of Directors, E, 25-26 (March 5, 1836).

[11] Morris to Fisk, August 1, 1835. A major objection to the construction of the dam in the main river was the engineering problem involved. The banks of the river where the dam was to be built sloped gradually from the rim of the valley. But the height of the freshets in the valley below required a very high dam to feed the canal at a level which would render it secure from floods. To erect a dam to the proper height would flood many valuable acres of rich bottom land. Yet a dam in the river had many advantages as an aid to trade, which the proposed dam in the South branch did not provide. The directors solved the question simply by taking no action.

[12] Report of the Committee on the location of the Canal from Dam No. 6 to Cumberland, October 9, 1835; filed in Letters Received.

adopted a low-level route along the river into the center of the town.[13]

After the passage of the Eight Million Dollar bill, construction began to recover from the low level to which it had fallen in 1835. But it was a slow, expensive, and difficult task to accumulate a large enough labor force to resume full-scale work. By August, 1835, the monthly estimates of work done had dropped to only $8,998. Averages per month for three-month periods thereafter rose grudgingly despite the increasing costs of construction.[14]

September, October, November,	1835—$21,068
December, January, February,	1836— 17,386
March, April, May,	1836— 31,201
June, July, August,	1836— 43,911
September, October, November,	1836— 45,055
December, January, February,	1837— 40,419
March, April, May,	1837— 63,273
June, July, August,	1837— 92,808
September, October, November,	1837—104,271

At this rate, the twenty-seven miles to Cacapon were not completed until 1839.[15]

The slow progress of the work was due largely to the persistence of three major obstacles to rapid construction. Throughout the decade there was widespread labor unrest along the canal line—especially in the latter thirties, a period of economic crisis and social unrest generally throughout the country. A second hindrance was the increasing cost of construction growing out of the inflation of the decade, the high cost of labor, and engineering difficulties arising from the nature of canal building. The third obstacle was the limitation of financial

[13] Notice of a Town Meeting (Cumberland, September 29, 1835), in Mayor Gephart and others to [President and Directors], October 1, 1835; Dr. J. M. Lawrence to [President and Directors], October 1, 1835; Report to 7th Annual Meeting (November 4, 1835), Proceedings of Stockholders, A, 417-419, 421; Proceedings of Directors, D, 423 (November 5, 1835).

[14] *10th Annual Report* (1838), Appendix 3, p. 31. This was always the case, and the threat of its repetition made the directors ever reluctant to suspend operations. They resorted to every conceivable device to keep the work going and hold the force together.

[15] *Niles' Register* LVI, No. 9 (April 27, 1839), 131-132.

resources resulting from a combination of the first two and general economic conditions throughout the Western World after 1837.

The accumulation and maintenance of an adequate working force on the canal had plagued the company since the beginning of its work. The experiment with the importation of indentured servants in 1829 ended in failure, and the proposal to purchase and employ Negro slaves met defeat at the hands of the stockholders in 1832. Despite the shortage of workers, construction went on. Beginning in 1832, reports of unrest among the workers on the line appear in the company records. In that year the cause of the disturbance was an ill-advised attempt to enforce the prohibition of the use of spiritous liquors by the workers.

In an effort to forestall the rioting and loss of time which resulted from excessive drinking, the directors ordered the enforcement of the condition contained in all contracts prohibiting the distribution of liquor to the workers. They had considerable difficulty enforcing the regulation in the absence of supporting Maryland laws, and eventually they reversed themselves and repealed the prohibition upon the report of the engineer that the enforcement of it was having the opposite effect from that intended.[16] Drunkenness had actually increased during the period of prohibition. The engineer reported that the men, deprived of a steady supply of spirits during the day, drank excessive quantities of liquor at neighboring grog shops in the evening. The amount consumed in the course of an evening, if spread over the whole day, could have been worked off without serious effects. Consumed all at once, it intoxicated them and led to rioting and disorder which lasted throughout most the night. Morning found many of the men lying on the ground where they had fallen exhausted, unfit for work that day. The approach of the sickly season was another excuse for restoring the controlled use of the customary "jiggers" as a preventive measure.[17]

The laboring force was the cause of anxiety on the part of the Board for other reasons. For one thing there was the

[16] Proceedings of Directors, C, 185-186 (July 11, 1832).
[17] Cruger to President and Directors, July 7, 1832.

continued demand for more men, especially skilled masons and stonecutters. The President carried the search for hands as far north as Philadelphia on one of his trips to secure funds for the company. In the fall of 1832, he reported that he had hired eight men there. The terms included: the advance of transportation money, the promise of a bonus, and the guarantee of work until December 10, 1832, at fair wages.[18] At the same time violence threatened to break out among the canal workers themselves. Ill feeling ran high between rival factions of the Irish workers, the Corkonians and the Longfords (sometime called Fardowners), but open warfare did not break out until 1834.

Later in 1832, the cholera epidemic disrupted work and scattered the working force. In the summer of 1833, there was another outbreak of the sickness on a less serious scale. This time it struck first farther up the river, near Williamsport.[19] Again the symptoms of panic and threatened dispersal of the workers appeared. The unrest spread to the neighboring village of Hagerstown because so many of the Irish workers were brought there for burial in the Catholic cemetery. A town meeting was held at which civil leaders expressed fear for the health and trade of the community. The town, the company, and the local priest took steps to provide other cemeteries closer to the line.[20] In this way the time lost from work during the solemnity and revelry of a funeral was reduced and the threat to the safety of the village removed. The epidemic gradually retraced its previous course down the river to Harpers Ferry and then disappeared.

In 1834 and 1835 open warfare broke out between rival factions of the Irish laborers, especially during the idle winter months. The first encounter in January, 1834, was in the nature of a preliminary skirmish between the Corkonians who were working near Dam No. 5, above Williamsport, and the Longfords, or Fardowners, from the vicinity of Dam No. 4,

[18] Mercer to Ingle, October 8, 1832.

[19] Purcell to Eaton, June 24, 1832 [1833]; Andrew Stewart to Ingle, July 10, 1833.

[20] "Resolutions of a Public Meeting in Hagerstown, July 27, 1833." Handbill in O. H. Williams, W. Price, E. Beatty to Purcell, July 31, 1833; Purcell to President and Directors, August 1, 1833.

below the town.[21] Several were killed in the clash before the militia arrived on the scene to restore order. Between the first and second encounters, the countryside took on the appearance of an armed camp. The Irish nursed their wounds and accumulated weapons while the local citizenry of Williamsport patrolled the Conogocheague aqueduct between the opposing sides to prevent further disorder. Notwithstanding these preventive measures, the Corkonians broke loose again in a few days, committing various acts of violence on the line. On January 24, the Longfords marched up in force, about three hundred strong, armed with guns, clubs, and helves.[22] They were permitted to cross the aqueduct when they announced that their intentions were merely to make a show of force. Farther up the line they were joined by three or four hundred more who had apparently crossed the Conogocheague behind the town. They met about three hundred Corkonians on a hill-top near Dam No. 5. Accepting a challenge they charged the latter's positions and overwhelmed them in a short pitched battle. At least five Corkonians were killed in the field and many more in the woods beyond during the flight that followed. The victorious Longfords marched back to Williamsport, disbanded, and returned to their shanties. Thereafter the local militia kept order until two companies of U. S. troops arrived from Fort McHenry.[23] Leaders of the rival factions were brought together in the course of the next week and a treaty of peace was signed.[24] Hostilities occurred briefly the following winter, but at no time did they reach a stage of seriousness comparable to the war of 1834.[25]

[21] *Niles' Register*, XLV, No. 22 (January 25, 1834), 336; Purcell to Ingle, January 23, 1834; Williams, I, 223. Purcell attributed the disturbances to an effort on the part of the rival organizations to oust the adherents of the other from the line of the canal. This presumably would have led to an increased rate of wages for those remaining.

[22] The account of the day's activities is based on the report of the Williamsport *Banner*, quoted in *Niles' Register*, XLV, No. 23 (February 1, 1834), 382-383, and on Williams, I, 223-224.

[23] *Niles' Register*, XLV, No. 23 (February 1, 1834), 383; Eaton to Janney, Smith, Gunton, January 31, 1834. Eaton suggested that the company take advantage of the presence of federal troops to discharge the trouble-makers. "The essential service . . . to us, will be, in staying the further progress of our works, at a time when it is evedent [*sic*] we cannot meet our fiscal engagements." See also Purcell to President and Directors, January 29, 1834.

[24] *Niles' Register*, XLV, No. 24 (February 8, 1834), 399; Williams, I, 224.

[25] Hagerstown *Torchlight* quoted in *Niles' Register*, XLVII, No. 25 (Febru-

The construction of the canal above Dam No. 5 was marred by recurring strikes and clashes among the workers. In January, 1836, another clash between the Irish factions occurred near Clear Spring.[26] Several men were wounded and two shanties burned in the encounter. It was said that the rival camps feared each other so much that they posted guards at night like armies.

The pattern of recurring disturbances during the idle winter months was soon broken, probably as a result of the rising cost of living. Violence occurred in the following spring. Two contractors had a large enough force at work on one section, "principally of Dutch and country borns, to have finished in April or May. . . . This force in April last [1836] was attacked by a body of Irish, beat and dispersed, since which we have been unable to collect a force. . . ." [27] It was reported from other sources that the turnout was general, although some few sections escaped it altogether. It was during these strikes that Lee Montgomery, the parson-contractor at the tunnel, proved his mettle and earned the plaudits of canal officials by holding his men on the job and resisting the efforts of the strikers to lure the workers from the tunnel. The Commissioner wrote in explanation of Montgomery's success:

Our Methodist parson-contractor [Montgomery] upon being asked how he escaped, replied that his men were generally picked men, and had provided themselves, he believed, with some guns and a few Little Sticks, and as it was supposed they would use them rather than be intruded on, the rioters thought it best not to stop as they were passing by — The truth is that in a good cause few men would probably use a "Little Stick" more effectively than himself, although he would *pray* at the same time against being obliged to "hold them uneasy." [28]

The unrest continued throughout the summer. Several of the contractors were threatened as well as non-cooperating workmen. Beatings, destruction of property, and other forms of physical violence were the usual methods of punishment to those who defied the "desperadoes." Canal officials attributed

ary 21, 1835), 429. See also Proceedings of Directors, D, 234 (February 9, 1835), 256-257 (February 25, 1835). This time the workers struck for higher wages.

[26] *Niles' Register*, XLIX, No. 20 (January 16, 1836).

[27] G. M. and R. W. Watkins to President and Directors, February 15, 1837.

[28] Bender to Ingle, May 8, 1836.

the disturbances to the activities of a secret terrorist society from New York, with branches in many states—probably an early labor union or Irish fraternal organization. So great was the fear of those punished that none dared testify against their tormentors.[29]

New outbreaks of rioting occurred in each succeeding year until the Board took effective steps to curb the violence. In May and June, 1837, the trouble centered around the tunnel, where parson Montgomery was working with his picked crew, augmented by laborers imported from England to increase his force and to resist the strikers. Notwithstanding the efforts of the contractor, the Irish succeeded in getting control of the work, driving off all but two of the forty new immigrants, and bringing operations to a halt. Again the company was partly to blame for its own misfortunes, for it had refused to press the cases against several of the trouble-makers at the tunnel after they had been arrested for pulling down shanties in broad daylight. The other workers gained the impression that the company was unwilling to bear the expense of the trial and punishment of the terrorists.[30]

Events of the next year gave no hope of early relief.

> On New Year's Day, 1838, a number of men [Irish] employed at the tunnel marched up to Oldtown, and made a raid on the place, almost demolishing Nicholas Ryan's tavern. Thomas Dowden, the Sheriff, summoned the Cumberland Guards, and other citizens, as a *posse*, and went down to quell the riot, but the disturbers had left.[31]

Several ringleaders were arrested and jailed to see what effect that action would have on the others. Apparently it made little impression in face of the continued uneasiness among the workers. They resorted to burning shanties in order to bring pressure to bear on contractors, and to drive away German laborers and newcomers to the line whose presence threatened to reduce the jobs for the Irish and to force down wages.[32]

[29] Bender to Washington, November 17, 1836. See also the enclosed copy of a placard.

[30] Fisk to Bender, May 15, 1838; Fisk to President and Directors, June 23, 1838.

[31] Lowdermilk, p. 342.

[32] Fisk to Washington, February 5, 1838, see especially pp. 12, 14, and 16.

Another riot was reported at the tunnel in February. In May, it was the nonpayment of wages by hard-pressed contractors that led to violence. The workers "insisted upon destroying the work they had done, since they were to receive no pay for it." [33] The company asked the local militia to protect canal property, but were embarrassed by the reluctance of the citizenry to turn out. The latter pointed out that both the state and the company had refused to pay their expenses last time. Besides many of them were convinced the company was partly to blame for withholding large sums from the contractors in such critical times.[34] "The officers reported that the men had positively refused to turn out, and that some of them had gone so far as to declare, that if they did they would 'fight for the Irish.'" [35] Nevertheless, the militia did march to the line, seize 140 kegs of powder from the relatively quiet workers, and return them to Hagerstown. Militia officers described the workers and their families as being "in a suffering and deplorable condition" but determined to prevent further work from being done until they were paid.[36] They rejected an offer of 25 cents on the dollar, and held fast to their positions. The local inhabitants assured them that they were in the right and supplied them with provisions on credit.[37]

In July and August, 1838, the Board finally took the long-delayed steps to curb the violence and remove the trouble-makers. A renewal of strife at the tunnel provided the opportunity, and the directors acted. Upon the recommendation of the engineer, they authorized the suspension of work at the tunnel and the dismissal and black-listing of disorderly persons.

[33] Fisk to Washington, February 15, 1838; Williams, I, 233.

[34] W. Price to Washington, May 11, 1838; O. H. Williams to Washington, May 16, 1838. The company refused to make further advances on contract prices, insisting that it had already done enough. It did offer to apply $4,000 of the withheld money to the payment of the workers' claims. Ingle to Bender, May 9, 1838, Letter Book D, 324; Ingle to Fisk, May 9 and 11, 1838, *ibid.*, pp. 325-326, 329-330; Washington to Williams, May 18, 19, 1838, *ibid.*, pp. 339-343.

[35] Williams to Washington, May 16, 1838.

[36] William H. Fitzhugh to Williams, May 16, 1838 (two letters); Williams to Washington, May 17, 18, 1838. The powder was stored on the courthouse lot in the center of town to the great alarm of the townfolk.

[37] Fisk to Ingle, May 19, 1838; Thomas Fillebrown, Jr. to Ingle, May 19, 1838; Williams to Washington, May 24, 1838.

On August 1, about one hundred and thirty men were discharged, mostly from the deep cut and the tunnel.[38]

There were no more untoward incidents until August and September, 1839. At that time, violence broke out near Little Orleans, between Cumberland and Hancock. Militia from both Allegany and Washington counties turned out, marched to the scene, seized from one hundred to two hundred firearms, tore down forty to fifty shanties and shops, arrested about thirty of the rioters and jailed them in Cumberland.[39] This time they were tried and all but two convicted. Those found guilty received fines and prison terms ranging from one to eighteen years.[40] A recurrence of the riot at the same place in November brought similarly harsh retaliation. For a while at least, the action seems to have been effective in restoring order.[41]

The second obstacle to the rapid completion of the canal was the increasing cost of construction. The work on the sections above Dam No. 4 proved more difficult, and consequently more expensive, than had been anticipated. One reason for this was that an assistant engineer, Charles Fisk,[42] again raised high the banner of perfection which the former president, C. F. Mercer, had carried so persistently. Writing more or less as an engineer and with apparently little knowledge of, or concern for, financial considerations, he proposed a revision of procedure in extending the canal. He urged greater care and expenditure in construction in order to reduce subsequent repair and maintenance costs.[43] Regardless of its economic and technical soundness

[38] Washington to Fisk, June 28, 1838, Letter Book D, 365-366; Fisk to President and Directors, July 3, 1838; Proceedings of Directors, E, 466 (July 12, 1838). See also the copy of a notice signed by C. B. Fisk, dated Chief Engineer's Office, August 1, 1838, filed in Letters Received.

[39] *Niles' Register*, LVII, No. 3 (September 14, 1839), 37-38, quoting Hagerstown *Torchlight* and Cumberland *Civilian*; Baltimore *Sun*, September 4, 1839; Lowdermilk, p. 346.

[40] Fisk to President and Directors, October 31, 1839; Lowdermilk, p. 346.

[41] Williams, I, 233. The canal company used an early form of labor spy in suppressing the outbreaks among the workers in 1839. James Finney received $100 for his "services." Proceedings of Directors, F, 405 (November 6, 1841).

[42] Judge Wright, the Chief Engineer, resigned in 1831 and refused all offers to return to the canal. Perhaps he foresaw that the mounting obstacles in the path of the proposed canal up the Potomac valley would eventually lead to the failure of the project.

[43] Fisk to President and Directors, March 30, 1835.

(and future experience left much room for doubt), it proved to be a politically disastrous course for the company in the thirties and forties. It also left the future success of the canal clouded by a staggering capitalization. Nevertheless, the Board apparently adopted the suggestion, if for no other reason than that it was the only completely conceived program at hand. The directors advanced Fisk to equal rank with Purcell as resident engineer and placed him in charge of the important new third residency upon which all construction was then concentrated.[44]

In 1836, the canal board repeated its insistence on perfection for the work above Dam No. 5, rejecting all proposals for expedients in construction.

> In the location and construction of the line of canal above dam No. 5, as well as that designed from Cacapon to Cumberland, the Board has acted on the principle that temporary works and expedients, to hasten the opening of the navigation to the coal region, cannot accomplish the object for which this magnificent improvement was designed, and would prove a failure alike discreditable to its projectors and managers, as well as to the community concerned; neither would the interest of the stockholders have been consulted by a plan of operation looking only to saving in cost and time. False and imperfect construction and location would necessarily induce frequent costly repairs, amounting eventually to more than the first cost of a perfect work; . . . they have endeavored to avoid false notions of economy in the construction of a work which is not designed to subserve the purposes of the present day or century, but is to endure for all time.[45]

As long as this attitude prevailed among the directorate, the completion of the canal would remain in doubt.

Another cause of the increased cost of construction was the absence of sufficient quantities of hard rock in the upper valley.[46] As early as May, 1835, Engineer Purcell reported from

[44] Proceedings of Directors, D, 311 (May 25, 1835), 319 (May 27, 1835).

[45] *9th Annual Report* (1837), pp. 6-7.

[46] The Board had optimistically reported in 1831 that it expected stone and lime to be more conveniently located, if not more plentiful, above the Blue Ridge. It also anticipated that the banks and walls would not be so high or the dams so wide. There would be no large aqueducts, and there would be plenty of food for man and beast. (3rd Annual Report [1831], Proceedings of Stockholders, A, 150.) Instead, however, costs mounted and materials remained scarce. Temporary bridges were thrown across the river in 1833 to procure material for embankments on Sections 193, 194 and 195. (Proceedings of Directors, C, 334-335 [May 4, 1833].) Later it was necessary to resort to the same procedure to obtain stone for the masonry.

Cumberland that he had never seen a region so destitute of good building stone.[47] A. B. McFarland, Superintendent of Masonry, made a more thorough inspection of the area, late in 1835, and confirmed the reported scarcity of high-quality rock. He found a large part of the strata to be composed of normally friable red sandstone, much of it already rotten. Good limestone was discovered at scattered points on both sides of the river, but at some distance from the stream. The best supplies were located near the mouth of the Cacapon on the Virginia side and at Town Hill on the Maryland side.[48] The Board considered several suggestions, old and new, to reduce expenses. The use of temporary wooden locks was suggested as an expedient until the opening of the canal provided cheap transportation for stone from the lower valley. Purcell revived the proposal to adopt slackwater navigation for some distance above the dams. Because the Maryland shore was so rugged, another engineer renewed the suggestion to shift the canal to the Virginia bank.[49] As a final device to overcome the construction problems in the upper valley, canal officials proposed a tunnel through a neck of land at the Paw Paw Bends of the Potomac to save five miles of tortuous river bed and cliffs.[50]

Land damages also added to the increasing expense of construction. Some proprietors in the upper valley had granted the right of way to the company in 1828, to give the canal preference over the railroad. But when the Chesapeake and Ohio agent tried to sound out the landholders as to damages he found them noncommittal, awaiting the decision on the final location of the line.[51] Juries in both Washington and Allegany

[47] Purcell to President and Directors, May 26, 1835. Fisk on the other hand optimistically reported that there was sufficient stone for the contemplated masonry below Cacapon. Report on the location of the canal from Dam No. 5 to Cacapon, Letters Received, 1835.

[48] McFarland to Bender, January 2, 1836. Three years later Fisk adopted substantially the same position regarding the scarcity of good building stone above Cacapon. Fisk to President and Directors, May 27, 1839.

[49] *7th Annual Report* (1835), p. 8-9; Purcell to Bender, June 3, 1835; Morris to Fisk, August 1, 1835.

[50] Bender to President and Directors, May 23, 1835; Morris to Fisk, August 1, 3, 1835. The engineers first suggested a tunnel at the Devil's Eyebrow on the Virginia side of the river below Paw Paw, near Doe Gully. The site of the present tunnel was adopted in December, 1835. Proceedings of Directors, D, 443 (December 21, 1835).

[51] B. S. Pigman to Bender, June 4, 1835.

counties continued to exact full satisfaction.[52] Although the company won a victory in one appeal to the courts, the hoped-for relief proved illusory.[53] Land costs averaged $2,290 a mile, more than double the estimates of 1834, ranging all the way from two and one-half to twenty-five times the estimated costs.[54] The Commissioner attributed the attitude of the inhabitants to a desire to force the company to abandon its work and surrender control to the state of Maryland. He cited the recent convention in Baltimore and the plea of one of the lawyers for the proprietors in which he referred to the Chesapeake and Ohio as "this great wealthy *foreign* Company [which] should not be permitted to tres-pass upon the Farmer without being made to pay *amply* for it." [55]

At least part of the rise in construction costs was due to increased labor and provision prices during the thirties. With the resumption of large-scale operations the shortage of workers again became acute. To relieve this condition, A. B. McFarland,

[52] W. Price and Merrick to President and Directors, July 23, 1835; Bender to President and Directors, August 10, 1835.

[53] Merrick to President and Directors, October 11, 1835. The juries were severely censured, but without effect.

[54] Bender to President and Directors, May 31, 1836:

	Estimated	Cost
Heirs of Dan. Smith	$1,000	$ 2,300
J. Charles, Jr.	100	2,500
Sam. Prather	1,000	2,960
Prather heirs	500	1,287
Tobias Johnson	1,150	10,600
Otto	225	1,775
Linn	400	1,575
Peter Miller (per agreement)	150	1,200
J. Chambers	625	2,350
Widow Bevans	575	1,600

Previous to this series of condemnations some proprietors in Allegany County had been willing to compromise, if only to avoid paying the lawyers' fees. The prices up to that time approximated the estimates of the engineers. Thereafter the prospects for extreme satisfaction were so promising that most landowners were willing to pay legal costs to gain the larger damages. The election of a strong Jacksonian as sheriff of the county in October, 1836, promised no improvement in jury awards in the immediate future. W. Price to Washington, October 25, 1836.

[55] Bender to Washington, May 7, 1836. Despite the passions of oratory a fairer rationalization would be probably that the small landholders of Western Maryland were determined to obtain the maximum damages from the company for their lands.

the Inspector of Masonry, went to New York and Philadelphia in 1837 to recruit additional hands.[56] Despite his efforts, the level of wages on the canal rose to \$1.18¾ and \$1.20 a day.[57] Many other public works had already been forced to suspend operations entirely beccause of the rising costs.[58] The Chesapeake and Ohio Canal failed to profit noticeably from these suspensions, for though the supply of labor increased, the continued high price of provisions prevented a marked decline in wages.[59]

As early as August, 1836, the contractors were in dire straits. The directors asked the engineer to recommend revisions of the estimates in view of the "unusual and unexpected increase [which] has taken place in the price of labour and of all provision usually required in the construction of extensive works. . . ." Fisk responded with a proposal to increase the estimates for eighteen contractors by about 8 per cent. The Board promptly adopted the recommendations without modification.[60] This, however, was just the beginning of a general increase in prices. In February, 1837, a directors' committee recommended a further advance of \$106,808 to the contractors on the twenty-seven miles.[61] In August, 1837, Fisk made out estimates for the fifty miles above Cacapon at a 30 per cent increase over January, 1836, prices.[62] A review of contract prices in 1838 indicated a continuing increase in costs. Five locks which had been let for 15 per cent below estimates in

[56] *10th Annual Report* (1838), Appendix 1, p. 22. Bender to Washington, February 22, 1837; Ingle to Bender, March 1, 1837, Letter Book D, 72-73; Bender to Ingle, March 20, 1837; Fisk to Bender, April 19, 1837; Bender to President and Directors, April 18, 1837.

[57] G. M. and R. W. Watkins to President and Directors, February 15, 1837; Fisk to Bender, August 3, 1837. In 1828, wages were \$8 to \$10 a month.

[58] Special Report to 8th Annual Meeting (April 21, 1837), Proceedings of Stockholders, B, 81.

[59] *9th Annual Report* (1837), p. 5; *10th Annual Report* (1838), p. 6.

[60] Proceedings of Directors, E, 126-127 (August 20, 1836), 129 (August 23, 1836); Fisk to Bender, August 22, 1836. See also the printed notice of the action of the Board, August 23, 1836, in Letters Received. This amounted to an increase of about 3 per cent on the total estimates for the twenty-seven miles.

[61] Ingle to Henderson, January 4, 1837, Letter Book D, 24; Ingle to Bender, Febuary 9, 1837; Report of the Committee of Directors, February 4, 1837, Letters Received.

[62] Fisk to Bender, August 3, 1837.

January, 1836, had been abandoned and re-let until the prices were 26 per cent above estimates. Many contracts had been re-let for increases of from 25 to 40 per cent.[63] Another indication of the advance in prices since December 1, 1837, was given by a comparison of costs for certain items on Sections No. 205 and 206: excavation was raised from 11 cents and 14 cents to 20 cents a cubic yard; puddling from 10 cents to 30 cents a cubic yard; walling from 45 cents to 75 cents a perch; and embankment from excavation from 18 cents to 30 cents a cubic yard.[64]

A fifth reason for the increased costs was the adoption of the Paw Paw tunnel and deep cuts. The driving of the tunnel was one of the most interesting and expensive projects on the entire line. It was the proudest achievement of the company and was let with great care. The Methodist parson-contractor, Lee Montgomery, who was working on the tunnel with a crew of carefully selected men, was treated with greater deference by the Board than most other contractors. Both his zeal and his character recommended him to the directors, and the importance of keeping the work moving on the heavy sections in order to prevent undue delay in the completion of the canal insured him their warmest support. The tunnel was being driven from both ends at the rate of 10 to 12 feet a week. By working simultaneously from two shafts sunk from the hilltop, Montgomery estimated that he could increase the rate of progress by 80 per cent. The work was pushed through hard but loose slate rock and proved much more difficult and costly than had been anticipated, and the contractor was soon in need of relief.[65] Notwithstanding additional assistance, he was in an impossible financial position in 1838. The engineer reported that costs on the tunnel were about 75 per cent above contract estimates, and the prices were again raised from $1.75 to $3.00 a cubic yard of excavation, depending on the type of work done.[66]

[63] "Report to the Maryland Legislature, February 5, 1838," in *10th Annual Report* (1838), Appendix 3, pp. 25 ff. The Board had passed one order for a flat 10 per cent increase on all prices.

[64] Proceedings of Directors, E, 389-390 (April 12, 1838).

[65] Bender to President and Directors, August 30, 1837.

[66] Proceedings of Directors, E, 384 (April 11, 1838).

The third major obstacle to the early completion of the canal was the inability of the company to secure adequate financial support for its work. The assistance provided by Maryland was usually late, always the minimum possible, and invariably in the form of state bonds which had to be sold to produce the aid granted. Pending the sale of the bonds, the company's current funds sometimes became exhausted, and the directors had to turn to bank loans to meet the expenses of construction.

The first financial crisis in canal affairs occurred in the critical year of 1832. Although the company still had extensive resources on paper, it was having difficulty in securing the payment of its calls and was becoming hard pressed for funds to push its ambitious construction plans. In June, the president sought unsuccessfully to obtain a loan of $300,000 on the pledge of company property.[67] In October, he made strenuous though futile efforts to secure loans in New York and Philadelphia on the pledge of Washington and Georgetown stock.[68] In November, the treasurer of the company went to Philadelphia to renew the attempt to negotiate a loan from the banks there. At the same time the directors made other efforts to obtain loans from the city of Washington. The Board also directed that memorials be prepared and submitted to the Virginia, Maryland, and Pennsylvania legislatures asking additional subscriptions from those states.[69] All efforts proved to be futile.

After the compromise of 1833 and the election of John H. Eaton to the presidency of the canal company had mollified the hostility of the state of Maryland and the Jackson administration, the Board renewed its efforts to obtain financial assistance in order to continue its work. Pending the success of the petitions to Congress and the several states, Major Eaton made the customary attempts to secure loans from private banks.[70] The appeal to Maryland was received favorably, and the

[67] Proceedings of Directors, C, 174 (June 23, 1832).

[68] Mercer to Ingle, October 8, 25 (two letters), 26, and 31, 1832.

[69] Proceedings of Directors, C, 240, 243-244 (November 23, 1832).

[70] See, for example, John H. Eaton to Biddle, August 9, 1833, Letter Book B, 115-116. See also Ingle to George Thomas, Cashier, and to J. Van Ness, President, Bank of Metropolis, November 5, 8, 1833, *ibid.*, B, 152, 154.

Assembly voted an additional subscription of $125,000 in March, 1834.[71] On the other hand, the company had in its possession $218,750 in Washington and Georgetown bonds which were currently unmarketable.[72] There was also $250,-000 due from delinquent stockholders in June, 1834. The Board made no effort to force payment in view of the tight financial conditions then existing.[73] Without substantial accretions to its resources, the canal was obliged to find other ways to continue construction. In 1834, the directors determined upon a new method, the issuance of canal scrip. They established a trust fund of $150,000 in bonds to redeem the notes as they were presented for payment.[74] Renewed efforts to secure bank loans late in the same year met with success. The Bank of the United States advanced $200,000 in September, and other banks assisted in the winter of 1834-1835 when further state aid seemed assured.[75]

The bonds issued by Maryland to cover the $2,000,000 loan of 1835 found a ready market and caused the canal company no trouble. But those issued to provide the $3,000,000 subscription in 1836 involved the company in a tangled and increasingly precarious financial situation. It had trouble at the very start in obtaining the bonds or the proceeds from their sale. There

[71] 5th Annual Meeting (December 9, 1833), Proceedings of Stockholders, A, 320-321 (March 24, 1834), 324-325.

[72] *6th Annual Report* (1834), p. 3. In June, 1834, the company vainly requested the cities to redeem their stocks at a moderate monthly rate. Washington to W. A. Bradley, Mayor of Washington, July 8, 1834, Letter Book B, 260-261; Washington to John Cox, Mayor of Georgetown, July 8, 1834, *ibid.*, p. 262.

[73] *6th Annual Report* (1834), p. 4; Proceedings of Directors, D, 79 (April 18, 1834). On July 16, however, the Board ordered the institution of suits against delinquent stockholders, *ibid.*, p. 128 (July 16, 1834).

[74] *Niles' Register*, XLVI, No. 9 (April 26, 1834), 133; *ibid.*, No. 10 (May 3, 1834) 149; *6th Annual Report* (1834), p. 4; Proceedings of Directors, D, 73-74 (April 11, 1834), 91 (May 16, 1834). The legality of the scrip was challenged, but the company's counsel upheld the issue. Proceedings of Directors, D, 75 (April 14, 1834), 76 (April 18, 1834).

[75] Ingle to R. H. Henderson, July 28, 1834, Letter Book B, 277; Ingle to Boteler and Reynolds, August 26, 1834, *ibid.*, p. 299; Washington to Ingle, September 14, 15, 16, 1834; Proceedings of Directors, D, 159 (September 18, 1834); Washington to the President of the Bank of the United States, December 17, 1834, Letter Book B, 366-367; Report to Special Meeting (April 22, 1835), Proceedings of Stockholders, A, 368. See also, Ingle to Henderson, April 10, 1835, Letter Book B, 438.

was some delay in putting the law into effect, and political distractions in Maryland caused the postponement of the appointment of state commissioners to negotiate the sale of the bonds.[76] By the end of March, 1837, the directors had decided to purchase the bonds on behalf of the company, if the state agents in Europe failed to sell them. A provisional contract was drawn up accordingly.[77] No difficulty was anticipated, however, in effecting the sale of the bonds by the agents as late as June, 1837, for Maryland's credit abroad was still high.

When the commissioners failed to negotiate the sale of the bonds for the required 20 per cent premium by December, 1837, the Board prepared to undertake the task on the same terms.[78] By this time more trouble was brewing at home, for some members of the Assembly had lost their early enthusiasm for internal improvements and were beginning to regret the passage of the Eight Million Dollar bill. Opponents of the public-works program also questioned the validity of the Maryland Canal Company subscriptions, organization, and certification. The legislature debated at considerable length the repeal of the act and the withholding of bonds not already issued.[79] The canal company insisted that the state was duty-bound to carry out the provision of the act, for the Board had already made advances to the Annapolis and Elkridge Railroad on behalf of the state, on the pledge of the bonds to be issued. The company had also made a very important concession in allowing the Baltimore and Ohio to construct its line west of Harpers Ferry.[80] The Assembly finally confirmed the bond issue in March, 1838, and placed the certificates in the company's hands.[81] The Board divided the bonds into equal sums

[76] 8th Annual Meeting (April 21, 1837), Proceedings of Stockholders, B, 79. The commissioners were not appointed until December, 1836. One left immediately for London, but the other two did not leave until spring. Special Report on the Completion of the Canal, p. 352.

[77] Proceedings of Directors, E, 226 (March 31, 1837); 8th Annual Meeting (March 31, 1837), Proceedings of Stockholders, B, 75; *9th Annual Report* (1837), p. 14.

[78] Special Report on the Completion of the Canal, p. 352.

[79] Washington to [Ingle], February 8, 1838; the partial report of the Committee on Ways and Means was favorable to the company. It left the question of the Maryland Canal to future study.

[80] Washington to Ingle, January 23, 1838.

[81] Ingle to Bender, March 8, 10, 1838, Letter Book D, 279, 280-281. Pro-

for sale here and abroad. There soon proved to be no market here because of the tightness in financial circles after the panic of 1837. The directors turned all hopes to negotiations in England.[82] There was no market in England for 6 per cent dollar bonds, and on the advice of their agents in London both the railroad and the canal companies prevailed upon the Maryland Assembly to convert the bonds to 5 per cent sterling.[83] After another debate on the propriety of refusing all aid,[84] the Assembly consented, and released the canal and railroad companies from the requirement of a 20 per cent premium. At the same time it subscribed an additional $1,375,000 to the canal stock.[85]

During these negotiations the Board resorted to several temporary arrangements to keep the work going. It instituted suits against delinquent stockholders to force full payment.[86] When the banking crisis of 1837 threatened the company's deposits, the directors took extraordinary measures to protect their existing resources, shifting their funds to specie-paying banks and demanding security for their safety.[87] Later in the year, while still awaiting the sale of the bonds for the $3,000,000 subscription, the Board resorted to loans from local banks

ceedings of Directors, E, 380-381 (April 2, 1838); *10th Annual Report* (1838), pp. 3, 11; *11th Annual Report* (1839), p. 3. The Assembly repealed the provision of the 1836 act requiring state commissioners to negotiate the sale of the bonds on March 12, 1839. Baltimore *Sun*, March 14, 1839.

[82] Proceedings of Directors, E, 388 (April 12, 1838); *10th Annual Report* (1838), p. 11.

[83] Special Report on the Completion of the Canal, p. 354.

[84] "Report of the Committee on Ways and Means in reference to the Chesapeake and Ohio Canal Company, March 14, 1839," *A Short History of the Public Debt of Maryland*, Appendix, Document P, pp. 76-78. There had been three separate investigations of the canal by successive legislatures, to the detriment of the canal's interests although it was vindicated in each case. See Washington to Peabody, May 18, 1839, Letter Book E, 225.

[85] Baltimore *Sun*, April 6, 7, 1839; Washington to Peabody, April 20, 1839; Special Meeting (May 11, 1839), Proceedings of Stockholders, B, 188-189; Special Report on the Completion of the Canal, p. 356. The subscription was the result of an admission as early as 1838 that because of the difficulty of construction and the high prices of the work, $1,500,000 more would be needed, over all resources available, to complete the waterway. Washington to Ingle, February 5, 1838.

[86] Ingle to Schley, February 28, 1837, Letter Book D, 71-72.

[87] Proceedings of Directors, E, 223-224 (March 20, 1837), 228 (April 1, 1837); Ingle to Bender, May 12, 1837, Letter Book D, 130.

on the pledge of Washington and Georgetown bonds. At first the efforts were successful only in Baltimore and Washington, but in November the Bank of the United States in Philadelphia granted a loan of $50,000 on the pledge of Washington stock.[88] After that the company secured loans in the District of Columbia and in Baltimore amounting to over $300,000 by June, 1838.[89]

Another temporary expedient was the renewed issuance of canal scrip. At first the directors limited the issue to notes of less than $5.00 in value.[90] The great scarcity of small coins and currency due to the disappearance of specie and the restriction on the issue of small notes by banks made the Board's action in August, 1837, generally popular.[91] In September, however, the directors began to issue larger notes of $5, $10, and $20 denominations, and what had started as a temporary convenience became a regular practice with dangerous potentialities. The company expanded the printing of scrip from time to time during the following year. By the end of May, 1838, $376,513.50 in canal notes had been issued under various authorizations and $80,000 more authorized but not yet issued.[92] After ordering the distribution of most of the latter, the Board called a halt to the printing of canal scrip for about a year.[93]

The law suits, the loans, and the scrip were all stop-gap measures pending the successful negotiations of the state bonds in England. Shortly after the Assembly confirmed the bond issue, the directors appointed George Peabody as their agent in England to effect the sale, but an offer by Auguste Belmont,

[88] Proceedings of Directors, E, 301 (August 9, 1837), 312 (September 6, 1837), 316 (September 22, 1837), 322 (October 4, 1837), 334 (November 8, 1837), 337 (November 26, 1837); Washington to Ingle, September 18, 1837; Biddle to Washington, September 19, 1837; Biddle to Gunton, November 24, 1837.

[89] Proceedings of Directors, E, 346 (December 20, 1837)—$30,000; 360 (January 27, 1838)—$40,000; 370 (February 28, 1838)—$38,000; 429-430 (May 30, 1838)—$100,000. Over $100,000 had been borrowed before December, 1837.

[90] Proceedings of Directors, E, 268 (June 7, 1837).

[91] Shriver to Ingle, June 29, July 12, 1837; Washington to Ingle, August 13, 1837; Ingle to Underwood, Bald, and Company, August 9, 1837, Letter Book D, 191-192.

[92] Proceedings of Directors, E, 298-299 (August 3, 1837), 317 (September 22, 1837), 426 (May 30, 1838).

[93] *Ibid.*, p. 459 (July 16, 1838): issuance of $60,000 of the $90,000 directed.

New York agent for Rothschild and Son, of London, to purchase $1,500,000 of the 6 per cent bonds was rejected, in May, 1838.[94] When no other bids were forthcoming, the Board decided to seek loans from banks on the pledge of the bonds while awaiting an improvement in the money markets. There followed one of the most disastrous episodes in the canal's history. It is not necessary to describe in detail the unpleasant course of affairs which followed. In a frenzy of hypothecation without effective safeguards, the Board floated loans both here and abroad on the pledge of Maryland bonds at 85. With the funds thus obtained, the directors rushed the completion of the canal in the face of mounting construction costs. By January 1, 1839, banks in the United States had loaned $490,000 and those in England, $1,258,925.08, including exchange differences.[95] After the substitution of 5 per cent sterling for 6 per cent dollar bonds had been effected and an additional subscription of $1,375,000 obtained, the company floated further loans in this country, bringing the total to $1,110,000 here, $1,258,-925.08 in England, and $2,368,925.08 in all.[96]

The wholesale hypothecation of Maryland bonds at 85 put the canal company in a very unpopular position. The directors' course undermined the state's credit both here and abroad. It threatened disaster to the canal as well. The actions of the Board were severely criticized on all sides, and the Assembly made a detailed investigation of the conduct of canal affairs.[97] Eventually, the general condemnation of the directors' practices and a political revolution in Maryland combined to overthrow the entire regime in 1839.[98]

[94] *Ibid.*, pp. 391-392 (April 16, 1838), 410 (May 16, 1838). Although the Board gave no reason for its action, the offer probably was for a sum below the 20 per cent premium required by the company's contract with the state.

[95] Washington to the Governor of Maryland, January 23, 1839, enclosing a statement of the debts and credits of the Chesapeake and Ohio Canal Company by John P. Ingle, clerk, January 1, 1839, *11th Annual Report* (1839), Appendix 1, p. 23.

[96] *11th Annual Report* (1839), p. 12. The Board had pledged the larger part of $3,200,000 in bonds from the subscription of 1836 and $1,375,000 from the subscription of 1839.

[97] "Report of the Committee on Ways and Means in reference to the Chesapeake and Ohio Canal Company, March 14, 1839," *A Short History of the Public Debt of Maryland*, Appendix, Document P, pp. 76-78.

[98] Washington to Peabody, March 5, 1839, Letter Book E, 194; Special

The principal problem facing the new directorate in June, 1839, was the liquidation of the staggering debt. At the same time the Board would have to find some means of pushing the construction of the canal to a successful conclusion or suspend all operations. In neither case were the prospects for success very bright.

The process of liquidation proved most disastrous and painful. For two months the new president, Francis Thomas, negotiated alone, unhampered even by a quorum of directors.[99] As his first move he made an agreement with the Baltimore and Ohio to cooperate in the sale of the bonds to maintain the state's credit and prevent sacrifices.[100] Unfortunately the canal company could not afford to await an improvement in the market. Its creditors were pressing for payment and threatening to effect a forced sale of the bonds hypothecated to them.[101] In the debacle that followed the bonds were sold for an average of 66 and 67 in New York, and 71 in England. Only in Baltimore and Washington did the company salvage even the 85 per cent hypothecated value. The total loss for the company on the $4,064,444.42 of bonds sold was $1,048,022.09, or 25.79 per cent of the par value.[102] Nevertheless, the president was able to report to the next annual meeting, in June, 1840, that

Report on the Completion of the Canal, p. 356. A Democrat, William Grason, was elected Governor in 1838, in the first popular canvass for Governor in the history of the state. He assumed office in January, 1839. (Baltimore *Sun*, January 9, 1839.) Thus he was in a position to use his influence to remove the Whig canal board and appoint Democratic officials in the next annual meeting of stockholders in June, 1839.

[99] Proceedings of Directors, F, 95-96 (August 28, 1839); Thomas to David Stewart, Chairman, Committee of Internal Improvement, February 8, 1840, Letter Book F, 49-50. The absence of his political allies caused some observers to remark that even Thomas' Democratic friends did not agree with his handling of canal affairs. See the letter of "Old Kent" in Baltimore *American*, September 15, 1841.

[100] McLane to Thomas, July 4, 1839.

[101] Thomas to Peabody, July 18, 1839, Letter Book E, 298-299. Thomas pointed out that the railroad was out of debt and could afford to wait. The canal's creditors, on the other hand, were pressing for payment. He then suggested that, despite the agreement he had just made with McLane, Peabody should not cooperate with the Baltimore and Ohio but should try to anticipate its moves and benefit thereby.

[102] *13th Annual Report* (1841), Appendix, p. 27; Baltimore *American*, September 11, 1841.

the entire debt of the company arising from the hypothecation of the 5 per cent bonds had been liquidated.[103]

Again faced with the alternative of suspending work or resorting to extraordinary measures, the Board decided on the latter course. On September 15, 1839, it authorized the issuance of $300,000 more in canal scrip. President Thomas insisted that he did not wish to issue the post notes except in case of utter necessity. Rather than abandon construction, however, the directors employed the paper money regularly. They again established a trust fund of 5 per cent Maryland bonds to redeem the scrip as it was received for tolls, rents, etc.[104] In April, 1840, they suspended the issuance of the notes, but resumed it in June under the general authority to print it as needed to pay the estimates of work done.[105] Again the experiment with paper money involved the company in legal and financial entanglements. A disagreement with the trustees over the conduct of their affairs and the misappropriation of the trust fund brought about a legal controversy which lasted into the next decade. Over 80 per cent of this latter issue was never redeemed.[106]

Meanwhile the Board attempted to continue the work on the unfinished portion of the canal. Apparently on the strength of the decision to issue scrip, it declared as abandoned sections

[103] *12th Annual Report* (1840), p. 3. See also Thomas to S. Pinckney, January 26, 1840, Letter Book F, 33. An investigation of Thomas' administration severely condemned his precipitous actions and alleged financial blunders. Baltimore *American*, September 7, 11, 1841.

While Thomas may have been guilty of inexperience, haste, and lack of tact, it appears that the canal company's finances were in an impossible condition. Both the old and new administrations were criticized, though for opposite reasons. No matter what course Thomas had pursued the consequences and the public censure would have been the same. Above all, the condition of the financial markets here and abroad allowed little choice.

[104] Proceedings of Directors, F, 108 (September 15, 1839), 150-151 (January 15, 1840); Thomas to Pinckney, November 1, 1839, Letter Book E, 388. Three bankers, James Swan and John S. Gittings of Baltimore and William Gunton of Washington, were made trustees, but Swan, President of the Western Bank, did most of the work and caused most of the trouble.

[105] Ingle to Chambers, April 8, 1840, Letter Book F, 98; Proceedings of Directors, F, 233-234 (June 17, 1840).

[106] Special Report on the Completion of the Canal, p. 358. See the *Letter of John Gittings to the Stockholders of the Chesapeake and Ohio Canal Company* (Baltimore, 1843).

upon which contractors had ceased work and re-let them in December, 1839.[107] Although the hoped-for aid from the Maryland Assembly was not forthcoming by the next spring, the Board continued to push the work rather than suspend operations, disperse the two thousand laborers on the line, and sacrifice $150,000 worth of tools, buildings, and materials.[108] By continuing construction the directors could also take full advantage of the falling price of labor and put an end to the outbreak of violence which had revived with the coming of hard times and the suspension of contracts.[109]

Accompanying the determination to continue construction on the basis of the unrestricted issuance of scrip was the first large turnover of canal employees. This was partly the result of a disagreement with the new policies and partly the effect of the application of the spoils system in the operation of the canal. Many old and reliable officials were dismissed or voluntarily retired, including the clerk, the treasurer, the chief engineer, several divisional superintendents, and many lesser officials.[110] The wholesale changes did not go without public notice, for the ousted officials carried into the newspapers their opposition to the directorate, and other observers expressed their opinions on the separations. A new legislature, elected during the same year, demanded in January, 1841, explanations of the Board's conduct and of company affairs.[111] When the Assembly adjourned in March without providing effective aid and the trust fund neared exhaustion, the directors reversed their former policy, forbade the issuance of more scrip until

[107] Proceedings of Directors, F, 137-138 (December 28, 1839); Ingle to M. C. Sprigg, December 28, 1839, Letter Book F, 8-9.

[108] Proceedings of Directors, F, 185-186 (March 28, 1840); *12th Annual Report* (1840), p. 6. Sale of these properties would bring only 50 per cent of their value, it was said.

[109] *12th Annual Report* (1840), p. 6.

[110] Proceedings of Directors, F, 246 (July 9, 1840), 256-257 (September 26, 1840); 259 (November 14, 1840); Ingle to President and Directors, June 10, 1840; Fisk to President and Directors, October 1, 1840; Fillebrown to President and Directors, November 21, 1840; Morris to Thomas, December 4, 1840. See also notices of dismissal in Letter Book F, 128, 130, 161, 170, 185-186, 195, and 210.

[111] Proceedings of Directors F, 279 (January 2, 1841), 284 (January 25, 1841).

means were provided to repay it, and prepared to suspend operations.[112]

In April, 1841, another revolution occurred in the directorate of the canal company. The state of Maryland, as the controlling stockholder, ousted the old Board and installed a new one. The latter, predominantly Whig, proceeded to reinstate as many of the old officials as were still available and to reform canal affairs. Company officials were forbidden to interfere in politics, the edict against scrip was continued, and proceedings against the trustees instituted.[113] The directors ordered tolls to be received one-third in current money after August 1.[114] They authorized final suspensions in the same month, although they agreed to accept drafts on the company by the contractors in order to encourage them to continue the work on their own until further aid was forthcoming.[115] An order requiring the payment of tolls in cash, effective April 1, 1842, brought to a close a period of disastrous financial experiments.[116] Work on the canal continued spasmodically a little longer, and then it too came to an end.[117]

[112] *Ibid.*, p. 297 (March 16, 1841). The Assembly did pass a bill to grant $2,000,000 in bonds to the canal company if the mine owners would guarantee to pay the state $200,000 a year beginning six months after the completion of the waterway. The latter refused, and the act lapsed. Baltimore *American* April 12, 1841, January 14, 1842.

[113] Proceedings of Directors, F, 301-302 (April 13, 1841), 308 (April 14, 1841), 315 (April 29, 1841); Morris to Sprigg, April 7, 1841; Fisk to President and Directors, April 29, 1841, Letter Book F, 262-264.

[114] Proceedings of Directors, F, 359 (July 15, 1841).

[115] *Ibid.*, pp. 377-378 (August 7, 1841), 381 (September 16, 1841).

[116] *Ibid.*, p. 433 (March 16, 1842).

[117] Fisk to President and Directors, December 1, 1842.

Chapter VII

THE COMPLETION OF THE CANAL (1842-1850)

After construction came to a temporary halt following the exhaustion of the company's immediate resources, Maryland paused in its promotion of the project to review the condition of the canal. In 1842 the waterway was completed as far as Dam No. 6, above Hancock, a distance of approximately 135 miles from Washington. The work thus far done had been accomplished under the most trying circumstances. A succession of obstacles had marred the construction, delayed the completion, and increased the cost of the work beyond all expectations. The dispute over the right of way, the cholera epidemic, continual labor, financial, and engineering problems, and political diversions all contributed their share. By 1842, over $10,000,000 had been applied to the construction of the canal and to incidental expenses.[1] In the process of supplying the major part of this sum, the state of Maryland had acquired the control and direction of the company's affairs from the federal government and the District cities. In the meantime, the time limit of twelve years allowed by the charter for the completion of the eastern section had expired in 1840.[2] The frontier had moved far to the west, and other established transportation lines were carrying the trade of the Ohio valley. Almost all hope for the construction of the western section had been abandoned.

The portion of the line from Dam No. 6 to Cumberland which had not yet been completed was commonly referred to as "the fifty miles." The region through which it passed included some of the most beautiful and most rugged country in the entire valley, but it was lacking in good building stone. Thus

[1] *13th Annual Report* (1841), Appendix, p. 28. Almost $2,000,000 more had gone into interest and losses.

[2] Coale to W. Price, December 8, 1843, Letter Book G, 121. Fortunately none of the parties to the charter had raised the question of forfeiture.

both excavation and masonry work promised to be expensive. Although all but eighteen miles of the section had been completed, the unfinished parts were scattered over the whole fifty miles and included most of the heaviest work—the tunnel, the deep cuts, etc. It was estimated in 1842 that $1,545, 000 was required to finish the eighteen miles.[3] The greatest difficulties would be in acquiring the funds and accumulating the necessary working force again.

The financial condition of the company in 1842 was deplorable, if not entirely hopeless. The officials publicly acknowledged debts of $1,196,400 above all means.[4] Many of the company's resources were tied up in the few remaining 5 per cent bonds it owned. These had been deposited with the Barings, in London, after Peabody had given up the agency,[5] and there they remained, for there was no market for them. This was especially true after Maryland failed to meet the semi-annual interest payment on them beginning July 1, 1841.[6] The Barings had agreed in 1839 to accept the drafts of the company for amounts up to £200,000 at a rate of £65 for every £100 of bonds, if not more than £30,000 were drawn in a month. After £30,151/8 had been so advanced by the end of 1842, the Barings, apparently hard pressed by the continuing stringency in the English money market, demanded some payment on the advances. If this were not forthcoming they announced that they would have to sell the bonds at market prices or buy them in themselves at 50 per cent.[7] The canal directors flatly refused to agree to these terms.

The latter proposed an alternate course to be followed in regard to the bonds. They suggested that the coupons for 1841 and 1842 be detached and sold to pay the interest due on the

[3] Fisk to President and Directors, December 1, 1842. The general decline of prices in the forties made it probable that the work could be done for much less in 1844, *16th Annual Report* (1844), p. 5.

[4] *Niles' Register*, LXI, No. 22 (January 29, 1842), 352, quoting Report of President. Many of the resources of the company were unavailable.

[5] Proceedings of Directors, F, 143-144 (January 8, 1840). It had been pending for several months. See *ibid.*, p. 112 (October 14, 1839).

[6] Turner to Barings, January 10, 1843, Letter Book G, 6; Turner to T. W. Ward, April 17, 1843, *ibid.*, p. 32.

[7] Barings to Peabody, November 27, December 6, 1839, quoted in Turner to Barings, January 10, 1843, *ibid.*, pp. 2-4.

advances made by the Barings. The Maryland legislature had authorized the receipt of the coupons in payment of state taxes, thereby restoring a large part of their value. The Barings consented to the sale of the coupons for July, 1842.[8] The canal directors then offered to settle the whole affair. They proposed to sell the Barings at 65 all bonds necessary to repay the advances made. The Barings would also take at 85 all coupons necessary to pay the interest due on the drafts paid. The Barings promptly accepted this offer in November, 1845.[9] The transfer of the remaining bonds from the Barings to the canal company, in the following March, formally completed the transaction.[10]

The state of Maryland had already taken steps ostensibly to compel the canal company to improve its financial condition. In the spring of 1842, the Assembly ordered the sale of all property owned by the Chesapeake and Ohio not strictly used for canal purposes. The directors were to receive canal scrip and other evidences of company debts in payment of the land.[11] In pursuance of this requirement the chief engineer made surveys along the entire line and submitted his report in July of the same year.[12] Sales took place by order of the Board during the rest of that year and 1843. The forced disposal of the property was completed by June, 1844. As might be expected the proceeds from the sales were very small, even when reckoned in depreciated canal scrip. The total amount received was $25,938.[13]

[8] Turner to Ward, April 17, 1843, *ibid.*, p. 33; J. H. B. Latrobe to Coale, September 25, 1843, quoted in Coale to Latrobe, September 30, 1843, *ibid.*, p. 101.

[9] Proceedings of Directors, G, 119-120 (October 10, 1843); Coale to Latrobe, October 10, 1843, Letter Book G, 103-104; Ward to Latrobe, November 21, 1843, Latrobe to Coale, November 25, 1843, quoted in Coale to Latrobe, November 27, 1843, *ibid.*, p. 115.

[10] Coale to Ward, March 26, 1844, Letter Book G, 143; *16th Annual Report* (1844), pp. 19-20. £15,500 5 per cent Maryland bonds with coupons from July 1, 1844 and £737/10 additional coupons of July 1, 1844, from the other bonds were returned to the canal company.

[11] *16th Annual Report* (1844), p. 18.

[12] Fisk to Young, Elgin, Rodgers, and Stone, April 6, 1842; Fisk to President and Directors, July 20, 1842.

[13] Ingle to Coale, June 11, 1844. The proceeds were probably nowhere near the cost of the lands to the canal company, but no accurate comparison of the prices paid and received by the company is possible because of the variance in the size of the lands.

During the suspension of work on the canal there was more or less general deterioration. This was equally true for both the unfinished and the completed sections. Freshets in the Potomac valley also wreaked their usual havoc on the more exposed portions of the line. The flood of April, 1845, which was described as the worst in the canal's history, was particularly destructive.[14] Besides these instances of unavoidable natural destruction, there were cases of deterioration which were just as clearly the result of neglect. Reports from a director and from the shippers themselves, in 1842, noted instances of delinquency of canal officials, lock gates out of repair, and the existence of sand and mud bars in the canal and the feeders. The same bars, or others, were still there in 1844.[15]

Plans for the completion of the canal went on apace in the early forties. There was, in fact, no break in the efforts of the canal company to obtain the means to finish the work. The suspension of construction on the line at this time merely indicated a shift of activity back to the political arena.

The earliest form which the proposals to finish the canal took was the attempt to secure the transfer of Chesapeake and Ohio stock held by the United States to the state of Maryland. At this time the federal government possessed $2,500,000 of the stock, including its own commitments for $1,000,000 and the subscriptions of the bankrupt District cities for $1,500,000. In return for the transfer of the stock, the state of Maryland offered a guarantee to complete the eastern section of the canal. A committee of the Maryland Assembly first suggested the transfer in a report on canal affairs in 1839.[16] Petitions to that effect were presented to Congress annually in the early forties.[17]

[14] Young to Turner, April 19, 1843; Fisk to Ingle, April 20, 1843.

[15] F. Tilghman to M. C. Sprigg, June 25, 1842; Thomas G. Harris and others to M. C. Sprigg, July 6, 1842; Fisk to Coale, September 19, 1844.

[16] "Report of the Committee on Ways and Means, March 19, 1839," *A Short History of the Public Debt of Maryland*, Appendix, Document P, pp. 76-78. The suggestion was also incorporated in the bill providing $1,375,000 for the canal. The act authorized the Governor to negotiate for the transfer on the promise that Maryland would complete the canal to Cumberland. Baltimore *Sun*, April 7, 1839.

[17] *Message on the Chesapeake and Ohio Canal from President Van Buren, transmitting a Letter of the Maryland Governor, William Grason, on the*

They were of course supported by memorials from Maryland citizens,[18] and vigorously opposed by the District cities.[19] In 1842, in a stinging indictment, a committee of the city of Washington effectively denounced what it termed the selfish attitude of the state of Maryland towards the canal.[20]

Transfer of Stock in the Chesapeake and Ohio Canal Company, January 6, 1840, 26th Cong., 1st sess., House of Representatives, Document No. 90; *Report of Senator S. S. Phelps on the Chesapeake and Ohio Canal Company Stock*, January 11, 1841, 26th Cong., 2d sess., Senate, Document No. 63; *Resolution of the Maryland Legislature for the transfer of Chesapeake and Ohio Canal Company Stock by the United States to Maryland*, January 18, 1843, 27th Cong., 3d sess., House of Representatives, Document No. 71; *Report of Representative Owen on the Transfer of Chesapeake and Ohio Canal Company Stock*, January 19, 1844, 28th Cong., 1st sess., House of Representatives, Report No. 56; *Resolution of the Maryland Legislature, urging the Transfer of the Chesapeake and Ohio Canal Company Stock to Maryland*, April 12, 1844, 28th Cong., 1st sess., House of Representatives, Document No. 227.

[18] See, for example, *Memorial of the Citizens of Allegany County for the Surrender of United States Stock in the Chesapeake and Ohio Canal Company to Maryland*, April 28, 1843, 27th Cong., 2d sess., House of Representatives, Document No. 202.

[19] *Memorial of the City of Washington against the Transfer of Stock Held by the United States in the Chesapeake and Ohio Canal Company*, March 11, 1840, 26th Cong., 1st sess., Senate, Document No. 277; *Memorial of the City of Washington against the Transfer of Stock of the United States in the Chesapeake and Ohio Canal Company*, December 28, 1840, 26th Cong., 2d sess., Senate, Document No. 30. Inevitably there was some support for the transfer in the District of Columbia. See *Matthew St. Clair Clarke to the Board of Aldermen and the Board of Common Council of Washington . . .* (Washington, 1842).

[20] The *Report of the Committee of the Corporation of Washington, against the Surrender of the stock* (Washington, January, 1842) stated in part: "Coupled with the act [of 1839] authorizing this last subscription, was a direction to the Governor to ask of Congress a surrender to the State of the $2,500,000 of stock, originally subscribed by the United States, and the Corporations of Washington, Georgetown, and Alexandria; and if granted, the State pledged herself to buy out all individual stockholders at 50 per cent. *But*, on the 23rd of February, 1841 (*fifteen days after the Senate of the United States had passed a resolution giving her the said $2,500,000 of stock*, and had sent it to the House of Representatives for concurrence, and when it was expected that the House would also pass it,) a bill was introduced into the Senate of Maryland, and instantly passed both branches of the Legislature, quietly revoking this obligation to which she had pledged herself to Congress to pay the private stockholders 50 per cent. This repealing bill was in the following brief and unostentatious form:

'A supplement to the act passed at December Session, 1838, chap. 396, entitled an "Act relating to the Chesapeake and Ohio Canal Company."

'*Be it enacted by the General Assembly of Maryland*, That the second and third sections of said act be, and the same are hereby, repealed.'"

Proponents of the transfer were unable to secure agreement in Congress on the resolution surrendering the stock.[21] In 1842 the Senate passed a joint resolution providing for the transfer of the stock to the state of Maryland and the District cities, on the condition that Maryland would agree not to foreclose its mortgage. The District cities promptly consented to this solution.[22] Maryland insisted, however, that it must receive the stock before it would borrow further to complete the work.[23] The canal company remained relatively indifferent to the outcome of the struggle, merely expressing the hope that the state, if successful, would pass a law for the completion of the eastern section.[24] All efforts to effect the transfer ultimately failed, and the question was dropped.

Another scheme advanced to provide for the completion of the canal was the proposal to sell the state's interest in the canal to parties that would undertake the task of finishing the work.[25] This plan was proposed even before the collapse of negotiations for the transfer of stock. It cleverly connected the settlement of canal affairs with the solution of Maryland's financial problems. The price finally decided upon in 1843 [26] was $5,000,000 in state bonds. There were no bidders. In the absence of any offers the canal company undertook to sell itself to likely purchasers.

[21] *Niles' Register*, LVIII, No. 21 (July 25, 1840), 330.

[22] *Ibid.*, LXII, No. 21 (July 23, 1842), 334, 336. *Memorial of Georgetown approving the transfer of United States Stock in the Chesapeake and Ohio Canal Company to Maryland and the District of Columbia cities*, June 29, 1842, 27th Cong., 2d sess., Senate, Document No. 343; *Resolution of Alexandria approving the Transfer of the Stock of the United States in the Chesapeake and Ohio Canal Company to Maryland and the District of Columbia cities*, June 29, 1842, 27th Cong., 2d sess., Senate, Document No. 344.

[23] *Niles' Register*, LXVI, No. 1 (March 2, 1844), 12. The position of the state was that the United States was responsible for the increased size and cost of the canal, and therefore should either assume the expense of its completion or assist the state to do it by direct relief or by the transfer of the stock held by the United States. See the *Speech of John M. S. Causin, Esq., in the House of Delegates of Maryland, on the Preamble and Resolution, Introduced by him, on the Subject of Relief to the States, by the Issue of Two Hundred Millions of Government Stock, Based upon a Pledge of the Proceeds of Public Lands* [January 31 and February 1, 1843] (Annapolis, 1843).

[24] Coale to W. Young, December 13, 1843, Letter Book G, 124.

[25] Proceedings of Directors, G, 11 (April 12, 1843).

[26] Baltimore *American* March 9, 10, 15, 1843. The bill was passed after a Democratic filibuster in the Senate was broken, and the disgruntled Democrats had left the chamber. *Ibid.*, March 13, 1843.

It pointed out that $5,000,000 in Maryland bonds at the current depreciated value (62½) would be a bargain.[27] The company even contemplated buying itself from the state by offering canal bonds to Maryland for $5,000,000 (presumably to be exchanged by the state for its own bonds).[28] The price set was far too high, and all efforts to bring about a sale were unsuccessful. The comic opera aspects of the whole episode were emphasized in a summary of the proposed sale by a contemporary observer.[29]

> But no sooner was this tack resolved upon, than up came a violent dispute about the price. And it was amusing enough to observe, almost the whole of those members who had invariably opposed the construction of the work, and insisted that it would never be worth anything to the state, suddenly became violent sticklers for demanding a price even beyond what the work had cost the state. Seldom has there been a more exciting scene in the legislature of any of the states in this union, than this question of price gave rise to in the Maryland state house last winter [1842-1843]. The executive was denounced for undue interference on the occasion; the majority in the house became completely divided, and the party split, and more bitterly denounced each other than the political parties before that, had done. The senate became for the first time in our state history, the arena of unparliamentary proceeding, which nothing but the prompt and energetic course of a most admirable presiding officer, averted from effecting absolute disorganization. . . .
>
> All this excitement proved to be of no other avail, than to save so far, the credit of the state. The canal, it appears, cannot be sold at present for even the *lowest* price which was in dispute. There has been in fact, no bidding for it. The reason assigned, if we understand aright, is not that the work would not be worth the money if finished, but the uncertainty of its being finished. The foreign capitalists say, "your canal would no doubt pay very well, if it were in operation, but you have such endless difficulties and delays; disputes with rival works,—law suits; injunctions taking you into chancery and keeping you tied up for years.—endless disputes in the legislature, session after session, about the right applications of the funds they grant,—disputes with the district cities—disputes with the authorities of the emporium of your own state—or rather, with the officers and contractors of the rival work which they are constructing alongside of you."

The plan which gave the greatest promise of acceptance and

[27] Coale to Ward, March 14, 1844, Letter Book G, p. 139.

[28] Proceedings of Directors, G, 40 (May 4, 1843); *15th Annual Report* (1843), p. 5.

[29] *Niles' Register*, LXIV, No. 24 (August 12, 1843), 372.

success was the proposal to waive the state's prior liens on canal revenues and permit the canal company to issue its own bonds to pay for the completion of its work. Like all other projects to provide for finishing the canal as far as Cumberland, this proposal was bitterly opposed by the railroad and by the city of Baltimore.[30] It was unpopular with others because it did not provide relief for the financial condition of the state. Thus it was looked upon as a last-resort measure; and as such it failed to pass while other schemes were being tried.

The first attempt was made during the December session, 1841. Disagreement between the Senate and House of Delegates prevented the passage of the bill before the Assembly rose in March, 1842, although the proposal itself at least required no further drain on the state treasury.[31] As a result, another year passed without action, during which dilapidation set in on the canal and the interest on the state bonds went unpaid. So disastrous were the consequences of the legislature's inaction that large meetings of citizens in western Maryland sent appeals to the Governor to call a special session of the Assembly.[32]

The attempt was renewed in the December session, 1842. Proponents of the measure again advanced the argument so often repeated in the thirties that "the completion of the public works was forever to exonerate them [the citizens of Maryland] from taxation on their or any other account."[33] Notwithstanding the pressure brought to bear for the bill, the enemies of the canal succeeded in defeating it again.

The proposition to waive the lien of the state in favor of contractors who would undertake to finish the canal, was very earnestly debated in the legislature, both last session and the session before, but did not prevail. The canal has been at a stand still, and it is probable will stand still, until the state either determines with its own resources or credit, to finish the work, or *otherwise* consent to forego its liens in favor of whoever will, with their own resources, finish it. The actual

[30] See, for example, the exchange of letters between "Delta" and "Maryland" in Baltimore *Sun* and the Baltimore *American*, January—March, 1841, for and against the completion of the canal, respectively. The letters of "Delta" are printed in *Delta: or What ought the State to do with the Chesapeake and Ohio Canal* [Baltimore, 1841].

[31] Baltimore *American*, March 9, 10, 11, 1842.

[32] *Niles' Register*, LXII, No. 4 (March 26, 1842), 52.

[33] *A Short History of the Public Debt of Maryland*, p. 48.

opponents of the canal, of which there is a party in the state, sorry we are to say, throw their weight first in one and then in the other scale, and thereby prevent either expedient from being adopted.[34]

The failure of the legislature to provide aid for the canal or to waive its prior lien caused general consternation among the neutrals in the fight between the internal improvement companies. There was nothing to look forward to, but, as in the past,

to listen week after week to long labored speeches, and to watch, session after session, the under currents, over currents, and counter currents, of innumerable little interests, each tugging as if for life, to accomplish its own design, without hardly for a moment regarding the public interest, ...[35]

The summer did not bring any substantial change in canal affairs. The attempt to effect a sale and to secure the transfer of U. S. stock in the Chesapeake and Ohio failed again. A contract with Letson and Rutter for the completion of the canal was annulled by the directors because of some undesirable conditions included in its terms.[36] On the other hand, agitation for a solution increased somewhat in the state at large. A Whig convention in Frederick County, for example, passed a resolution in September urging the waiver of the state's lien. On reconsideration, the convention withdrew the endorsement in order to keep the canal out of politics as much as possible. At that time, both parties in Frederick County favored the completion of the canal.[37] Governor Thomas also referred to the urgency of providing for ways and means of finishing the eastern section in his annual message to the legislature in December, 1843.[38]

The proposal to waive the state lien was re-introduced in the December session of the Assembly. Opponents of the measure again resorted to all kinds of pretexts to defeat it. Some members held out for a canal all the way to Savage River.[39] There was a distinct element of obstructionism in this position,

[34] *Niles' Register*, LXIV, No. 24 (August 12, 1843), 373.

[35] *Ibid.*, p. 372.

[36] See below, pp. 148-150.

[37] *Niles' Register*, LXV, No. 2 (September 9, 1843), 19.

[38] *Ibid.*, No. 18 (December 30, 1843), 276.

[39] Ingle to Coale, January 29, 1844.

for there were many legislators favorably disposed to the canal who would be against such a proposal. The Baltimore and Ohio interests argued that the railroad, already completed as far as Cumberland and having made an arrangement for the coal trade with the canal, should be used as a feeder for the latter, and the extension of the canal dispensed with entirely.[40] Of the city of Baltimore itself, it was said, "all [is] in a ferment about the Canal Bill & every kind of element is in motion to defeat it." [41] Feelings also ran high at Cumberland, where it was said "the railroad people" intended to erect "a pole, as high as the gallows of Haman . . . at the railroad depot, with a banner floating from its top, on which is to be inscribed something signifying defiance to the canal company." [42]

The bill met defeat in the House of Delegates, early in March, 1844, by a vote of 42 to 35. Among the victorious opponents of the bill were all the few, but vociferous, Baltimore representatives. The Assembly then took under consideration a modified bill for the same purpose. Agitation in favor of the canal broke out anew, and friends of the project in Cumberland held a mass meeting. However, the second measure also lost out shortly after the first one.[43] Ironically, the canal company had enough influence in the legislature to bring about the defeat of all bills sponsored by the Baltimore and Ohio interests in the same session.[44] Thus the two internal improvement companies, by combining with the opponents of both projects and with other members already concerned over the wretched financial condition of the state, were able to prevent the progress of either work.

[40] Coale to Ward, March 14, 1844, Letter Book G, 139. The pressure of the railroad company was strongly resisted by the canal's friends, who stressed the inconsistency and selfishness of the former's position. See, for example, the *Speech of John Johnson, Esq., . . . on the Bill to Provide for Completing the Chesapeake and Ohio Canal from the Revenues of the Work* [February 27 and 28, 1844] (Annapolis, 1844).

[41] Coale to Turner, February 3, 1844.

[42] W. Price to Coale, March 4, 1844.

[43] *Niles' Register*, LXVI, No. 2 (March 9, 1844), 17; *ibid.*, No. 3 (March 16, 1844), 38; Cumberland *Civilian*, March 14, 1844, quoted in *ibid.*, p. 48; Coale to Ward, March 14, 1844, Letter Book G, 139.

[44] *Niles' Register*, LXVI, No. 3 (March 16, 1844), 38 [39]. The Baltimore and Ohio sought laws reducing fares on the Washington branch and providing for the extension of the main line west of Cumberland.

While awaiting favorable action on the proposal to waive the state's prior lien on canal revenues to permit the issuance of bonds to complete the canal, the directors prepared for the resumption of construction. As early as the fall of 1841, they solicited contracts for the following spring in anticipation of aid from the Maryland Assembly.[45] In both 1842 and 1843 the Board received additional offers, but the latter were usually conditioned on the waiver of Maryland's claims. The only exception was the ill-fated Letson-Rutter proposal which the directors rejected in 1843. The Board also sent inquiries to England concerning the availability of funds to complete its work if the state waiver became law.[46] Despairing of direct or indirect aid from the Maryland Assembly, the directors appealed once again to Congress for a further subscription. They suggested that the United States subscribe $2,500,000 thus bringing its investment to the same figure as Maryland's ($5,000,000), or that the federal government set aside two million acres of public land for the canal, as was proposed in the pending measure providing aid for the Illinois and Indiana canals.[47] In neither case were the company's appeals successful.

Early in May, 1843, the Board definitely established the terms under which the contract for the completion of the canal would be negotiated.[48] The contractor was to receive canal company bonds maturing in twenty years, bearing 6 per cent interest payable semi-annually. Work was to begin in sixty days and the canal should be completed in two years. The maximum price at which the instrument would be negotiated was the chief engineer's estimate in 1842. As security for the repayment of the bonds, the canal company offered a pledge of all revenue, subject to existing mortgages. The latter phrase was the stumbling block, for the state had consistently refused to waive its sizable prior liens.

The incident which led to the definition of contract terms was the Letson-Rutter episode. Late in 1842, it was suggested to the Chesapeake and Ohio that if William C. McNeill were chosen president, out-of-state capital might be secured to com-

[45] Proceedings of Directors, F, 398-399 (November 5, 1841).

[46] Coale to Peabody, August 23, 1843, Letter Book G, 57-58.

[47] Coale to John P. Kennedy, December 21, 1844, Letter Book G, 214-215.

[48] Proceedings of Directors, G, 38-40 (May 4, 1843).

plete the canal. M. C. Sprigg, the incumbent, promptly resigned.[49] The state, always anxious to try any scheme to finish the canal and put it on a paying basis without making any further advances itself, then elected Captain McNeill president. He failed to take office, however, until April 12, 1843. On the next day the first proposal from Letson and Rutter was received. The directors were dissatisfied with some of the terms, and tabled the offer. On May 4, McNeill proposed a second contract on behalf of Letson and Rutter. The Board rejected this proposal too, for it was substantially the same as the first. It was at this meeting that the directors formally defined the terms they would accept in a contract.[50] The Board received several other proposals but accepted none, for all required the state's waiver as a prior condition.[51]

Early in July, 1843, the president entered the company office in Frederick during the absence of the Board and the clerk, forcibly seized the official seal, and executed a contract with Letson and Rutter.[52] At the regular meeting of the Board, July 20, 1843, he was able to announce that construction had already been resumed. The directors refused to be stampeded into approval of the arrangement, and demanded instead an explanation of his conduct and the authority upon which he made the agreement.[53] They subsequently rejected the answer of the president and annulled the contract. The Board insisted that the purported contract did not meet the requirements previously established as acceptable and pointed out that other

[49] M. C. Sprigg to Stockholders, December 3, 1842. McNeill, an ex-Captain in the U. S. Topographical Engineer Corps, had first-hand knowledge of the canal from a survey which he had made for the company in 1833. See *Report on the Chesapeake and Ohio Canal by Lewis Cass, Secretary of War, transmitting the Information Required by a Resolution of the House of Representatives of the 24th Ultimo, in Relation to the Chesapeake and Ohio Canal,* January 14, 1834, 23d Cong., 1st sess., House of Representatives, Document No. 38.

[50] Proceedings of Directors, G, 16 (April 13, 1843), 37-39 (May 4, 1843); Report of Directors, 15th Annual Meeting (August 16, 1843), Proceedings of Stockholders, C, 153-154.

[51] Report of Directors, 15th Annual Meeting (August 16, 1843), Proceedings of Stockholders, C, 156.

[52] *Ibid.*, pp. 160-161; McNeill to Ingle, July 10, 1843.

[53] Proceedings of Directors, G, 72-73 (July 20, 1843); W. Price to Coale, July 13, 1843; Ingle to McNeill, July 13, 1843.

offers, some of them lower than this one, had been received.[54] Neither side was entirely right or free of prejudice in the affair, as a contemporary summary of the episode pointed out.

The Frederick *Examiner* states, that offers were before the board at their prior meeting, to do the work for $200,000 less than the president subsequently contracted for, upon condition that the state's prior lien were waived. The Torch Light says that said offers were twenty-five per cent. less than the contract.—The Frederick Herald says for fifteen per cent. less. It is asserted on the other side that all the other offers before the board, were only to *contract for a contract*, but that those contractors bind themselves to begin the work westward, at any time within sixty days after being required so to do by the company. And it is urged as a motive for preferring this contract, that all the others postpone operations until the state's lien is waved [*sic*], whereas this proposes to progress instantly, thereby saving, they say, nine months' interest upon the $10,200,000 at present invested in the canal, amounting to $459,000, so that even if the contract be fifteen per cent. higher than other offers, that per cent. upon the two millions [the contract price for the canal to the Savage river above Cumberland] would be only $300,000, thus saving, in fact, $159,000 by progressing forthwith. This calculation however, predicates upon the nine months' delay being totally obviated by operating under the contract.—Again, it is urged, that the evidence of an actual bonafide contract to finish the work, and for a given sum, is the only expedient by which capitalists could be induced to adventure their money in purchasing the canal, and that without that assurance, no hopes can be entertained of finding purchasers.[55]

The majority of the stockholders, that is, the state of Maryland, agreed with the position taken by the directors. At a general meeting in August, 1843, it upheld the action of the latter in annulling the Letson-Rutter contract. The state then removed McNeill from the presidency of the canal company and chose James M. Coale, one of the directors, as his successor.[56]

The reorganized Board promptly took steps to improve the position of the canal as a transportation agency pending the

[54] Proceedings of Directors, G, 75-87 (July 20, 1843), especially pp. 75 and 87. The reasons advanced by the Board for its action were about as weak as the excuse of the president. See *ibid.*, pp. 84-86.

[55] *Niles' Register*, LXIV, No. 24 (August 12, 1843), 372. See also the defense of President McNeill in *Letter to the Stockholders of the Chesapeake and Ohio Canal Company by One of their Number* (Baltimore, 1843).

[56] 15th Annual Meeting (August 17, 1843), Proceedings of Stockholders, C, 175-178.

successful culmination of continuing efforts to provide for its completion. It opened negotiations with the Baltimore and Ohio for a temporary arrangement to give the canal access to the Cumberland iron and coal trade. The railroad agreed to transport coal from Cumberland to the canal at Dam No. 6, at 2 cents a ton per mile, as long as the amount of coal so carried did not interfere with its own business or require a material increase in facilities. The final arrangements were made on September 21, 1843, and the railroad promptly began construction of the necessary sidings at Dam No. 6.[57]

The agreement proved to be more harmful to the canal's interest than it was beneficial. The amount of coal shipped under the arrangement was inconsequential.[58] On the other hand, the railroad company made political capital out of it. The Baltimore and Ohio interests in the Assembly urged that the arrangements be made permanent, that the railroad act as a feeder for the canal.[59] The argument was persuasive and apparently won considerable support both in the legislature and in the state at large. To offset the effect of the Baltimore and Ohio's proposal, President Coale made a thorough analysis of the whole question in a special report in November, 1843.[60] He cited the experiences of railroads and canals in England, the comparative costs of transportation on the Baltimore and Ohio and the Chesapeake and Ohio as now constructed, the size of the Maryland investment in the canal, and the amount of trade required to pay the interest on the bonds issued for the canal. This latter factor was the decisive point in the report. It would require 289 cars daily (or rather 578 cars, since the distance was 45 miles and allowance would therefore have to be made for empties making the return trip) in 22 trains of

[57] McLane to Coale, September 17, 1843; Proceedings of Directors, G, 97-100 (September 14, 1843), 115 (September 21, 1843); Special Report to 15th Annual Meeting (November 16, 1843), Proceedings of Stockholders, C, 192-193.

[58] McLane to Coale, May 7, 1845. *Statistics of the Cumberland Coal Trade*, a broadsheet printed by the canal company in 1878 reviewing the division of trade among common carriers from 1842 to 1878, lists no tonnage for the canal until 1850, so small was its share of the trade before that year. See also below, Appendix, Table IV.

[59] Coale to Ward, March 14, 1844, Letter Book G, 139.

[60] Special Report to 15th Annual Meeting (November 16, 1843), Proceedings of Stockholders, C, 195-228.

13 cars each to supply enough coal to the canal for it to be able to pay anything to the state on its investment.[61]

The new Board also devoted a large proportion of its attention to the task of securing legislative approval of the state waiver. There was considerable excitement during 1844, which was both a national and a state election year. Two big issues in the local campaign were the related subjects of the state credit and the condition of the canal. In some instances friends of the canal went down in defeat. On the whole, however, the result was favorable to both issues. The governor-elect and many members of the new Assembly proved to be friendly to the canal.[62]

Following the usual procedure, proponents of the canal introduced a bill in the new legislature to provide for the waiver of the state lien. This time after a long and bitter fight it met with success. Both the canal bill and a stamp act to provide effective means of meeting the interest on the state debt, after being defeated, were reconsidered and passed in the crucial House of Delegates by one vote, 38 to 37. The canal bill provided that the Chesapeake and Ohio could issue $1,700,000 of preferred construction bonds on the mortgage of its revenues, when it received guaranties from interested parties for 195,000 tons of trade annually for five years.[63]

The passage of the acts was met with mixed reactions. Baltimore was furious, demanding a redistribution of seats in the House of Delegates to give the city greater representation and calling for the repeal of both acts. The report of a committee of the City Council stated in part:

> Thus we see on all sides, the palpable evidence, that Baltimore is to be made to bear the burden, and that unless she rises up in her whole united strength, she will be crushed by that mountain of imposition which is constantly accumulating around her. Baltimore in point of fact is subject to taxation without representation. If she had been

---

[61] *Ibid.*, p. 208; Williams, I, 214.

[62] Mandeville to Price, October 5, 1844; *A Short History of the Public Debt of Maryland*, p. 49. William Price, a canal director, lost out in Allegany County. Price to Coale, October 4, 1844.

[63] *Niles' Register*, LXVIII, No. 1 (March 8, 1845), 16; *ibid.*, No. 2 (March 15, 1845), 23-24; "Report of the Joint Committee of Both Branches, Proceedings of the Baltimore City Council, May, 1845," *A Short History of the Public Debt of Maryland*, p. 84.

fairly represented in the Legislature of the State, the obnoxious laws complained of, never could have been passed! How was it with the Canal Bill and Stamp Act of the last session!—Both rejected,—then reconsidered, and passed by *one vote*—and that *one* vote given under such circumstances as to fix upon it the suspicion of foul corruption.[64]

An observer less congenial to the city's point of view, took it severely to task for its conduct during and after the passage of the acts.

Not contented, however, with heaping their maledictions on the majority of the Legislature, they must also make an attack on an honest, able and virtuous Chief Magistrate, whose fault in their eyes, is, that after having while a member of the Legislature, sagaciously but vainly endeavored to protect the state from what he conscientiously deemed measures ruinous to her interests and imprudent in their concoction had the courage and wisdom to recommend and carry others, which are calculated to protect her honor and character. . . . Some have even had the audacity to accuse him of having effected the passage of the Canal and Stamp Bills by sheer bribery; . . . .[65]

Western Maryland, on the other hand, was wildly jubilant over the long-awaited success, and the District cities joined in the celebration.

The intelligence of the passage of the bill occasioned in the western parts of Maryland unbounded rejoicings. Judging by the papers from thence, they must be in ecstacies. A week ago they were at the depth of despondence, at the defeat of the former bill. The authorities of Georgetown have directed a general illumination in celebration of the event. One hundred guns were fired at Alexandria on the news reaching that city.[66]

The canal company and its friends hastened to secure the guaranties required and to insure the full benefits of the act. The president went to Boston and New York to confer with officials of the Cumberland coal companies.[67] There he found evidence of interference by the Baltimore and Ohio interests. "I am induced to believe," he wrote later to the president of the Maryland Mining Company, "that the Balt. & Ohio R.

[64] "Report of the Joint Committee, etc.," *A Short History of the Public Debt of Maryland*, p. 84.

[65] *A Short History of the Public Debt of Maryland*, p. 49.

[66] *Niles' Register*, LXVIII, No. 2 (March 15, 1845), 23.

[67] Proceedings of Directors, G, 228 (March 19, 1845); *Niles' Register*, LXVIII, No. 6 (April 12, 1845), 85.

Road interest, as their last throw of the die are endeavoring to prevent the fulfilment of the guaranties."[68] An article reputedly inspired from Baltimore was published in the New York *Herald* casting great doubt on the value of the canal. It exaggerated the duration of enforced suspension during the winter months. It emphasized the more frequent handling and transshipment of coal via the canal route and the greater damage to the coal. The canal president refuted these assertions, but the effect of their publication among financial interests in New York was undoubtedly harmful.[69]

At the same time the Board conducted an extensive correspondence throughout March and April, 1845, in its efforts to assure the guaranties. Friends of the canal were also active all along the Potomac River.

> Public meetings are held in the upper counties, and spirited addresses are made to enlist confidence in the completion of the work. . . . An ordinance has passed the corporation of Alexandria, to indemnify any of their citizens that may sign the bonds [of guarantee].[70]

Twenty-eight instruments, including both personal and corporate ones, were eventually signed and delivered, for a total of 225,000 tons. The Governor formally accepted the guaranties and certified his approval in August, 1845.[71]

After the guaranties were approved, the canal board proceeded to the letting of the contract. It rejected the first proposals of prospective contractors in August, 1845, and granted a ten-day delay for the submission of new offers.[72] On September 23, 1845, the directors accepted the offer of Walter Gwynn, William Thompson, James Hunter, and Walter Cunningham. The state agents promptly gave their approval, and the contract was drawn up and executed. The additional mortgage to the state of Maryland, required by the legislature, was also drawn

[68] Coale to Horatio Allen, May 8, 1845, Letter Book G, 258.

[69] Coale to Allen, May 13, 1845, Letter Book G, 263-264.

[70] *Niles' Register*, LXVIII, No. 6 (April 12, 1845), 85.

[71] Special Report, 17th Annual Meeting (July 22, 1845), Proceedings of Stockholders, C, 497; Proceedings of Directors, G, 288 (August 12, 1845); *18th Annual Report* (1846), pp. 4-5. The effective total was only 195,000 tons, because many of the guaranties were simply bonds to insure a certain quantity of trade if it were necessary to fill out the total required.

[72] *18th Annual Report* (1846), pp. 6-7.

up and executed on January 5, 1846.[73] By the terms of the contract, Messrs. Gwynn and Company agreed to provide the materials of the required quality in workmanlike manner according to the specifications of the chief engineer, to begin work within thirty days, and complete the canal by November 1, 1847, to raise $100,000 for the use of the company (to pay its contingent expenses), and to cash the bonds of the canal company at par, paying the interest on them until January 1, 1848. The price to be paid for the work was fixed at $1,625,000 in canal bonds.[74]

The making of the contract proved a much more simple task than carrying its terms into effect. All the sections were sublet in October, 1845, and the contractors placed a token force on the job on November 1, pending successful negotiations for the necessary funds to finance large-scale construction. By May 1, 1846, however, the work done amounted to only $55,384, and " the force employed on the work . . . [had] actually diminished, and at the middle of last month it was merely nominal." The contractors seemed earnest enough, but were unable to improve their efforts due to war conditions and the collapse of financial arrangements. The Board threatened to declare the contract abandoned, but it was obvious that unless the means could be obtained no real work could be undertaken.[75] The number of laborers at work on the canal dwindled from a total of fifty at the end of May to only ten by the end of June, 1846. After negotiations for the sale of the bonds collapsed in July, work on the canal ceased entirely.[76] All construction on the line was suspended during the rest of 1846 and most of 1847. In February, 1847, the directors considered

[73] Proceedings of Directors, G, 317-318 (September 23, 1845), 320-321 (September 24, 1845), 322-323 (September 25, 1845), 353-354 (January 5, 1846).

[74] *18th Annual Report* (1846), pp. 8-9.

[75] *Niles' Register*, LXIX, No. 8 (October 25, 1845), 128; *18th Annual Report* (1846), pp. 10-11. There is an accurate account, as far as it goes, of the negotiations to give effect to the contract in *Application of Hunter, Harris & Company to the Chesapeake and Ohio Canal Company for Relief* [August 1853] (Baltimore, 1853).

[76] Fisk to President and Directors, June 25, 1846; C. Cox to Coale, July 10, 1846; Proceedings of Directors, G, 443 (July 16, 1846).

cancelling the contract and offering the bonds to the state of Maryland, but they took no action on the plan.[77]

Negotiations for the sale of the bonds had been under way since before the formal signing of the contract. Efforts of Daniel Webster and of the company itself to effect a loan in England failed when the Barings declined to take any part in it.[78] Subsequent attempts to complete the necessary arrangements seemed to be making progress in May and June of the following year, 1846. The hopes proved to be overly optimistic, however, for all efforts to interest London merchants failed. The contractors then turned to local capitalists for assistance. Here conversations reached the point of assigning definite quotas to be subscribed by interested bankers (New York, $400,000; District of Columbia, $200,000 or $300,000; contractors, $200,000; Richmond, $100,000; leaving $100,000 or $200,000 of the estimated $1,100,000 needed still to be acacounted for), but these arrangements also failed.[79]

Another year passed before negotiations again reached an advanced stage which gave some promise of success. By this time, several events had measurably improved the prospects affecting the sale of the bonds. The state of Maryland had finally provided for the payment of the arrears on its debt and for the prompt payment of the semi-annual interest in the future. This measure helped the credit of both the state and the canal company. The Virginia Assembly had authorized the state treasurer to guarantee $300,000 of the canal bonds. The corporations of Georgetown and Washington had authorized the loan of $25,000 and $50,000, respectively, to the contractors in exchange for the canal bonds, while the citizens of Alexandria took up a private subscription for $25,000 for the same purpose. The net effect of these activities by the District cities in April, 1837, was to guarantee to take $100,000 of the bonds. Thus when the time came to make another attempt to negotiate for the sale of the preferred construction bonds, some of the quotas had already been guaranteed. Tentative arrangements provided for the distribution of the entire sum of $1,100,000 cash needed to finish the work among Virginia ($300,000),

[77] *Ibid.*, H, 8-11 (February 10, 1847).
[78] *Ibid.*, G, 311 (September 22, 1845).
[79] *18th Annual Report* (1846), p. 11; C. Cox to Coale, July, 10, 1846.

District cities ($100,000), Boston interests ($200,000), the Barings ($300,000), and the contractors ($200,000).[80] The arrangements were temporarily threatened by the withdrawal of the Barings because of the tightness of the international money market, but it was fully expected that this time local capitalists could be persuaded to step into the breach. The negotiations were finally carried to a successful conclusion by Messrs. Davis, Hale, and Allen, acting as agents for the contractors.[81] The Board drew up and executed the mortgage of the canal's revenues in the fall of the same year. It named Phineas Janney of Alexandria, W. W. Corcoran of Washington, David Henshaw and George Morey of Boston and Horatio Allen of New York, as representatives of the twenty-nine capitalists in New York, Boston, and Washington who had undertaken the sale of the bonds. By the terms of the final agreement, the capitalists agreed to take $500,000 of the bonds and the subcontractors $200,000, in addition to the $400,000 already pledged by the state of Virginia and the District cities.[82]

Work was resumed on November 18, 1847, under a slightly modified contract. The old company was reorganized and a new one succeeded to its contract with the canal board. Messrs. Gwynn and Cunningham retired, but the remaining partners, Hunter and Thompson, continued with the addition of a third partner, Thomas Harris.[83] The directors adopted various economy measures to facilitate the completion of the canal. They decided to substitute kyanized wood for stone in the locks, and they postponed the construction of lock-keepers' houses and the arching of the tunnel until after the canal was formally opened to Cumberland.[84] At last all efforts were con-

[80] *19th Annual Report* (1847), pp. 4-5; *Niles' Register*, LXXII, No. 12 (May 22, 1847), 179.

[81] *Niles' Register*, LXXII, No. 19 (July 10, 1847), 293; Proceedings of Directors, H, 92 (October 26, 1847), 95 (October 27, 1847); *20th Annual Report* (1848), pp. 3-4.

[82] Proceedings of Directors, H, 94-96 (October 27, 1847); *20th Annual Report* (1848), pp. 5-6.

[83] *20th Annual Report* (1848), pp. 7-8. Prices in the new contract were not to exceed the 1845 allowances by more than 12½ per cent, and the work was to be completed by October 1, 1849.

[84] Proceedings of Directors, G, 285 (July 24, 1845). The kyanizing process

centrated on the one object of completing the canal in some manner at the earliest possible date.

Of course, some of the old problems, such as sickness and the scarcity of workers, returned to hinder construction. "It is true, that, for a great part of the time, severe sickness prevailed among the laborers, and it was difficult to procure additional hands or even to retain those employed, ..."[85] And there were the ever-present financial troubles which were the consequence of the slow sale of bonds and the excess of costs over estimates.[86] In spite of these distractions, however, the force employed on the line increased to 1,447 men and 594 horses, mules, and oxen, in May, 1849. The contractors also built about nine miles of railroad to facilitate the transportation of supplies for the work.[87]

In April, 1850, the troubles came to a head when the financial difficulties of the contractors brought about a suspension of the work for several days and the threat of violence. The workers, who had been unpaid for some time, were demanding satisfaction. The trustees, Davis, Hale, and Allen, took over the contract on assignment from Hunter, Harris, and Company, and resumed work. The date for the completion of the canal was extended to July 1 and then to August 1.[88] It was all in vain, however, for in July the trustees' resources were exhausted and work again stopped. The Board promptly declared the contract abandoned and negotiated a new one with Michael Byrne providing for the completion of the canal for $3,000 cash and $21,000 in bonds.[89] Under this contract the work was finally completed in the fall of the same year, eight years after the railroad had reached Cumberland and three years before it reached the Ohio River.

While pushing the completion of its work, the company also turned its attention to that portion of the canal below Dam

consisted of dipping the timbers in "a corrosive sublimate" to prevent early decay. William Easby to Ingle, January 8, 1840.

[85] 21st Annual Report (1849), Proceedings of Stockholders, D, 160.

[86] Proceedings of Directors, H, 274-275 (July 18, 1849).

[87] 21st Annual Report (1849), Proceedings of Stockholders, D, 163.

[88] Proceedings of Directors, H, 349 (April 17, 1850), 365 (June 25, 1850); 22d Annual Report (1850), Proceedings of Stockholders, D, 260.

[89] Proceedings of Directors, H, 369-371 (July 17, 1850), 372 (July 18, 1850). Fisk notified the Board that work had ceased July 15, 1850.

No. 6. This, the old part of the line, was now badly in need of repair.[90] Once again the state of Virginia came to the rescue of the Chesapeake and Ohio. This time it authorized the guarantee of $200,000 of repair bonds to be issued by the canal company. The money was to be applied to the renovation of the canal from Dam No. 6 to the Potomac Aqueduct.[91] Maryland questioned the authority of the canal board to accept the Virginia act and issue the repair bonds, but the decision of the Attorney-General of Maryland removed all doubts on that score. The work of renovation was then pushed so as to have the entire line in readiness for the formal inauguration of the canal.[92]

The eastern section of the Chesapeake and Ohio canal, the only part ever to be completed, was formally opened to trade at Cumberland, Thursday, October 10, 1850.[93] Preparation for the ceremonies appropriate to the occasion had been underway for some time. On the day before the opening invited guests and curious visitors began arriving from all parts of Maryland, Virginia and the District of Columbia. Colonel Pickell, a director, brought along a band of the Independent Blues of Baltimore which was especially welcome. They responded to the reception given them by the local populace and "electrified an immense multitude of our citizens with their unsurpassed instrumental performance."

Thursday "dawned upon the mountains in all the richness of the early autumn. . . ." Ceremonies got under way at the usual early hour. There was already a large crowd assembled in front of the United States hotel and Barnum's at 8:30 in the morning. The Eckhart Artillery, a local unit, entertained the throng for a while with "various military evolutions in a manner that would have done credit to a veteran corps." The procession to the canal formed at nine o'clock and included the visiting state and canal officials, local dignitaries, the military units, and the citizenry. At the outlet locks of the canal the ceremonies were opened by passing "five canal boats, laden

[90] *Ibid.*, p. 127 (January 12, 1848).

[91] *Ibid.*, pp. 251-257 (April 18, 1849).

[92] 22d Annual Report (1850), Proceedings of Stockholders, D, 262-265.

[93] The following account is based on the report in the Cumberland *Civilian* (n. d.) as reprinted in Proceedings of Stockholders, D, 390-395.

with the rich product of the mines of Allegany, and *destined for Eastern Markets*, . . . through the locks, amid the salvos of artillery from the Eckhart company, accompanied by the brilliant performances of the bands."

After two long speeches of welcome and eulogy, the official visitors and some of the local citizens boarded the packet ship *Jenny Lind* and the newly-refitted canal boat *C. B. Fisk* for a short trip down the waterway. Another procession was formed, this time composed of canal vessels. Following the two lead craft was another carrying the artillery unit, and bringing up the rear were the five coal boats, *Southampton, Elizabeth, Ohio, Delaware*, and *Freeman Rawdon.* The bands provided music for the trip, and occasional salutes from the cannon punctuated the festivities. About ten miles down the line, the party stopped for a banquet and the coal boats continued on their way to the East.[94] After partaking "of an abundant collation . . . to which zest was imparted by a copious supply of the finest and choicest wines," the visitors returned to Cumberland where another banquet was given by the townfolk. On this gratifying note the ceremonies officially came to an end.[95]

After twenty-two years of intermittent enthusiasm and despair, the Chesapeake and Ohio Canal was completed to Cumberland.

[94] Of the five boats, one went only to Williamsport, two reached Alexandria, and two got stuck above Dam No. 6, because of the low level of water in the canal. The latter drew four feet with their load, instead of three and one-half, which would have passed. (Fisk to Coale, October 20, 1850.) The *Freeman Rawdon* won the race with the *Southampton* reaching Washington about 6 p. m., October 17, 1850. Horses and mules were requisitioned along the way to maintain the speed, and the boats arrived within a short time of each other. (Elgin to Coale, October 18, 1850.)

[95] The Board ordered that a marble slab or block be placed "in a conspicuous position in the masonry of, or on the line of the Canal" with the names of the president, directors, officers, state agents, and the date of completion. Proceedings of Directors, H, 384 (November 27, 1850). It stands, a short obelisk, near the Wisconsin Avenue bridge over the canal in Georgetown.

CHAPTER VIII

THE CANAL AND ITS BRANCHES

The Chesapeake and Ohio Canal, as completed in 1850, extended for 184½ miles along the northern bank of the Potomac River from Rock Creek in the District of Columbia to Wills Creek at Cumberland. Included in its works were seven rubble or masonry dams in the bed of the river, eleven stone aqueducts over the northern tributaries of the Potomac, seventy-five stone or composition locks with a lift averaging 8 feet, many score culverts to carry the smaller streams under the trunk, a quarter-mile long tunnel, a towpath 12 feet wide along the river side of the canal, and a waterway 6 to 8 feet deep, ranging in width from 50 to 80 feet.[1]

The eastern terminus of the canal, for all practical purposes, was a basin 3 feet above tide at the mouth of Rock Creek, between Georgetown and Washington. The pool was formed by damming the waters of the creek behind a broad mole which was built across its mouth. On this embankment and along the sides of the basin were many docks and warehouses. Here goods were taken from the boats and stored or transferred directly to coastal vessels lying on the river side of the mole. There was also a tidal or outlet lock to the river, permitting canal boats to enter or leave the basin. The pool was a source of many problems: questions pertaining to traffic, unloading facilities, berth privileges, etc., required the Board's constant attention. In addition, the creek brought down large quantities of silt, making it necessary to dredge the basin and outlet lock frequently in order to keep them in navigable condition.

[1] For a detailed description of the canal and its works in 1831 and 1833, see the reports of Abert and Kearney and of W. G. McNeill in the *Memorial of the Chesapeake and Ohio Canal Company*, December 3, 1831, 22d Cong., 1st sess., House of Representatives, Document No. 18, and *Report on the Chesapeake and Ohio Canal by Lewis Cass, Secretary of War*, . . . January 13, 1834, 23d Cong., 1st sess., House of Representatives, Document No. 38. Many of the original structures can still be seen in substantially the same form in which they were first built. See also the property maps of the canal company now in the possession of the National Parks Service, Department of Interior, Washington, D. C.

From Rock Creek the canal extended westward through Georgetown. It rose abruptly by means of four locks to a level 35 feet above tide, though below the town itself. The high route which it followed required heavy embankments on the river side to sustain the weight of the water in the canal. The Georgetown level [2] extended all the way to Little Falls, about five miles up the river. On this stretch, the trunk was excavated to a width of 80 feet (except where confined to 70 feet by the Little Falls road) and a depth of from 7 to 8 feet. The larger dimensions of the work provided ample water for navigation, for branches to Alexandria and Baltimore, and for sale to mills and manufactories along the canal bank.

From Little Falls to Harpers Ferry the canal was generally 60 feet wide and 6 feet deep. It should be noted in passing, however, that on the entire line the maximum effective width was 15 feet, the dimensions of the locks and aqueducts. The sixty miles from Georgetown to Harpers Ferry encompassed the greatest ascent in the whole distance. In this, the first third of the eastern section, almost half of the locks (32 out of 75) and the dams (3 out of 7) were located. It was on this part of the work that the most serious obstacles were encountered and the early mistakes were made.

Above the Ferry, the canal was only 50 feet wide. Instead of becoming easier, however, the construction had proved fully as difficult over much of the remaining distance. At places the river became very narrow; it generally followed a more winding course; and at some points its banks became precipitous cliffs. The canal company had to resort to expensive modifications of its plans. It frequently chose to carry its works over the obstacles by high-level construction. At other times the embankments were built in the river bed itself. Despite its consistent and determined opposition to slackwater navigation, the Board finally turned to it as a temporary solution in a few places.[3] When the rugged nature of the country made even these measures undesirable or inadequate, the directors authorized expensive deep cuts and a tunnel.[4] Scarcity of stone and

[2] A level is that part of the canal between two lift locks.

[3] *7th Annual Report* (1835), p. 9.

[4] Proceedings of Directors, Journal D, 443 (December 21, 1835); 11th Annual Meeting (1839), Proceedings of Stockholders, B, 251-252.

money affected the work on the western end of the canal, and necessitated the adoption of composition wood locks, the construction of frame lockhouses, and the use of houseboats for canal employees.

The locks and lockhouses on the canal had been matters of great concern to the Board. After much discussion the directors had decided to use single locks on the canal, although estimates were requested for both single and double locks.[5] The company adopted a 15-foot clearance for the chambers to conform with the dimensions of those in use on the New York, Ohio, and western Pennsylvania canals.[6] The locks were constructed of stone throughout and were so placed as to leave ample room on the berm side for another one if required at a later date. The engineers and directors experimented repeatedly with ways and means of speeding the passage of boats through the locks. The time required to fill and empty a lock chamber was eventually reduced to three minutes. Some hope was held that this might be cut still further to two and one-half or possibly two minutes.[7] The Board also experimented with the lock-gates, the only perishable structures on the entire line. It even tried iron gates, but they proved unsatisfactory in practice and were not generally adopted.[8] The directors then sought to prolong the life of the wooden gates by having them painted.[9] This too was later abandoned, probably for lack of money and demonstrable success. The lockhouses were built on a simple rectangular plan like those on the Erie Canal. They were also of stone construction, except in the upper valley, and cost between $900 and $1,000 each, or $1,200 for double ones.[10] The masonry work on the houses was not always the best, and there were reports of bulging walls in later years.

[5] Proceedings of Directors, A, 80 (September 19, 1828).

[6] Report to Special Meeting (September 10, 1828), Proceedings of Stockholders, A, 19.

[7] Wright to William Archer, September 1, 1829; Supplementary Report, November 26, 1830, *2d Annual Report* (1830), p. 32.

[8] Memorandum of Clement Smith, Treasurer, 1829, Letters Received.

[9] J. W. McCalley to Chesapeake and Ohio Canal Company, July 16, 1830; Van Slyke to President and Directors, September 20 [1830].

[10] Martineau to President and Directors, October 1, 1828; Proceedings of Directors, E, 36 (March 30, 1836), 256 (May 10, 1837); Ingle to Watkins James and Otho Baker, March 31, 1836, Letter Book C, 269; Ingle to John D. Grove, May 21, 1836, *ibid.*, p. 309.

The Board sought to anticipate some of the problems which the canal might have to face in the future and to prevent further serious trouble. In order to increase the permanence of the work and to facilitate the use of steamboats on the waterway, the directors ordered the trunk to be paved with stone wherever it was plentiful and readily available.[11] They authorized the introduction of numerous small streams into the waterway as feeders in order to reduce the srength of the current flowing down the canal from the main feeders and to insure an adequate supply of water for all purposes in all seasons. The Board thought that the existence of so many feeders, providing greater access to the waterway from the Maryland side, would be beneficial to the farmers as well as to the trade of the canal.[12]

As the canal advanced up the valley it promoted the development of many towns which depended largely upon it for a livelihood. Seneca, the first western terminus of the waterway, held the spotlight for a while. The Board anticipated that a small community would develop there on the strength of the canal trade, the large pool formed by the Seneca dam, and the possibility of water-powered manufactories along the canal banks. The directors named the site of the prospective development Rushville, in honor of Richard Rush, ex-Secretary of the Treasury, who had negotiated the loan from the Dutch capitalists, enabling the District cities to pay their subscriptions to the canal stock. The company planned a similar future for a settlement at Great Falls to be called Crommelin, after the Dutch banking family which had been instrumental in effecting the loan.[13] Neither of these projects, however, reached an advanced stage of development.

Later, a flourishing commercial entrepôt sprang up at Point of Rocks, an exchange point with the Baltimore and Ohio Railroad. A contemporary description of the community noted that:

[11] Report to Special Meeting (September 10, 1828), Proceedings of Stockholders, A, 19.

[12] 1st Annual Report (1829), Proceedings of Stockholders, A, 53; 3d Annual Report (1831), *ibid.*, p. 136; Proceedings of Directors, B, 267 (March 23, 1831), 384-385 (June 10, 1831), C, 35 (December 2, 1831).

[13] Proceedings of Directors, B, 382-383 (June 10, 1831).

The Point of Rocks is now the point of attraction, and really presents, as we are told, an animating scene. Rail road cars and canal boats, constantly arriving, interchanging passengers and cargoes and then departing—the bustle and confusion of a little village sudden arisen, as it were out of the earth and actually doing the business of a commercial emporium—its inhabitants hardly yet acquainted with each other, and very often outnumbered by the transient strangers who throng thither in pursuit of business and pleasure—the very novelty itself, of two great public enterprises so long at war with each other, just going into harmonious operation upon the spot which may be called the battleground . . . .[14]

But the prosperity of the village was only temporary, and it declined rapidly as the end of track and of navigation moved westward towards Harpers Ferry.

Farther up the river, another rural community, Weverton, blossomed under the influence of the railroad and the canal. It also proved to be favorably located for the utilization of water power. Many mills and manufactories took their places along the canal in the middle of the century. The chief engineer finally called a halt to further expansion in 1866, fearing there would not be enough water left for navigation.[15] Weverton remained a representative canal town, its fortunes shifting with those of the waterway itself. Other valley communities, like Knoxville and Brunswick, took on renewed life under the combined impetus of the railway and the waterway.

Harpers Ferry in turn succeeded Point of Rocks as a commercial emporium. It had many more advantages than the latter, because of its location at the mouth of the Shenandoah River. It served as both the outlet for the trade of that valley and as the point of deposit for that of the upper Potomac. Its commercial position was not solely dependent on the railroad or the canal, nor was it of recent development. Harpers Ferry already had a long history as an entrepôt for North-South and East-West trade. Thus its increased prosperity under the influence of the railroad and the canal was better grounded and more permanent than that of the lower valley settlements.

[14] Frederick *Times*, quoted in *Niles' Register*, XLV, No. 13 (November 23, 1833), 199.

[15] Proceedings of Directors, K, 490 (May 10, 1866); George Rothbury, Agent, Henderson Steel and Wire Manufacturing Company, to Coale, October 17, 1850; C. P. Manning to President and Directors, April 12, 1866.

Above Harpers Ferry the most promising site for industrial and commercial development was Williamsport.[16] Here again conditions were favorable to the establishment of mills and manufactories utilizing water power. Dam No. 5, located only eight miles above the town, fed a relatively short stretch of the canal. There would be ample surplus water available. Williamsport might also become the channel for the trade of Hagerstown with the Eastern markets via the canal. The railroad was stopped momentarily at Harpers Ferry, and when finally released from that restriction, constructed its line to the West through Virginia, rather than Maryland. When the canal reached Williamsport in 1835, the scene at Point of Rocks was repeated, as the town took on new life. Some fifty or sixty canal boats passed through the locks on the first day.

> " It was a glorious sight to see " the numerous boats as they lay in the basin by night, each illuminated by a glowing coal fire, which cast " a long level rule " of light across the water; and the silence of night was not unpleasantly interrupted by the cries of the hoarse boatmen, as they were disturbed from their moorings by new arrivals, and driven to closer contact with their neighbors.[17]

Unlike Point of Rocks, Williamsport settled down to become perhaps the outstanding canal town along the route of the Chesapeake and Ohio.

Above Williamsport, the next major objective of the canal was Hancock. At this point contact would be made with the turnpike from the West. Here it was hoped the canal might secure some of the wagon traffic from as far west as the Ohio. Great interest was shown on all sides over the prospective rise of another point of exchange. However, the anticipated business did not develop because the canal was so late in reaching Hancock, but the town continued to act as a center for local trade.

The town of Cumberland at the mouth of Wills Creek is

[16] Cruger and Purcell to President and Directors, July 4, 1832. A portion of the western trade would also be available at Williamsport. Washington to Colston, January 31, 1835, Letter Book B, 400.

[17] Williamsport *Banner*, April 11, 1835, quoted in *Niles' Register*, XLVIII, No. 8 (April 25, 1835), 135. See also Williamsport *Banner*, April 4, 1835, quoted in *ibid.*, XLVIII, No. 6 (April 11, 1835), 89; and *Niles' Register*, XLVIII, No. 8 (April 25, 1835), 134-135.

perhaps the greatest accomplishment of the Potomac trade route. Founded by the Ohio Company in 1749, it served as a natural center for the business and commerce of the upper valley and for the transmontane trade. The completion of the railroad and the canal to Cumberland, in 1842 and 1850, respectively, brought to the town a dependable means of transportation to the Eastern markets and a large transfer business in coal from the mines at Frostburg and farther west.[18] Cumberland was also the last "end-of-navigation" town for the canal. It undoubtedly secured a large amount of trade from the boatmen between runs and during the winter. At any rate, the prosperity of the town, its land values and trade were closely associated with the fortunes and misfortunes of the canal.[19] By the time the coal fields had been exhausted and the canal had become a magnificent ruin, the town had developed an independent and permanent basis of prosperity and continued as an important industrial and commercial center.

Actually, of course, the canal was not "completed" when it reached Cumberland. The projected connection of the Eastern and Western waters via the Potomac and the Youghiogheny or Monongahela rivers was never achieved. The ambitious mountain section, with its 246 locks and its four-mile tunnel, 1,900 feet above sea level, and the more gently sloping western section failed to advance beyond the planning stage. The early optimism and enthusiasm over "the great national project" disappeared in the face of the unexpected difficulties encountered in the construction of the eastern section. All that remained was the unfinished segment lying alongside the Potomac River. And yet the proposed continuation of the canal to the Ohio occupied much of the company's time and exerted a definite influence on canal policy at least until 1876. Specula-

[18] During the agitation for the completion of the canal, in the forties, the proposals to extend the canal beyond Cumberland to the Savage River brought protests from Cumberland citizens who were already anticipating the valuable transfer business the waterway would bring. The revival of the project in the seventies caused another flurry of protests. See Letters Received, 1843 and 1875.

[19] The intimate connection between Cumberland's commercial prosperity and land values and the Chesapeake and Ohio Canal was demonstrated as early as 1836, when the announcement of the suspension of work on the canal caused a brief panic in the city. *Niles' Register*, XLIX, No. 25 (February 20, 1836), 426. See also *ibid.*, LXII, No. 4 (March 26, 1842), 52.

tion on the prospective value of the project persisted into the present century.

In the first years of the company's existence the directors assumed that the construction of the western section was to be the logical conclusion of their work. Consequently the amount of time devoted to preparations for the extension of the canal beyond Cumberland was proportionately greater. Furthermore, one of the conditions of the Pennsylvania assent to the charter was that work should begin on the western section within three years.[20] The Board was, of course, anxious to accommodate the wishes of the state for the immediate commencement of the work. Representative Andrew Stewart, the director from the Keystone state, secured the necessary land rights along the proposed route of the canal as early as September, 1828. The engineers undertook the survey and location of the line in 1829 and completed it in the same year.[21] The surveys indicated that a canal via Wills Creek would have a sufficient supply of water if a four mile tunnel were adopted on the summit level.[22] On the basis of these findings, the company petitioned Pennsylvania for an extension of the time permitted for the commencement of the western section, and at the same time memorialized Congress for permission to begin the western part of the canal before finishing the eastern leg. The directors also requested subscriptions of $1,000,000 from Congress and $500,000 from Pennsylvania.[23] The suspension of work in the

[20] Act of the Pennsylvania Legislature, passed February 9, 1826, *Documents Relating to the Chesapeake and Ohio Canal*, July 11, 1840, pp. 31-34. The charter itself provided that the eastern section must first be completed.

[21] Stewart to President and Directors, September 29, 1828, May 27, July 18, 1829; 1st Annual Report (1829), Proceedings of Stockholders, A, 48-49; Proceedings of Directors, A, 336 (August 26, 1829).

[22] The prospect of driving a tunnel through a coal region excited proponents of the scheme to speculate on the possibility of being able to shovel the coal directly into waiting canal boats, thus making the work pay for itself. *Communication from William Archer, Esq. to the Stockholders of the Chesapeake and Ohio Canal, on the Subject of the Location of the Tunnel Through the Allegany Mountain* (Washington, 1835), pp. 3-4. Much of the speculation was based on Roberts' report of 1829 (in Letters Received).

[23] 1st Annual Report (1829), Proceedings of Stockholders, A, 49; Mercer to General Abner Lacock, February 1, 1830, Letter Book A, 169-170; *Niles' Register*, XL, No. 6 (April 9, 1831), 91; Ingle to Mercer, February 11, 12, 1831; Stewart to Mercer, February 22, 1831. Friends of the project even petitioned Congress for the right to use troops in the excavation of the tunnel. *2d Annual Report* (1830), pp. 25-27.

east due to the railroad injunction contributed to the wish to start the western section ahead of schedule. Unfortunately, the necessary financial assistance was not forthcoming.

During the thirties and forties the problem of the completion of the eastern section thrust the question of the western extension of the waterway into the background. So great was the success and prosperity of the canal in the seventies, however, that many took its record as a demonstration that railroads could never hope to compete with canals in the low cost of transportation. Agitation revived for the construction of additional waterways between the Middle West and the Atlantic Coast. In September, 1873, for example, a rally of the friends of the Chesapeake and Ohio was held at Cumberland.[24] Eventually, Congress took an interest in the movement and authorized surveys of the several routes proposed for the connections. The report on the extension of the Chesapeake and Ohio to the Ohio River brought out several interesting points. For one thing, the preliminary report in 1874 stated that the Pittsburgh branch of the Baltimore and Ohio Railroad had appropriated almost the exact route originally recommended for the canal via Wills creek. The extension of the main line to the west, up the Potomac did not interfere with an extension of the canal, however, for the railroad had to allow room for the waterway in the Potomac valley, pursuant to the court decision in 1832.[25]

Nevertheless, the route via Wills Creek was so obviously the best possible one that the engineer requested special permission to concentrate on it notwithstanding the specific prohibition against it in the authorization of the surveys. The report stated further that the cost of any canal from Cumberland to the Ohio would be so great that local advantages must be subordinated to the primary object—the connection with the Ohio. For this purpose the best possible route should be taken regardless of local interest. The engineer then observed that for practical purposes the dimensions adopted for the extension should be

[24] Proceedings of Directors, M, 121 (August 8, 1873). The meeting was scheduled for September 10, 1873. See also *45th Annual Report* (1873), p. 18; *46th Annual Report* (1874), pp. 19-20.

[25] *Letter of the Secretary of War on the Extension of the Chesapeake and Ohio Canal*, April 14, 1874, 43d Cong., 1st sess., House of Representatives, Executive Document No. 208, pp. 5 and 9.

the same as those of that part of the canal already in operation. Also, the Ohio River must be dredged so as to be 6 feet deep at all times, if the advantages of the canal were to be fully utilized. The cost of the canal 54 feet wide (30 feet at the bottom) and 6 feet deep, from Cumberland to Pittsburgh, was estimated at $28,801,313.[26]

The final report in 1876 confirmed most of these findings and concluded that the canal, while difficult and expensive, was still practicable. The dimensions of the proposed waterway were increased to 70 feet wide and 7 feet deep, and the locks to 120 feet long and 20 feet wide to enable the route to compete with the proposed James River and Kanawha connection.[27] Despite the larger size of the canal, the total cost was reduced to $24,237,080 by the utilization of slackwater navigation on the Youghiogheny below Connellsville.[28] Nothing further was done to bring about the extension of the Chesapeake and Ohio. The canal board retained hopes, however, that at least the waterway would be extended up the Potomac to the heart of the coal region, but even this proposal failed to win support.[29]

The decline of the canal in the eighties and nineties once again put an end to talk of its extension to the West. The project was speculatively revived during and after the World War, but it was never seriously contemplated.[30]

In addition to the main line of the Chesapeake and Ohio Canal from Rock Creek to Cumberland, several branches were considered by the directors and by other interested promoters. Among these were a half-dozen or more feeders in the Potomac valley and three extensions from the eastern terminus of the waterway.

At one time or another almost every major tributary of the Potomac was considered as the site of a possible feeder. One

[26] *Ibid.*, pp. 5, 7-8.

[27] *Letter of the Secretary of War transmitting report of Engineer Merrill on Chesapeake and Ohio extension*, March 2, 1876, 44th Cong., 1st sess., House of Representatives, Executive Document No. 137, p. 2. The locks would be 10 feet longer and 2 feet wider than the Erie Canal.

[28] *Ibid.*, p. 26.

[29] *Ibid.*, p. 31; *47th Annual Report* (1875), p. 19.

[30] See, for example, Washington *Evening Star*, October 25, 1929; Washington *Sunday Star*, July 17, 1927; May 4, 1930; September 30, 1934. The cost was estimated at $219,000,000 in 1930, and $242,000,000 in 1934!

projected branch up the Monocacy River to Frederick was frequently discussed during the early years of the company. In 1829, the Board suggested that a connection between the Monocacy and the Susquehanna might be effected, thus providing an inland waterway to New York.[31] Dr. John Martineau surveyed the route of the proposed Monocacy improvement in 1829, and estimated the cost of the work at $296,389 for the twenty-four miles.[32] The citizens of Frederick soon lost interest in the waterway, however, and turned again to the railroad. The canal directors, who had looked upon the branch primarily as a feeder for that part of their own canal above the Seneca dam, were greatly disappointed by this lack of cooperation.[33]

The Board also showed some interest in the development of the Shenandoah trade, in 1832, but the strained financial condition of the company made it impossible to undertake any major work on that river.[34] In fact, as its resources neared exhaustion the improvement of any tributaries of the Potomac by the Chesapeake and Ohio in the immediate future was impracticable. In 1831, the company waived its rights to those branches in favor of any enterprises that might undertake to improve them.[35]

There were three projects for independent canals to tap the trade of the main stem at its eastern terminus, two of which were ultimately carried to completion and put into operation. The long-talked-of Maryland Canal was never constructed, but the Washington and Alexandria canals were finished, and the latter became an important outlet for the trade of the Chesapeake and Ohio.

The Maryland, or "cross-cut," canal was among the first of

[31] 1st Annual Report (1829), Proceedings of Stockholders, A, 53.

[32] Frederick *Examiner*, quoted in *Niles' Register*, XXXVI, No. 19 (July 4, 1829), 302; *Niles' Register*, XXXVIII, No. 4 (March 20, 1830), 69.

[33] R. Potts to [Ingle?], November 29, 1828; 3d Annual Report (1831), Proceedings of Stockholders, A, 132. The Monocacy was again considered as a feeder in 1831, as were Broad Run, Abraham's Branch, and other streams below Point of Rocks. (Proceedings of Directors, B, 287 [March 23, 1831], 384-385 [June 10, 1831,] C, 35 [December 2, 1831].) The canal company was seeking ways and means of utilizing its waterway above the Seneca feeder while the railroad injunction was still in effect.

[34] Charles A. Stewart to President and Directors, February 10, 1832.

[35] 3d Annual Meeting (December 3, 1831), Proceedings of Stockholders, A, 190-191.

the branches to be mentioned.[36] It was a factor in the interest of Baltimore, and to that extent in the support of the state, in the Chesapeake and Ohio Canal Conventions of 1823 and 1826.[37] Enthusiasm for the "great national project" in Maryland varied in direct proportion to the optimism with which Baltimore merchants viewed the possibilities of effecting the proposed connection. The first Maryland Canal Company was incorporated, March 6, 1826, by the same act which subscribed $500,000 to the stock of the Chesapeake and Ohio.[38] Preliminary surveys by state commissioners for a route through Montgomery County, however, seemed to indicate the impossibility of tapping the main canal far enough up the river to afford the city of Baltimore much chance for a fair share of its trade.[39] Baltimore merchants and capitalists thereupon turned to another means of securing the trade of the West, in competition with Philadelphia, New York, and Boston. The solution which they thought they had found for their own peculiar problem of a waterless, mountainous route was the railway. At this early date, the latter was still strictly in its early experimental stage as a transportation agency in the United States. Nevertheless the Assembly chartered the Baltimore and Ohio Railroad Company in 1827 and the citizens of Baltimore immediately organized the corporation that was to construct the road.[40]

Meanwhile, William Howard, a United States engineer, made another survey of possible routes for a canal between the Chesapeake and Ohio and the city of Baltimore. The local merchants followed the surveys with great interest, seeking the reassurance of an alternate means of communication with the

[36] The following account of the Maryland Canal project is the substance of my article appearing in the *Maryland Historical Magazine*, XLI, No. 1 (March, 1946), 51-65.

[37] See, for example, *Niles' Register*, XXV, No. 10 (November 8, 1823), 145.

[38] Opinion of Chief Justice Buchanan, Baltimore and Ohio Railroad Company *vs.* Chesapeake and Ohio Canal Company, 4 Gill and Johnson 155.

[39] *Letter of the Secretary of War, J. Barbour, transmitting a Report of the Engineer on the survey of a route for the proposed canal to connect the Chesapeake and Ohio canal with Baltimore*, January 11, 1828, 20th Cong., 1st sess., House of Representatives, Document No. 58, pp. 6, 8.

[40] Answer of the Chesapeake and Ohio Canal Company, 4 Gill and Johnson 33-34.

West in case the railroad did not prove satisfactory. Mr. Howard ran his lines in 1827, and reported his findings to Congress in 1828. He accepted the conclusions which the Maryland commissioners had made earlier that there was no practicable route through Montgomery County (or above and to the west of it). Instead he concentrated his attention on a line indicated by them through the city of Washington to the Eastern Branch of the Potomac River (the Anacostia), and then in a northeasterly direction to Baltimore. This course he found to be practicable, although expensive. The estimate for the whole line, excluding land costs, was $2,980,815.40.[41] The route itself was distasteful enough to Baltimore, offering little likelihood of securing much trade. The high cost of the connection quickly brought all talk of the project to an end. Although the dam and feeder at Little Falls and the Georgetown level were planned with a view to supplying the needs of a Maryland canal (and other branches),[42] no more was said of the proposal until the middle thirties.

The project for a cross-cut canal to divert the prospective trade of the Chesapeake and Ohio was revived in the thirties after the legal victory of the latter in the Maryland Court of Appeals. This verdict and the compromise act of 1833 seemed to have halted the railroad at Harpers Ferry, at least temporarily. As the need for some connection with the main canal became greater the reluctance of the Baltimore merchants to accept the findings of the early surveyors as final increased. The Maryland Canal project had become a convenient political device in the thirties. Inasmuch as both the Baltimore and Ohio and the Chesapeake and Ohio needed further financial assistance by 1836, they united with the supporters of the cross-cut canal and other internal improvement schemes to push through the Assembly the omnibus bill providing eight million dollars for public works. The act released the grants to the Baltimore and Ohio and to the Chesapeake and Ohio only after the state treasurer certified the successful organization of the Maryland Canal Company with sufficient capital to begin the construction of the long-awaited connection. The company was duly formed,

[41] *Letter of the Secretary of War*, January 11, 1828, pp. 6-7, 8 ff.
[42] Special Report on the Completion of the Canal, p. 333.

the subscriptions made, and the fact of organization formally recognized by the treasurer in the same year.[43] After the subscriptions to the major works were released, the company lapsed into inactivity. A legislative investigation in 1838 revealed the sordid details of the incident, but it was then too late to rescue the project.

The problems which remained unsolved and which prevented the proposed canal from becoming a reality were the location and cost of the connection. Several surveys of possible routes were made during and after the agitation for the construction of the waterway. Fisk, the Chesapeake and Ohio's engineer, and Hughes, the state engineer, made examinations in 1836 of three lines entirely within the state, that is, the Westminster, the Monocacy-Linganore, and the Seneca routes. They reported in March, 1837, that all three were impracticable because of an insufficient water supply on the summit levels. In the meantime, the mayor of Baltimore appointed Isaac Trimble, an engineer experienced in the construction of railroads, to make his own surveys. He reported in the same month that the Seneca route was practicable on certain conditions and at a cost of $6,324,300.[44]

At this point the citizens of Montgomery County, through which the proposed canal would pass, intervened and requested further examination of the disputed route. The Assembly recalled the three engineers and questioned them further, but all confirmed their original findings. In March, 1838, the Maryland legislature ordered its subscription to the Maryland Canal Company withheld unless the cross-cut canal was constructed via an all-Maryland route. At the request of the Governor of the state a United States engineer, Col. John J. Abert, reexamined the three routes in question, concentrating especially on the one in dispute. In his report in December, 1838, he confirmed the conclusions of Fisk and Hughes that all three were impracticable. At the same time he reported the discovery of

[43] *A Short History of the Public Debt of Maryland*, pp. 44-46; Special Report on the Completion of the Canal, pp. 346-348.

[44] Special Report on the Completion of the Canal, pp. 349-350. See Charles B. Fisk and George W. Hughes, *Report on Surveys and Examinations for a Canal between Baltimore and the Chesapeake and Ohio Canal* [March 6, 1837] (n. p., 1837).

a fourth, from Seneca to the Patapsco River via Brookeville.[45] In response to a request for a further study and estimate, he reported in February, 1839, that for the summit level, 21¾ miles in length, the probable cost of construction would be $11,670,000—an average of over $500,000 per mile.[46] This staggering figure put an end to all speculation about the connection at that time.

The project died hard, perhaps because of a lurking fear that the railway would not be able to compete successfully with the waterway as a transportation agency. At any rate, the proposal for a cross-cut canal was revived in the fifties shortly after the completion of the Chesapeake and Ohio.[47] By this time the Baltimore and Ohio was established firmly enough to dispel all ideas as to the desirability of the connection.[48] Yet the question came up again in the seventies at the height of canal prosperity, when talk of the extension of the Chesapeake and Ohio was also revived. The Assembly chartered a company to build the long-delayed Maryland Canal, but it was never organized.[49]

A second branch of the main canal was the Washington, or city, canal. The project for an artificial waterway through the capital to connect the Potomac and the Anacostia rivers was as old as the city itself.[50] The first company abandoned the

[45] Special Report on the Completion of the Canal, p. 350; Baltimore *Sun*, January 18, 1839; John J. Abert, *Report on a Canal to Connect the Chesapeake and Ohio Canal with Baltimore*, p. 35.

[46] Special Report on the Completion of the Canal, p. 351.

[47] 23d Annual Report (1851), Proceedings of Stockholders, D, 414; *Report of the Committee of the Baltimore City Council on the Cross-Cut Canal* (Baltimore, 1851), pp. 3-4.

[48] Letter of Thomas Swann, President of Baltimore and Ohio Railroad Company, in *Report . . . on the Cross-Cut Canal*, pp. 5 ff.

[49] *46th Annual Report* (1874), p. 24.

[50] De B. Randolph Keim, *Washington and Its Environs* (24th edition, Washington, 1887), p. 50. The best account of the early history of the Washington Canal is that found scattered through the two volumes of Wilhelmus Bryan, *A History of the National Capital* (2 vols., New York, 1914-1916). The following summary is based largely upon his work, supplemented by a re-examination of the sources he cites and by the use of other materials not available to him. In the former category is a volume of newspaper clippings and manuscript notes on the Washington Canal in the Manuscripts Division of the Library of Congress. This volume, entitled "Canal and Sewerage," contains most of the materials referred to by Mr. Bryan, and apparently was extensively used by him.

original plan to unite the Tiber and St. James (or James) creek in the early nineties because of straitened financial conditions. Maryland authorized a lottery in 1795 in an effort to provide funds for the company to continue its work, but the receipts were negligible.[51] In 1802, Congress chartered another enterprise to carry on the work, but interest was so slight that no company was actually organized. Vain attempts were even made to raise money in England.[52] The failure was attributed to the momentary suspension of the Potomac Company's work for lack of funds, the sparse settlement on the Anacostia (and hence weak support for the whole scheme), and the general indifference of the citizens.[53]

In 1809, Congress chartered another company to undertake the work. This time the business of organization proceeded more rapidly. Subscription books were promptly opened, but such was the poverty and apathy of the city that only half of the authorized capitalization of $100,000 was raised. Nevertheless work began within a year. Appropriate inaugural ceremonies were held, on May 9, 1810, near the present intersection of New Jersey Avenue and E Street, S. E. The President of the United States, James Madison, turned the first spadeful of earth.[54] The company adopted two routes for the canal: one extending from the Tiber to the foot of New Jersey Avenue at the Eastern Branch, the other, following the course of James Creek from a junction with the first route near the point at which the inaugural ceremonies had been held to the Anacostia River east of Greenleaf point (the present-day War College).[55] Irish immigrants worked on the canal for about a year before

[51] Bryan, I, 243, 493.

[52] Washington *National Intelligencer*, September 6, 1817. Two years elapsed before the subscription books were even opened to the public. See the public notice of the event, in *ibid.*, June 15, 1804, signed by Thomas Tingey, Daniel Carroll, Thomas Law, and Daniel C. Brent, June 11, 1804. See also *ibid.*, September 5, 1803, quoting letters of Law dated May 30 [1803].

[53] Communication from a meeting of citizens of Washington, in *ibid.*, May 18, 1807.

[54] Bryan, I, 499-500; Washington *National Intelligencer*, September 6, 1817. The *Intelligencer* of that date has a short account of the early history of the canal project in a letter of "A Stockholder." Payments on the capital stock that was sold extended over a two year period. *Ibid.*, June 30, 1811.

[55] Bryan, I, 501, n. 2. See also any contemporary map of Washington or the District of Columbia.

bankruptcy threatened to halt construction. The company had almost exhausted its resources when Congress came to its rescue in 1812 and revived the old Maryland law permitting a lottery to provide additional funds for construction.[56]

After five years of effort, including a brief interruption during the British invasion of the city in 1814, the company finally completed the 2¼-mile waterway. The canal was formally opened on November 21, 1815, with the usual ceremonies conducted by city and company officials and accompanied by the Marine Band.[57] When the directors attempted to collect wharfage fees in 1817 (following a two years' delay during which a lock was repaired), the local citizens objected vigorously. They complained that the cost of provisions was increased by the charges, and asserted indignantly that the terms of the charter had not been met. In support of the latter contention they pointed out that at low tide the bottom of the canal was exposed in some places.[58] The company insisted that it had complied with the charter and that the work had been duly accepted.[59] The canal proved to be very unsatisfactory in operation and was the subject of repeated complaints. For example, the middle section was soon filled up by the deposits of the tides in the Potomac and the Anacostia.[60] By 1817-1818 the condition of the canal had so deteriorated that the city was already discussing its purchase and restoration.[61]

The organization of the Chesapeake and Ohio Canal Company revived interest in the city canal as a means by which the trade of the former could be brought into Washington. The city and the Chesapeake and Ohio reached a compromise in

[56] *Ibid.*, I, 500; See also the letter by "A Stockholder" in Washington *National Intelligencer*, September 6, 1817.

[57] Bryan, II, 104; Washington *National Intelligencer*, October 27, November 22, 1815.

[58] Washington *National Intelligencer*, September 2, 1817; Bryan II, 105.

[59] *Report of the President and Directors of the Washington Canal Company*, January 31, 1817, quoted in Bryan, II, 105-106. See also the letter by "A Stockholder" in Washington *National Intelligencer*, September 6, 1817.

[60] Washington *National Intelligencer*, September 6, 1817; Report of Benjamin Severson, in *Journal of the 64th Council* [of the city of Washington] p. 591 (April 22, 1867) quoted in Bryan, II, 106.

[61] Letter of John P. Ingle, November 11, 1830, in Washington *National Intelligencer*, November 15, 1830.

1828 by which the latter agreed to extend its waterway to a basin which the city undertook to construct at the mouth of Tiber Creek.[62] When Washington was slow in taking advantage of this agreement, the Chesapeake and Ohio considered extending its own line to the Anacostia by a different route, generally around the northern fringe of the city.[63] The local authorities finally purchased the old Washington Canal in 1831 and began the work of renovation and improvement. The Chesapeake and Ohio thereupon extended its waterway along the Potomac to the Tiber.[64]

Although this canal remained one of the possible outlets for the trade of the Potomac valley until the 1880's, for various reasons it was seldom used. The tide was constantly at work filling the channel, requiring continual dredging to keep it open for even the lightest draft boats. Furthermore, in the early years, the trade on the main canal and the demand of the city markets were not great enough to provide much business for the local waterway. When the Chesapeake and Ohio finally reached Cumberland, the city again put its canal in repair at a cost of $140,000.[65] Local traders anticipated great trade benefits, pointing out that the Potomac channel on the Georgetown side was rapidly filling up, and that soon large boats would be unable to fully load there. The commercial advantages of the Anacostia wharves would bring the trade of

[62] Special Meeting (September 10, 1828), Proceedings of Stockholders, A, 23-24; *ibid.* (September 17, 1828), p. 28.

[63] 1st Anual Meeting (1829), Proceedings of Stockholders, A, 58; *Memorial of the Chesapeake and Ohio Canal Company*, December 6, 1828, 20th Cong., 2d sess., House of Representatives, Document No. 12, pp. 4-5, 7-8; Report [of Roberts and Purcell] on the Extension of the Chesapeake and Ohio Canal to the Navy Yard on the Eastern Branch of the Potomac, filed in Letters Received, 1832.

[64] 4th Annual Report (1832), Proceedings of Stockholders, A, 224-225. See also the letters of P. Rodier, engineer in charge of the construction of the Washington branch, Letters Received, 1832; and *Laws of the Corporation of Washington*, 1831, ch. 30: Act for the purchase of the Washington Canal and the completion thereof by the Corporation of Washington, passed January 3, 1831. The canal was finally completed in 1837 at a cost of $310,000, of which Congress appropriated $150,000. The operation of the waterway was under the control of a commission appointed by the city council. It was a public highway, toll-free. Keim, p. 50; Bryan, II, 110.

[65] Messages of the Mayor of Washington, 1852 and 1855, quoted in Bryan, II, 265.

the main stem to that branch of the Potomac.[66] Unfortunately by the time the Chesapeake and Ohio was completed, the canal boats had become so large that navigation under the low Georgetown bridges was inconvenient. Thus trade with both Georgetown and Washington declined as the boats crossed the Potomac Aqueduct to reach tidewater at Alexandria.

After the Civil War, the Chesapeake and Ohio finally raised the bridges and cleaned out the basin. The city of Washington again took up the task of cleaning and renovating its canal. The work had barely begun when the city lost its self-government. Congress, which took over the direction of city affairs in 1874, was not interested in the commercial development of the city as much as it was in its role as the national capital. The city canal was neglected, and eventually became a nuisance until it was finally filled in and covered over.[67]

The third and most important of the proposed extensions of the Chesapeake and Ohio was the canal to Alexandria. This town had the longest history as a Potomac port of any of the District cities. In the eighteenth century, it had served as the hub of the trade between the Ohio Company agents on the frontier and the English market. It had also been one of the most active supporters of the Potomac Company. But when Alexandria was included in the federal district, it entered a period of eclipse from which it never emerged. Washington, the new city which was created for the seat of national government, obtained all the public buildings and all the favors. At the same time the commercial position of Alexandria received a setback when Congress ordered the construction of a causeway closing the western channel of the main river in order to accom-

[66] Letter by "H." in Washington *National Intelligencer*, November 1, 1848. See also the letters by "J. C. B." in *ibid.*, October 16, 27, November 3, 8, 15, 1848.

[67] There was virtually no trade on the canal after 1855. (Communication from the President, 43d Annual Meeting [December 29, 1871], Proceedings of Stockholders, E, 185.) Congress established a territorial form of government for the District of Columbia in 1871. Three years later it replaced this regime with the present form, a Board of Commissioners. (Bryan, II, 576, 626.) The canal was gradually filled in and covered over, beginning in 1879. (*Ibid.*, p. 266; and John C. Proctor "Along the Old Washington Canal," Washington *Sunday Star*, March 18, 1845.) The James Creek section was not covered over until the World War. (See Washington *Post*, October 8, 1940.)

modate the post road to the South. Congress granted the application of Alexandria authorities for permission to cut a canal through the causeway, but the War of 1812 intervened before the passage was opened.[68] The sealing of the western channel closed a relatively quiet waterway to Alexandria and forced the river traffic into the more turbulent main channel. Thus the position of Alexandria as a port for the river trade was compromised.

The organization of the Chesapeake and Ohio Canal Company revived Alexandria's interest in the valley trade. The merchants and bankers of that city actively supported the company collectively and individually. When Washington forced the company to bring its waterway down to Rock Creek and eventually to Tiber Creek. Alexandria, like Georgetown, feared the effect that such an extension would have on its competitive position. Its leaders professed to have understood that the canal would terminate at Little Falls, at which point, they asserted, all three cities would have had more or less equal opportunities to secure their share of the trade.[69] To obtain a reasonable proportion of the anticipated increased commerce under the new conditions the local merchants took the lead in the formation of the Alexandria Canal Company.[70]

The purpose of the new company was to construct a tidewater canal along the south bank of the Potomac from an aqueduct across the river above Georgetown to Alexandria. The connection with the main waterway was made just to the west of the city of Georgetown. The major undertaking

[68] *Memorial of Alexandria for Government Aid to Complete the Chesapeake and Ohio Canal to Alexandria*, December 22, 1836, 24th Cong., 2d sess., House of Representatives, Document No. 47, p. 2. See also U. S. Law, June 17, 1812, and *Annals of Congress*, 23d Cong., 1st sess., p. 966 (January 8, 1835), quoted in Bryan, I, 496-497.

[69] *Memorial of Alexandria*, December 22, 1836, p. 3.

[70] "Memorial of the City of Alexandria, December 3, 1828," *Memorial of the Chesapeake and Ohio Canal Company*, December 6, 1828, 20th Cong., 2d sess., House of Representatives, Document No. 12, p. 9; *Memorial of the Corporate Authorities of Alexandria*, June 13, 1836; 24th Cong., 1st sess., Senate, Document No. 53, p. 3. See also Bryan, II, 110. The company was chartered by Congress in 1830. *Memorial of the Alexandria Canal Company*, January 31, 1831, 21st Cong., 2d sess., House of Representatives, Document No. 71, pp. 1-3.

in the project was the Potomac Aqueduct.[71] It was soon discovered that a wooden trunk on wooden piers would not bear the weight of the canal water in the turbulent current of the Potomac.[72] The use of stone piers made the aqueduct a much more formidable and expensive task than had been anticipated. As finally completed, the canal cost $1,250,000 instead of the $202,552 estimated.[73] There was some opposition in Congress to building a canal where nature had already provided one.[74] Furthermore, the promoters of the Alexandria Canal had to overcome the hostility of Georgetown authorities.[75] These officials, representing the local merchants, looked with disfavor on the project as a threat to their monopoly of the valley trade. Notwithstanding this opposition, the company was formally organized, and construction began on July 4, 1831.[76] With the help of a Congressional appropriation of $400,000, work progressed as well as might be expected. Company officials finally overcame Georgetown's hostility in the Supreme Court and surmounted the failure of the Chesapeake and Ohio to build the northern abutment of the aqueduct (as was required of it).[77]

[71] "Memorial of the City of Alexandria, December 3, 1828," p. 9; *Letter from the Secretary of War transmitting a Report and Estimate of the Chesapeake and Ohio Canal to Alexandria in the District of Columbia*, April 18, 1828, 20th Cong., 1st sess., House of Representatives, Document No. 254, pp. 6, 13-14. A description of the aqueduct as built, written by M. C. Ewing, December 18, 1845, is contained in Alexandria Canal Company Miscellaneous Papers, Manuscripts Division, Library of Congress. The structure was over 1,500 feet long, 30 feet wide and 5 feet deep. Eight stone piers rising from the bed of the river and two stone abutments on the north and south banks carried the wooden trunk (itself over 1,000 feet long) across the Potomac, 30 feet above tide. The trunk was heavily insured against damage by fire.

[72] *Report of the Committee of the District of Columbia* [on the Memorial of the President and Directors of the Alexandria Canal Company], May 30, 1834, 23d Cong., 1st sess., House of Representatives, Document No. 498, p. 3; Bryan, II, 111.

[73] *Letter from the Secretary of War*, April 18, 1828, p. 14. *Annual Report of the Alexandria Canal Company* (1849), quoted in Bryan, II, 110.

[74] *2d Annual Report* (1830), p. 9; *Register of Debates*, p. 790 (December 15, 1834), cited in Bryan, II, 112.

[75] Georgetown used the location of the Northern abutment as the reason for its opposition. *Register of Debates*, p. 1053 (June 2, 1832), cited in Bryan, II, 114.

[76] Thompson F. Mason to Mercer, June 29, 1831; *Niles' Register*, XL, No. 19 (July 9, 1831), 328.

[77] Bryan, II, 114, 131; Georgetown *vs.* Alexandria Canal Company, *U. S. Supreme Court Reports*, 12 Peters 91.

After twelve years of unrelenting effort the canal was completed and formally opened December 2, 1843.[78] Shortly thereafter, Congress retroceded the territory in the federal district south of the Potomac to Virginia. That state promptly came to the relief of the city by subscribing to a large block of Alexandria Canal Company stock.[79] When the Chesapeake and Ohio Canal was finally completed, the Alexandria branch became its primary outlet to the river, for the Rock Creek basin was greatly filled in and generally out of repair. During the Civil War, the federal government drained the aqueduct and used it as a bridge, to the detriment of the trade of both canals.[80] After the war, the Georgetown bridges were raised and the basin was cleaned out. Thus in the postwar years Alexandria had to share the coal trade from the Cumberland fields with Georgetown. In the face of this competition, trade on the canal gradually declined until it became negligible. Meanwhile, the government was casting covetous eyes on the sturdy aqueduct. In 1887, Congress appropriated funds to purchase it and convert it to a bridge, thus closing the connection with the Chesapeake and Ohio Canal and bringing to an end the turbulent existence of the Alexandria Canal.[81]

[78] Washington *National Intelligencer*, December 6, 1843; Coale to Col. Charles M. Thruston, December 6, 1843, Letter Book G, 119.

[79] Virginia Assembly, Laws, March 1, 1847, cited in Bryan, II, 263. It subsequently also guaranteed some of the company's bonds.

[80] Washington *Evening Star*, December 5, 16, 23, 1861.

[81] Proceedings of Directors, N, 362 (June 23, 1887). Some coal companies continued to ship their produce down the river to Alexandria for transshipment there, until the destruction of the Chesapeake and Ohio Canal in 1889.

Chapter IX

THE CANAL IN OPERATION BEFORE 1850

Such as it was—and in its own time it was the largest in the United States—the Chesapeake and Ohio Canal was gradually extended and opened for trade. The first stretch completed was that from Seneca to Little Falls. By 1831, the whole line from Seneca to Georgetown was in use. In 1834, the canal reached Harpers Ferry, sixty miles from Washington.[1] As it advanced it brought trade and prosperity. With only the section from Little Falls to Seneca completed, the cost of transporting flour down the river dropped from $1.00 to 30 or 50 cents a barrel.[2] When the canal was opened all the way to Rock Creek, these expenses continued to fall to 7 cents a barrel, including tolls. Some thirty thousand barrels of flour were shipped in the first ten days, as well as many other goods.[3]

The opening of the waterway to trade from Georgetown to Seneca, in 1831, marked the beginning of a new period in the affairs of the company. Thereafter the canal directors were concerned with both the construction and operation of the waterway. With characteristic thoroughness the Board issued a comprehensive set of rules and regulations covering navigation on the canal and the conduct of boatmen and officials.[4] The first stipulation was that all boats or floats on the waterway must be propelled by a towing line drawn by men or horses. Other provisions required that the greatest care be taken at all times to prevent injury or damage to the canal and to those navigating it. The regulations prohibited the use of iron-tipped poles in particular and forbade the operation of pointed boats

[1]Proceedings of Directors, B, 194 (October 4, 1830); *Niles' Register*, XL No. 6 (April 9, 1831), 91; *ibid.*, XLVI, No. 8 (April 19, 1834), 119.

[2]A. Lee to Mercer, January 13, 1831.

[3]*Niles' Register*, XL, No. 6 (April 9, 1831), 91, 95.

[4]"Regulations for Navigating the Chesapeake and Ohio Canal," Proceedings of Directors, B, 410-419 and 419-421 (July 16, 1831), revised and brought up to date, *ibid.*, D, 240-252 (February 18, 1835). The major change in the revision was the modification of rule 1, to permit the use of steamboats on the canal.

and craft with iron-shod corners. Traffic was to keep to the right in passing, and a system of preference was established to facilitate navigation: boats had the right of way over rafts, descending boats over ascending craft, packets over freight boats at all times, and packets carrying the mail over all others. Vessels traveling at night were required to have a light on the bow. Due notice must be given upon approaching a lock to permit the tender to open the gates; and only if the latter failed to do his duty was the boatman to lock his own craft through, showing at all times proper care for the safety of the company's property. Boats were to tie up only on the berm side of the canal to prevent interference with traffic on the towpath. Finally, all craft must be registered and plainly marked on both sides with name, number, and marks denoting the draft of the vessel.[5] The regulations that applied to canal officials, collectors, and lock-keepers warned against neglect of duty, urged the greatest care at all times, and assigned responsibility for the protection of company property and interests.[6]

The canal was divided into large segments of fairly uniform length, each with a superintendent in charge. Although the exact boundaries of the divisions changed, they usually coincided with the arrangements of dams or were centered around the principal valley towns, Georgetown, Catoctin, Harpers Ferry, etc. New sections were added as more of the waterway was finished. Each superintendent was responsible for all matters affecting the canal in his zone, but he usually received insufficient authority to do his job effectively. The Board also assigned work gangs and bosses to each division to expedite repairs. Because of the lack of authority and at times the indifference of the incumbent, the operational organization of the canal broke down in practice. It was frequently incapable of enforcing the proper degree of efficiency among the employees and was not always successful in anticipating trouble or remedying it promptly. This condition was not helped by the frequent changing of officials which began in this early period and became routine after the completion of the canal.

[5] See also *ibid.*, B, 290 (March 25, 1831). Provisions against the use of poles and requiring registration and proper marking were adopted even before the general code of regulations.

[6] *Ibid.*, pp. 419-421, 422-429 (July 16, 1831).

The organization of the line became in effect a mere formality, for the Board retained too much authority for itself. As a result, the character and the conduct of the superintendents were not so important in the operation of the canal as they might have been. On the whole, however, the men who held office during most of the early period were not so inefficient as might have been anticipated on a new work—or as their successors were. If not exceptionally capable, they at least became experienced, and they made some effort to perform their tasks conscientiously. The same may be said for the conduct of the collectors and other officials in the early period.

In the absence of an effective line of authority, the character of the lock-keepers became important to the welfare of the canal. On the basis of what little is known of the early lock-tenders, they do not, as a group, seem to have been outstanding for their enthusiasm or reliability. Despite the important role which devolved upon them in the course of the Board's conduct of canal affairs, apparently little was expected from them. For his services at any hour, day or night, the lock-keeper received his house, an acre of land for a garden, and $150 a year. For each additional lock under his care, he received $50 extra, up to three locks and $250; but he was expected to provide his own assistants to tend the extra locks.[7] Married men were preferred and large families favored—the more hands to do the work. At times women held the position of lock-tender, but these were usually the widows of the original keeper. In March, 1835, the Board decided that all women lock-keepers would be discharged May 1, in the interest of more efficient operation.[8] Exceptions were subsequently made in at least four cases: Mary Ross, Susan Cross, Mrs. O'Riley and Mrs. James Davis, all the widows of former keepers.[9] Male tenders, how-

[7] *Ibid.*, B, 135 (July 7, 1830), 188 (September 25, 1830), H, 144-145 (February 4, 1848). Actually tenders of a single lock received but $100 a year. It was not until July 1, 1831, that their wages were raised to the $150 minimum. *Ibid.*, B, 396 (July 1, 1831).

[8] *Ibid.*, D, 264 (March 18, 1835). This was not necessarily a reflection on the ability of the women. The operation of a lock required no little physical strength and endurance. It was a task better suited to men.

[9] Mary Ross to President and Directors, March 24, 1835; Proceedings of Directors, D, 267 (March 25, 1835), E, 36 (March 30, 1836), F, 512 (December 20, 1842), G, 146 (April 16, 1844).

ever, were not always blameless. Many were dismissed for drunkenness, neglect of duty, and absence without notice or without providing a substitute.[10] Frequent complaints were made about the sale of liquor by lock-keepers to boatmen and workers, and the disorderly results of this practice. The Board repeatedly forbade the illicit trade, but apparently with little effect.[11]

The formulation of detailed regulations and the organization of canal employees did not insure the orderly operation of the work. On the contrary, every conceivable abuse was reported at one time or another. The Board immediately saw the necessity of securing some definite delegation of police power from the parties to the charter in order to gain the authority to enforce its regulations.[12] Canal property was misused, tools were lost and stolen, repair materials damaged or stolen, and the towpaths and aqueducts used as wagon roads and bridle paths.[13] Repeated directions for the enforcement of the rules indicate a laxness or indifference on the part of the officials and boatmen alike. Regulations which were singled out for enforcement involved the use of iron-shod poles for propulsion, the navigation of the canal by boats and scows that did not conform to regulations, and damage to the locks by the negligence of boatmen and tenders.[14]

The boatmen themselves were a rough and ready lot.[15] They

[10] *Ibid.*, B, 328 (June 3, 1831), 396 (July 1, 1831), D, 80-81 (April 25, 1834), G, 209-210 (November 8, 1844); Stone to Coale, August 29, 1844; Elgin to Coale, March 5, 1846. In the last two cases, the men did not lose their jobs. See also Ingle to Rodgers, August 30, 1837, Letter Book D, 205.

[11] Proceedings of Directors, E, 69 (June 4, 1836), G, 210-211 (November 8, 1844), H, 179 (June 5, 1848).

[12] *Ibid.*, B, 206 (October 19, 1830); 3d Annual Report (1831), Proceedings of Stockholders, A, 173.

[13] Elgin to President and Directors, July 10, 1833; F. Thomas [sr.] to F. Thomas [jr.], December 15, 1837; Elgin to President and Directors, September 15, 1841; Proceedings of Directors, C, 401 (July 19, 1833), D, 206 (December 24, 1834), E, 345 (December 20, 1837); Ingle to Elgin, December 20, 1837, Letter Book D, 243.

[14] W. H. Bryan to Ingle, August 15, 1831; Proceedings of Directors, B, 290 (March 25, 1831), C, 30 (November 19, 1831), 368 (June 4, 1833), 392 (June 28, 1833); W. Easby to President and Directors, December 9, 1838.

[15] The description of the boatmen is based on interviews with George Nicolson, General Manager of the Chesapeake and Ohio Canal, 1890-1938, "Charley" Egan, and Harvey Mayhew, former boatmen, and Frank Lee Carl, newspaper

usually formed a class apart from their neighbors, intermarrying within their own group. Their children were frequently born and raised in the trade, knowing no other life. The boatmen received little, but often cared less. They were constantly brawling among themselves for precedence at locks, because of some real or fancied slur, or for exercise; and with others for almost any reason. Their life was at best irregular and unpredictable, and the canallers were like their trade. Many dawdled along the line, taking their time in making the run. Others were more ambitious, driving their teams and boats at full speed night and day, caring little for themselves, their mules and boats, or for others—least of all for canal property.[16] The men were constantly at odds with the company over freight charges and the toll rate and in the early days took unusual ways of expressing their dissatisfaction. One master of a packet staged a demonstration in Georgetown.

> . . . we heard a thundering noise of wild music and saw a large Cavalcade Colours flying & having got near, it proved to be Mr. Fenlon, with his teams & crew with the Colours of the packet floating in high glee; he proceeded and paraded down Bridge Street, and made a Stop upon the new Bridge and—*refreshing* himself and his crew after much music gave the word of command for High Street—reeling in Saddle all the way; a gang of negroes & boys thronging the street.[17]

Usually, however, the canallers shunned the towns, for it cost too much to feed their teams, and they felt out of place. Even while wintering along the line they had their own settlements on the fringes of the towns or often quite far from them.

A point of particular grievance to the directors was the quality of the boats operating on the canal. No one was willing to undertake to fulfill their dreams of steamers and double-decked packets.[18] In fact, the boatmen were reluctant to meet even the minimum requirements of the regulations. Complaints

correspondent and local historian, Cumberland, Maryland; also with Edward Oswald, Clerk of the Circuit Court of Washington County, Maryland.

[16] The boatmen particularly resented the priority granted to packets, and often engaged in fights among themselves for preference at the locks. See, for example, Van Slyke to President and Directors, April 2, May 26, 1831.

[17] P. Rodier to Ingle, September 8, 1831. In later years, after the boatmen had become organized under the duress of the seventies, they resorted to strikes as a more effective way of securing their ends.

[18] 1st Annual Report (1829), Proceedings of Stockholders, A, 47.

were frequently made of iron-shod boats, leaky scows, drifting rafts, and sunken wrecks obstructing navigation.[19] By the enforcement of regulations, the provision of drydocks, the assessment of fines, and by other devices the company sought to drive undesirable craft off the waterway and to encourage the construction of new and larger boats. In this they were partly successful, assisted by the growing demands of the trade. The size of the boats increased steadily until they reached the maximum dimensions permitted by the locks. The directors also levied a rate discrimination of 100 per cent against rafts.[20] Nevertheless, the lumber trade and the incidental trade of the farmers, who built their own craft designed to last for only one trip (usually to be sold at Georgetown for firewood), made the struggle for better boats a never ending one.

The Board also sought to encourage the development of passenger travel and packet service on its waterway. It kept on the lookout for and published information on experiments with new types of boats on European canals. The directors offered attractive terms to would-be promoters of packet lines, including the privilege of operating toll-free for one year after the inauguration of the service.[21] They made the same offer to the builder of the first successful steamer to be placed in operation on the canal.[22] The company even built a novel all-iron boat of its own as a model packet.[23] In the end, the best it could achieve was a daily packet service, toll-free, but with the privilege of free use by canal employees when traveling on official business.[24] Later on, a ferry service was established across the Potomac Aqueduct. No successful steamer was put into operation on the waterway in the early period.

[19] Proceedings of Directors, C, 30 (November 19, 1831); J. Y. Young to [Ingle?], October 25, 1838. William Easby to President and Directors, December 9, 1838; J. G. Stone to Ringgold, June 6, 1847.

[20] Proceedings of Directors, D, 284-285 (April 23, 1835).

[21] *Ibid.*, B, 194-195 (October 4, 1830), D, 358 (July 3, 1835), F, 115 (November 2, 1839).

[22] *Ibid.*, D, 220 (January 13, 1835).

[23] Ingle to Zachariah Offutt, March 22, 1834, Letter Book B, 203. It cost about $1,400, but was found to be unsatisfactory for its purpose and was offered for sale as scrap for $300 in 1836. Ingle to Hugh Smith, December 16, 1838, *ibid.*, D, 9.

[24] Proceedings of Directors, D, 398-399 (September 11, 1835), E, 87 (July 6, 1836); O. M. Linthicum to President and Directors, June 29, 1836.

The business of the canal in these early years was almost wholly the transportation of agricultural produce. As long as this continued the company was barely able to meet expenses, and all hopes of the promoters had to be expressed in terms of future prospects. But the canal board refused to accept a comparison of its trade with that of the Potomac Company. Instead it preferred to point to the great lumber and coal resources of the valley and the valuable trade to and from the West. If any comparison had to be made, the directors used the successful Erie Canal as the measure of the future prospects of their waterway.[25] Nevertheless the company did not ignore the river trade. Until its own works were completed, it kept the Potomac Company's locks and canals in repair.[26]

In 1834, the Board established the first comprehensive rates of tolls.[27] A revised list of charges went into effect on July 1, 1835, at which time all tolls for river traffic (except where slackwater navigation in the Potomac bed was technically a part of the canal) were abandoned.[28] The tolls of 1835 also made the first distinction between short- and long-distance trade, providing lower rates per mile for additional distances over fifteen miles. A second revision occurred in 1841 when the directors raised the charges on the major agricultural products and provisions to a flat 2 cents a ton per mile. The tariff on coal and lime remained at 1 cent a ton per mile.[29] In 1843

[25] *2d Annual Report* (1830), pp. 12-15; *5th Annual Report* (1833), p. 11; *11th Annual Report* (1839), p. 7.

[26] Proceedings of Directors, A, 312-313 (July 7, 1829), 342 (September 9, 1829), B, 30 (February 24, 1830). This consideration toward river traffic remained a fixed policy in the construction of the canal all the way to Cumberland. In 1833, for example, the Board ordered the construction of a temporary lock around the abutment of Dam No. 5 to permit the continuation of river trade while the dam was being built. *Ibid.*, D, 13 (November 15, 1833).

[27] *Ibid.*, D, 67-69 (April 4, 1834). Until 1834, the rate was the same as that established by the Potomac Company. (*Ibid.*, B, 194 [October 10, 1830].) In preparation for the establishment of the new schedule of tolls, the company requested information on charges made upon other canals. See, for example, Ingle to Dr. Silas Condict, Morristown, N. J., and Ingle to Edward Everett, Boston, October 5, 1830, Letter Book A, 256-257.

[28] Proceedings of Directors, D, 284-286 (April 23, 1835), 333-334 (June 15, 1835); Ingle to Collectors and Lock-keepers, June 26, 1835, Letter Book C. 40.

[29] Proceedings of Directors, F, 295-296 (March 15, 1841).

a new Board reduced the tolls to approximately the levels of 1835. Reductions below the latter rates could be made early with the consent of the state agents according to the terms of the mortgage of 1835.[30]

The agricultural nature of canal trade which was indicated by the toll schedules and testified to by the company officials was also demonstrated by the annual analyses of trade on the waterway. Although accurate and detailed listings did not begin until 1842, by which time the canal had already reached Dam No. 6, the chief articles transported were still flour, wheat, and corn. Lumber, lime, stone, and some coal were also shipped in varying quantities.[31] Depending as much as it did on agricultural produce, the canal's business was subject to fluctuation according to the size of the local crops.[32] Recognizing the intimate relationship between canal trade and local agricultural prosperity, the Board reduced charges on fertilizers, in cooperation with the Virginia Society for the Advancement of Agriculture, in order to help increase the productivity of the soil and thus indirectly stimulating trade.[33]

On the whole, however, the problem of developing business for the canal was not clearly or fully recognized during the early period. The directors were prone to look upon their work as a magnificient enterprise to which trade would naturally be attracted. They conceived their task to be merely the construction and maintenance of the waterway. Thus the efforts of the Board to increase canal trade were not at all consistent. At the same time that it lowered tolls on manures in order to increase agricultural production, it refused to have any connection with the business of transportation. Although the directors tried to encourage boat-building, they did nothing to establish and operate a freight line for the company. They manipulated tolls

[30] *Ibid.*, G, (May 3, 1843). See below, Appendix, Table VII, for rates.

[31] See Appendix, Table IV. In 1851, the company destroyed waybills and toll returns for the period prior to 1847, inasmuch as the accounts were closed and the papers were "of no value for future reference." Proceedings of Directors, H, 449 (June 2, 1851).

[32] *5th Annual Report* (1833), p. 11; Washington to T. W. Veazey, Governor of Maryland, February 4, 1837, Letter Book D, 94; Report of the General Committee, 10th Annual Meeting (1837), Proceedings of Stockholders, B, 137.

[33] Proceedings of Directors, H, 214 (October 10, 1848), 239 (February 7, 1849).

so as to compete with the railroad for business, but made no effort to control all the charges of transportation, including freights, wharfage, etc. The company spent large sums on dredges, ice-breakers, and repair gangs to keep the canal open for navigation, but forbade its employees to have any connections with persons or businesses operating boats on the canal. Although the Board sought to develop manufactories along its waterway by the disposal of surplus water power, it looked upon the sales primarily in terms of immediate profits rather than as stimulants to further trade. Yet at the same time the directors frequently cited the value to the state of New York of the Erie Canal *in terms of the trade it produced for the state* as much as the profits earned by the canal itself. Subsequently the Chesapeake and Ohio Canal Company reversed itself on all points except the sale of water power.

Trade grew slowly before 1850. After the enthusiasm of the first year, 1831, the total business on the canal remained almost stationary until 1838. Then it rose abruptly, doubling within four years to over 60,000 tons in 1841. Thereafter there was another period in which trade fluctuated irregularly about the new level. In the three years prior to the completion of the canal, commerce on the waterway again increased rapidly, to 86,436 tons in 1848, 102,041 tons in 1849, and 101,950 tons in 1850.[34]

Two factors tended to discourage the growth of trade: the interruptions to navigation due to breaches and floods, and the competition of the Baltimore and Ohio Railroad.

The minimum task set by the canal company, the maintenance of the waterway, proved to be an unending job. During the early years of operation there were many breaks resulting in suspensions of trade for hours, days, or weeks.[35] Most of these could be attributed to any one of several causes: the

[34] See Appendix, Table IV.

[35] Purcell to President and Directors, November 26, 1830; Van Slyke to President and Directors, October 2, 15, 1830; Van Slyke to Ingle, June 7, 1831; Purcell to Ingle, October 4, 1831; Young to President and Directors, July 5, 1836; Barnard to Coale, April 1, 1844 (mentions breaches in August, 1842, April, August and September, 1843). See also Proceedings of Directors, B, 191-192 (October 2, 1830); 236 (November 26, 1830), 382 (June 10, 1831); C, 12-13 (October 7, 1831); D, 233-234 (February 9, 1835), etc.

newness of the works, the high banks required in some places, the inexperience of the employees, the poor quality of construction, insufficient knowledge of soil conditions in the region, and even the depredations of muskrats.[36] On the other hand, there were also frequent complaints of low water in the canal resulting from droughts in the valley, sand and mud bars washed into the waterway by freshets, and leaking dams.[37] Other obstructions to trade during the early years of the canal included sunken wrecks, loose boats, bodies of dead animals, and fallen rocks and earth.[38] The basin at Rock Creek was the source of much trouble on two points, the obstruction of traffic by boats tied up irregularly along its sides, and the rapid filling up of the basin by the silt which the creek brought down.[39]

The most serious threat to the trade of the canal was the danger of floods in the Potomac valley. Although the worst freshet in the history of the Potomac Company, in 1810, had left its works relatively undamaged, the Chesapeake and Ohio Canal Company was not so fortunate. Floods occurred more frequently and with greater destructiveness. Substantial damage was inflicted by the freshets of 1836, 1843, 1846, and 1847, but these were by no means the only floods to ravage the canal.[40] Each freshet was a twofold blow at company fortunes, for it deprived the latter of its sources of revenue and at the same

[36] There was a reward of 25 cents for each muskrat presented to canal officials if evidence was given that it was killed on the line of the canal. Proceedings of Directors, C, 111-112 (March 24, 1832).

[37] G. G. Johnson to President and Directors, November 21, 1838; Petition of Thomas G. Harris and others, July 6, 1842; F. Tilghman, director, to M. C. Sprigg, June 25, 1842; Fisk to Coale, September 19, 1844.

[38] Proceedings of Directors, C, 30 (November 11, 1831), D, 323 (May 29, 1835); Dan Boyle to Washington, June 27, 1838.

[39] Proceedings of Directors, C, 112 (March 24, 1832). See also the correspondence with O. H. Dibble, Letters Received, 1832.

[40] Purcell to Mercer, January 11, 1832; John C. Lackland to President and Directors, May 10, 1832; Purcell to Ingle, January 15, 1834. Full reports on the 1836 flood are contained in: Young to Ingle, June 3, 4; Fisk to Ingle, June 3, 4; Rodgers to Ingle, June 4; Elgin to President and Directors, June 6, 1836. The 1843 freshet is described in: Fisk to Coale, September 17, and Ingle to Coale, September 18, 1843. The crest of the river in 1846 was lower than the one of September, 1843, but higher than a minor one in April, 1843. Elgin to Coale, July 8; Fisk to Coale, July 8, 1846. The flood of 1847 surpassed all previous marks. Elgin to Coale, October 8, 9, 11; Stone to Coale, October 8, 10, 12; J. Lambie to Ringgold, October 9, 1847.

time made necessary the expenditure of large sums of money for repairs. The canal suffered immediately from both causes, and its future was threatened by the reputation for the unreliability of navigation it was gaining and by the growing burden of debt under which it was laboring.

The competition of the railroad was another obstacle to the growth of canal trade before 1850. The rival enterprises clashed at several points in the Potomac valley in the early years of their existence. The first encounter occurred during the joint construction of their respective works from Point of Rocks to Harpers Ferry. Shippers complained that the waterway was filling up and becoming dangerous for navigation because of the rocks which were falling or being thrown into the canal from the railroad which was building farther up the slope.[41] The parallel course of the rival enterprise brought up other questions of interference. The compromise of 1833 required the Baltimore and Ohio to erect a board fence between its tracks and the canal before using steampower on that part of its line. The Chesapeake and Ohio had insisted on this provision in order to protect the business on its waterway by shutting off from the view of the canal mules the terrifying sight of the locomotives.[42] The railroad company wanted to experiment with the use of steam without raising the fence.[43] It suggested that a rail fence be built, if necessary, on the river side of the towpath to prevent the mules from bolting into the stream. After a long dispute the canal company finally agreed to accept $2,723 from the Baltimore and Ohio and build the rail fence on the towpath as suggested.[44]

The accommodation of the railroad bridge at Harpers Ferry led to another series of controversies. By the terms of an agreement formally entered into early in 1835, establishing the location and dimensions of the viaduct, the railroad company consented to the construction of a tracking path for canal trade

[41] Proceedings of Directors, D, 323 (May 24, 1835).

[42] Washington to Thomas, June 17, 1835, Letter Book C, 29-30.

[43] Proceedings of Directors, D, 272 (April 8, 1835); P. E. Thomas to McCulloh, May 31, 1835. By this time the former's demands were becoming more forthright and blunt, more insistent.

[44] Proceedings of Directors, E, 166 (November 9, 1836); 172-174 (November 23, 1836).

across the river alongside the bridge.[45] It further agreed to carry part of the canal's business across the Potomac over its own tracks at prevailing rates. The bridge and tracking path were built shortly thereafter in accordance with the compact between the rival works.[46] Early in 1837, however, the canal company discovered that the right of access to the path at the Virginia end of the viaduct was not included in the arrangement and was in imminent danger of being completely lost. In anticipation of a profitable transfer business with the railroad, Gerard B. Wager, the owner of the property at the south end of the bridge and an old enemy of the canal, had begun the construction of a brick warehouse which was located so as to take full advantage of the rail traffic and which incidentally effectively blocked access to the tracking path.[47] The canal board took the matter up with the Baltimore and Ohio directors who politely and sadly protested their innocence and helplessness in the affair.[48] Wager then decided to permit trespass to the path upon the payment of an appropriate toll.[49] The canal company sought to condemn the land needed but was unsuccessful, and the tracking path remained practically unused.[50] Wager eventually secured a virtual monopoly of storage facilities at Harpers Ferry,[51] and in an effort to complete the monopoly he sought, in 1839, to lease a site for a warehouse at Lock 33, opposite the town. The canal board consented to

[45] *Ibid.*, 214-217 (January 13, 1835), 235 (February 11, 1835).

[46] *Ibid.*, p. 436 (December 4, 1835).

[47] Elgin to President and Directors, April 19, 29, 1837. For a brief summary of Wager's interest in the bridge, see the MS Bill of Complaint, May 6, 1936, Harpers Ferry and Potomac Bridge Company *vs.* Baltimore and Ohio Railroad Company and State Roads Commissioners of Maryland, in Equity No. 2447, District Court of the United States for the District of Maryland (Baltimore, Md.), especially pp. 3-4.

[48] Proceedings of Directors, E, 239 (April 19, 1837), 248 (May 3, 1837); Ingle to President and Directors of the Baltimore and Ohio Railroad Company, April 27, 1837, Letter Book D, 115-116; Ingle to J. W. Patterson, President of the Baltimore and Ohio Railroad Company, May 5, 1837, *ibid.*, p. 120.

[49] Elgin to President and Directors, September 6, 1837.

[50] Proceedings of Directors, E, 310 (September 6, 1837), 481-482 (September 5, 1838); Ingle to Wager, April 26, 1839, Letter Book E, 205. The Board ordered installation of a swinging ladder at the Virginia end of the tracking path, communicating with the river.

[51] Starbuck to Smith, April 13, 1839. The monopoly was the subject of much complaint.

make the lease in return for a satisfactory arrangement about the tracking path.[52] Wager protested his inability to come to any agreement on that basis, but continued negotiations, effectively preventing competition by any other warehouse on the site. Eventually, the directors despaired of coming to terms with him and granted the warehouse site to another applicant.[53]

The struggle between the railroad and the canal for the Shenandoah trade at Harpers Ferry was renewed in the early forties. At least three points of friction were present: the tracking path, the railroad charges on traffic over the bridge, and the flour trade. In May, 1841, the Baltimore and Ohio tore down the tracking path and refused to rebuild it.[54] The company's engineer insisted that the railroad and not the canal had originally paid for it, contrary to the terms of the agreement.[55] After a delay of over a year, during which the canal was deprived of even the relatively small use of the path and consequently placed at a convenient disadvantage in its rivalry with the railroad, the latter finally rebuilt the tracking, amid profuse apologies.[56] During the interlude in which there was no tracking path, the railroad fixed the rates for carrying goods across its bridge by rail at 50 cents a ton, far above the maximum rates permitted by its charter or charged by the company, again contrary to the agreement which made possible the construction of the viaduct.[57] It also refused to furnish Baltimore and Ohio cars for the trade and at the same time exacted a fee for permitting the Winchester and Potomac Railroad cars to use the bridge. Even after the tracking path had been restored, canal shippers protested that the rates charged by the Baltimore and Ohio made their trade unprofitable, if not impossible.[58]

[52] Proceedings of Directors, E, 497-498 (September 28, 1838); Ingle to Wager, July 26, 1838, Letter Book D, 410.

[53] Proceedings of Directors, F, 54-55 (May 16, 1839). Wager claimed he no longer was the sole owner of the property in dispute at the bridge. It was, he said, in common with the other warehouse sites at Harpers Ferry, held by a group of capitalists, of whom he was merely one.

[54] Elgin to President and Directors, May 10, 1841, July 14, 1842. The local officials of the railroad ignored the protests of canal representatives and refused their claims about previous payment before destroying the path.

[55] Fisk to M. C. Sprigg, July 21, 1842.

[56] Fisk to Latrobe, December 7, 1842.

[57] Elgin to President and Directors, May 10, 1841.

[58] W. L. Clarke, President of the Winchester and Potomac Railroad, to

The same sort of maneuvering occurred in connection with the struggle for the flour trade. Until May 1, 1841, the charges by rail from Harpers Ferry to Baltimore were 34 cents a ton plus 3 cents for handling. On May 1, the railroad raised the rate to 50 cents per ton, including handling. It then petitioned the legislature to compel the canal company to raise its toll to a " profitable rate." The latter raised its charges at the request of the railroad without awaiting the action of the Assembly. Within a month, on June 3, 1841, the railroad reduced its rates to 34 cents a ton, including handling. The charges from Frederick to Baltimore at the time were said to be 30 cents. Thus the additional charge for the twenty-one miles from Frederick to Harpers Ferry was only 4 cents. Between June and December, 1841, the flour trade on the canal from the Ferry fell off 4,411 barrels as compared to the 1840 figures. A large amount of this decrease was attributed to the actions of the railroad company.[59] Again, in 1844, Alexandria citizens complained of the loss of the flour trade to the Baltimore millers.[60]

The struggle for the Cumberland coal trade which began in the forties proved to be the decisive factor in the course of canal trade and prosperity. From December, 1843, until March, 1845, the railroad and the canal cooperated in the handling of the lucrative business. According to their agreement the railroad, which had already reached Cumberland, undertook to carry all the coal offered for shipment via the waterway over its own tracks at special rates to the western terminus of canal navigation at Dam No. 6. The passage of the canal bill in March, 1845, brought to an abrupt end all pretense on the part of the Baltimore and Ohio of an interest in the canal's future welfare. The railroad and its ally, the city of Baltimore, began a large-scale assault on the trade of its arch competitor which threatened to deprive the latter of all possible chance of success, even before it was completed.

Coale, September 3, 1843. This road was a short feeder line from Winchester to Harpers Ferry, entering the latter via the Shenandoah valley.

[59] Elgin to Ingle, December 23, 1841. Elgin closed the letter with the blunt statement, "I am at all times provoked when on such a subject."

[60] Resolutions of Citizens of Alexandria, October 14, 1844; Thomas M. Maccubbin to Turner, November 6, 1844.

The city of Baltimore paved the way for more effective competition by the railroad.

Meantime the corporation of Baltimore are actively engaged in measures which have a tendency to frustrate the objects of the canal company. An ordinance has passed both branches of the city council allowing the Baltimore and Ohio railroad company to run their locomotives into the city with coal, iron ore &c, and also to lay tracks to a new depot on the south of the basin, where vessels may lay free of port charges, and other expenses which they have heretofore been subjcted to. The report of the committee of the councils to whom the subject was referred, suggested, that if it became expedient so to do, the railroad company might put the price of bringing down coal and iron to a mere nominal sum and defy competition. This we should suppose would encourage the coal and iron companies and the western county people to keep up the spirit of a competition, which however ruinous to canals and railroads, would enable them to get their material wealth and products to market, for a mere song; the very thing for them.[61]

The railroad struck its blows wherever it could reach its enemy, specifically at the two main sources of canal revenue, present and prospective, the flour trade and the coal trade. It abruptly terminated its arrangement for the transportation of coal from Cumberland to Dam No. 6 at 2 cents a ton per mile. The rates were raised to 4 cents a ton per mile for coal and 6 cents for iron. The excuse for the action, curiously enough, was not the increased facilities required by the size of the trade, but that the amount of business was "so inconsiderable as scarcely to authorize a longer continuance of our preparation for its accommodation at present rates." Besides, the Baltimore and Ohio was making arrangements for a more extensive trade to the city of Baltimore, which was more important to the railroad.[62] The canal company refused to recognize the abrogation as an act in good faith, but made no sustained protest. President Coale poignantly observed to the president of the railroad company,

Whether the reasons given in your letter are sufficient to authorize a departure from the arrangement entered into between the two Companies in Sept: 1843, & whether the interests of "the public gener-

[61] *Niles' Register*, LXVIII, No. 6 (April 12, 1845), 85.

[62] McLane to Coale, May 7, 1845; Proceedings of Directors, G, 252-253 (May 21, 1845).

ally" will be subserved by the imposition of a *prohibitory Tariff* between Cumberland & Dam No. 6, are questions upon which I think impartial men will differ with you.[63]

At the same time the Baltimore and Ohio intensified its efforts to win the flour trade from the canal.[64] The competition for the Harpers Ferry business continued, with the railroad throwing every possible obstacle in the way of the transfer of the canal trade across the river. It continued to charge at the rate of 20 cents a ton per mile for goods shipped one-quarter mile over the viaduct, although the charter permitted a maximum rate of only 8 cents a ton per mile. It refused to allow the use of its own cars, and those of the Winchester and Potomac Railroad were compelled to pay a high fee to participate in the trade. There was always a great delay in the handling of what little business was offered on these terms.[65] Of course, all these actions were contrary to the agreement with the canal company under which the bridge was built.

While engaged in the construction and operation of the waterway, the directors looked about for other means of increasing their resources. Two ways of exploiting the canal attracted the Board's interest at an early date. A road along the berm side of the waterway above Georgetown was necessary for the transportation of supplies to the line. Inasmuch as the existing public road was unsatisfactory, the directors suggested that in return for their improvement of that highway (improvement was inevitable for the purposes of the company anyway) they be permitted to operate it as a turnpike, charging tolls for its use.[66] The Board also briefly considered opening the towpath as a toll-road for horseback travel. In this way, the traffic on the path would pay for its maintenance.[67]

The most obvious source of additional revenue was the sale of surplus water from the canal to mills and manufactories

[63] Coale to McLane, May 9, 1845, Letter Book G, 260.

[64] Milton Reizenstein, *An Economic History of the Baltimore and Ohio Railroad, 1828-1852*, pp. 82-83.

[65] J. H. Elgin to Coale, November 2, 1845.

[66] Proceedings of Directors, B, 206 (October 19, 1830); 3rd Annual Report (1831), Proceedings of Stockholders, A, 172. The canal had occupied the site of the original road in 1829. (Proceedings of Directors, A, 154 [February 2, 1829].) Permission was not granted.

[67] 3d Annual Report (1831), Proceedings of Stockholders, A, 173.

along its banks. The Board looked for a twofold advantage: the financial return from the sale of the water and the added business which the industrial establishments would bring. Unfortunately, in the continued financial straits of the company, the first advantage came to outweigh the second. Thus the suggestion of contemporaries that the company might give away its surplus water in return for the benefits of increased trade from the factories never received much consideration.[68] The early promoters of the canal also thought that small establishments would spring up all along the line, at every lock at which waste and flume power would be available.[69]

In the beginning the canal company did not even possess the right to dispose of its surplus water by sale to manufacturers. The charter had granted the undertaking rights to only that water which was essential for purposes of navigation.[70] The Board soon petitioned for the necessary grant of authority from the parties to the charter, but only gradually did the directors overcome the opposition of the valley inhabitants. Local proprietors on the Maryland side of the river were particularly hostile to the company's request, for it represented an infringement of their own rights.[71] Virginia, whose citizens had the least to lose, gave the necessary authority in February, 1829. Maryland assented, in 1833, in return for the consent of the Chesapeake and Ohio to the extension of the railroad to Harpers Ferry.[72] Congress gave its approval in March, 1837.[73] The only restriction on the power received under these acts

[68] Washington *National Intelligencer*, May 26, 1835.

[69] See, for example, 3d Annual Report (1831), Proceedings of Stockholders, A, 151. In 1835 the company was told to expect sales only near cities. Zachariah Allen to C. C. Starbuck, January 1, 1835. But the Board continued to believe that water power could be sold at the locks as late as 1874, despite the obvious failure of earlier expectations to be realized. *46th Annual Report* (1874), p. 19.

[70] G. C. Washington to William Steuart, January 20, 1836. See also the *Resolution of the Maryland Assembly*, 1830, ch. 36, February 19, 1831.

[71] A. Lee to Mercer, February 15, 1829; Cruger to Mercer, February 13, 1831.

[72] Act of the Virginia Assembly, February 27, 1829; *Maryland Laws*, 1832, ch. 291, passed March 22, 1833.

[73] Act of Congress, approved March 3, 1837. It was introduced on March 3, 1836; passed the House of Representatives during the next session, January 20, 1837, and the Senate shortly thereafter, March 2, 1837. *Congressional Globe*, IV, 110; V, 114, 217.

was the stipulation of the Maryland law that no water could be sold within the state for the manufacture of grain, a prohibition that would exclude competition with the Baltimore millers. This provision was not repealed until the 1870's.[74]

Even after the legal authority was secured, the title of the company to the surplus water from Dam No. 1 at Little Falls, the most valuable source of potential water power, was not clear. The claims of John K. Smith under the Potomac Company, which had been the subject of much correspondence after 1816, had been inherited by Amos Binney, a Boston capitalist. The latter, or rather his heirs and his agent, William Steuart, took his claims into court after failing to come to an understanding with the canal directors.[75] Several cases brought by him lingered in the courts for many years. The canal company won repeatedly, but there was always another case or an appeal.[76] After having won most of its points, the company compromised the few remaining ones, and obtained clear title to the water.[77] Thus it was ready to take full advantage of its rights when Congress consented to the sale of surplus water in 1837.

In preparation for exercising its new authority, the company studied carefully the procedures on other canals and modeled its own rules after them.[78] It provided a gradual scale of increasing rents and for the location and control of water

[74] *Maryland Laws*, 1832, ch. 291, passed March 22, 1833; *46th Annual Report* (1874), p. 19.

[75] Mercer to Ingle, August 9, 19, 1829.

[76] Amos Binney *vs.* Chesapeake and Ohio Canal Company in Chancery Court, quashed, September, 1829, Letters Received; Petition of Thomas Swann and Richard Coxe, April 9, 1834; Chesapeake and Ohio Canal Company *vs.* Binney, 4 Cranch C. C. 68; Binney *vs.* Chesapeake and Ohio Canal Company, 8 Peters 201.

[77] Special Report to 8th Annual Meeting (July 18, 1836), Proceedings of Stockholders, B, 36-38.

[78] Roswell and Colt to Charles Nourse, January 11, 1831 [1832]; Conditions for letting water power in the District of Columbia, March 25, 1839, Letters Received.

Rights to water power at various points in Maryland not in dispute had been sold in 1835. Having sold these rights, however, the Board discovered that there was not enough water in the canal for navigation, much less for sale as surplus. The directors were unable to return to Washington via the canal, but made the journey by stage. Proceedings of Directors, D, 311-315 (May 25, 1835).

gauges. It granted rights at several places along the canal, Williamsport, Weverton, Georgetown, etc., but the most important development was at Georgetown. Here the greatest opportunity was available for the establishment of industries because of the nearness to markets, labor supply, and capital, the location of Dam No. 1 at Little Falls, the large dimensions of the feeder and the Georgetown level, and the absence of restrictions on the use of the water. Millers, founders, and textile manufacturers were the chief users of water power in Georgetown. Despite the irregularity of service at times, the development of new sources of power, and charges and countercharges of abuse, several of these establishments are still using surplus water from the canal, under what are said to amount to perpetual leases, that is, twenty-year leases, renewable indefinitely upon certain conditions.[79]

The actual beginning of water-power leases in 1837 did not mark the end of the contest over the disposal of canal water. The concentration of industrial establishments in Georgetown because of the more favorable location and laws there put an end to the struggle with Amos Binney's heirs. In the forties, however, the Alexandria Canal Company stepped forward with its claim for a share of the surplus water from Dam No. 1.[80] This claim was supported by the state of Virginia in the act of 1849 guaranteeing $200,000 of repair bonds for the restoration of the Chesapeake and Ohio Canal below Dam No. 6. The terms of the act restricted the use of the proceeds from the bonds to that part of the canal above the Potomac Aqueduct. In addition they stipulated that the Chesapeake and Ohio must consent to an arrangement with the Alexandria Canal Company concerning its unpaid obligation for the construction of the northern abutment of the aqueduct and the allotment to that company of one-half of the additional water power (later fixed at 1,200 square inches) resulting from the tightening of Dam No. 1 and the enlarging of the feeder. The Chesapeake and Ohio readily agreed to the conditions, and secured the bonds.[81]

[79] Opinion of George Nicolson. The validity of the leases has been tested in the courts.

[80] Proceedings of Directors, G, 406-407 (April 16, 1844).

[81] *Ibid.*, H, 252-257 (April 18, 1849).

Afterwards, it always found some excuse for refusing to grant the required water power (or to pay for the abutment). A survey of water power leases in force in 1855 revealed that 1,295 inches had been granted on a regular basis and 300 inches on a temporary basis.[82] Subsequently (in 1860) temporary grants amounting to 1,200 inches were made permanent despite the agreement with the Alexandria Canal Company.[83]

[82] *Ibid.*, I, 159 (April 6, 1855). The report advised against the grant of more than 1,200 inches in addition to the 1,295 inches already leased on a permanent basis. Thus the Alexandria Canal Company would be entitled to only 600 inches instead of the 1,200 inches originally agreed upon. (*Ibid.*, pp. 162-164 [April 6, 1855].) The Alexandria company was given four months to accept the terms. Meanwhile the Chesapeake and Ohio leased 200 inches to Robert Dodge. (*Ibid.*, p. 168 [May 5, 1855].) The Alexandria Canal Company refused the new terms and insisted upon receiving the share allotted to it under the original contract. (*Ibid.*, p. 193 [August 4, 1855].) It was supported in its stand by the stockholders of the Chesapeake and Ohio Canal Company, but in vain.

[83] *Ibid.*, K, 166-167 (April 5, 1860).

Chapter X

VICISSITUDES OF WAR AND PEACE (1850-1870)

After the completion of the canal to Cumberland in 1850, the company prepared to enter a new phase of its existence. As the first step the Board completely revised the organization of the line. For purposes of more efficient operation it established six fairly equal divisions: Georgetown, Monocacy, Antietam, Williamsport, Hancock, and Cumberland. For the superintendents of these sections it retained the incumbents on the lower line and named former assistant engineers familiar with the upper canal to the new divisions. It also appointed the lock-tenders for the recently completed stretch of the canal.[1] The directors then issued a new set of resolutions to govern navigation on the canal and the conduct of the line officials.[2] These rules were largely a confirmation of the existing regulations, modified and brought up to date by the lessons of the first revisions. In spite of the usual opposition of the boatmen to the determination to enforce rules previously ignored, the president reported satisfaction with the operation of the new regulations in 1851.[3]

The canal itself was in fairly good condition after the thorough renovation of the whole line. As a matter of fact the work of improvement was still in progress in 1851.[4] In that year, for example, it was necessary to restrict the draft of the boats to approximately 4 feet, or about 100 to 110 tons burden. Although the water was generally 6 feet deep, bars in the trunk and low banks reduced the effective depth to 5 feet in some places.[5] Progress continued to be made in the restoration of the original prism, and by the next year the

[1] Proceedings of Directors, H, 391-393 (November 27, 1850).

[2] *Ibid.*, pp. 407-414 (February 27, 1851), 431-434 (March 1, 1851).

[3] 23d Annual Report (1851), Proceedings of Stockholders, D, 409.

[4] *24th Annual Report* (1852), p. 4. In 1851, $90,402.75 was spent on repairs and improvements.

[5] 23d Annual Report (1851), Proceedings of Stockholders, D, 410.

water level had reached a minimum of 5 feet 8 inches on the entire line.[6]

Upon the completion of the canal, the Board took under consideration revision of the existing toll rates. As coal soon became the principal article of trade, the charges on that product became the chief source of canal revenue. The directors offered to fix the toll on coal at 2 mills per ton, if the mine owners would guarantee to ship 500,000 tons a year via the canal. The companies were unable to take advantage of the offer, and the toll remained at ¼ cent a ton per mile.[7] Other preliminary modifications of the existing charges, adopted in February, 1851, affected a variety of non-agricultural products: sand, gravel, earth, paving stones, fire brick, ice, bricks, and salt, as well as some farm produce and fish.[8]

These early rate changes continued the downward trend of tolls in the forties and anticipated the general reductions which were incorporated in the revised list. The new permanent schedule went into effect in June, 1851. It divided all articles transported on the canal into six classes. Reductions below the rates established in 1835 ranged from 25 to 75 per cent, the greatest decrease being that in the toll on coal. Classes I and II, including general merchandise, spirits, and most agricultural produce, called for the highest rates. Class III was reserved for salt. Classes IV and V included heavy freight—lumber, bricks, cement, and manufactured iron. The most important and most highly competitive bulk freight was placed in Class VI upon which the lowest tolls were charged. Included in this group were coal, limestone, and iron ore.[9]

[6] *24th Annual Report* (1852), p. 6.

[7] Proceedings of Directors, H, 403 (January 9, 1851); 23d Annual Report (1851), Proceedings of Stockholders, D, 412-413.

[8] Proceedings of Directors, H, 423 (February 28, 1851). See below, Appendix, Table VII, for rates.

[9] Proceedings of Directors, H, 449-452 (June 2, 1851). The rates per ton per mile according to classes, were:

	First 20 miles	Thereafter
I	2c.	1c.
II	1c.	1c.
III	1c.	¾c.
IV	1c.	½c.
V	1c.	¼c.
VI	¼c.	¼c.

There were some modifications of these schedules in the course of the first decade. In an effort to encourage boat-building and indirectly to stimulate the lagging coal trade, the company again offered in 1852 to reduce the toll on coal to 2 mills as soon as one hundred new first-class boats were registered.[10] This condition was not fulfilled, however, and the charges remained the same. In 1857, there were some slight changes within and between classifications: salt shifted from Class III to Class IV rates; corn and fish from Class I to Class II; boards, shingles, staves and headings from Class II to Class V.[11] In 1860, on the eve of the Civil War, the Board reduced rates on all commodities in Class I to the level of those in Class II.[12]

Canal trade followed an irregularly upward course during the decade. Tonnage doubled between 1850 and 1851, soaring to 203,893 tons. Thereafter it moved to new peaks in cycles of two- and three-year duration. By 1859 it had reached 359,-716 tons per year.[13] The increasing number of boats registered and built on the canal reflected the expanding business.[14] Nevertheless the fluctuations experienced were discouraging at best. The frequent interruptions of navigation due to floods and breaches were partly responsible for the indifferent course of canal prosperity in the fifties. The volume of coal shipped via the canal proved to be disappointing in the early years of the decade. At the same time poor crops and the competition of other transportation agencies limited the amount of agricultural produce carried on the waterway.[15]

The directors tried various ways of stimulating commerce. They granted permission for the construction of basins on the Georgetown level to encourage the development of transfer

[10] *Ibid.*, p. 570 (December 9, 1852).
[12] *Ibid.*, K, 209 (August 15, 1860).
[11] *Ibid.*, I, 333 (January 8, 1857).
[13] See Appendix, Table IV.

[14] The number of boats registered on the canal rose from 154 in 1851 (including 78 new ones, usually over 100 tons each), to 215 in 1852 (of which 61 were new), to 343 in 1856. Of these, however, it was said many were out of repair and that only 250 could be counted upon. But over a hundred new boats were added for the 1857 season. 23d Annual Report (1851), Proceedings of Stockholders, D, 412; *24th Annual Report* (1852), p. 12; *28th Annual Report* (1856), pp. 8-9; *29th Annual Report* (1857), p. 12.

[15] *27th Annual Report* (1855), p. 12; *28th Annual Report* (1856), p. 4; *29th Annual Report* (1857), pp. 6-7.

facilities there.[16] They requested the Alexandria Canal Company to keep its locks open later at night, until 8 p. m.[17] And they deprived packets of their right of way over loaded freight boats descending the canal in order to reduce the delays in the passage of the trade on the waterway.[18] To augment the small coal trade the canal company directed the Baltimore and Ohio Railroad to permit the construction of a spur from the Cumberland Coal and Iron Company's railroad across the former's tracks to a projected wharf on the canal.[19]

The Board also considered several proposals for the improvement of the canal itself to facilitate the expansion of trade. There were plans for raising the Georgetown bridges, for the installation of a steam pump near the mouth of the South Branch (the original site for Dam No. 7 which had never been built), for repairs to all the Dams from No. 1 to No. 5, and for the renovation of the Washington branch.[20] The most important of these for the trade of the canal was the raising of the Georgetown bridges. The latter had originally been planned and constructed according to the practice prevailing on the Erie Canal in 1828 and 1829. They allowed a clearance of only 8 feet above the normal level of water in the canal. By 1850, the boats had become so large that although they could pass fully loaded under the bridges they could not return empty until the water level in the canal was lowered. Thus long and costly delays occurred which hampered trade to and from the Rock Creek basin and soon forced most of the business on the waterway to pass over the aqueduct and down the Alexandria Canal to the river at that city. To reopen the route through Rock Creek and into Washington, eight bridges and the market-house in Georgetown, one bridge over the basin, and two in Washington woud have to be raised so as to allow

[16] Proceedings of Directors, H, 426-429 (February 28, 1851).

[17] *Ibid.*, I, 248 (March 6, 1856).

[18] *Ibid.*, pp. 251-252 (April 3, 1856).

[19] *Ibid.*, pp. 267-268 (June 13, 1856). This procedure had been provided for in the contract of 1851 between the canal company and the Baltimore and Ohio, by which the former permitted the railroad to effect a connection at Cumberland with the western section of its main line. See p. 245, n. 71 below.

[20] 23d Annual Report (1851), Proceedings of Stockholders, D, 411; *24th Annual Report* (1852), pp. 4-6; *26th Annual Report* (1854), pp. 5-6; *27th Annual Report* (1855), pp. 4-5, 7.

at least a twelve-foot clearance.[21] The Board first proposed this in 1851, estimating the cost of the improvement at $12,-500.[22] The directors again referred to the project in 1852 and emphasized the importance of it. On closer examination, however, the subject was found to involve greater expenses and property infringements than had been anticipated, and in 1854 the matter was dropped, as far as independent action by the canal company was concerned. An appeal to Congress for financial assistance in carrying out the proposed improvement failed to pass the House of Representatives, in 1855, after winning the approval of the Senate.[23] Nothing more was done before the outbreak of the war.

The irregular course of canal fortunes in the fifties was largely the result of the unreliability of the canal as a carrier. This in turn was due principally to the occurrence of a disastrous series of freshets and the interference of local politics in the administration of the canal. Before the newly completed waterway was able to get fully started on the new phase of its existence, it was struck a double blow at its future prospects of success. The worst flood in the history of the Potomac, to that date, devastated the entire line in 1852. In the same year, political influence again resumed a major role in the direction of canal affairs.

The flood of 1852 was as great a surprise to the canal board as it was a disaster to the waterway itself. The directors had raised the embankments at the most exposed places above the level of the highest freshets in the history of the valley. They based their action on the levels attained in the flood of 1847, which had been the worst in sixty years. The precautions proved to be in vain, for in April, 1852, the river rose six feet higher, in some places, than the levels attained in 1847. At Great Falls it reached the unprecedented height of sixty-four feet. Had the

[21] Proceedings of Directors, H, 516-517 (March 16, 1852); *24th Annual Report* (1852), pp. 4-6. See also, Col. D. H. Rucker to Brig. Gen. M. C. Meigs, Quartermaster General, April 25, 1862, MS, in Records of Quartermaster General's Office (War Department Archives, National Archives).

[22] Proceedings of Directors, H, 516-517 (March 31, 1852). East of Congress Street, Georgetown, the bridges were to be raised to allow 10½ feet clearance.

[23] *24th Annual Report* (1852), pp. 4-6; *26th Annual Report* (1854), p. 9; *27th Annual Report* (1855), pp. 14-15.

crest been only two or three feet lower, the waterway might have escaped serious injury. As it was, by the time the work of restoration was completed the cost of repairs amounted to $100,000.[24] The canal itself was weakened by the disaster, but the effect on its trade and its financial condition was even more serious, as company officials admitted later.

> The disaster occasioned by the flood in the spring of 1852, was very detrimental to the interests of the company, in causing not only a large debt, and heavy expenses in repairing the canal, and the loss of three or four months revenues during the suspension of navigation that year, but had a still more unfavorable influence by the loss of confidence in the stability and reliability of the work as a means of transportation.[25]

Hard on the heels of the destruction wrought by the flood there was an equally devastating assault on the fortunes of the canal by political interference in its management and operation. At the annual meeting in June, 1852, the controlling stockholder, the state of Maryland, acting through its representatives, appointed a new administration for the company. The dominance of the state in company affairs meant, in effect, that the political party in power in Maryland also controlled the selection of the canal board, and indirectly the many subordinates on the line. The latter became the objects of party patronage. Canal positions had been used for party purposes once before in the early forties. At that time there had been two successive sweeps of offices, as the one party installed its political friends and the other promptly reinstated the older officials when it returned to power.[26] Thereafter there had been no large-scale interference for about a decade. The new administration in 1852 proceeded to revive the spoils system in the management of the canal, reaching all the way down to the lock-tenders and bosses in the thoroughness of its sweep.[27] Thereafter, more or less complete reorganizations, reflecting the unsettled con-

[24] *24th Annual Report* (1852), pp. 3-4; *25th Annual Report* (1853), p. 3. The towns of Alexandria and Georgetown, and banks in the District of Columbia advanced the necessary funds.

[25] *27th Annual Report* (1855), p. 12.

[26] See above, pp. 136-137.

[27] Proceedings of Directors, H, 537-541 (July 15, 1852), 550-551 (September 30, 1852), 556 (October 1, 1852).

ditions in Maryland politics, occurred regularly during the fifties and early sixties. As new Boards succeeded the old ones, they promptly replaced their political enemies with party favorites.[28] There was little or no concern for the welfare of the canal.

The serious effects which the continued political interference had on the fortunes of the canal were later graphically described by a group of dissatisfied bondholders.

> Therefore [after 1850] as the State administration changed, so did the management of the canal, until about 1870, when it was ascertained that during the twenty years preceeding [*sic*] there had been a dozen different administrations and executive heads in the management of this once popular and magnificent State Work. As an inevitable consequence of this too much-management the canal became a magnificent failure; transportation was uncertain; the big ditch was gradually filling up; the culverts were delapidated [*sic*]; interest on the bonds was unpaid and largely in arrears; and the bonds themselves sunk in the market to a point below sale or quotation.[29]

For this state of affairs Maryland was solely responsible, the bondholders continued, for

> the State . . . by virtue of her ownership of five Eights of the Capital Stock, has had . . . the Exclusive Management, and has absolutely shaped and controlled the policy of the Company.
>
> Administering its affairs by officers chosen by her; changing those officers with every change of her politics; removing one year officials who had just begun to be familiar with the duties and responsibilities of their position, . . . it is no wonder this great Enterprise has languished. . . . Without a fixed and Stable policy; without a Corps of trained and Experienced officers; without Judicious and systematic Economy, paralysed by perpetual Changes in its administration; the victim of abuses, Mismanagement and lavish Expenditures; its power and influence Constantly used in the Service of [the] political organization which, for the time, appointed its officers and regulated its direction. . .[30]

The wonder is that the waterway survived the frequent shifts

[28] *Ibid.*, I, 181 (June 30, 1855), 277-282 (June 27, 1856), K, 1-10, (March 30-31, 1858), 14-16 (April 15-16, 1858), 19 (May 5, 1858), 183-184 (May 16, 1860), 192-193 (June 2, 1860), 272-275 (February 12, 1862).

[29] "Memorial of Certain Bondholders of the Chesapeake and Ohio Canal Company to the Board of Public Works of Maryland," 53d Annual Meeting (1881), Proceedings of Stockholders, E, 341.

[30] *Ibid.*, p. 343.

of personnel and the variety of reorganizations which it underwent.

The forces of nature continued their assaults on the canal after 1852. No year passed without some interference with navigation. In 1853, a severe drought in the valley caused a five-week suspension of trade in June and July because of low water in the levels below Dams No. 4 and 5. Another dry spell hindered, but did not stop, traffic on the canal in August and September of the same year.[31] Low water in the canal below Dam No. 6 resulted in the loss of two months' trade in 1854. To prevent a recurrence of these failures the Board contracted for a steam pump early in 1855.[32] It was installed at the mouth of the South Branch as proposed in 1852, and was completed in 1856. The first tests proved it to be defective, but, after further work, the company finally accepted it in 1858.[33] In August, 1855, a flash flood washed out a road culvert and caused a partial suspension for three or four weeks. The opening of the canal for business in 1856 was delayed because of the severity of the winter. When another drought in August of the same year brought a renewal of complaints of low water in the canal below Dams No. 4 and 5, the company determined to put an end to the nuisance permanently.[34] In 1853 it had been content merely to repair the old brush and rubble dams.[35] In 1856, it decided to replace them with new, tight, masonry dams, at a much greater expense. Contracts were let for Dam No. 4 in October, 1856, and for Dam No. 5 in January, 1857.[36]

No sooner were the new dams contracted for than a great ice freshet roared down the valley in February, 1857. In fact, not

[31] 25th Annual Meeting (August 3, 1853), Proceedings of Stockholders, D, 471-472; *26th Annual Report* (1854), p. 6; *29th Annual Report* (1857), p. 6.

[32] Proceedings of Directors, I, 143 (January 26, 1855); *27th Annual Report* (1855), p. 6.

[33] *28th Annual Report* (1856), p. 7; Report of the General Committee, 29th Annual Meeting (1857), Proceedings of Stockholders, E, 46; Proceedings of Directors, K, 38 (June 30, 1856).

[34] *28th Annual Report* (1856), pp. 3-4; *29th Annual Report* (1857), pp. 9, 11.

[35] *26th Annual Report* (1854), p. 6; *27th Annual Report* (1855), pp. 4-5.

[36] Proceedings of Directors, I, 298-299 (August 27, 1856), 316 (November 7, 1856); *29th Annual Report* (1857), p. 11.

one, but four successive floods swept over the canal in 1857. The first one badly damaged Dam No. 4 and carried out 500 feet of Dam No. 5. On April 12, after temporary cribs had been installed closing the gaps, a second freshet occurred, undoing some of the work previously thought to be secure. Repairs had again reached an advanced stage and were within a few days of completion on May 4, when the river rose for a third time and poured over the dams. Although workmen waged a four-day struggle to save the structures, the torrent carried off half the repairs that had been made. A fourth flood in the middle of the month delayed repairs for a few days and tore a hole in Dam No. 4.[37]

The disasters of 1857 all but wrecked the company financially. It had never been in better than a precarious condition since the completion of its waterway.[38] Debts had continued to pile up during the decade to add to the already staggering burden of acceptances, balances due, scrip, state loan, and the repair bills after the freshet of 1847.[39] The directors had borrowed heavily from Selden, Withers and Company to pay the semi-annual interest on the construction bonds until the canal could get on its feet.[40] The flood of 1852 suspended even these efforts to meet the most pressing obligations and saddled the company with an additional repair debt.[41] The irregular course of trade in the early fifties and the necessity of making unavoidable repairs prevented the canal boards from reducing the debt

[37] *29th Annual Report* (1857), pp. 12-13.

[38] The expenditure of $100,000 for repairs was authorized, of which $71,000 was borrowed. Proceedings of Directors, I, 356 (May 29, 1857), 366 (August 4, 1857).

[39] *24th Annual Report* (1852), p. 4; *25th Annual Report* (1853), pp. 5-6; Proceedings of Directors, I, 124 (November 8, 1854). Debts that were officially recognized amounted to $1,653,382.92. They were listed under the following categories:

Canal Scrip.........	$457,593.75	Balances due to contractors	$ 89,673.29
Acceptances	154,369.00		
Bonds for Post Notes	6,928.00	Interest (to January 1, 1855)	709,000.00
Bonds for contractors	235,818.88		

This does not include the state loan of $2,000,000 in 1834.

[40] Proceedings of Directors, H, 398 (January 8, 1851), I, 132 (December (1854); *24th Annual Report* (1852), p. 10. In all $143,000 was borrowed.

[41] Proceedings of Directors, H, 532 (June 24, 1852); *24th Annual Report* (1852), p. 10; *27th Annual Report* (1855), p. 12.

burden substantially.[42] The flood of 1857, coming on top of all these debts, almost drove the company into bankruptcy. By a new device, toll certificates, which were sold to the coal companies at 75 per cent of their face value, the directors were able to raise funds to repair the canal and to continue for a while the work on the new dams. Over $116,118.78 secured in this way between 1858 and 1860 was still outstanding in the latter year.[43] By the end of the decade the company was in partial default to the workers and officials on the line for their wages.[44] Bankruptcy and foreclosure were close at hand on the eve of the war and were freely predicted by the canal officials.[45]

The outbreak of the war in 1861 came at a time when the fortunes of the waterway seemed to be approaching their lowest point.[46] As a result of the secession of Virginia, the canal found itself on the border between the Union and the Confederacy, in the path of the contending armies. Consequently during the first two or three years of the conflict, its trade was greatly reduced and its works alternately occupied and/or destroyed by the opposing forces. The condition of the company and its properties materially deteriorated from even the gloomy pre-war status. Only toward the end of the war when interference with navigation declined did its trade and financial status improve.

During the first few years of the war, great destruction was wrought upon the canal and its trade. In 1861 and 1862

[42] On the contrary, the company increased its obligations by assuming the debt of Hunter, Harris and Company, contractors for the completion of the canal, to the amount of $260,000. *27th Annual Report* (1855), p. 9. See also, *Application of Hunter, Harris & Co. to the Chesapeake and Ohio Canal Company for relief* [August, 1853].

[43] Proceedings of Directors, K, 80-81 (January 6, 1859); *33d Annual Report* (1861), pp. 5-6. The Board requested holders of the certificates not to use them before August 1, 1859, and then required tolls to be paid at least 50 per cent in current money. See Proceedings of Directors, K, 91 (March 3, 1859).

[44] Proceedings of Directors, K, 152-153 (January 6, 1860). The Board however, refused to issue toll certificates to pay the workers.

[45] There were gloomy predictions of failure as early as 1856. See, for example, *28th Annual Report* (1856), p. 6.

[46] The account of the canal during the Civil War is the substance of my article published in the *Journal of Southern History*, XI, No. 1 (February, 1945).

Southern troops cut its embankment at vital places, tried to blow up some of the dams, and attempted other spot destruction in order to halt trade on the waterway. At the same time they tried to prevent repairs by harassing the canal workers.[47] In September, 1862, advance forces of Lee's first invasion of Maryland again breached the banks and damaged some of the locks to stop canal traffic. Repairs which had been begun with federal aid after the repulse of the Confederates were delayed by further raids in October and November.[48] Lee's second invasion in June and July, 1863, wrought the same type of destruction and again the activities of rebel pickets hindered repairs after the withdrawal of the main forces.[49] In 1864, other raids, this time by Early, Mosby, and White, caused widespread damage to the canal. Boat-burning and mule-stealing had become regular occurrences by then, while the more permanent and expensive works—locks and aqueducts—continued to be damaged or destroyed.[50] The raids lasted from June to November despite the pleas of canal officials for adequate protection at the numerous ferries across the upper Potomac, especially during periods of low water in the river.[51] If any-

[47] Baltimore *American*, June 11, 1861; Washington *Evening Star*, June 11, 14, 1861; A. Spates to W. S. Ringgold, Clerk, June 13, 1861; A. K. Stake to A. Spates, June 26, July 6, 1861; A Spates to Ringgold, August 13, 1861; S. P. Smith to Ringgold, October 23, 1861. See also the purported copy of Confederate orders for the destruction of Dam No. 6, dated October 20, 1861, in an anonymous pamphlet, *To the People of Maryland: The Canal and its Management Vindicated* (n. d.).

[48] G. Spates to Ringgold, September 13, October 6, November 26, 1862; J. Masters, to Ringgold, September 22, 1862; A. Spates to Ringgold, October 6, 1862; T. Hassett to Ringgold, October 14, 1862; Washington *Evening Star*, September 26, 1862.

[49] L. Lowe to Ringgold, June 20, 1863; G. Spates to President and Directors, June 30, 1863; Masters to Ringgold, July 19, 1863; H. Miller to Ringgold, July 22, 1863; A. C. Greene to Ringgold, July 25, 1863; Masters to President and Directors, August 4, 1863.

[50] A. Spates to Ringgold, July 5, 1864; G. Spates to Ringgold, July 16, 1864; Masters to Ringgold, July 18, 1864; Miller to Ringgold, July 18, 1864; L. Benton to Ringgold, July 20, 1864; Lowe to Ringgold, July 25, 1864; G. Spates to President and Directors, July 25, 1864. In all, about sixty boats were burned during Early's raid.

[51] Greene to Ringgold, September 2, 1864; Greene to A. Spates, September 29, 1864; Masters to President and Directors, October 3, 1864; G. Spates to Ringgold, October 16, 1864. The Washington *National Intelligencer*, July 15, 1864, contains a masterly and devastating summary and criticism of the Lincoln administration for its lack of an effective Shenandoah policy.

thing, the destructive purpose and results of the raids became more vicious in the latter years of the war, although they did not cause such long suspensions of navigation or interfere with the revival of trade on the waterway.

In addition to the damage caused by the battles raging across its line, the canal suffered as the result of the occupation of its works from time to time by the rival armies and by the federal government. In the course of their belligerent operations, Confederate troops seized and held portions of the canal during the summer of 1861, 1862, 1863, and 1864. Federal troops moved into position along the line in 1861, and remained for protection and patrol throughout most of the war. The federal government also occupied portions of the canal property, including the Rock Creek mole,[52] the Potomac Aqueduct, and at times fleets of canal boats. The government took over the aqueduct in 1861, drained it and converted it to a bridge, thus depriving the canal of its only practicable outlet to the river at tidewater.[53] In March and April, 1862, during the panic accompanying the spectre of the Merrimac running wild on the Potomac and bombarding Washington, the government seized about one hundred canal boats.[54] These were taken to Georgetown and held there for use in case of emergency. As the period of forced inactivity lengthened, shippers and canal officials became restless and complained bitterly about government interference and red tape.[55] Amid rumors and premature

[52] It was still occupying portions of the mole as late as 1867. Proceedings of Directors, L, 56 (October 23, 1867); William Godey to Ringgold, January 10, 1868.

[53] Skirmishing occurred at the aqueduct as early as May 2, 1862. On May 24, Federal troops occupied the Virginia shore opposite Washington. By December 5, the bridge over the aqueduct was being built. On December 16, the water was drawn off to permit the erection of the trestling for the bridge, and by December 23, a dam had been placed across the Georgetown entrance of the aqueduct, closing it to the trade of the canal. Washington *Evening Star*, May 2, 24, December 5, 16, 23, 1862.

[54] J. Wolfe to Ringgold, March 10, 1862; Greene to Ringgold, April 11, 1862. On the panic of the Cabinet, see *Diary of Gideon Welles* (3 vols., Boston, 1911), I, 61 ff.

[55] Greene, an agent of the Borden Mining Company as well as a director of the canal, wrote that in his opinion nothing "stronger than redtape or indifference" was holding the boats in Georgetown, and that it looked almost like a "conspiracy" between the government and Pennsylvania interests to destroy the coal trade of Maryland in favor of that of its northern neighbor. Greene to Ringgold, April 11, 1862.

announcements of their pending release, about thirty-six of the boats were loaded with rock and taken down the river. There they were to be sunk if necessary to block the channel. Some six or eight of them eventually were sunk. The other craft were subsequently released and returned to their owners.[56] Later, however, in October, 1862, and in June and July, 1863, more of the boats were seized by the government for briefer periods.[57]

A third way in which the war adversely affected the fortunes of the canal was in the destruction of its markets and the damage wrought to some of the mills along the course. The mere existence of a state of war reduced the coastal trade which had created some of the demand for canal coal. The Treasury Department soon stepped in and restricted the coastwise shipment of coal to the region north of the mouth of the Delaware river.[58] In this area, Cumberland coal faced severe competition from Pennsylvania coal.[59] The institution of the Potomac blockade by federal forces also handicapped the coastal trade of canal coal from the port of Georgetown.[60] The subsequent easing of both the shipping restrictions and the blockade came none too soon.[61] The effect of the war on some of the mills along the canal can be seen in the experiences of two widely

[56] Ringgold to Greene, March 24, April 16, 1862, Letter Book M, 31, 36; Greene to Ringgold, April 26, 1862; *Diary of Gideon Welles*, I, 66-67. See also, War Department Order No. 44, April 21, 1862, in *The War of the Rebellion: A Compilation of the Official Records of the Union and Confederate Armies* (129 vols. and index, Washington, 1880-1901), Series I, Vol. XII, Part III, p. 97. Cited hereinafter as *Official Records*.

[57] War Department Circular, October 24, 1862, confirming Order No. 44, filed in Letters Received, December, 1863; Washington *Evening Star*, July 15, 1863.

[58] Washington *National Intelligencer*, April 21, 1862. Two of the better markets for canal coal were South America and the British West Indies. These would be eliminated by the prohibition as first issued. See *45th Annual Report* (1873), p. 16.

[59] Greene to Ringgold, April 7, 11, 1862. In the second of these letters, Greene wrote. "In the meantime the Penna. interests are moving heaven and earth to maintain themselves in the ground they were enabled to occupy by our disasters last summer." They had reduced charges 30 cents a ton, he continued, and would go further, "in order to exclude us from market another year, when an attempt to regain it on our part will be almost impossible."

[60] Washington *Evening Star*, May 2, 1861. There was much unemployment among river pilots because of the blockade and the stagnation of trade.

[61] Washington *National Intelligencer*, April 21, 1862. The Treasury department modified the prohibition to read: "ports north of Cape St. Rogue, South America, and west of that longitude."

separated examples. A large cotton factory in Georgetown, a user of water power from the canal, was cut off from its supply of raw material and forced to shut down in 1861.[62] Farther up the river, another mill was caught in the ebb and flow of the military operations, and was alternately occupied by troops and idle because of the lack of water power from the damaged canal.[63]

The effect of the restrictions and destruction of the war on the business of the canal was almost disastrous. Military operations resulted in the virtual extinction of canal trade from late April to early August, 1861.[64] September and October, always the best months for the canal, showed only a slight revival.[65] From a business standpoint, the following year 1862, was on the whole even worse. Although there was no single month as poor as May, June or July, 1861, between the seizure of the canal boats in the spring and the rebel raids in the summer and fall, no month witnessed a satisfactory amount of business.[66] So complete was the severance of trade that in

[62] J. Pryor Williamson and Co. (Pioneer Cotton Factory) to President and Directors, June 20, 1861. The reasons assigned for the shut-down were: high wages, high prices and scarcity of raw cotton, lack of markets for finished goods, and ruined credit.

[63] Jacob Miller to President and Directors, May 1, 1863. He wrote that his mill was occupied by troops in the spring of 1862. After that, the water was out of the canal from July 1 to 12, for twelve days in August, and from September 14, 1862, on. During the last named period of suspension his mill was again occupied by troops, first as a hospital after the battle of Antietam and then as a pickets' rendezvous. When the soldiers moved out, they left the mill a wreck, taking everything movable with them and destroying what they could not carry off. By then it was too late in the year to resume operation, even if the repair materials had been available.

[64] *33d Anual Report* (1861), Appendix C, p. 14; *34th Annual Report* (1862), Appendix B, p. 9.

	1860	1861		1860	1861
May	$19,214.19	$657.36	July	$23,051.10	$ 16.94
June	18,529.60	206.27	August	28,005.02	2,444.07

So complete was the suspension of trade in 1861 that the President reported there was "comparatively no business on the Canal before September." *34th Annual Report* (1862), p. 3.

[65] *33d Annual Report* (1861), Appendix C, p. 14; *34th Annual Report* (1862), Appendix B, p. 9. Tolls received:

	1860	1861
September	$33,084.04	$10,509.22
October	32,547.54	17,793.22

[66] *35th Annual Report* (1863), Appendix B, p. 8.

August an agent of one of the coal companies and a director of the canal wrote in exasperation, "There has been no real through navigation on the canal this year."[67] Even after the revival of trade in 1863, the canal was harassed and often set back in its recovery by rebel activity. Lee's second invasion and the raids which followed it in 1863 reduced trade from the middle of June until early in October. July of that year was the worst single month for canal navigation since July, 1861.[68] Early's raid in July, 1864, followed by Mosby's and White's incursions in August and September halted for a while what promised to be the best year in the canal's history. The month of August saw no through navigation at all, giving the canal its new low for a single month since July, 1861.[69] By this time, even the threat or rumor of a raid was sufficient to send the boatmen scurrying for shelter.[70] But perhaps the most severe set-back in business experienced by the canal due at least in part to the irregularity of navigation during the war was the loss of two-thirds of its share of the flour trade.[71] In the years before the canal reached Cumberland and the coal fields, this trade had practically supported the company through its darkest days and even after coal had supplanted it as the principal

[67] Greene to Ringgold, August 11, 1862. Of course the invasion in September and October of that year ruined the trade on the canal for these months. Tolls fell to $5,282.48 and $538.78, respectively. *35th Annual Report* (1863), Appendix B, p. 6.

[68] *36th Annual Report* (1864), Appendix B, p. 10. Tolls for July, 1863, amounted to $480.06.

[69] *37th Annual Report* (1865), Appendix B, p. 10. Tolls for August amounted to only $398.80. See also Washington *Evening Star*, August 22, September 13, 1864.

[70] Greene to Ringgold, September 2, 1863; Greene to A. Spates, September 29, 1864; G. Spates to Ringgold, October 16, 1864.

[71] Charles Embry and Son to H. W. Dellinger, a canal director, April 26, 1862. The Baltimore and Ohio Railroad had made a determined effort to win the flour trade away from the canal in the forties. (Reizenstein, pp. 82-83.) Notwithstanding those efforts, the flour trade continued to be one of the larger though erratic sources of canal revenue. From 14,880 tons in 1843, it rose to 25,761 tons in 1851 and fell to 11,087 tons in 1860. In 1861 it had dropped to 7,067 tons, and after a slight recovery it had declined to 5,962 tons and 5,383 tons in 1864 and 1865 respectively. *16th Annual Report* (1844), Appendix No. 11, p. 46 (10½ barrels equals a ton), for 1843; *24th Annual Report* (1852), Appendix b, p. 26, for 1851; *33d Annual Report* (1861), Appendix C, p. 16, for 1860; *34th Annual Report* (1862), Appendix B, p. 11, for 1861; *37th Annual Report* (1865), Appendix B, p. 12, for 1864; *38th Annual Report* (1866), Appendix C, p. 15, 1865.

article of trade, it remained a large and lucrative business for the canal.

The sharp reduction in its business was accompanied by declining revenues. This added to the financial crisis which the canal had faced at the beginning of the war. While the company's income dropped from $191,890.20 in 1860 to $75,-741.90 in 1861 and $72,624.95 in 1862, its operating expenses maintained themselves at an irreducible minimum of approximately $100,000 a year.[72] Thus the canal was forced to struggle through several more bleak years by means of further loans from the coal companies in the form of toll certificates and by continued partial non-payment of salaries to its employees.[73] Receipt of the toll certificates was almost immediately suspended in the face of continued business failure, and the redemption of them was only gradually restored in the latter years of the war.[74] Meanwhile the rising cost of living brought demands from the canal employees for higher wages.[75] In view of the immediate and pressing needs of the company for every cent of its revenue, necessary repairs were poorly and hastily made, and important improvements—the raising of the Georgetown bridges or the construction of an inclined plane above the aqueduct—were postponed.[76]

The canal experienced many lesser difficulties or annoyances

[72] *33d Annual Report* (1861), Appendix B, p. 12; *34th Annual Report* (1862), Appendix A, p. 7. *35th Annual Report* (1863), Appendix A, p. 6.

[73] *34th Annual Report* (1862), Appendix G, p. 16. The extent of the non-payment of wages is shown by the following comparison of expenses and expenditures.

	1860	1861	1862
Expenses	$32,636.15	$32,257.65	$28,537.37
Amount paid	28,247.06	14,701.82	18,285.91

33d Annual Report (1861), Appendix B, p. 12, and D, p. 17; *34th Annual Report* (1862), Appendix A, p. 7, and C, p. 12; *35th Annual Report* (1863), Appendix A, p. 6, and C, p. 11.

[74] Proceedings of Directors, K, 238 (October 1, 1861). Certificates worth more than $17,000 were still outstanding on May 31, 1865. *37th Annual Report* (1865), Appendix H, p. 20.

[75] Petition, numerously signed, to President and Directors, April, 1863; G. Spates to President and Directors, March 31, 1864.

[76] Testimony of Alfred Spates, before the committee of the Maryland General Assembly investigating the Chesapeake and Ohio Canal, *Report of the Joint Standing Committee . . . in the Chesapeake and Ohio Canal Investigation* (Annapolis, 1880), pp. 494-495.

during the course of the conflict which are directly attributable to the war. Disloyalty among the canal officials and employees was an ogre which continued to harass the Board of Directors. In January, 1861, a director and former president of the company wrote sympathetically of the divided sentiment in Frederick, his home town, towards the impending break-up of the Union.[77] Apparently he was more discreet in the expression of his sentiments after the outbreak of war than was the wartime president of the company, Alfred Spates. The latter was thrice arrested and detained by military authorities for disloyal conduct.[78] An engineer engaged in the construction of the new masonry dam (No. 5) was also imprisoned briefly in 1863 for the same reason.[79] In 1862 and 1863 there were several complaints of disloyalty against George Spates, a superintendent on the Monocacy division, and against several of the men under him.[80]

The effect of the draft was greatly feared, although in operation it was not so serious. The first announcement of the scheme elicited a letter from the company requesting blanket deferment for canal employees.[81] Several lock-keepers who were eventually drafted borrowed money and paid for substitutes, and then petitioned the company for the payment of overdue wages.[82] In another case, where no substitute could be obtained, the lock-keeper's family carried on his work.[83]

The disposition of troops along the line was the cause of some excitement. The discovery of gold at Great Falls by California troops stationed there caused a momentary flurry.[84]

[77] L. J. Brengle to Ringgold, January 1, 1861.

[78] Baltimore *American*, September 3, 1863, January 25, 1864; Fred Fickey, Jr., Maryland Commissioner of Public Works, to Ringgold, September 1, 3, 1863; Brengle to [Ringgold], September 15, 1863; Greene to Ringgold, January 25, 1864.

[79] Brengle to [Ringgold], September 15, 1863; Stake to Brengle, September 17, 1863; Washington *Evening Star*, September 2, 1863.

[80] Capt. R. C. Bomford to Directors, August 28, 1862; Proceedings of Directors, K, 361 (December 17, 1863).

[81] Ringgold to Stanton, August 21, 1862, Letter Book M, p. 56.

[82] J. G. White to Board of Directors, April 10, 1863.

[83] G. Spates to Directors, October 30, 1864.

[84] E. B. Swanson to A. B. Cammerer, October 26, 1938, MS, in National Capital Parks, File 1460 (Chesapeake and Ohio Canal), in Department of Interior, Washington D. C.

The presence of so large a body of soldiers also brought problems of health to plague canal officials.[85] Finally, the proximity of the battlefield on occasion resulted in the hasty conversion of canal property to hospitals and morgues.[86]

Meanwhile, the older problems of the canal continued to interfere with its success. Political influence brought about the wholesale turnover of employees in 1860 and 1862.[87] Although these appointments were the last during the war years, the men who were appointed in 1862 were not particularly attentive to their duties, according to the testimony of canal officials as well as others.[88] And the top officials continued to intrigue in state politics throughout the war.[89] The canal also experienced the usual trouble with floods and droughts. Freshets were especially severe in the dark years of 1861 and 1862,[90] while serious droughts were noted in the summers of 1862 and 1863.[91] The latter were of great concern both for the effect on trade and for the increased danger of rebel raids from across the river during periods of low water.

Despite the troubles of the early years, the canal was an important transportation agency during the war. Between raids and repairs the canal did yeoman service for the Union, hauling troops and supplies, particularly the precious coal which the government hoarded so jealously.[92] The canal provided the

[85] Baltimore *American*, June 8, 1861; Washington *Evening Star*, October 28, 1861; S. P. Smith to Ringgold, October 23, 1861.

[86] J. Miller to President and Directors, May 1, 1863. G. Spates to President and Directors, November 30, 1864.

[87] Proceedings of Directors, K, 183-184 (May 16, 1860), 192-193 (June 2, 1860), 273-275 (February 12, 1862).

[88] Ringgold to Greene, August 8, 1862, Letter Book M, 56; Greene to Ringgold, August 11, 12, 1862; Capt. R. C. Bomford to Directors, August 28, 1862; Chambers to Directors, December 10, 1862; Hassett to president and directors, May 4, 1863.

[89] A. Spates to Ringgold, May 12, 1863. There was to be no meeting of the Board of Public Works that year, to avoid a reorganization of it. See also, B. B. Bootman, lock-keeper, to directors, April 4, 1862.

[90] Baltimore *American*, April 16, 19, June 11, 1861; Washington *Evening Star*, April 17, 1861; C. Embry and Son to Dellinger, April 26, 1862 (reporting the seventh highwater in seventeen months); Greene to Ringgold, April 29, 1862; Masters to Ringgold, April 13, 1864.

[91] Greene to Ringgold, August 6, 1362; September 2, 1863.

[92] Baltimore *American*, May 27, 30, 1861; Washington *National Intelligencer*, March 10, 1862; Washington *Evening Star*, September 12, 1862.

sole direct link between Washington and Harpers Ferry for the transportation of men and materials to that important post, as well as to other points in the Potomac valley. Only late in the war did the government begin to realize the importance of Harpers Ferry and the whole Shenandoah valley, and only then did the weakness of the connection provided by the waterway become apparent.

The canal, together with the river, was a natural defense line for the Union troops, and it was used as such during a large part of the war on the upper Potomac. The canal also provided the government with an established route of communication, staffed by sufficient personnel, along the boundary between North and South. In December, 1862, the Treasury Department took cognizance of this fact by appointing six of the employees along the line to act as revenue agents.[93]

The bleakness of the early years of the conflict was largely reversed toward the end of the struggle. Despite continuing raids and occupation, business on the canal began to revive in 1863 and improved steadily until the end of the war. Trade rose from a low of 126,793 tons in 1862 to 265,847 in 1863 and 290,772 in 1864.[94] The improvement in business was paralleled by increasing revenues. The general inflationary tendency of prices toward the end of the war also permitted the toll on coal to be raised from ¼ cent a ton per mile to 5/16 cent a ton in April, 1863, to ⅜ cent a ton in April, 1864, and finally to ½ cent a ton in July, 1864.[95] Annual revenues soared to $163,024.10 in 1863, $234,699.30 in 1864 and $359,734.56 in 1865.[96]

On the strength of this sudden financial prosperity, and at the expense of effecting permanent repairs, the company raised the wages of its employees[97] and began to pay off its debts. It was immediately deluged with requests for relief from long-suffering claimants. The federal government demanded the

[93] A. Spates to Ringgold, December 1, 1862; Proceedings of Directors, K, 315 (December 11, 1862).

[94] See Appendix, Table IV.

[95] Proceedings of Directors, K, 329 (April 10, 1863), 382 (April 15, 1864), 395 (July 28, 1864).

[96] See Appendix, Table V.

[97] Proceedings of Directors, K, 383 (April 15, 1864).

payment of its tax on canal revenues, amounting to 2½ per cent of the gross receipts. This claim the Board of Directors rejected, insisting that by its charter, the canal was tax exempt.[98] By 1865, the Board was able to boast that it had paid off all debts contracted by it and about $150,000 of the more recent obligations of its predecessors.[99]

The canal emerged from the war on both a somber note and a hopeful one. The waterway itself had suffered great physical damage from the depredations of the opposing armies. Furthermore, the government continued to occupy the Potomac Aqueduct and part of the Rock Creek mole, to the detriment of the canal's business.[100] On the other hand, the company's finances had measurably improved as a result of the revival of trade in the latter years of the conflict. Bankruptcy no longer seemed to be so near. And the improved commercial and financial status of the company made it possible to undertake necessary and long-delayed repairs and improvements.

The physical condition of the canal in 1865 was much worse than it had been before the war. Despite growing trade and revenues and some increase in repair expenditures toward the end of the conflict, the waterway had for the most part been badly neglected. The destruction of its works in the war had been serious. In addition it had not received the attention required for normal maintenance. The Board had made only the most necessary repairs, and then usually in a hasty and slipshod fashion.[101] The Rock Creek basin was largely filled in by the deposits of the creek, and was being infringed upon by the extension of the city streets.[102] The tidal lock was also out of repair after being damaged by government occupation and

[98] R. B. Ferguson, Assistant Assessor, U. S. Bureau of Internal Revenue, to Ringgold, August 27, 1864.

[99] A. Spates to the Speaker of the Maryland House of Delegates, March 13, 1865, Letter Book M, 176.

[100] Proceedings of Directors, K, 511 (September 5, 1866); *ibid.*, L, 56 (October 23, 1867); Bvt. Lt. Col. James Moore to Ringgold, May 28, 1866; William Godey to Ringgold, January 10, 1868 (reporting that the government was about to surrender its portion of the mole).

[101] Manning to President and Directors, May 31, 1866.

[102] James C. Clarke to the Governor and Board of Public Works of the District of Columbia, November 8, 1871, Proceedings of Directors, L, 459 (October 11, 1871).

operation.[103] The lower dams, Nos. 1, 2, and 3, were reported to be in poor condition.[104] The heavy traffic on the towpath had worn it down, and necessitated repairs at many points.[105] The prism of the trunk itself was shrinking as a result of deposits on the inner slopes and the floor of the canal. The Washington Canal and the Tiber Creek extension of the Chesapeake and Ohio were said to be impassable because of bars and refuse in the waterway.[106] The occurrence of many breaches in the spring and summer of 1865 indicated the general state of deterioration of the canal.[107]

Sorely needed improvements had been postponed and those in progress had come to a halt during the war years.[108] Work on the new masonry Dam No. 5 continued intermittently during 1861 and 1862, and then stopped. Although the closing of the Potomac Aqueduct seriously inconvenienced canal trade, the company had no funds with which to raise the low bridges in Georgetown or to construct the proposed inclined planes from the canal to the river above the aqueduct.[109] In 1863, Congress finally appropriated $13,000 to raise the bridges, after having deprived the company of the use of the aqueduct in the preceding year. The actual work did not get under way until after the war, however, for no contracts were let until April, 1865.[110]

The restoration and improvement of the canal began almost immediately after the conclusion of the war.[111] Construction of the masonry dam replacing the temporary structure at Dam No. 5 was resumed, and by 1866 over half of it had been completed. The Board also considered plans for the improve-

[103] Proceedings of Directors, K, 489 (May 10, 1866); *39th Annual Report* (1867), p. 5.

[104] *38th Annual Report* (1866), p. 5.

[105] John Cameron to President and Directors, November 9, 1865.

[106] Proceedings of Directors, K, 489 (May 10, 1866).

[107] See the numerous letters of complaint, Letters Received, April-July, 1865.

[108] Manning to President and Directors, May 31, 1866.

[109] Testimony of A. Spates, *Report of the Joint Standing Committee . . . in the Chesapeake and Ohio Canal Investigation*, pp. 494-495.

[110] Proceedings of Directors, K, 325 (March 12, 1863), 422 (April 12, 1865).

[111] Manning to President and Directors, February 1, May 31, 1866.

ment of Dams Nos. 1 and 3.[112] In the same year, the company finally came to an agreement with the corporate authorities of Georgetown concerning the manner of raising the bridges over the canal. The work began promptly, and the new structures were ready by 1867. The directors ordered the basin to be cleaned out and the outlet lock repaired in anticipation of the resumption of trade through Georgetown.[113] Several proposals were made without success for the resolution of the extension from Rock Creek to Tiber Creek.

The postwar years were not without their difficulties, however. Heavy floods occurred in the Potomac valley in 1865 and 1866. The freshet in the latter year swept away sixty feet of the temporary coffer Dam No. 5. In the spring of 1868, an ice freshet carried off one-half of Dam No. 1.[114] The end of the war also brought a depression in trade as the demand for coal declined from the wartime peaks. At the same time wage disputes broke out between the miners and the coal companies, interfering with the coal trade in May and June, 1865, and again in the spring of 1866.[115] In the face of the deflationary tendency of coal prices and the decreasing demand for that product, the Board reduced tolls to 4 mills per ton in September, 1866, and back to ¼ cent a ton per mile in March, 1868.[116] The interference of local political influence also returned after the war. The brief period between 1865 and 1870 witnessed no less than four changes in canal administration. Along with the frequent political upheavals charges of fraudulence were

[112] *38th Annual Report* (1866), pp. 4-5; Proceedings of Directors, K, 491-492 (May 10, 1866).

[113] *39th Annual Report* (1867), p. 5. See also the Ordinance of the Corporation of Georgetown, June 26, 1866, permitting the substitution of iron bridges for stone ones, so as to prevent a change in street grades. (Letters Received.)

[114] *39th Annual Report* (1867), p. 5; Isaac Mans to President and Directors, July 11, 1868.

[115] *37th Annual Report* (1865), p. 6; *38th Annual Report* (1866), pp. 3, 5; *39th Annual Report* (1867), p. 3; Manning to Ringgold, April 22, 1866; Greene to Ringgold, April 27, 1866 (reporting the backbone of the strike broken).

[116] Proceedings of Directors, K, 511 (September 5, 1866); *ibid.*, L, 82 (March 26, 1868). See also the petitions of the coal companies, June 12, 1865 and March 16, 1866; Greene to Ringgold, March 16, 1866, and the petition of Allegany County citizens, March, 1868.

placed against the former administrators. The wartime president, Alfred Spates, was accused of falsely obtaining for his own purposes appropriations for work already paid for.[117] Although the evidence presented indicates a strong probability of misconduct, a later administration, apparently more favorable to Mr. Spates, dropped all charges without further investigation.[118]

Despite unsettled trade conditions, political interference, and the appropriation of large amounts for the work of restoration and improvement, the financial condition of the company continued to improve. Canal trade recovered quickly from each setback, rising to a new high each year and reaching a peak of 723,938 tons in 1869. Receipts averaged over $375,000 a year except in 1868.[119] By 1867, the company had paid off all but $10,000 of its floating debt of $300,000, which had been acquired since the late forties.[120] It was then ready to resume the payment of its long-term obligations according to the priorities laid down by the court in the case of Commonwealth of Virginia *vs.* the Chesapeake and Ohio Canal Company.[121] The first on the list were the repair bonds of 1849 and the interest on them. Repayment on these finally began in 1869.[122]

[117] Proceedings of Directors, L, 233-245 (December 9, 1869). There were no less than nine separate charges in the accusation.

[118] Thomas Anderson, counsel, to J. C. Clarke, July 15, 1870; Proceedings of Directors, L, 380-381 (December 8, 1870).

[119] See Appendix, Tables IV and V.

[120] *39th Annual Report* (1867), p. 6 ($301,024.25).

[121] Commonwealth of Virginia *vs.* Chesapeake and Ohio Canal Company, 32 Maryland 501.

[122] Proceedings of Directors, L, 226-231 (December 9, 1869).

CHAPTER XI

THE GOLDEN AGE OF THE CANAL

(1870-1889)

The appointment of James C. Clarke as president of the canal company in June, 1870, marked the beginning of the most stable and prosperous period in the history of the waterway. During his administration and that of his successor, Arthur P. Gorman, the canal enjoyed five years of unprecedented financial profits. For the first time the waterway gave promise of fulfilling the hopes of its promoters. The brief reign of President Clarke paved the way for the spectacular prosperity of the canal under A. P. Gorman. The Board of Directors continued the program of restoration and improvement, fostered the growth of trade to record levels, and continued payments on the long-term debts of the company.

Despite the repairs already made, there was still much to be done. The chief engineer recommended a thorough overhauling of the canal in 1871, including repairs to locks, aqueducts, and the waterway itself.[1] The restoration of the Washington branch was discussed, but no agreement was reached for either its improvement or its abandonment. Inasmuch as few boats had used it in the past fifteen years and none since 1860, nothing was done.[2] The Board considered ways and means of expediting traffic through the tunnel. The great increase in canal trade had resulted in frequent and long delays at the tunnel while the boats awaited their turn to enter the long and narrow passage. There were two proposals, one for a system of signals to show when the boats might enter and the

[1] Proceedings of Directors, L, 439 (September 12, 1871); *Report for the Year 1870* (February, 1871), p. 9. The cost of the proposed repairs was set at $78,000.

[2] Proceedings of Directors, L, 463 ff. (November 10, 1871). Yet the canal could not be abandoned without the consent of the city of Washington. See also 43d Annual Meeting (December 29, 1871), Proceedings of Stockholders, E, 184; *ibid.* (January 4, 1872), pp. 196-197.

other for the assignment of a watchman to direct traffic. The directors adopted the latter method.[3]

Trade continued to improve somewhat irregularly. After reaching a total of 723,938 tons in 1869, commerce on the waterway fell off slightly to 661,772 tons in 1870, but soared to a record peak of 968,827 tons in 1871.[4] A minor freshet in 1870, a strike of boatmen and dock laborers in 1871, and a drought which lasted from August to October in the same year did not perceptibly interfere with the rapidly expanding prosperity of the waterway.[5] Business was so active in 1871 and 1872 that canal shippers found it difficult to obtain enough coasting vessels to load coal at Georgetown. Stocks piled up on the wharves forcing a deliberate curtailment of shipments over the canal.[6]

The method of expediting trade on the Georgetown level soon became the major obstacle to the continued growth of business. Unloading and transfer facilities were unable to handle the increasing tonnage which was brought to them. As a result, boats lined up in the canal awaiting their turn to unload. Not only were the delays annoying and costly to the boatmen, shippers, and company alike, but the congestion on the Georgetown level was a problem in itself. The waterway was not wide enough to accommodate both the ordinary traffic to and from the basin or the aqueduct and the clamoring boatmen awaiting access to the coal wharves. The president of the company summarized conditions in the following words in December, 1871.

> As it now is, it is not unfrequently the case that from sixty to eighty boats have to lie along the Canal bank singly, so as to allow sufficient room in the Canal for boats to pass in opposite directions. Often a string of loaded boats from half mile to a mile in length is seen lying

---

[3] *Report for the Year 1870* (February, 1871), pp. 7-8.

[4] See Appendix, Table IV.

[5] Proceedings of Directors, L, 365 (October 12, 1870), 392 (January 11, 1871); *Report of the President for the Year 1871* (December, 1871), p. 5; 43d Annual Meeting (December 29, 1871), Proceedings of Stockholders, E, 182. The tonnage of boats was reduced from 100-115 to 85-90 tons during the drought.

[6] *Report for the Year 1871* (December, 1871), p. 5; Proceedings of Directors, M, 14 (May 10, 1872).

above the Collector's Office in Georgetown, waiting their turn to get to the wharves to discharge their cargoes.[7]

There were two courses which the Board might follow to alleviate the congestion at the eastern end of the canal. One grew out of the greater demand for water for purposes of navigation as a result of the increased trade. The easiest way to supply this need was by stricter control of water leases and to stop the abuses that had come about in the use of the surplus water. This could be best accomplished by compelling the return of the water gauges to the canal bank where they could be controlled by the company. The Clarke administration attempted to carry out this policy but was unable to achieve complete success in the face of the bitter opposition of the millers.

The other course which the Board adopted to reduce the delay in unloading on the Georgetown level was the construction of outlet locks above the aqueduct, connecting with the river. This alternative had been proposed during the Civil War after the government took over the aqueduct, but had been postponed because of the lack of funds. The present administration, while admitting that the locks were the obvious answer to the problem it faced, refused to undertake the expense of construction. It preferred to devote its sizable profits to the payment of interest on the bonds of 1844. Fortunately, private capital was willing to build the locks if guaranteed the right to charge a fee for the use of them sufficient to insure a return on the investment. This arrangement was satisfactory to the canal company, as long as it retained the option to purchase the locks whenever its funds would permit. On these terms a contract with H. H. Dodge was made in the spring of 1872.[8]

The commercial prosperity which the canal enjoyed at the opening of the decade made possible a further improvement in its financial condition. The repayment of the long-term obligations of the company, which had begun in 1869, proceeded

[7] Report of the President, 43d Annual Meeting (December 29, 1871), Proceedings of Stockholders, E, 187-188.

[8] 43d Annual Meeting (December 29, 1871 and January 4, 1872), Proceedings of Stockholders, E, 187, 198-199; *ibid.*, (April 23, 1872), pp. 215-222; Proceedings of Directors M, 19-24 (May 10, 1872).

rapidly according to the order of priority laid down by the courts. By 1871, the Board had paid in full the last of the interest and principal of the repair bonds of 1849.[9] The directors then turned immediately to the payment of the back interest on the construction bonds of 1844. The last coupon paid on these bonds had been the one in January, 1852. An earlier Board had funded coupons falling due in July, 1852, January and July, 1853, and January, 1854.[10] The Clarke administration therefore began with the first of the unprotected coupons, for July, 1854, and January, 1855. In May and June, 1872, it authorized the payment of these coupons, marking the beginning of a new era in canal finances.[11]

In June, 1872, another revolution occurred in the direction of the Chesapeake and Ohio Canal Company. The regular Democratic party secured control of the Maryland Board of Public Works which promptly chose Arthur P. Gorman to be the new president of the company. The choice was not a popular one because of the political connections of the appointee and the office and because the two years of the Clarke administration had been the most successful in the canal's history. The new incumbent was an ambitious young member of the Maryland legislature, a delegate from Howard County. Contemporary observers expected him to run the company as an adjunct of Democratic party patronage. He proceeded to live up to expectations, and in so doing built a machine that carried him to the leadership of his party in the state and to an influential position in national party councils. However, he also applied his energy and acumen to the problems of the waterway, perhaps considering it a challenge to his ability. In him the canal company gained for the first time a politically powerful president, who was an energetic promoter of its interests and an able antagonist of the Baltimore and Ohio's dominance in the state. During his administration the Chesapeake and Ohio Canal Company reached the zenith of its prosperity and influence.

The new directors took over the program of reconditioning and improvement undertaken by the Clarke regime. They carried

[9] Proceedings of Directors, L, 412 (June 22, 1871).
[10] *Ibid.*, I, 37 (July 29, 1853).
[11] *Ibid.*, M, 15 (May 10, 1872), 31 (June 10, 1872).

to completion the restoration of the canal to its original satisfactory condition. By 1874, the waterway had regained its full prism, and the strength of its banks had so increased that a freshet which completely submerged the canal on the levels below Dams No. 4 and No. 5 did no appreciable damage.[12] Improvements beyond the mere restoration of the waterway included the macadamizing of a part of the towpath on the Monocacy division, on which the clay was so bad that the path was hardly passable in wet weather. The president also suggested the purchase of additional steam stone-crushers and the macadamization of the entire towpath.[13] The extent of canal improvements was at least partially reflected in the increased tonnage carried by the freight boats. The annual average rose from 109½ tons in 1872 to 112 tons in 1873 and to 113½ tons in 1874.[14] One boat passed over the entire line in 1873 carrying 131 tons of coal.[15] In addition to the work of repair and improvement, the Board collected materials along the line in anticipation of future trouble. It sought thereby to expedite the actual work of repair and to reduce the interruptions to navigation.

The directors continued the struggle for control of the water gauges. Like the Clarke administration, the new regime sought to restore them to the canal banks, where the original leases of water power had stipulated they should be placed.[16] In this way the company could check closely the use of water power by the Georgetown millers and put an end to the many abusive practices which had arisen. The bitter opposition of the millers to this phase of the program continued as it had under the earlier administration. The increasing demand for water for the purpose of navigation on the Georgetown level, however, made strict regulation of water power leases imperative.

The need for these improvements, if the canal were to continue to carry its large and prosperous trade, was demonstrated

[12] *46th Annual Report* (1874), pp. 11-12; Monthly Report of the President, Proceedings of Directors, M, 154-155 (April 15, 1874).

[13] *47th Annual Report* (1875), pp. 8-9.

[14] *Ibid.*, p. 9.

[15] Monthly Report of the President, Proceedings of Directors, M, 114 (July 8, 1873).

[16] Proceedings of Directors, M, 44-47 (August 14, 1872), 80-81 (December 12, 1872).

by a severe drought in 1872 and a flash flood in 1873. The drought in the Potomac valley during the months of August, September, and October, 1872, emphasized the necessity of securing for the company an adequate control of the use of water by the Georgetown manufacturers.[17] The low water in the river and in the canal led to the adoption of various measures to maintain navigation on the waterway. The Board cut off the supply of water to the millers in the daytime, for a brief period in September, and reduced the draft of canal boats from 4½ to 4 feet in October and November. It considered the replacement of Dam No. 1 by a tighter structure and ordered the re-installation of the steam pump at the mouth of the South Branch. To prevent a recurrence of the experiences of 1872, it withdrew the permission previously granted for the use of water power to unload boats in Georgetown.[18] Finally, it called upon the government to restore the feeder from the dam at Great Falls and to repair Dam No. 1, in order to assure the canal enough water for the purposes of navigation, according to the agreement of 1853.[19]

The freshet of 1873 showed the precarious nature of the canal's prosperity. In September, a flash flood following fourteen days of rain so swelled the smaller tributaries of the Potomac that the culverts under the canal were not able to pass the miniature rivers. Many of them were washed out by the torrents. The total destruction was the greatest experienced by the canal from natural causes since 1852. Repairs were delayed and in some cases undone by a succession of storms which struck them while in an exposed stage of construction.[20]

With the help of the improvements and despite momentary interruptions of navigation, trade continued at a high level between 1872 and 1875. At first it fell off slightly from the

[17] Monthly Report of the President, Proceedings of Directors, M, 53-54 (September 16, 1872), 62 (October 3, 1872), 68-69 (November 7, 1872).

[18] *Ibid.*, M, 53-54 (September 16, 1872), 68-70 (November 7, 1872), 81-82 (December 12, 1872).

[19] Communication of A. P. Gorman to the Stockholders, January 4, 1873, Proceedings of Directors, M, 85 (January 7, 1873). See also Proceedings of Directors, H, 568 (December 9, 1852).

[20] Monthly Report of the President, Proceedings of Directors, M, 124 (September 10, 1873); *46th Annual Report* (1874), p. 11. The Baltimore and Ohio Railroad sent special relief trains carrying workmen and repair materials.

record peak of 1871, but it recovered quickly and in 1875 surpassed the achievement of any preceding year. Detailed figures show a decline to 923,581 tons in 1872 and 880,630 tons in 1873, followed by a recovery to 909,959 tons in 1874 and 973,805 tons in 1875.[21] During this period the Board discovered a new source of business in the gas coal trade. It granted drawbacks—the first on this canal—to encourage the development of this new trade.[22] Later, however, gas coal wastes became a source of much trouble for the company.[23]

Both the coal companies and the canal board undertook to encourage the increasing trade. The former built ninety-one new boats at Cumberland in 1873 and put them into service, increasing the number of vessels plying the canal to 554, with an average capacity of 112 tons.[24] In 1876, six steamers navigated the waterway, realizing for the first time the great dream of the canal's founders. Regular steamboat operation continued thereafter until 1889. The directors watched the first craft

[21] See Appendix, Table IV. It is interesting to note that commerce flourished despite the existence of many hindrances. A score of incidents disrupted navigation for brief periods. The towpath became so muddy after a heavy rain that it was impassable at some points. Broken lock gates, unexpected sand bars, and small leaks delayed trade anywhere from a few hours to several days while repairs were being made before a serious breakdown occurred. The drought in the late summer and fall of 1872 and the flood of 1873, already mentioned, resulted in more serious restrictions of trade. An early and severe winter forced the waterway to close before the usual date in 1872. Strikes of boatmen and miners in March and April, 1873, delayed the opening of the canal in that year. Also in 1873, sickness stripped the boats of their crews for a brief period and was responsible for the loss of many canal mules. Proceedings of Directors, M, 62 (October 3, 1872); Monthly Report of the President, *ibid.*, p. 107 (May 13, 1873); *45th Annual Report* (1873), p. 3.

[22] Proceedings of Directors, M, 152 (March 17, 1874), 206 (January 13, 1875); *45th Annual Report* (1873), pp. 16-17. In 1874 the drawback was 4 cents a ton for 50,000 tons or more; in 1875 it was 5 cents a ton for 100,000 tons or more and 6 cents for 200,000 tons or more. The gas coal trade declined almost as rapidly as it had developed because of the excessive amount of sulphur in the West Virginia gas coal and the strict inspection standards in the District of Columbia. See B. H. Bartol, President, Washington Gas Light Co., to Gorman, April 3, 1878. However, some of the Youghiogheny gas coal was shipped via the canal.

[23] Testimony of A. Spates, *Report of the Joint Standing Committee . . . in the Chesapeake and Ohio Canal Investigation*, p. 495. The tar which resulted from the burning of the gas coal was dumped into the Washington branch of the canal. When the company workmen sought to clean it out, the acid in the tar burned their clothes and legs.

[24] *46th Annual Report* (1874), p. 14.

carefully for signs of damage to the canal resulting from the speed of the boats or the action of the propelling mechanism. The Board finally decided that serious damage occurred if the steamers exceeded the speed limit (five miles per hour), but that if they adhered to the rules no appreciable harm was done.[25]

The canal company, as its part, abolished the sporadically enforced Sabbath law prohibiting Sunday runs. It maintained that the canal was a public highway and as such was open to traffic at all times.[26] The directors tried to rush the construction of the outlet locks on the Georgetown level above the Potomac Aqueduct, in order to relieve the congestion at that end of the waterway. When the financial stringency in the country postponed even the commencement of the work, the Board purchased a steam dredge and cleaned out the Rock Creek basin.[27] This improvement came none too soon, for in July, 1874, a large breach occurred on the Alexandria Canal, leaving the basin as the only remaining means of communication with the river.[28] The directors also planned extensive improvements in the Cumberland basin, but dropped the proposals in the interest of economy, after making an arrangement with the Consolidation Coal Company for increased accommodations at its wharf.[29] To promote the continued expansion of trade in both agricultural produce and coal the canal company sought to

[25] *48th Annual Report* (1876), p. 8; *49th Annual Report* (1877), p. 9.

[26] Proceedings of Directors, M, 57 (September 16, 1872), 106 (April 15, 1873).

[27] Monthly Report of the President, Proceedings of Directors, M, 133 (December 4, 1873); Proceedings of Directors, M, 163 (June 16, 1874); *46th Annual Report* (1874) p. 12; *47th Annual Report* (1875), p. 8. The dredge cost $10,000. In 1873 alone, it removed 32,230 cubic yards of sand and mud at a saving of $11,079.22 over the previous cost of removing it by hand during the suspension of navigation. Thus, the dredge paid for itself in one year, and gave the additional benefit of keeping the canal open for maximum draft boats during the entire boating season. In 1874, it removed 25,685 cubic yards more, thus adding to its record of service and economy. The latter figure also gives a good indication of the rate at which the basin and the Georgetown level filled up in the course of a year.

[28] Monthly Report of the President, Proceedings of Directors, M, 171-172 (July 14, 1874).

[29] W. R. Hutton, Chief Engineer, to A. P. Gorman, May 1, 1874, Proceedings of Directors, M, 160 (May 11, 1874); Proceedings of Directors, M, 168-170 (June 16, 1874).

facilitate the construction of the Cumberland Valley Railroad and the Western Maryland Railway where those lines touched upon the canal's rights.[30]

As trade increased, company income and profits also mounted. In 1873 and 1874 receipts exceeded a half-millon dollars and net income for each year was over a quarter of a million dollars.[31] The Board applied the excess of revenues over current expenses to the tremendous task of restoration and improvement and to the payment of the back interest on the preferred construction bonds. In the first three and one-half years of its tenure, to December, 1875, the Gorman administration paid off nineteen coupons, representing nine and one-half years' interest, amounting to $902,457.88[32] The financial condition and reputation of the canal rose perceptibly from even the high levels to which the Clarke regime had carried it.[33]

Despite the great prosperity of the canal (especially in view of the widespread depression in trade and industry after 1873) and the substantial improvements already made, President Gorman was not yet satisfied. He recommended the continuation of the general program of improvement and expansion designed to modernize the canal as a carrier and establish more firmly its future as a transportation line. In a long report made in 1875, he cited the reasons for his stand and the course he

[30] *45th Annual Report* (1873), pp. 16-17. The Cumberland Valley Railroad was a short line extending from Harrisburg to Winchester, crossing the canal just below Williamsport. The anticipated increase in trade arising from the construction of the Western Maryland did not materialize. The Chesapeake and Ohio, which had expected to carry most of the railroad's coal business from Cumberland to its western terminus at Big Pool (above Williamsport), attributed its disappointment to the failure of the Western Maryland to obtain adequate terminal facilities in Baltimore. *46th Annual Report* (1874), p. 18.

[31] Receipts totalled $507,660.52 and $517,412.22, respectively. See Appendix, Table V.

[32] *48th Annual Report* (1876), p. 10. Of the $200,000 repair bonds, $199,-000 had been paid off, with interest, by 1873. The next in order according to the court decisions were the preferred construction bonds. *45th Annual Report* (1873), p. 8.

[33] *Testimony of Hon. A. P. Gorman before U. S. Commissioner G. Morris Bond* [Baltimore, May 31, 1880], U. S. Circuit Court for the District of Maryland, D. K. Stewart *vs.* the Chesapeake & Ohio Canal Company (Baltimore, 1880), p. 2. The average price of bonds was 57 in 1872, 100 to 105 in 1873, 92 in 1874, and 115 in 1875. During 1876, the market price of the bonds declined to 110. Thereafter it fell rapidly to 70 in 1877 and 65 in 1878.

proposed to take. It is worthwhile to quote parts of the recommendations in detail, so clearly were the canal's past and present condition and future prospects described.

In reviewing the changing position of the canal in the Cumberland coal trade, the president cited the reasons for undertaking a program of far-reaching improvements to strengthen its competitive position.

It is well known when this work was constructed it was then of larger dimensions than any other Canal in this country; and the carrying capacity of the boats sufficient to make the cost of shipping coal, much less than by any of the then competing lines.

Since then, but comparatively little attention has been paid to making improvements, so as to reduce the cost to a minimum. While on the other hand, *the best talent of the country has been employed in perfecting the system of railroad transportation and with wonderful results.*

When this Canal was completed in 1850, it was not supposed that a ton of coal could be profitably moved by rail for less than two (2) cents per ton per mile, whereas it is now transported from Cumberland to Baltimore for a fraction over one cent per ton per mile.

It is true, that during the same time, reductions have been made in tolls and wharf charges by the Canal, so that a proper difference has always been maintained in its favor. But further improvements are being rapidly pushed forward by other transportation companies, which, when completed may, and probably will, require further reductions on our part.

Up to this time the Baltimore and Ohio Railroad has been our only formidable competitor.

The *able* and *comprehensive minds* who direct the affairs and shape the policy of that Company, have long since recognized the necessity for *greater reductions in the cost of transportation, and to that end,* have been for some years constructing its third track from Baltimore to Cumberland, *which, when completed will enable it to reduce the cost of delivering a ton of coal from the mines on board of vessels in the harbor of Baltimore to a minimum railroad rate*, which, together with the superior facilities of the port of Baltimore, as compared with Georgetown and Alexandria, for shipping to Northern Ports, will make it absolutely necessary that a corresponding reduction in cost and improved facilities shall be furnished by this Company.

Within the past four years another competing line has been constructed to the coal fields, which is owned and controlled by the Pennsylvania Railroad Company; the very able and astute managers of which recognize the great value and importance of securing the transportation of a large portion of the products of the Maryland mines, ...

The older, Maryland transportation agencies, he continued, have advantages of distance and economy.

But the Pennsylvania Railroad Company owns and controls the Canals leading up the Juniata, and have for some years been making extensive improvements by enlarging them, and it is now proposed and recommended by their accomplished engineers to expend only one million dollars more, which would complete their enlarged Canal and slack water to a point within 80 miles of our mines.

Then by railroad of only 80 miles, and a Canal of sufficient capacity for section boats of 300 tons passing through to Philadelphia and New York, they claim that a large portion of the tonnage of this Canal, as well as of the Baltimore and Ohio Railroad must be diverted.[34]

After a brief justification of his activities during the first three years of his administration, he outlined his program of improvements and the present state of its achievements.

Early in our administration, but after a careful examination of the various questions involved in this subject, we were convinced that no time should be lost in inaugurating a general system of improvements, involving the expenditure of considerable sums to complete them, but distributing it over a series of years, so as not to diminish our payments on account of debts. The improvements already made and results obtained, have been fully set forth.

CONTEMPLATED IMPROVEMENTS.

The improvements contemplated and deemed necessary, were:

First. To restore gradually the water-way of the Canal to its original dimensions, so that with the present locks, the tonnage of the boats should be increased from 109 to 120 tons.

Second. To control the amount of terminal charges.

Third. To secure such a control as would enable us to fix and maintain a uniform rate of freight charges.

Fourth. Enlarge the locks of the Canal so as to increase the capacity of the boats to two hundred and fifty (250) tons.

To complete these improvements, and supply the work with improved steam appliances, would necessarily involve the expenditure of a large sum of money.

But that they are desirable, if not absolutely necessary, no one can question, and that they can be completed within a reasonable time, without diminishing the usual payments, on account of indebtedness, we do not doubt.

---

[34] *47th Annual Report* (1875), pp. 14-15.

To that end we have, within the past three years, purchased improved steam machinery to pump water, steam dredge to widen and deepen the Canal, and furnish an outlet to the Potomac River, at Georgetown, so as to give ample opportunity for wharf facilities, and thus reduce the cost at that point.

2nd. We have leased, during the present year, sufficient wharf facilities at Cumberland, to control the cost of wharfage at that point.

3rd. We have made some progress in preparing material to enlarge the locks.[35]

These improvements, he insisted, must be continued and expanded, in the manner of those already described on the Pennsylvania canals. Furthermore, the canal company must forget past concepts of its function as a carrier and devise new ways and means to control effectively all charges on its waterway. Thus the last vestiges of distinction between the railroad and the canal would be obliterated (excepting physical differences).

Another difficulty in the successful management of this work, arises from the fact, that it is not within the power of the Company to fix the rate of charges for freights. The theory was, that as a public highway, free to all boats who paid certain charges, free competition in the carrying trade would insure the lowest freight charges. The practical operation has been and is, that a combination of a few interests can dictate these charges, with no power on the part of the Company to control them. Indeed it has gone so far as to reverse it, and dictate to the Company what its rate of tolls shall be.

The time has now arrived, when this company must adopt some measure, whereby those charges can be fixed and controlled by it, so that the boatmen may have a uniform and *remunerative rate for his* [*sic*] *labor and investment*, while at the same time, we can inform the Coal Companies, before the opening of navigation, each spring, what rate of charges will be made for the year.[36]

The insistence on continued efforts to improve the canal's position as a transportation line was not premature, even in the banner year of 1875. There were already ample indications of rough sailing ahead. In August, 1874, trainmen on the Cumberland and Pennsylvania Railroad went on strike. The boatmen, who had organized in 1873 to resist reductions in boating

[35] *Ibid.*, pp. 16-17.

[36] *Ibid.*, p. 18. The proposal for the canal company to operate its own transportation line aroused bitter opposition of coal agents and boat builders. See C. O. Hammond to Gorman, November 21, 1877.

charges, also struck on August 25, 1874, demanding $1.35 a ton freight rates from Cumberland to Georgetown.[37] The investigation of the strike by the canal board uncovered serious abuses in the system of boating then in operation on the canal which tended to support the boatmen's position.[38] The urgency for the resumption of business, however, did not allow time to remedy these grievances. The judicious use of strike-breakers and police soon brought the boatmen to terms.[39] In addition to these troubles, there was always the threat of a rate war among the competing coal carriers. The volume of coal shipped via railroads fell off as early as 1874 although the canal's trade continued to improve.[40] In the spring of 1875 the Board ordered a general reduction of charges, including tolls, wharfage, and freights,[41] in order to maintain its position in the trade. As a result, although tonnage on the waterway increased slightly in 1875, canal revenues declined from the peak year of 1874.[42]

In 1876 the great nation-wide depression finally reached the canal. Trade fell off sharply to 709,112 tons; and that part of it which was retained was kept only by lowering the rate of tolls and wharfage from 51 cents to 46 cents per ton from Cumberland to Georgetown.[43] In addition to this reduction, the canal board adopted for the first time a system of drawbacks on published rates for coal companies shipping large quantities of coal via the canal.[44] President Gorman accurately identified

[37] Monthly Report of the President, Proceedings of Directors, M, 173 (August 7, 1874); *ibid.*, pp. 176-177 (September 10, 1874). The Boatmen's Benevolent Society of Cumberland had been active in 1873 protesting toll charges, liquor traffic, etc. See, for example, Proceedings of Directors, M, 94 (February 13, 1873), 102 (March 11, 1873).

[38] Report of the Committee on the Boatmen's petition; *ibid.*, M, 180-185 (September 17, 1874). The committee found the cost of the boats exorbitant and the terms of their purchase unfair. It also criticized sharply the practice of shippers in their dealings with the boatmen.

[39] *Ibid.*, pp. 182-183, 184 (September 17, 1874).

[40] *47th Annual Report* (1875), p. 10.

[41] Proceedings of Directors, M, 210-211 (April 6, 1875). Over-all charges were reduced 20 cents: tolls--8 cents, freight—10 cents, and wharfage—2 cents. Receipts fell from $517,412.22 in 1874 to $473,218.40 in 1875.

[42] See Appendix, Tables IV and V.

[43] Proceedings of Directors, M, 255 (April 18, 1876); *48th Annual Report* (1876), p. 10. The Baltimore and Ohio Railroad had reduced its charges from $2.30 a ton to $2.02 a ton to Baltimore.

[44] Proceedings of Directors, M, 246 (January 5, 1876). Drawbacks were granted to the Consolidation Coal Company and the Maryland Mining Company.

the causes of the depression in company affairs when he noted that:

> The continued depression in all branches of industry has so lessened the demand for coal as to seriously affect our business.
>
> The depression has also induced the shippers of coal from other regions and transportation lines leading to tide water, to reduce the price of coal at commercial centres, so that [a] large reduction in prices was necessary in Cumberland coal.[45]

In an effort to compete with other carriers for the declining trade, the Board gave the president blanket authority to reduce tolls on all commodities at competing points on the canal to whatever rates were necessary to retain the trade. As the first move under this authority, President Gorman lowered the toll on flour to ¾ cent a ton per mile from all such points between Williamsport and Weverton.[46] In an attempt to reduce the cost of canal coal and to stimulate trade, the president secured the passage of a law by the Maryland Assembly to compel the Cumberland and Pennsylvania Railroad (which carried most of the coal from the mines of western Maryland to the canal at Cumberland) to reduce its charges from 3 cents to 2 cents a ton per mile. The railroad resisted the move, however, and the reduction did not take effect until the Maryland Court of Appeals upheld the validity of the law in 1877.[47] The Board directed surveys to be made up the north branch of the Potomac in 1876 with a view to extending the canal to the mouth of Savage River and establishing a direct connection with the coal fields.[48]

Notwithstanding all efforts to stimulate trade, reduce charges, and provide direct connections with the fields, the coal trade (and consequently the total trade) on the waterway continued to drop as the production of the Cumberland region fell off markedly. The unsatisfactory state of affairs was succinctly summarized in the annual report for 1876.

[45] *48th Annual Report* (1876), p. 10.

[46] Proceedings of Directors, M, 255 (April 18, 1876), 258 (May 17, 1876). See also Cockrell and Engle to Gorman, January 26, March 9, 1877, on the effects of rate-slashing by railroads on the flour trade via the canal.

[47] *49th Annual Report* (1877), p. 3; Proceedings of Directors, M, 296 (May 10, 1877).

[48] *47th Annual Report* (1875), p. 19; Proceedings of Directors, M, 283 (December 12, 1876); *49th Annual Report* (1877), p. 10.

> The business from the Maryland Coal region during the year, has proved one of the most unsatisfactory in its history. The decrease in the number of tons of coal shipped from this region to tide water amounts to 507,692 tons, equal to a decrease of twenty-one (21) per cent, as compared with 1875.
>
> This large decrease in the business of that region, is attributable to the general depression that has followod [*sic*] the financial crisis of 1873, coupled with the fact, that the Cumberland and Pennsylvania Rail Road Company, over which all the coal from the Cumberland basin to [the] Canal must pass, refused to comply with an Act of the Legislature of this State, reducing its charges, thereby preventing our coal from being put in market at such a price as to compete successfully with other coals.[49]

The decrease in trade and the reduction of tolls caused canal revenues and profits to fall to approximately two-thirds and one-fourth of their respective levels for 1875.[50] The Board suspended most of the improvements which had been projected or were in progress. The work of lengthening the locks was curtailed—only three of them,. all on the Georgetown level, were finished during the winter of 1876-1877. The company leased for twenty-five years at a cost of $15,000 a year the outlet lock at Georgetown which was finally completed by the end of 1876.[51] By the time the lock was put into operation, the decline of commerce had relieved the canal of the immediate need for it. The directors authorized the payment of only one coupon on the construction bonds in 1876.[52]

The year 1877 promised no improvement in canal trade or revenue. The country was still in the grip of the depression, and a rate war among the transportation lines was in the offing. The Baltimore and Ohio reduced its charges 22 cents below the published rate for 1876 (to $1.81), and was reportedly offering even lower rates to canal shippers for their trade. Canal directors believed that the railroad had offered rebates of 18

[49] *49th Annual Report* (1877), p. 3.

[50] *Ibid.*, p. 4; see below, Appendix, Table V.

[51] *49th Annual Report* (1877), p. 9; Proceedings of Directors, M, 286-287 (January 11, 1877), 283 (February 13, 1877). The locks were said to have cost $146,556.77. Technically, the state of Maryland leased the locks, but the canal company paid the rent--an arrangement which caused a considerable tempest in the eighties.

[52] *49th Annual Report* (1877), p. 9; Proceedings of Directors, M, 281 (December 12, 1876). The coupon for July, 1864, was the last one ever paid.

to 20 cents in 1876, and they assumed that the rebates offered in 1877 would be at least as large.[53] Although the Cumberland and Pennsylvania Railroad finally reduced its charges to 2 cents a ton per mile, the competition of the Baltimore and Ohio Railroad interests and the Pennsylvania Clearfield anthracite coal was so great that the canal board decided early in April it would be impossible to make any profit on the coal trade that year, and that the important thing was to hold the trade which the waterway already had.[54] The Board thereupon plunged into the thick of the rate war. It reduced tolls several times in the course of the year, from 41 cents in April to 22 cents a ton from Cumberland to Georgetown in August.[55]

The troubles of the canal in 1877 were only beginning, however. On June 21, the boatmen struck again, tying up on the first level above Seneca. There they awaited some redress from their grievances, far from the reach of the coal companies and the canal board. The strike lasted for two months, during which trade on the waterway sank to negligible proportions. The men finally resumed their runs on August 20. By that time many canal shippers had made arrangements with the railroad for the transportation of their business for the rest of the year. The canal directors fixed tolls at a nominal rate and attempted to make up as much of the lost ground as possible in the few months of navigation that remained.[56]

Three months later—fortunately near the end of the boating season—the last of the series of misfortunes which befell the waterway in 1877 occurred. On November 24 another great

[53] Monthly Report of the President, Proceedings of Directors, M, 293-294 (April 10, 1877).

[54] Monthly Report of the President, Proceedings of Directors, M, 296 (April 10, 1877). See also the letters to Gorman from William Borden, President, Borden Mining Company, March 26, 1877; G. P. Lloyd, President, American Coal Company, March 28, April 6, 1877; J. George Repplier, President, Hampshire & Baltimore Coal Company, March 31, 1877; and Henry Loveridge, President, Maryland Coal Company, April 7, 1877; in Proceedings of Directors, M, 298-302 (April 10, 1877).

[55] Proceedings of Directors, N, 4 (August 21, 1877); *50th Annual Report* (1878), p. 6. Tolls were 46 cents on April 1, 1877 (including wharfage) and 25 cents on September 1, 1877 (including wharfage). See below, Appendix, Table VII.

[56] *50th Annual Report* (1878), pp. 3, 6; Proceedings of Directors, N, 4 (August 21, 1877).

flood swept down the Potomac valley. This one was the worst in 150 years of the recorded history of the region. In its wake it left the canal almost a total wreck and, of course, brought trade to an end for the season. In all there had been only 161 days of navigation during the year.[57] The crest of the flood was generally two feet higher than the previous record established in 1852. At Great Falls, the water reached a point seventy feet above the low-water mark. Damage was generously scattered along the entire line, but the middle section suffered the most. There were fourteen breaches on the Cumberland division, and the walls and towpath were badly washed in many places. In addition, the abutments of Dams No. 5 and 6 were seriously damaged. On the middle division the worst blow was the destruction of Dam No. 4. The river tore a gap about 200 feet wide in the middle of this new masonry structure which was thought to be one of the best of its kind in the country. There were also many breaches and washes, and the canal was completely filled at some points. On the Georgetown division the damage was limited to heavy washes and large breaches. All along the line, quantities of repair materials, stores, and cargoes were lost.[58]

The work of restoration began immediately. As in the case of every disaster that struck the canal many observers believed the waterway to be finished as a transportation agency. The Board of Directors did not give up so easily. Repairs began on November 26, as soon as the waters had receded and the nature and extent of the damage was ascertained. As an economy measure the company suspended all lock-keepers, collectors, and other officials on the line, but most of them probably found employment directing and making the repairs. All winter long the work continued as rapidly as possible.[59] All available company resources were used, augmented by a loan of $115,000 from coal companies, banks, and individuals.[60] The canal re-

[57] *50th Annual Report* (1878), p. 3; Proceedings of Directors, N, 11 ff. (December 12, 1877).

[58] There is a full report of the damage to the canal in Proceedings of Directors, N, 11-13 (December 12, 1877). See also, *50th Annual Report* (1878), pp. 9-10; and the Baltimore *Sun*, November 26, 29, 1877.

[59] Proceedings of Directors, N, 14, 17-20 (December 12, 1877—April 10, 1878).

[60] *50th Annual Report* (1878), p. 11.

opened for business on April 15, 1878, only one month later than usual. But the magnificent effort had cost the company $238,500.21 and had left it exhausted, saddled with a debt of $196,463.96.[61]

Once again President Gorman went to the state legislature for help. By the terms of an earlier court decision the right of the company to issue bonds for repairs on a pledge of its revenues was recognized as legally unrestricted. To insure a market for the bonds, however, it was deemed necessary to limit the right to a sum that might reasonably be repaid.[62] Upon the request of the canal company, the legislature passed an act in February, 1878, specifically waiving the state's prior lien on canal property for repair bonds up to $500,000 in amount. The additional pledge of property for the repayment of the bonds was considered necessary to strengthen the market value of the issue. At first the directors authorized the sale of only the few bonds required to cover repair costs, for these obligations were not subject to cancellation before maturity.[63] More than ever the company needed a revival of trade at profitable rates in 1878 to enable it to get out from under the new burden of debt and to resume payments on the construction bonds.

Prospects for a marked recovery, however, appeared to be slight. Business remained generally depressed, and coal prices continued their deflationary tendency. The price of a ton of coal on board vessels at Georgetown, which had been $4.65 in 1872, fell to $2.60 in 1878 and 1879.[64] The railroads also continued their cut-throat competition and rate wars.[65] Under these conditions trade remained slow, and revenues had little opportunity to rise. For a third time the state legislature, came to the aid of the waterway. In 1878, it passed an act curbing

[61] Proceedings of Directors, N, 20 (April 10, 1878); *50th Annual Report* (1878), p. 10; *52nd Annual Report* (1880), p. 8.

[62] Baltimore *Sun*, January 28, 1878. The case was: Commonwealth of Virginia *vs.* Chesapeake and Ohio Canal Company, 32 Maryland 501, 35 Maryland 1.

[63] Act of the Maryland Assembly, 1878, ch. 58, approved February 27, 1878. This act is printed as an appendix to the *50th Annual Report* (1878). See also Proceedings of Directors, N, 22 (April 10, 1878); 49th Annual Meeting (April 30, 1878), Proceedings of Stockholders, E, 302-303; *50th Annual Report* (1878), p. 11; and *51st Annual Report* (1879), p. 8.

[64] *52nd Annual Report* (1880), p. 7.

[65] *51st Annual Report* (1879), p. 11.

the competitive practices of the Baltimore and Ohio Railroad.[66] On the strength of this act the canal board raised tolls from 25 cents to 40 cents a ton from Cumberland to Georgetown.[67]

Meanwhile the company turned to other ways and means of improving its position as a carrier. At least four courses of action were possible: to secure an independent connection with the coal fields; to gain control of freight rates on the canal; to reduce operating expenses; and to come to some agreement with competitors. All four ways were tried.

The object of securing an independent connection with the coal fields was to reduce the cost of transportation for the coal companies and to free the canal of its dependence on the Baltimore and Ohio and its subsidiaries. The company made special arrangements with the owners of the Davis mine in West Virginia in 1879 for the transportation of coal from that mine.[68] It sought to facilitate the construction of no less than four independent railroad connections with the canal at Cumberland. Among these was one which proposed to build a line all the way down the Potomac to the canal basin at Cumberland. This road, the Georges Creek and Cumberland Railroad, received the assistance of the canal company in its attempt to force the Baltimore and Ohio to permit a crossing of its tracks in order to reach the canal basin.[69] Two other roads, the Bloomington and Fairfax and the Potomac and Piedmont, agreed in 1880 to build short feeder lines to the Baltimore and Ohio Railroad on the promise of special rates from the canal

[66] Act of Maryland Assembly, 1878, ch. 155; Frederick *Examiner*, February 27, March 3, 1878. The terms of the act are given in the latter issue. See also, *50th Annual Report* (1878), p. 12. Hostility toward the Baltimore and Ohio was increasing in the legislature and in the state generally. It reached a peak in the state elections of 1875 when the railroad company cast off its allegiance to the Democratic party which was dominated by Gorman. In one of the bitterest canvasses in Maryland history, Gorman and his friends in both parties overcame the power of the railroad in state political circles and secured control of the legislature. It was in 1875 that the "Canal Ring" in Western Maryland was born amid fierce denunciations by its opponents and vigorous denials of its existence by its alleged members.

[67] Proceedings of Directors, N, 20 (April 10, 1878). The revised charges represented 15½ per cent of the total cost of transportation via the canal, compared to only 12 per cent in 1872. *52nd Annual Report* (1880), p. 7.

[68] *52nd Annual Report* (1880), p. 12.

[69] *Ibid.*

for coal shipped over it.[70] In the same year, the canal board invoked the agreement of 1851 at the request of the Pennsylvania Railroad to compel the Baltimore and Ohio to permit the former road to cross its tracks in order to enter Cumberland.[71]

The purpose of the endeavor to gain control of freight rates on the canal was to reduce the profits of the various agencies involved in canal transportation so as to enable the company to reduce over-all charges while maintaining a profitable rate of tolls. It was even said that President Gorman intended to institute a canal transportation line controlled by the company in order to reduce freight charges.[72] Although this is entirely likely, nothing was accomplished in that way before the turn of the century. The assault on another of the agencies in the canal trade was more successful. The rates charged by the owners of wharf facilities at Cumberland and Georgetown were the cause of great concern to the Board of Directors. The wharf owners received a handsome return on their relatively small capital outlay, and at the same time their rates were so high that they forced the canal directors to reduce their charges on the coal trade in order to compete with the railroads for business. The low rate of tolls, on the other hand, did not produce enough revenue to pay anything on the great invest-

[70] *Ibid.*, p. 13; Proceedings of Directors, N, 99-100 (February 18, 1880), 112 (July 20, 1880).

[71] Proceedings of Directors, N, 114-115 (July 20, 1880), including the letter of Henry Loveridge, Vice President of the Pennsylvania Railroad Company (in Maryland) December 19, 1879, and the resolutions of that company.

All four of these railroads required the assistance of the canal directors to reach the Cumberland basin because of the location of their respective roads in relation to the Baltimore and Ohio tracks. The latter closely paralleled the canal below and at Cumberland (on the berm side), and followed the approximate route of the proposed extension of the waterway in the Potomac valley above the town. Thus any railroad from the mines in Frostburg, Georges Creek, and Savage River districts of Western Maryland would have to cross the Baltimore and Ohio to reach the canal. Realizing this, the Chesapeake and Ohio had required the latter, in 1851, to permit its tracks to be crossed by other railroads seeking to reach the canal basin, when so requested by the canal directors. The Baltimore and Ohio had agreed to this arrangement in order to secure the approval of the canal board for the proposed route of the railroad in Cumberland. This approval was necessary in view of the decision of the Court of Appeals in 1832 sustaining the claim of the canal company to the right of prior location of its waterway in the Potomac valley.

[72] *Act of Maryland Assembly*, 1878, ch. 58, sect. 4. See also C. O. Hammond to Gorman, November 21, 1877, and the Baltimore *Sun*, January 28, 1878.

ment of capital in the canal company. The Board dredged the Rock Creek basin and repaired the outlet lock in order to make the river bank available for wharf facilities thus seeking to force wharfage fees at Georgetown down to a fair level. At Cumberland, the canal company leased the Potomac wharf and cut rates until others were forced to reduce theirs. Later it purchased the largest wharf on the basin and secured a permanent control over wharfage at that end of the canal.[73]

The company attempted to reduce its own operating expenses by introducing improvements of various types. It sought thereby to permit a toll rate which would lower the over-all costs of transportation, but which would still leave the canal a profit. One improvement, completed and in operation by October, 1879, was the installation of a telephone line along the waterway. There were forty-three stations so located as to be within easy reach of any point on the canal. It was at that time the longest single circuit in existence.[74] Another proposed improvement was the lengthening of locks. It was estimated that twenty-seven locks must be lengthened to 120 feet each if any benefit was to be derived from the improvement. Only fourteen had been extended by 1882, however. Thus the advantages anticipated from the operation of double boats were denied to the coal shippers and the canal.[75]

The efforts to come to terms with the competitors involved both force and compromise. The company enlisted the assistance of the Maryland Assembly to bring the Baltimore and Ohio

[73] Proceedings of Directors, M, 291 (March 14, 1877), N, 56 (September 17, 1878); *Testimony of A. P. Gorman before U. S. Commissioner G. Morris Bond,* (Baltimore, May 31, 1880); U. S. Circuit Court for the District of Maryland, D. K. Stewart *vs.* the Chesapeake and Ohio Canal Company (Baltimore, 1880), pp. 22, 28. See also testimony of Henry Winship, *Report of the Joint Standing Committee . . . in the Chesapeake and Ohio Canal Investigation*, p. 162. Wharf owners made $344,000 income in 1874 alone on their investment of $300,000. The revenue for the canal company in the same year was approximately $428,-000 on an investment of over $11,000,000.

[74] J. Frank Morrison, Telephone Engineer, to A. P. Gorman, November 1, 1879, Proceedings of Directors, N, 94-97 (November 26, 1879); *Testimony of A. P. Gorman*, p. 18; Testimony of A. Spates, *Report of the Joint Standing Committee . . . in the Chesapeake and Ohio Canal Investigation*, p. 500; *52d Annual Report* (1880), p. 11. The telephone followed the exact route of the canal, except for the tunnel. There it went over the hill instead.

[75] Special Meeting of the Stockholders (March 21, 1882), Proceedings of Stockholders, E, 353-355.

to terms in 1878. It voluntarily cooperated with the latter and the Pennsylvania Railroad Company to fix charges on the coal trade at profitable levels. This arrangement enabled the Board to raise canal tolls in April, 1880.[76]

The attempts of the Gorman administration to improve the position of the canal as a transportation line were not carried out without obstruction. In 1879 there was a strike of miners, from September 4 to October 8, and a serious drought to hinder the recovery of the canal.[77] In 1880 a strike of boatmen interfered with navigation for eight weeks beginning in the latter part of June. Trade dropped from an average of 21,374 tons to 13,870 tons a week during the strike.[78] Hardly was the strike settled than the river lock at the Rock Creek basin gave way and was abandoned.[79] In the same year a bondholder, Daniel K. Stewart, challenged the right of the company to sell repair bonds of 1878 to raise funds for lengthening locks.[80] The influence of local politics was manifested in 1882, after the company had won a doubtful victory in the Stewart case, when Governor Hamilton, an opponent of President Gorman, expressed his doubts as to the legality of using the bonds for that purpose.[81] The opposition of these two men ruined the market value of the bonds and brought the improvements to a halt. Meanwhile the Georges Creek and Cumberland Railroad was having trouble securing the necessary permission to cross the Baltimore and Ohio tracks to the canal basin. Thus as late as 1881 the waterway was still without its independent connection with the mine fields.[82] Another severe drought in August and September of the same year so reduced the water in the river

[76] Proceedings of Directors, N, 101-102 (April 14, 1880), including letter of W. H. Smith, General Freight Agent, Baltimore and Ohio Railroad Company, to A. P. Gorman, March 5, 1880.

[77] *52d Annual Report* (1880), p. 4.

[78] Report of the President, Proceedings of Directors, N, 117-118 (September 22, 1880).

[79] J. J. Moore to A. P. Gorman, August 26, 1880, Proceedings of Directors, N. 119 (September 22, 1880).

[80] *52d Annual Report* (1880), p. 10.

[81] "Special Report of the President to the Stockholders, March 21, 1882," *54th Annual Report* (1882), Appendix B, p. 21.

[82] Proceedings of Directors, N, 148-149 (July 19, 1881). The canal company finally cancelled its agreement with the Georges Creek and Cumberland Railroad. *53d Annual Report* (1881), pp. 7-8; *54th Annual Report* (1882), p. 7.

and in the canal that boats could be passed only in fleets every six or eight days. Water was collected by the upper dams and then passed through the canal along with the boats down to the lowest levels.[83] Finally, in 1882, another strike occurred among the miners lasting until August, during which there was virtually no trade on the canal. By the time the miners agreed to go back to work there were only three months of navigation remaining and many of the boatmen had left the canal, despairing of doing any further boating that year.[84]

During the great strike of 1882, President Gorman left the company. He had been trying to resign ever since his appointment to the United States Senate in 1880. In June, 1882, he refused re-election, and formally retired from the administration of the company.

Following the ten-year reign of Senator Gorman as president of the canal company, there was a succession of short administrations by political appointees. In the background there was always the shadow of the Senator, still the political boss of the Democratic party in Maryland. The canal itself went into a period of decline from which it never emerged. Under the continuing depressed state of trade there was little the officials could do to put the waterway back on its feet. Indeed it was scarcely possible to keep the canal in shape for navigation. The dilemma in which the Board found itself was set forth in 1886.

> . . . the work cannot for any considerable period be kept in good navigable condition unless the amount expended on it is increased nor can its revenues . . . be maintained unless the canal is improved so as to keep pace with the increased facilities that are constantly being made by rival lines of transportation.[85]

On the whole, the story of the canal in the last decade of its independent existence presents a dreary picture of trade stagnation, financial depression, physical deterioration, political interference, and outside intrigue. The heyday of the canal had definitely passed.

[83] Gambrill, General Superintendent, to Gorman, October 5, 1881, Proceedings of Directors, N, 151-152 (October 6, 1881). The draft of canal boats was reduced from 5¾ feet to 4 ½ feet. Printed also in *54th Annual Report* (1882), Appendix A, p. [15].

[84] *54th Annual Report* (1882), p. 9; *55th Annual Report* (1883), p. 8.

[85] *58th Annual Report* (1886), p. 5.

The business on the waterway by this time was almost entirely dependent on the demand for coal. In view of the continued depression in industry this demand remained relatively stagnant in the early years of the decade. The competition of the great railroad lines also acted to keep the coal shipments via the canal at a minimum.[86] In 1884 the canal's business was curtailed by the efforts of the coal companies to force the Board to lower its charges.[87] The general paralysis of business led to the suspension of navigation for four of the first six months of 1885. Rate wars and strikes also interfered.

> Freight warfares between trunk lines of railroads have added to the decrease in receipts of all carrying companies, and compelled a marked reduction in the tolls heretofore charged by this Company. Strikes or threatened strikes in the coal regions have caused also a diminished shipment of coal.[88]

The general stagnation of the canal's trade was clearly reflected in the annual tonnage figures for the early eighties. With the

[86] *58th Annual Report* (1886), pp. 6-7.

"The improvement in the motive power of railroads, whereby one crew of hands can now do the work which formerly required three crews, has tended greatly to cheapen the cost of transportation. . . .

"But in canal transportation such improvements have not yet been reached. The same number of horses or mules are required to draw the boat and the same number of hands are now employed to man it as were needed when the Canal was first opened. Canals have not kept place [*sic*] with the improvements and money saving inventions introduced into the service of other carriers.

"Until some means shall be devised to diminish the cost of the motive power on the Canal, and until the locks shall be lengthened so that double boats may be passed through them, or some other means found to cheapen the cost of transportation, successful competition is almost hopeless.

"Whatever the means needed or adopted to lessen the cost of canal carrying may be, the C. & O. is utterly unable to supply them.

". . . it is powerless to aid itself."

[87] Report of the President, Proceedings of Directors, N, 260 (June 20, 1884). Pressure on the canal to lower its tolls was by no means novel. As recently as 1878, leading coal companies in the Cumberland region had brought concerted pressure to bear on Gorman to reduce tolls. The arguments used are significant as an indication of a tendency that was then present—though not so serious as the coal companies would have one believe. The decline in popularity of Cumberland coal, the growing demand for anthracite, the greater handling and breakage of canal-shipped coal, the obsolescence of Georgetown as a port, and the dependence of the canal on the coal trade were all mentioned. William Borden to Gorman, April 1, 1878; Henry Loveridge to Gorman, April 15, 1878; George Repplier to Gorman, April 19, 27, 1878.

[88] *57th Annual Report* (1885), p. 6.

single exception of 1883, coal shipments averaged slightly over 300,000 tons a year from 1882 to 1888.[89]

Canal revenues declined irregularly in the face of the bitter competition among the coal carriers.[90] The directors lowered canal tolls from 40 cents (including wharfage at Cumberland) in 1883 to 36 cents in 1884 and finally to 26 cents in 1885 to offset the reductions in charges by the railroads and to stimulate trade.[91] In 1885 the Baltimore and Ohio Railroad was carrying coal to deep-water docks at Locust Point for $1.30 a ton whereas as late as 1865 it had charged $5.58 a ton.[92] The decline in revenue made the financial position of the debt-ridden, obsolescent canal very precarious. If the interest on the repair bonds went unpaid for too long (two years according to the decision of the U. S. Circuit Court in 1886), the bondholders might obtain a foreclosure.[93] On the other hand, if the canal's income were used to pay this interest, the company would not have the funds to make the improvements necessary to enable the waterway to compete with the low freight charges of the railroads and thereby to obtain the money to repay the loans. The repeated somber warnings of the canal officials show that they were fully aware of the waterway's dangerous financial position.

To resolve its financial dilemma as well as it was able, the company resorted to several devices. First, it cut the ordinary expenses of operation whenever and wherever possible. During the suspension of trade in 1882 pending the end of the miners' strike, it reduced the salaries of lock-keepers, bosses, and laborers on the line by approximately 50 per cent. The wages were only partially restored after the strike ended, and it was not until the following May that the Board returned them to their

[89] See Appendix, Table IV. The coal trade soared to 707,486 tons in 1883.

[90] Also with the exception of 1883 the canal's receipts from all sources averaged less than $150,000 a year from 1882 to 1888. In 1883 receipts amounted to $329,527.07. Expenditures, on the other hand, averaged slightly less than $200,000 a year. See Appendix, Table V.

[91] Proceedings of Directors, N, 220 (June 13, 1883), 251 (April 10, 1884), 308 (February 6, 1885). See also *57th Annual Report* (1885), p. 7; *58th Annual Report* (1886), p. 6.

[92] *58th Annual Report* (1886), p. 9. It was reported that the railroad frequently carried coal for as low as $1.00 a ton.

[93] *Ibid.*, pp. 8-10.

former level.[94] During the winter months of 1883-1884, the directors again halved lock-keepers' salaries, and discharged 105 laborers.[95] Still further reductions in the working force in May, 1884, brought the total number of employees down to about one-half the 1882 force.[96] In June, 1884, the Board lowered the regular salaries of the employees by 20 to 25 per cent, and in July it abolished the offices of general superintendent, engineer, assistant superintendent, and assistant collector at Georgetown. At the same time, it cut the salaries of the office staff 20 per cent.[97]

The canal company also applied its economy measures to the work of maintenance and improvement.[98] The Board authorized only the most essential repairs to the waterway. It suspended work on the comprehensive program of improvements laid down by the Gorman administration, except for the payments on the purchase of the Basin Wharf at Cumberland.[99] The directors kept the Rock Creek basin clear by continual dredging, but this became imperative, after the purchase of the Potomac Aqueduct by the government in 1887 for conversion into a bridge.[100] The company also had to raise the guard bank at Great Falls to protect the canal after the government raised its dam there, but Congress provided the necessary funds for that work.[101] At one time the Board reversed its stand on improvements and resolved to sell repair bonds to lengthen the locks, but another challenge by the bondholders of 1844 de-

[94] Proceedings of Directors, N, 189-190 (August 31, 1882), including Report of Gambrill to President and Directors, August 31; *ibid.*, N, 214 (May 10, 1883).

[95] Report of the President, Proceedings of Directors, N, 246 (February 14, 1884).

[96] Gambrill to L. Smith, May 14, 1884, Proceedings of Directors, N, 257-258 (May 15, 1884).

[97] Report of the President, Proceedings of Directors, N, 267-268 (June 20, 1884); *ibid.*, p. 274 (July 24, 1884); Proceedings of Directors, N, 276 (August 21, 1884).

[98] *57th Annual Report* (1885), pp. 5-6, 9-10.

[99] Proceedings of Directors, N, 376 (April 19, 1888). Only $22,000 was still due.

[100] *Ibid.*, p. 362 (June 23, 1887).

[101] James G. Berret to Major E. I. Lydecker, engineer-in-charge of the aqueduct, May 4, 1883, Berret to President and Directors, May 10, 1883, Proceedings of Directors, N, 212-214 (May 10, 1883).

stroyed the market value of the bonds. Even the decision of the court was not clear on the legality of the use of bonds for that purpose. Until other funds could be obtained the work came to an end.[102] As a result of the limited expenditures on maintenance the canal experienced a gradual but general deterioration. Two indications of this were the filling up of the outlet lock at Cumberland and the virtual abandonment of the Tiber Creek branch.[103]

Even these economy measures proved insufficient, and the company found itself unable to pay all its obligations to its employees in the early years of the decade. By December, 1884, there was a floating debt of $170,862.94, "a large portion of it due to employees who had worked hard and faithfully to earn what is due them, and who have waited with unprecedented patience and forebearance for their wages."[104] In a desperate effort to wipe out these debts, the Board resorted to the sale of repair bonds on a large scale. Before 1885 only $125,000 of them had been sold to pay for the repairs and improvements of the waterway after the great flood of 1877.[105] In September, 1885, the directors sold $189,000 of them to Robert T. Baldwin, at 86, but they confessed that,

> Until the right to consummate the sale shall be settled, we are wholly unable to relieve the distress of many who have been deprived of their wages for more than a year, and whose sufferings for the bare necessaries of life have been great and painful during the past winter.[106]

Although the company succeeded in paying off all indebtedness for wages incurred in 1885, there was still a debt of $120,540.96 remaining from an excess of expenditures over receipts between 1878 and 1885.[107]

The following year was a critical one for the canal. In 1886,

[102] *58th Annual Report* (1886), pp. 10-11.

[103] Proceedings of Directors, N, 361 (May 25, 1887), quoting a letter from Col. George Schley; *59th Annual Report* (1887), pp. 10-11. In neither case, however, was the deterioration vital to canal trade.

[104] *57th Annual Report* (1885), pp. 5-7.

[105] Proceedings of Directors, N, 300 (December 8, 1884).

[106] *Ibid.*, pp. 317-319 (September 1, 1885); *57th Annual Report* (1885), p. 8. Baldwin also took an option to purchase $71,000 more within two years. This proved to be the beginning of a scramble to secure control of the canal through a majority holding of the repair bonds.

[107] *58th Annual Report* (1886), pp. 8, 11-12.

the period in which there had been no major disasters came to an end.[108] The trouble began early in March with a general strike of miners.[109] On April 1, a flood swept down the entire length of the upper Potomac valley, tearing a great hole in Dam No. 6, and generally wreaking havoc along the waterway.[110] On April 5, another freshet widened the gap in the dam and added to the destruction of the canal proper. At that time a complete report of the damage caused by the two floods revealed that over 200 feet of the dam had been entirely swept away, leaving 125 feet on the Virginia side weakened though still standing and 150 feet on the Maryland side which was described as old and rotten. In addition there were the usual large breaches in the banks, the partial filling of the canal by bars washed into the trunk, large rocks and earth slides, and heavy washes on the towpath.[111] A third flood, on May 9, widened the hole in Dam No. 6 to 237 feet, added fresh damage to the canal, and retarded the repairs already in progress.[112]

About the only hopeful sign in the otherwise black record for the year was the completion of the Piedmont and Cumberland Railroad.[113] An independent connection with the West Virginia coal fields had at last been realized. This railroad had built its line down the Potomac valley to the south of the Baltimore and Ohio, and therefore was not balked in its efforts to reach the canal by the refusal of that road to permit a crossing of its tracks. The ill-fated Cumberland and Georges Creek Railroad had been blocked in this way for many years, and as late as April, 1888, was still requesting the canal company to compel the Baltimore and Ohio to permit the crossing it

[108] Between 1882 and 1886, for example, there had been only one flood, in Washington County, in July, 1884. Although untimely and expensive, it was a relatively minor one. Report of the President, Proceedings of Directors, N, 273 (July 24, 1884).

[109] *Ibid.*, p. 328 (March 9, 1886).

[110] *59th Annual Report* (1887), pp. 5-6. See also the reports of Superintendents Biser and Mulvaney, *ibid.*, Appendix A, pp. 15 ff., Appendix B, pp. 23 ff.

[111] Report of S. Gambrill, Proceedings of Directors, N, 329-331 (April 22, 1886).

[112] Report of Superintendent Biser, *59th Annual Report* (1887), Appendix B, p. 25.

[113] *59th Annual Report* (1887), p. 11.

wished.[114] The Piedmont and Cumberland Railroad approached the basin from the other direction and easily gained the consent of the canal board to build its tracks across the waterway to a connection with the basin wharf.[115]

To meet the costs of the restoration of the canal after the floods of 1886, the company began to sell the remaining repair bonds of 1878 without restraint. On April 22, it ordered the firm of Robert T. Baldwin, or his assignees, Robert A. Garrett and Sons, to exercise the option to purchase $71,000 of the bonds.[116] Subsequent sales authorized and made in the same year accounted for $113,000 more, making a total of $498,000 sold by January, 1887. The average price of the bond sales was 80 per cent of par.[117] The $189,000 sold in 1885 had brought 86; the price required by the option for the $79,000 was 80; John A. Hambleton and Company bought $75,000 of the bonds in August at 78; and the final sale, at the end of the year, was for $38,000 at 76.[118]

The bonds were particularly desirable, for they carried a preferred mortgage on the physical property of the canal, not merely a claim against its revenues. By the middle eighties the life of the canal under its present management was believed by many to be of short duration. In the reorganization that would inevitably follow its bankruptcy, the waterway would probably be sold. Hence the bonds were a good investment. Railroad companies, eyeing the canal right of way as a possible roadbed, were especially interested, for the control of the 1878 bonds could force the sale of the canal in the bankruptcy proceedings. Two companies that were vitally concerned in the route occupied by the canal were the Baltimore and Ohio which feared a competitor on its flank, and the West Virginia Central which sought an outlet for its line from the West Virginia coal fields to Cumberland. The sale of $260,000 of the bonds to Baldwin and his assignee, Garrett, ultimately gave control of the

[114] Proceedings of Directors, N, 376 (April 19, 1888).

[115] *Ibid.*, pp. 345-346 (December 14, 1886).

[116] *Ibid.*, pp. 332-333 (April 22, 1886), including a letter of L. Victor Baughman, President, to R. T. Baldwin and R. Garrett & Sons, April 22, 1886.

[117] *59th Annual Report* (1887), p. 6.

[118] Proceedings of Directors, N, 317-318 (September 1, 1885), 332-333 (April 22, 1886), 338-339 (August 5, 1886), 344 (August 26, 1886), and 348-349 (January 5, 1887).

bonds to the Baltimore and Ohio. Meanwhile, the West Virginia Central interests, including several Senators, among them A. P. Gorman, began buying up the bonds. They soon discovered that the Baltimore and Ohio already possessed a majority and suspended their purchases.[119]

Notwithstanding the gloomy predictions of its impending failure and the struggle for control that was already developing, the financial condition of the canal improved somewhat in 1887 and 1888. Coal tonnage declined but slightly and revenues actually increased in 1887 and 1888, on the strength of higher tolls.[120] For the first time the Board made a distinction in toll charges between coal destined for the Washington market in which there would be less rivalry and that which was intended for transshipment to other Eastern markets. The directors fixed the rate for the latter at 34 cents a ton from Cumberland to Georgetown while locally consumed coal paid 40 cents a ton in 1887 and 44 cents a ton in 1888.[121] However, the tolls were still too low to produce revenues or profits on the scale of those in the prosperous postwar years. They were not, in fact, insufficient to provide enough money to pay the ordinary expenses of operation, much less to meet the interest on the repair bonds. Balances due to employees for unpaid back wages continued to mount rapidly, until by September, 1888, over $93,000 was owed to the men.[122] The omission of the payment of coupons on the repair bonds increased the threat of foreclosure. By July 1, 1888, the Board had passed three successive coupons.[123] One more would complete two years without payment, making the canal liable to foreclosure. Thus while the condition of the canal company had improved in comparison to 1886, its future had not measurably brightened by the end of 1888.

[119] Washington *Evening Star*, June 6, 1889. The West Virginia Central was formerly called the Piedmont and Cumberland.

[120] Canal trade amounted to 295,415 tons in 1886, 277,688 tons in 1887, and 286,183 tons in 1888. Canal receipts rose from $94,138.19 in 1886, to $129,-206.82 in 1887, and $129,469.87 in 1888. See Appendix, Tables IV and V.

[121] Proceedings of Directors, N, 360 (April 21, 1887), 372 (February 14, 1886).

[122] Report of the President, Proceedings of Directors, N, 392 (September 20, 1888).

[123] *Ibid.*

The new year soon gave indications that it would be a repetition of the disastrous year of 1886. Successive misfortunes assailed the canal from almost the opening day of navigation. On March 24, a large break occurred in the limestone region above Shepherdstown, interrupting navigation until April 2. On April 8, a rock slide occurred in the deep cut at the lower end of the tunnel, completely filling the waterway for a hundred feet. After ten days' effort, the repair gang finally removed the rocks, some of which weighed 20 to 50 tons. All year long the Rock Creek basin proved particularly troublesome. It had already been dredged twice by May 8, and was reported to be rapidly filling up again.[124]

Between May 30 and June 1, disaster again struck the canal. A titanic flood swept down the Potomac, the crest of which was higher than any ever before recorded in the history of the valley. It began with a disturbance that was described as a cyclone which entered the valley near Martinsburg, West Virginia, and crossed the river a few miles above Williamsport.[125] It was followed by heavy rains which swelled the Potomac until it poured over its banks.[126] The story was pretty much the same all along the canal. At Cumberland the water rose both in the main river and in Wills Creek until it completely submerged the land between them. At Hancock, it reached a point three feet above previous records set in 1877.[127] At Williamsport the crest was 44⅓ feet above the low-water mark, 7½ feet above 1877 levels. The junction of the Potomac and the Conococheague was described as a huge lake.[128] At Sandy Hook, opposite Harpers Ferry, the water rose to a point eight feet higher than the railroad tracks which were seventeen feet above the canal itself.[129] At Washington the crest was three feet above the level of the 1877 flood.[130]

[124] *Ibid.*, p. 413 (May 8, 1889).

[125] Cumberland *Evening Times*, May 30, June 1, 1889. The storm crossed back into West Virginia at Falling Waters. Washington *Evening Star*, June 1, 1889.

[126] Hagerstown *Mail*, June 7, 1889.

[127] Cumberland *Evening Times*, June 1, 1889.

[128] Hagerstown *Mail*, June 7, 1889.

[129] Frederick *Examiner*, June 5, 1889. The river rose to the tops of locomotives which had been run onto the bridge at Harpers Ferry to prevent it from being swept away. Hagerstown *Mail*, June 7, 1889.

[130] Washington *Evening Star*, June 1, 1889.

The damage caused by the rampaging river was fully as impressive as the record heights established by the flood.[131] There were the usual large breaks in the canal's banks, especially on the lower division. The torrent swept away many lock-houses, storehouses, and sheds, including all the company's buildings, tools, and materials at Sandy Hook. It was reported to be

> one of the peculiarities of the freshet of 1889 that the stone-work of the walls, &c., is more generally involved than on any previous occasion of the kind. The telephone wires [also] have been swept away, . . . and every bridge for which the canal company is responsible is down.[132]

Many frame buildings in the valley were torn from their foundations and carried downstream by the river.[133] Attempts to save the buildings at Knoxville by roping them to trees and stumps failed.[134] Additional damage to the canal itself included the destruction of Dam No. 6, in which the Potomac opened a 100-foot gap, and heavy washes of the towpath and the banks.[135] The flood waters carried away canal boats, teams, and cargoes, destroying the boats or depositing them crazily along both sides of the valley.[136] The swirling current also damaged mills, warehouses, and wharf facilities along the canal and at Georgetown.[137] Preliminary reports estimated the damage to the canal at from $500,000 to $1,000,000.[138] One fact was clear to all: the canal was a total wreck.

[131] The full report of the damage is in the Special Report of the President and Directors, June 13, 1889, to the 61st Annual Meeting, in Circuit Court for Washington County (Md.), *George S. Brown, et al.* vs. *the Chesapeake and Ohio Canal Company* (Equity No. 4191), pp. 6-9.

[132] Cumberland *Evening Times*, June 11, 1889.

[133] Hagerstown *Mail*, June 7, 1889.

[134] Frederick *Examiner*, June 5, 1889.

[135] Special Report of the President, etc., June 13, 1889, pp. 7-8.

[136] Washington *Evening Star*, June 1, 3, 1889; Cumberland *Evening Times*, June 5, 1889; Hagerstown *Mail*, June 7, 1889.

[137] Washington *Evening Star*, June 1, 3, 1889; Hagerstown *Mail*, June 7, 1889.

[138] Washington *Evening Star*, June 4, 1889, quoting Gambrill.

Chapter XII

THE LAST YEARS OF THE CANAL

After the river had receded to its normal level, the full extent of the damage to the canal became apparent. Early estimates placed the amount of the destruction along the waterway at between a half million and a million dollars.[1] The blow to the company did not end with the damage done to its works. The flood had scattered the canal boats, which carried its declining trade, all along the river, on both banks, often at some distance from the nearest water. It had swept others downstream and smashed them against the aqueduct and the Long Bridge. It left still others to rot in the dry canal bed.[2] The freshet put several hundred persons out of work through the destruction of the waterway. These included some two hundred and fifty employees and their families, from two to three hundred boatmen and their families and mules, and countless others in related occupations.[3] Many of these people lost the only means of livelihood they had ever known. Large numbers of the boatmen lounged around the company offices in Georgetown, stunned by the blow and more or less at a loss to know what to do.[4] Those towns which were closely associated with the canal in their prosperity were reported to be particularly hard hit.[5]

The destruction wrought by the river affected the life of the entire valley. The loss of the waterway as the primary line of transportation and communication was only one side of the picture, although it may well have been the most important. An indication of the far-reaching effects of this one result of the flood can be seen in the statement that the entire road system

[1] Washington *Evening Star*, June 4, 1889.

[2] *Ibid.*, June 3, 4, 1889; Cumberland *Evening Times*, June 5, 1889; Hagerstown *Mail*, June 7, 1889.

[3] Washington *Evening Star*, June 6, 1889; Hagerstown *Mail*, June 14, 1889.

[4] Washington *Evening Star*, June 4, 1889. The beginning of the dispersal of the boatmen from the Potomac valley was noted in the Hagerstown *Mail*, August 2, 1889.

[5] Cumberland *Evening Times*, June 15, 1889.

of the valley on the Maryland side was keyed to the canal. Only inferior connections existed with the railroad and the main highways.[6] Another effect on the valley as a whole was the destruction of the small industries along the river. Mills, warehouses, and feed stores were damaged or entirely swept away all along the Potomac.[7] Property values plummeted as the full extent of the flood damage became apparent.[8] Industries in Georgetown were particularly hard hit, because of their dependence on the canal for their water power and their raw materials. Flour mills and lime kilns suffered the most, although none escaped. The Borden Mining Company closed its agency in Georgetown permanently.[9] The Meredith and Winship wharves were wrecked and a large part of their stores washed away.[10] Millers fumed over the loss of water power.[11] At least three of the largest lime kilns went out of business, adding to the widespread unemployment and loss of purchasing power.[12] Prices of canal-shipped goods, wood, coal, and lime especially, rose rapidly.[13]

The valley above Georgetown and outside of the canal towns suffered from the damage to the land and the canal. The storm accompanying the flood and the waters of the river devastated hundreds of acres of rich farm land in four counties of western Maryland.[14] Thus the farmers lost part of their means of subsistence in addition to being deprived of the cheap access to markets which they had enjoyed via the canal. Valley inhabitants lost the not inconsiderable business which was subsidiary to the canal—feed-stores, boat-building, repair docks, warehouses, etc.[15] There was widespread poverty in the valley immediately after, and as a direct result of, the destruction wrought by the flood. On top of all else, the empty canal, with

[6] Washington *Evening Star*, June 10, 1889.

[7] Hagerstown *Mail*, June 7, 1889.

[8] Cumberland *Evening Times*, June 15, 1889.

[9] Washington *Evening Star*, June 5, 1889.

[10] *Ibid.*, June 1, 3, 1889.

[11] *Ibid.*, June 4, 1889.

[12] *Ibid.*, June 5, 1889.

[13] *Ibid.*, The price of wood rose 50 cents a cord, lime prices were up 10 to 16 cents a barrel, and coal cost 75 cents to $1.00 a ton more.

[14] *Ibid.*, June 10, 1889; Hagerstown *Mail*, June 14, 1889.

[15] Hagerstown *Mail*, June 14, 1889.

its stagnant pools and exposed murky bottom, constituted a real menace to the health of the suffering citizens.[16]

As soon as the extent of the wreckage of the canal was apparent, speculation on its future became rife. The subject had already been widely discussed by state newspapers even before the flood of 1889. The press of western Maryland was particularly active in the debate. The excuse for the seemingly premature outburst of speculation had been the repeated assertion of canal officials that the waterway was a failure.[17] The Hagerstown *Mail* was perhaps the first to take up the agitation for the disposal of the canal (which was of no direct assistance to its city). The gist of the *Mail*'s argument was that the section of the canal above Williamsport should be sold to the Western Maryland Railway to give the latter access to the Cumberland coal trade and to enable it to compete with the Baltimore and Ohio.[18] The *Mail* believed that the railroad could be compelled to keep the canal below Williamsport open for local trade.[19] To those who disagreed that the canal was a failure, especially the citizens of Cumberland who had a stake in it, the *Mail* replied that they simply refused to face the facts.[20] To those who were unwilling to see the canal destroyed for the benefit of Hagerstown and its railroad, the *Mail* asserted belligerently that it was only fair that the state's metropolis, Baltimore (eastern terminus of the Western Maryland Railway), should profit from the expenditure of the state rather than a foreign port (Georgetown).[21] In its stand it was supported by other papers whose communities had a stake in the railroad, for example, the Westminster *Sentinel*, and opposed by those interested in the canal, such as the Cumberland *Times* and the Montgomery (County) *Advocate*.[22] All papers and interests were inevitably thinking in selfish terms of the net value to themselves. When accused of this, the *Mail* frankly admitted it, but triumphantly called for a majority decision on the question of the future of the canal.[23]

[16] Cumberland *Evening Times*, June 15, 1889.

[17] See, for example, Hagerstown *Mail*, April 5, 12, 1889.

[18] *Ibid.*, April 5, 1889.

[19] *Ibid.*, April 12, 1889.

[20] *Ibid.*

[21] *Ibid.*, April 26, 1889.

[22] *Ibid.*, April 5, 19, 26, 1889.

[23] *Ibid.*, April 26, 1889. This would, of course, have meant a decision in the interests of the city of Baltimore, aided and abetted by Hagerstown.

After the flood, speculation increased by leaps and bounds. On one point there was fairly general agreement, at least in the period of shock that immediately followed the disaster. As the Cumberland *Times* observed, "It is the opinion of nearly everyone living along the river that the canal is irreparably injured." [24] The state press agreed generally, and usually without regrets.[25] State and canal officials, including Senator Gorman, Director Berret, the Honorable George Peter, Speaker of the Maryland Senate, ex-president James Clarke, and President Gambrill, all thought so.[26] The *Coal Trade Journal*, reflecting the opinions of shippers on the canal, agreed.[27] And the boatmen themselves were reported to be generally pessimistic over the future of the waterway.[28]

The next question was the disposal of the canal company, its rights, and its magnificent wreck. On this point there was no general agreement. Rumors as to the course of action that was to be taken were rampant. One report said that the company was going to secure a loan of one million dollars from a group of capitalists in Amsterdam for the purpose of restoring the waterway.[29] Another version was that ex-president Clarke would head a syndicate of American capitalists who would take over the canal, restore it, and operate it "without political interference." [30] A third rumor claimed the company would issue $300,000 in toll certificates to repair the canal. This provoked the *Mail* to observe that canal securities on the pledge of revenues under the mortgage of 1844 were selling for $5 to $10 each, and that there would probably be no market for the certificates which would have in effect the same security.[31]

The most popular rumor was that the canal would be sold, presumably to a railroad company, for the construction of a towpath railway. This was the last stage in the development of the speculation. Popular imagination soon pictured the Western Maryland, the Pennsylvania, and the West Virginia

[24] Cumberland *Evening Times*, June 5, 1889.

[25] The indifference of the state press was particularly irritating to the sober Hagerstown *Mail*. See especially June 14, 1889.

[26] Washington *Evening Star*, June 3, 4, 6, 10, 1889.

[27] Quoted in the Cumberland *Evening Times*, June 17, 1889.

[28] Washington *Evening Star*, June 4, 1889.

[29] *Ibid.*

[30] *Ibid.*, June 12, 1889.

[31] Hagerstown *Mail*, July 12, 1889.

Central railroad companies as all interested in the canal.[32] This brought up in turn the question of the attitude of the Baltimore and Ohio toward the waterway, for it had emerged as the majority bondholder under the mortgage of 1878. Opinion was divided as to whether the Baltimore and Ohio would foreclose its mortgage or not.[33]

Inevitably there was a reaction in favor of the canal from the depths of gloom and despair that had followed the flood. The early estimates of repair costs were soon reduced officially to $250,000 or $300,000.[34] The Georgetown millers had been anxious for the restoration of at least the Georgetown level ever since the extent of the damage had been ascertained. But they had been unable to convince others in the District of Columbia that their interests also required the repair of the canal, and the millers were unwilling to undertake the expense themselves.[35] The large number of business failures, actual or impending, helped bring about the reaction in favor of piecemeal restoration of the waterway, along the lines laid down by the millers.[36] The same reaction brought informal offers to repair sections of the canal at Cumberland and Williamsport.[37] The Maryland Canal Union at Cumberland undertook a correspondence with a New York society to secure information on the relation of the state of New York to the Erie Canal, looking forward probably to a revival of the *Times'* earlier suggestion that the state of Maryland take over the waterway and operate it as a free public highway, in imitation of the Erie.[38] A

[32] Washington *Evening Star,* June 5, 6, 1889; Hagerstown *Mail,* August 2, 1889.

[33] Colonel Berret said that the minority bondholders would sue for foreclosure if the Baltimore and Ohio procrastinated. (Washington *Evening Star,* June 6, 1889.) On the other hand, President Gambrill expressed doubt that the railroad would try to foreclose, pointing out that the latter would probably prefer to have a crippled canal as a competitor than another railroad. (Cumberland *Evening Times,* June 22, 1889.)

[34] Special Report of the President, etc., June 13, 1889, *George S. Brown, et al.* vs. *the Chesapeake and Ohio Canal Company,* p. 9.

[35] Washington *Evening Star,* June 4, 8, 1889.

[36] *Ibid.,* June 13, 1889. There were renewed proposals for the restoration of the canal with loans from the coal companies. The state was prohibited from extending its credit to public works companies.

[37] Hagerstown *Mail,* July 19, 1889. Gambrill denied that any definite offers had been made.

[38] Cumberland *Evening Times,* June 21, 1889. The proposed convention of

convention of friends of the canal met in Georgetown to consider ways of restoring the waterway, perhaps by a lease to capitalists.[39] Even the *Mail* was swept up in the general enthusiasm and conceded that the canal had been invaluable to the farmers and miners of the state as well as profitable to shippers.[40]

The admission on the part of the canal company that it was unable to raise funds to repair its works and that it was bankrupt brought to an end the preliminary speculation over the future of the canal. At the same time the Baltimore and Ohio Railroad emerged as the majority owner of both the 1878 and the 1844 bonds, thus holding preferred mortgages on the physical property and the revenues of the canal. Seemingly it would be the one to decide the future of its former great rival. The railroad company weighed the comparative costs of a forced sale to a possible competitor (or to itself at a high price) and the restoration of the canal at its own expense. It chose the latter course. In December, 1889, it petitioned the court for the appointment of receivers under the mortgage of 1844.[41] In January, 1890, it also petitioned the court for the sale of the canal under the mortgage of 1878, in order to prevent others from filing the petition by default.[42] It pushed its claims under the first petition.

The next question was what court would be competent to appoint a receiver for the entire canal. The Chesapeake and Ohio Canal Company had been chartered by Virginia, Maryland, Pennsylvania, and the United States. It owned property in Virginia, Maryland, and the District of Columbia; and did business in Maryland and the District of Columbia. The solution to this problem was the simultaneous petition for receivers

the canal to a state-owned public waterway had been vehemently rejected by the Hagerstown *Mail*, April 12, 1889.

[39] Cumberland *Evening Times*, September 10, 1889.

[40] Hagerstown *Mail*, February 28, 1890.

[41] *George S. Brown et al.* vs. *the Chesapeake and Ohio Canal Company*, Circuit Court for Washington County (Maryland), No. 4191 Equity, p. 1. The bill of complaint was filed December 31, 1889.

[42] *George S. Brown et al.* vs. *the Chesapeake and Ohio Canal Company*, Circuit Court for Washington County, No. 4198 Equity. The bill of complaint was filed January 31, 1890. One petition for sale had already been filed by Anna M. Hughes and Thomas Hughes. *Ibid.*, pp. 38-39.

in Maryland and District of Columbia courts.[43] The choice of the Maryland court was a curious one. Apparently after much thought, the railroad company passed over the state courts and brought suit in the Circuit Court for Washington County. Was a county court legally competent to decide the fate of the canal which extended through several counties? Many observers thought not. They reckoned without the presiding judge of the court. Justice Alvey was a proud and ambitious jurist in an ambitious county, and he was destined to go far in state political and judicial circles. Judge Alvey believed that he was quite competent to sit in judgment on the case, and he so ruled. Deliberate or accidental, the choice of the Washington County Circuit Court proved to be a fortunate one, for Judge Alvey and his successors consistently ruled in favor of the railroad's interests on almost every point of legal interpretation while the canal was under the court's jurisdiction.

Another interesting point in the case that was shaping up was the position of the state of Maryland, the majority stockholder and secondary mortgage-holder in the canal company. Many professed to see in the stand which the state took an indication of the position of A. P. Gorman, the political boss of the majority party. Maryland intervened in 1890, and requested the sale of the canal.[44] The trustees of 1844, acting for the Baltimore and Ohio Railroad, the majority bondholder, objected to the intervention and petition of the state on the ground that it had already waived its prior liens, and urged therefore that the request for the sale of the canal should not be granted.[45] It is possible Senator Gorman hoped that by forcing the sale of the canal the West Virginia Central Railroad, in which he and several other Senators were interested, could secure an outlet to tidewater. He probably had the support of Baltimore

[43] *George S. Brown et al.* vs. *Chesapeake and Ohio Canal Company*, Supreme Court of the District of Columbia, 12,240 Equity, Docket 30.

[44] George S. Brown et al. *vs.* Chesapeake and Ohio Canal Company, Nos. 4191 and 4198 Equity, pp. 31-32.

[45] *Ibid.*, pp. 35-36. Senator Gorman was a director of the West Virginia Central and Pittsburgh Railroad Company from 1884 to 1887 and from 1894 to 1902. See the list of directors in the 2d, 3d, 4th, 5th, 12th, 13th, 14th, 15th, 16th, 17th, 18th, 19th, and 20th *Annual Reports of the West Virginia Central and Pittsburgh Railroad Company* (1884-1887, 1894-1902). Senators Davis, Elkins, and Blaine also served as officials of the company for some years.

interests, although for a different reason. The city controlled the Western Maryland Railway which it had built during the reaction against the Baltimore and Ohio, but which had stopped short of Cumberland and the coal fields. The Western Maryland hoped to buy enough of the canal right-of-way, that is, from Williamsport to Cumberland, to extend its tracks to the coal fields.

The proceedings of the case are noteworthy for the evidence they contain of the interplay of rival pressure groups seeking to gain control of the canal for their own purposes. The Baltimore and Ohio's conduct can be explained by its intention to prevent the canal from falling into the hands of a potential competitor, at the lowest possible expense to itself. The state urged the sale of the waterway, ostensibly to realize some return on its $2,000,000 loan and $5,000,000 investment in canal stock, but really to bring about the ends sought by the various interests supporting the state's position.[46] Minority bondholders of 1878 accused the Baltimore and Ohio of seeking receivership under the mortgage of 1844 merely to prevent the sale of the canal to a competitor. They urged instead the disposal of the waterway, each for his own personal reasons.[47] President Gambrill on behalf of the board of directors, requested the sale of the canal, but insisted that it be sold *in toto*.[48] This position may have reflected most clearly the real wishes of Senator Gorman, brother-in-law of the president.

After hearing all parties concerned, Judge Alvey rendered his decision.[49] He confessed that he was unable to see the basis of the canal company's appeal for immediate sale, for that would inevitably mean its self-imposed destruction. On the other hand, he accepted without question the contention of the trustees of 1844 that the waterway might be operated profitably if restored and freed from political control (a very convenient and over-worked epithet of damnation). He decided that the canal should be given another chance, and agreed to

[46] *George S. Brown et al.* vs. *Chesapeake and Ohio Canal Company*, Nos. 4191 and 4198 Equity, pp. 31-32, 34, and 69.

[47] Answer of Anna Hughes and Thomas Hughes, Trustees, *ibid.*, pp. 38-39.

[48] *Ibid.*, p. 81.

[49] Opinion of the Court, *ibid.*, pp. 80-89.

appoint receivers under the mortgage of 1844 to restore and operate it.[50]

The early reports of the receivers glowed with optimistic statements of probable repair costs and of the willing cooperation of the coal companies (at least one of which was controlled by the railroad company).[51] Then a note of gloom settled over the receivers and the court.[52] The latter agreed that the restoration of the waterway could not be achieved at a cost that might reasonably be expected to be repaid. On September 1, 1890, Judge Alvey announced himself ready to issue an order for the sale of the canal *in toto*.[53] At some time during the following month, the railroad company must suddenly have come to life and decided that restoration of the canal was after all the cheapest policy. At any rate, the receivers announced that they had changed their minds and were ready to repair and operate the canal.[54] On October 2, Justice Alvey, not in the least upset by this apparently capricious conduct, ordered the sale as promised, but suspended it on the condition that the trustees of 1844 promptly restore the canal.[55] The decision of the District of Columbia Court followed the same course as that of the Washington County Court.

Under the threat of a forced sale, the Baltimore and Ohio undertook the restoration of the waterway. The actual work of repair took much longer and was more expensive than had been anticipated. At least part of the additional cost of the work was due to the delay in commencing repairs.[56] The repairs were

[50] *Ibid.*, p. 89. Receivers were appointed, March 3, 1890.

[51] 2d Report of Receivers, June 9, 1890, *ibid.*, pp. 111-133. As exhibits, the receivers filed estimates of engineers that the total cost of restoration would be $268,698, and that counting the work already done locally on the Cumberland, Williamsport, and Georgetown levels, the cost would be only $180,198. Furthermore, they stated that the coal companies had guaranteed an annual tonnage of 450,000 tons for four years, which would be equivalent to $134,360 tolls per year. See also 4th Report of District Receivers, *ibid.*, pp. 180-181.

[52] The change in tone of the petitions was abrupt. It is obvious in the petition of the trustees of 1848 [1844] that the canal must not be sold to the Cumberland and Washington Railroad Company, to whom it surely would go if a sale was to be ordered then. *Ibid.*, p. 198.

[53] Opinion of the Court, September 1, 1890, *ibid.*, p. 211.

[54] Final Opinion of the Court, October 2, 1890, *ibid.*, p. 217.

[55] *Ibid.* The order for the sale of the canal was issued, October 2, 1890. *Ibid.*, p. 226.

[56] Report of Trustees, January 30, 1894, in *Chesapeake and Ohio Canal Company* vs. *the Western Maryland Railway Company*, January 18, 1904, Maryland Court of Appeals, pp. 109-110.

finally completed by September, 1891, and the canal was reopened for business. The total cost of the restoration of the canal was $430,764.43, all of which had to be borrowed from outside sources.[57]

Canal trade recovered quickly, but was unable to expand beyond the low averages of the eighties.[58] Many of the boatmen had left the valley or had turned to other occupations. The position of Georgetown as a port had suffered greatly as a result of the prolonged suspension of canal navigation. The rate of tolls established for the coal trade, 40 cents a ton from Cumberland to Georgetown plus 4 cents wharfage less 10 cents rebate, was not likely to divert much of the trade from the Baltimore and Ohio Railroad. It is not unlikely that the probable result was a consideration in the establishment of the rate. At that the low toll charges did not attract enough business to meet expenses. At no time after 1890 did the canal operate profitably.

The railroad company resorted to a shadow corporation to enable the waterway to show a profit, as the court order had required. It organized the Chesapeake and Ohio Transportation Company which entered into a contract with the canal receivers in 1894. In return for the latter's guarantee to keep the waterway in a navigable condition, the transportation company agreed to provide whatever boats were necessary to carry the trade offered, in addition to the boats already in service. It further guaranteed the canal company an annual profit of $100,000.[59] The court ratified the contract over the protest of the state, and extended until 1901 the time limit before the order for the sale of the canal would become effective.[60] With the annual "profits" the receivers proceeded to pay the costs of receivership, the loans for the restoration of the waterway, and the bonds of 1878, in the sequence established by the court. In

[57] *Ibid.*, p. 110.

[58] *Ibid.*, pp. 110-112.

[59] *Ibid.*, pp. 114-116; the contract was dated January 30, 1894. It went into effect, January 1, 1896. Report of the Trustees, April 6, 1901, *ibid.*, p. 129. The letter books of the company are deposited in the National Archives.

[60] Answer of the state of Maryland, February 15, 1894, *ibid.*, pp. 117-120; Opinion of the Court, February 15, 1894, *ibid.*, p. 121. The state of Maryland appealed the decision on July 30, 1894, but the Court of Appeals affirmed the decision of the lower court, June 17, 1896 (State *vs.* Cowen, et al.). *Ibid.* pp. 121-122, 129.

1901, the court again extended the time limit four years, until December 31, 1905.[61] In 1905 it approved a revised contract between the receivers and the transportation company by which the latter agreed merely to guarantee the canal company against loss. Thereafter, the time was automatically extended each year upon evidence that the canal was not operating at a loss.[62]

The obvious purpose and result of the contract with the transportation company was to postpone indefinitely the order for the sale of the canal. The Baltimore and Ohio Railroad, as the chief bondholder under the mortgages of 1878 and 1844, had restored the waterway as the cheapest method of preventing it from falling into the hands of a competitor. The unexpectedly high cost of reconstruction and the insistence of the court that the canal show a profit from its operations forced the railroad to use the device of an intermediary company to absorb the operational losses of the canal. In effect, the railroad loaned the canal receivers the funds which made possible the restoration of the waterway. It then created a dummy corporation through which it paid the canal enough money to cover its expenses and to repay the loans from the railroad. When the railroad had repaid itself for its own advances, and given itself something on account of the bonds of 1878 (pursuant to court order), it modified the contract arrangement to provide merely that the canal should be guaranteed its expenses. The court was thus satisfied that on paper the canal was not operating at a loss, and the railroad was assured of security from competition at the cost of the restoration and operation of the canal, plus the small expenses of receivership.

In 1902 the receivers took another step towards the establishment of a complete control over freight charges on the water-

[61] Report of the Trustees, April 6, 1901, *ibid.*, pp. 129-130. The trustees said that the transportation company would continue its contract for the full ten years if the court would extend the time allowed the trustees. The state of Maryland objected, on the grounds that its interest would in effect be destroyed if the canal were not sold, but the time extended. The court, as usual, ruled in favor of the trustees, April 29, 1901. The state appealed the decision, May 4, 1901, but the order of the lower court was affirmed, January 15, 1902. *Ibid.*, pp. 133-136.

[62] Report and Petition of the Trustees, December 13, 1905, and Court decree, December 27, 1905, filed in Canal Cases, Circuit Court for Washington County, Hagerstown, Maryland. The location of these manuscripts will be cited hereinafter as Canal Cases.

way. The Canal Towage Company was organized along the lines first suggested by A. P. Gorman.[63] The primary function of this enterprise was to provide economy and regularity in the runs of the waterway. To do this the company supplied the boats, teams, and equipment, and established a regular schedule for the boatmen to follow. It also cut freight rates and controlled the distribution of cargoes. There is no doubt that the company improved the service and the efficiency of canal navigation, but in so doing it destroyed the last shred of independence for the canallers. They could still sing their songs, heap scorn on passers-by, blow their silver or brass horns, and shout, "Hey-y-y, Lock!" but the canal had lost much of its romance.[64] Boats were numbered instead of named; they were uniform and utilitarian rather than colorfully individualistic. Spirited, unruly, and lackadaisical boatmen were alike undesirable to the company; the rougher ones were not permitted to use its boats. Traffic became regularized on a time-table basis.

The transition in the position of the boatmen in the changing canal scene had been in progress for many years. The growth of marked distinctions in canal society in the latter half of the nineteenth century—officials, shippers, and canallers—mirrored the development of the capitalist, middle, and laboring classes in the country as a whole. The emergence of the waterway as a money-making, big business enterprise in the seventies tended to increase the differences by exerting pressure on all groups to maintain the *status quo* in order not to disturb the canal's prosperity. If anything, the impact of the depression after 1875

[63] Information on the operation of the Canal Towage Company was obtained from an interview with George Nicolson, former engineer and general superintendent of the canal, and from the letter books of the company during the receivership period, in the National Archives. See also Washington *Evening Star*, July 11, 1905

[64] Interviews with former boatmen, canal employees and valley inhabitants. One of the better songs, accurately descriptive, had as one verse (there was a stanza for each section of the journey . . . many of them unprintable):

> I was comin' down the Log Wall an' give a mighty yell—
> the hames catched afire an' the driver catched hell;
> The cap'n played the fiddle; the steerman played the flute,
> The cook poured the coffee in the old man's boot—
> Git along, old bones, git along!

For other songs and stories of the canal see Lee McCardell's series of articles in the Baltimore *Evening Sun*, August 9, 10, 11, 12, and 13, 1937.

heightened the pressure on the boatmen. The directors insisted that nothing should interfere with the attempts of the canal company to maintain itself. The long-term benefits of maintaining the waterway as a going concern outweighed, in the Board's opinion, the immediate hardships to the canallers which might result. For this reason strikes of boatmen, like the one in 1876, were crushed, wages and freight charges slashed, and canal trade regularized. The canallers were caught in a squeeze between the efforts of the coal companies and the canal company to reduce expenses. The coal companies, which built and owned most of the canal boats, sought to maintain boat rents and sale prices at high levels. To meet these continuing expenses, boatmen needed high freight charges. But the canal company, seeking to cut transportation costs and maintain tolls at a profitable level, demanded lower freight rates. The Canal Towage Company, sponsored by the Consolidation Coal Company and the canal receivers (both dominated by the Baltimore and Ohio), represented the culmination of the late nineteenth-century trends towards lower charges and complete control over coal transportation. Independent boatmen could not compete with the Towage Company and its sponsors. A comparison of receipts and expenses of independent boatmen before the organization of the Towage Company and the boats operated by that company clearly demonstrates the relative disadvantage of the independent canallers.[65]

BALANCE SHEET

(PER TRIP)

Independent Boatmen		
Receipts		
90 tons @ 65c. a ton		$58.50
Expenses		
Boat Rent..	$15.00	
Mule Hire..	16.00	
Way bills...	4.80	
Feed	5.00	
		40.80
Profit per trip.........		$17.70

Canal Towage Company Boats		
Receipts		
90 tons @ 45c. a ton		$40.50
Expenses		
Way bills....	$4.80	
Feed	5.00	
		9.80
Profit per trip.........		$30.70

[65] Washington *Evening Star*, July 11, 1905.

The chief articles in the trade offered for transportation on the canal in the latter period of its existence were coal, lime, building materials, and some flour.[66] Of these commodities the most important was coal, which accounted for almost the entire amount of business on the waterway. The Consolidation Coal Company, owned by the Baltimore and Ohio, supplied over 99 per cent of the business. The former transported the coal from its mines in western Maryland to its own wharf at the canal basin in Cumberland via the Cumberland and Pennsylvania Railroad, also owned by the Baltimore and Ohio. It shipped the coal from Cumberland to Washington in its own fleet of boats, operated by the Canal Towage Company which had been created by the Consolidation Coal Company in cooperation with the canal receivers. These boats navigated on the Chesapeake and Ohio Canal, which had been restored and maintained by the Baltimore and Ohio and its subsidiary, the Chesapeake and Ohio Transportation Company. Thus, in effect, the trade on the waterway in the receivership period was limited primarily to that supplied by the Baltimore and Ohio interests for consumption in the local market. The domination of canal affairs by its erstwhile rival was complete.

On the whole, trade on the waterway after 1890 was rather uneventful.[67] Although the farmers who brought their crops to market via the canal continued to cause the company some anguish with their makeshift boats and irregular habits, they were the last representatives of an age which had long since passed. The receivers prohibited the operation of steamboats on the canal as too destructive to the banks. They cooperated, however, in experiments with the use of tractors as motive power on the towpath. But the tests soon demonstrated that the old mule teams and wooden barges provided the cheapest and most efficient means of transportation. During the World War the canal carried coal for the government proving grounds

[66] "Summary of the History and Present Status of the Chesapeake and Ohio Canal," George Washington Memorial Parkway Commission, File 500-10, Section 2, Department of Interior (Washington, D. C.); Statistics of the Coal Trade, 1909-1924, Records of the Chesapeake and Ohio Canal Company (receivership papers). The trustees argued in 1924 that it was inadvisable to repair the canal for other than the coal trade. Report of the Trustees for 1922, 1923, 1924, filed February 6, 1925, Canal Cases. See below, Appendix, Table IV

[67] Information supplied by Mr. Nicolson and former boatmen.

at Indianhead, Maryland, down the river.[68] For the first time tugs regularly hauled canal boats with their precious cargoes up and down the Potomac below tidewater.

At no time did the amount of trade on the canal justify the continued operation of the waterway. It became, in fact, ever smaller despite the growth of the city of Washington and the demands of the World War. The lack of aggressive leadership for the canal undoubtedly contributed to this decline. The obsolescence of the waterway as a means of transportation, of Georgetown as a port, and of the Potomac River as a channel for trade also hurt the competitive position of the canal. Irregularity of navigation played its part, although the length of time had been reduced. The freshets, occasional breaches in the trunk—especially in the lime sinks of the upper valley, and innumerable incidental occurrences all interfered with navigation. Above all, the Cumberland coal region, which had been referred to so often in the early nineteenth century as inexhaustible, was almost worked out. The miners' strike in 1922 was evidence of the declining productivity of the mines, and was itself almost a death-blow to the coal fields and the canal alike.[69]

The importance of the waterway in the receivership period was not so much in the trade it carried or in its position as a transportation agency; it was rather its role in the struggle between the railroads for control of the route it occupied.

The focus of this struggle was the attempt of George Gould to extend his inland railroad empire to the Atlantic coast during the first decade of the twentieth century.[70] Several

[68] Washington *Evening Star*, September 26, 1918. The government built five boats for the canal trade and was to add five more. The Canal Towage Company had about eighty boats in operation. It is interesting to note that the war brought a revival of many of the same troubles the canal experienced during the Civil War: strikes, inflation, the draft, etc.

[69] The influence of the depression in the Cumberland coal trade and particularly the effect of the miners' strike was noted in the Report of the Trustees for 1922, 1923, and 1924, filed February 6, 1925, Canal Cases. The exhaustion of the Cumberland mines was generally cited as a cause for the decline of canal trade by former boatmen and local inhabitants in Cumberland. It is also shown by statistics on coal production in the United States.

[70] See especially, *Report of the Committee on Interstate Commerce on Railroad Combination in the Eastern Region*, February 6, 1940, 76th Cong., 3d sess.

changes had occurred in the control of the competing roads in the western Maryland and West Virginia coal fields. The Baltimore and Ohio had gone into receivership in 1896 and had fallen under the control of its rival, the Pennsylvania Railroad, between 1899 and 1901.[71] In 1902, the city of Baltimore sold its control of the Western Maryland Railway to a syndicate representing the Gould interests.[72] Another syndicate in which Gould was represented had purchased the West Virginia Central Railroad.[73] Even so, Gould's line to the east was not unbroken. There were several gaps in the system, among which one of the most formidable was that between the western terminus of the Western Maryland at Big Pool on the Chesapeake and Ohio Canal, near Williamsport, and the eastern terminus of the West Virginia Central at Cumberland.[74]

In 1903, the Western Maryland Railway Company petitioned the Maryland Board of Public Works for permission to extend its line up the Potomac valley to Cumberland, crossing and recrossing the canal en route.[75] The state legislature, representing several converging interests, supported the petition. The Assembly was still very hostile to the Baltimore and Ohio Railroad, partly because of the legacy of opposition from the seventies and eighties and partly because it had fallen under the domination of a foreign corporation, the Pennsylvania Railroad. The Board of Public Works granted permission to cross the canal and approved the plans for the crossings. The court confirmed the arrangement over the protests of the trustees that the proposed bridges would interfere with navigation and infringe upon canal property.[76] The state approved

Senate, Report No. 1182, Part 1 (*Before 1920*), Ch. III ("George Gould moves Eastward") and IV ("More Community of Interest and the Collapse of Gould").

[71] *Ibid.*, pp. 18, 22-24. See also *ibid.*, Appendix 3, pp. 85-91.

[72] *Ibid.*, p. 36.

[73] *Ibid.*

[74] *Ibid.*, p. 37; see also the map in *ibid.* between pp. 36-37.

[75] Petition of the Western Maryland Railway Company, June 13, 1903; Order of the Court, June 13, 1903; Petition of Western Maryland Railway Company, October 5, 1903; in *Chesapeake and Ohio Canal Company* vs. *Western Maryland Railway Company*, pp. 140-149. See also Act of Maryland Legislature, 1904, ch. 56, passed March 9, 1904, in Special Report of the Trustees, January 26, 1905, *ibid.*, pp. 315-317.

[76] Answer of Trustees, October 5, 1903; Order of the Court, October 17,

the grant in 1904.[77] The receivers thereupon made the best of the situation by using the payments for abutment sites to continue to satisfy the claims against the canal company in proper sequence.[78] In effect this meant that the Baltimore and Ohio, after failing to prevent the construction of a competing line, accepted the money for the lands surrendered and paid itself on account of its holdings of 1878 bonds. Notwithstanding his victory in Maryland, Gould failed to complete his projected line to the Atlantic coast, partly because of the effective opposition of the Pennsylvania and New York Central interests and partly because of the financial difficulties in which he became involved in 1907.[79]

Meanwhile, in 1904, the state proceeded to dispose of its holdings in the canal company for whatever price they would bring. The authority for the disposal of its stocks on these terms had been granted to the Board of Public Works by the state constitution and by a subsequent act of the legislature. Payment was to be made in state bonds—a revival of the old connection between public works and state finances. Fairfax S. Landstreet, a vice president of the Western Maryland Railway Company, bid $155,000 for the $2,000,000 loan rights and over $5,000,000 of canal stock. The bid was accepted in December, 1904, and the transfer consummated.[80] When the Gould properties went into receivership in 1907, the Western Maryland's holdings of canal stock eventually fell to the Baltimore and Ohio Railroad.[81] At the same time, the Pennsylvania Railroad began to sell its holdings in Baltimore and Ohio stock, fearing the intervention of the Interstate Commerce Commission and the federal courts and the possible forced sale of the stock under less favorable conditions.[82] The Baltimore and

1903, October 20, 1903; Special Report of the Trustees, January 26, 1905; *ibid.*, pp. 157-159, 172-173, 315.

[77] Act of the General Assembly of Maryland, passed March 9, 1904, in Special Report of Trustees, January 26, 1905, *ibid.*, pp. 315-317.

[78] *Ibid.*, pp. 320-325, 341-346.

[79] *Report on Railroad Combination in the Eastern Region*, I, 58-59.

[80] *Chesapeake and Ohio Canal Company* vs. *Western Maryland Railway Company*, pp. 326-328.

[81] The deed, dated July 29, 1907, filed in Washington County Liber 126, Folio 209, records the transfer of stock to the Continental Trust Company of Baltimore. See also Auditor's 10th Report, August 9, 1841, Canal Cases.

[82] *Report on Railroad Combination in the Eastern Region*, I, 65-66. See also *ibid.*, Appendix 3, pp. 85-91.

Ohio thus resumed its independent existence, and the relationship between the canal and the railroad returned to the status of 1895.

The receivers disposed of other canal properties from time to time, with the consent of the court. The Baltimore and Ohio secured the right to lay a spur track beside the canal from a point on its Metropolitan branch just outside the District of Columbia to the Rock Creek mole. It also secured several valuable parcels of land on the mole and in Cumberland for the erection of warehouses. Proceeds from the transaction were used to pay the interest and principal of the bonds of 1878, so the sales really cost the railroad nothing.[83] The canal company was unable to prevent these inroads on its domain because the railroad now controlled a majority of both bonds and stock.

The receivers granted permission to the Potomac Light and Power Company for the erection of a power station at the dam near Williamsport.[84] Virginia properties of the canal company at Great Falls, inherited from the Potomac Company, were sold on the order of the courts over the protest of the trustees. The purchaser was the Great Falls Power Company, but the proposed development never advanced beyond the planning stage.[85] Even the federal government became a party to the piecemeal disposal of the canal, beginning in 1915, when it sought to obtain all or part of the mole in order to reopen the mouth of Rock Creek in connection with the Rock Creek and Potomac Parkway project.[86] In all cases, the proceeds of

[83] On the acquisition of lands in Cumberland by the Baltimore and Ohio, see Auditor's Report No. 3, ratified by the court order of November 19, 1910, Canal Cases. Lands on the mole were reserved by the terms of the contract of sale to the United States.

[84] Report and Petition of Trustees, July 23, 1906, and copy of the agreement with the Martinsburg Power Company (predecessor of Potomac Light and Power Company), Canal Cases.

[85] The original agreement between the trustees and the Great Falls Power Company was dated March 19, 1901, Canal Cases. However, the litigation in the case was not finally settled until 1925. See the opinion of Chief Justice Holt, in Chesapeake and Ohio Canal Company *vs.* Great Falls Power Company, Circuit Court for Fairfax County (Virginia), Special Court of Appeals, October 1, 1925.

[86] Notes on a conference between J. G. Langdon and George Nicolson, January 15, 1915, "Informational Material in *re* the Chesapeake and Ohio Canal," MS, Records of the Rock Creek and Potomac Parkway Commission, Department of Interior Archives (National Archives). The government was

the sales, amounting to about $800,000, eventually found their way to the Baltimore and Ohio Railroad in payment of the principal and interest on the 1878 bonds.[87] During the entire receivership period not one penny was ever paid to the bondholders of 1844, under whose mortgage the court authorized the restoration and operation of the waterway.

In March, 1924, a long over-due flood in the Potomac valley wrecked the canal for the fifth time in its history.

The canal had not wholly escaped the ravages of floods in the interval since 1890.[88] On the contrary, freshets had occurred with depressing regularity, the most serious ones in 1897, 1902, 1907, and 1914. The work of repair and restoration went on unceasingly. As soon as the rough spots from one freshet were smoothed out, another would bring in new bars, cause new breaches, and wash the towpath again. None of the floods, however, was so disastrous that the railroad hesitated to repair the damage, and none approached the proportions of the freshets of 1877 and 1889.

On March 29, 1924, the waters of the Potomac began to rise at Cumberland. Heavy rains swelled the river so that it mounted at a rate of thirty inches an hour to levels approaching the record crest of 1889.[89] At Williamsport the river reached a point twenty-eight feet above normal, seven feet below the mark of 1889. A brief cold snap momentarily halted the rise of the Potomac on March 30, and even reversed it.[90] The next

still trying to reach some agreement with the trustees in the matter in 1929. U. S. Grant, 3rd, to R. Walton Moore, House of Representatives, February 15, 1929, George Washington Memorial Parkway Commission, File 500-10.

[87] See, for example, the agreements with the Western Maryland Railway Company, January 16, 1905 (ratified March 7, 1905), May 28, 1912 (ratified June 26, 1912), and July 10, 1912 (ratified July 20, 1912), for the sale of lands and rights valued at $500,000, $167,500, and $2,000 respectively. The proceeds of these sales went to the Baltimore and Ohio Railroad Company or its officials in repayment of principal and interest on the trustees' notes which were issued to repair the canal after 1890 and on the repair bonds of 1878, all of which were owned by the railroad company. After all these sums had been paid out, there was still $132,500 unpaid on the principal of the repair bonds. See Auditor's Report No. 4, July 30, 1912, Canal Cases.

[88] Information on the freshets and the effects on the canal was supplied by Mr. Nicolson.

[89] Hagerstown *Daily Mail*, March 29, 1924; Washington *Evening Star*, March 29, 1924; Washington *Sunday Star*, March 30, 1924.

[90] Hagerstown *Daily Mail*, March 31, 1924.

day the river rose again, but by that time the threat of a major disaster was past, as much of the run-off had occurred.[91] A survey of the damage in the valley revealed that the flood was not nearly so serious as had been feared. There was really little destruction outside of the canal, which had been badly mauled at Cumberland where the torrent in the river had leveled some of the banks.[92] The dams survived the onslaught of the river fairly well, and the lower valley escaped serious damage altogether.[93]

The flood of 1924 provided the opportunity for the railroad to relieve itself of the expense of operating the canal. The receivers made no effort to restore the canal beyond the Georgetown level. They authorized enough repairs to protect what was left of the waterway and to enable them to assert that the canal could quickly be put into navigable condition if sufficient business was presented to warrant the effort.[94] The canal was left a magnificent wreck, but technically a going concern in which the water rents received from the Georgetown factories paid the expenses of the minimum operating staff. The court accepted the position of the receivers, and ruled that the canal had not forfeited its rights by non-operation, but that the "other" aspect of its business, the maintenance of a canal for purposes of navigation, was merely suspended temporarily in the absence of remunerative business.[95] Both the receivers and the court continued to maintain the ludicrous contention that the canal was not abandoned, and could easily and quickly be

[91] Hagerstown *Morning Herald*, April 1, 1924.

[92] Washington *Evening Star*, March 31, April 1, 1924; Hagerstown *Morning Herald*, April 1, 3, 1924.

[93] Washington *Sunday Star*, March 30, 1924; Washington *Evening Star*, April 2, 1924; Hagerstown *Morning Herald*, April 1, 1924.

[94] Reports of the Trustees for 1922, 1923, and 1924, and for 1925 and 1926, filed February 6, 1925, and May 6, 1927, respectively, Canal Cases.

[95] United States of America *vs.* the Chesapeake and Ohio Canal Company, Supreme Court of the District of Columbia, in Equity, Spring term, 1935. The court chose to adopt this interpretation, in line with the decision in Canton Company *vs.* the Baltimore and Ohio Railroad Company, on the grounds that abandonment is a matter of intention, not appearance. The decision is interesting in view of the 20th section of the canal company's charter which states: "And if, after the completion of the said canal and locks, the president and directors shall fail to keep the same in repair for twelve months at any time, then, in like manner, the interest of the company in the navigation and tolls shall cease, and their charter be forfeited."

put into navigable condition if trade were offered—even after dams and feeders filled up and washed out, locks and lock-houses deteriorated into a hopelessly unusable condition, and saplings two, three, and four inches in diameter grew in the trunk, destroying the puddling and often obscuring the canal itself.

After the obvious abandonment of the canal, except for purposes of legal fiction, speculation again broke out as to the future of the historic old relic. This time most proposals centered on the purchase of the right of way, or at least part of it, by the federal government. Early plans called for the construction of a scenic highway in place of the canal, perhaps as a continuation of the George Washington Memorial Parkway from Mt. Vernon to Great Falls.[96] Another suggestion called for the conversion of the canal into a fish and wild-life refuge.[97] The government was still interested in the mole for the extension of the Rock Creek and Potomac Parkway.[98]

The attitude of the Baltimore and Ohio towards the discussion over the future of the waterway was typical of its dealings with the canal.[99] For the most part, it waited and said nothing. Officially its position was that the canal was not abandoned, and it successfully defended this contention in court. It was determined that if any sale were made the contract should guarantee that under no circumstances would the canal fall into the hands of a competitor. Once again, the railroad gave

[96] Much of the early material in George Washington Memorial Parkway Commission, File 500-10, Section 1, contains discussions, proposals, and action looking toward the acquisition of at least a part of the canal bed for a highway. See also Blanche C. Howlett, "Great Boulevard from Capital May Follow Old Canal Course," Washington *Evening Star*, May 15, 1925; *ibid.*, August 6, 1926; and Washington *Post*, August 8, 1926.

[97] The idea of converting the canal into a wild-life sanctuary persisted as late as 1938. See Charles J. Smith to the Director, MS, National Parks Service, February 7, 1938, National Capital Parks, File 1460 (Chesapeake and Ohio Canal), Section 1.

[98] U. S. Grant 3rd to R. Walton Moore, February 15, 1929, MS, George Washington Memorial Parkway Commission, File 500-10. See also "Informational Material in *re* Chesapeake and Ohio Canal," MS, Records of the Rock Creek and Potomac Parkway Commission.

[99] On the attitude of the Baltimore and Ohio, see the MS account of an interview with Nicolson in the office memorandum of Fred G. Coldren, Secretary, Park and Planning Commission, November, 1926, George Washington Memorial Parkway Commission, File 500-10, Section 2.

evidence of its abiding fear of the threat to its business represented by the canal, a fear that was exaggerated in the thinking of Baltimore and Ohio officials beyond any possible injury which a competing line along the canal bed could cause. If the waterway was sold, the Baltimore and Ohio wanted a good price for the magnificent wreck.

The interest of the federal government in the acquisition of the Chesapeake and Ohio Canal was limited at first to the section between Rock Creek and Point of Rocks. Only gradually did the idea of buying the entire canal and restoring it as a national park and a historic shrine gain widespread acceptance.[100] Early negotiations, in 1934, were conducted in reference to the canal below Point of Rocks. The cost of that section was estimated at between $1,250,000 and $1,500,000.[101] While the project worked itself out, the government took steps to improve its bargaining position. In 1936 it sought unsuccessfully to establish that the canal was no longer a going concern, and therefore was subject to the forfeiture of its rights.[102]

At this point, a new development altered the picture and reversed the relative position of the government and the railroad. The Baltimore and Ohio, hard hit by the depression in the thirties, applied to the Reconstruction Finance Corporation in December, 1937, for an additional loan.[103] As collateral for this increased indebtedness, the railroad company scraped the bottom of its property holdings and produced along with other security the title to the Chesapeake and Ohio Canal. On February 1, 1938, the credentials officially changed hands.[104] The railroad expressed itself willing to dispose of the entire canal

[100] On the development of the idea of buying the entire, see the brief history of federal interest in the project, in "Memorandum on the Chesapeake and Ohio Canal Company," MS, George Washington Memorial Parkway Commission, File 500-10, Section 2.

[101] F. A. Delano to the Secretary of the Interior, December 26, 1934, referring to a recent conference with President Willard of the Baltimore and Ohio. See also A. B. Cammerer to Frank C. Wright, May 2, 1938, *ibid.*, Section 1. Mr. Cammerer reported that the Commission had no plans for the acquisition of the canal above Point of Rocks.

[102] T. S. Settle to Mr. Delano, April 2, 1936, *ibid.*, Section 1.

[103] Memorandum from T. S. Settle to Delano, December 29, 1937, *ibid.*, Section 2.

[104] Frank C. Wright to Harold L. Ickes, February 1, 1938, *ibid.*, Section 2.

for $2,500,000 or $3,000,000. The proceeds of the transaction would be applied to its $80,000,000 debt to the Reconstruction Finance Corporation.[105] After several months of negotiation the transfer was finally agreed upon for approximately $2,000,000.[106] Ownership formally changed hands in September, 1938. After almost exactly one hundred years the United States again found itself in control of the canal.

The federal government promptly set about to restore the waterway as a scenic natural recreation area.[107] As an experiment, it planned first merely to reconstruct the twenty-two miles to Dam No. 2 at Seneca. Eventually it would continue to work on up the canal to Cumberland. A threat to the ultimate restoration of the entire canal was disclosed almost immediately. Some of the reservations which the Baltimore and Ohio had made in the contract of sale related to certain parcels of land at Point of Rocks, which the railroad conceived to be essential to its future welfare as the site of additional tracks. The effect of these reservations would have been to exclude any practicable room for the canal and to render the complete reconstruction of the waterway impossible. The matter is not as yet settled, but for once it is the government and not the railroad which is employing the delaying tactics.[108]

The dedication of the canal as a public park was celebrated on Washington's Birthday, 1939, with appropriate ceremonies in which the leading participant was Mutt, a thirty-eight year old canal mule.[109] The canal was opened as far as Seneca in

[105] *Ibid.* The debt of the Baltimore and Ohio to the Reconstruction Finance Corporation on December 29, 1937, was $79,842,923. The additional loan, secured in February, 1938, was for $8,233,000. See the memorandum from Settle to Delano, December 29, 1937.

[106] Contract of sale, Trustees of the Chesapeake and Ohio Canal Company to the United States of America, August 6, 1938, *ibid.*, Section 2; press release, August 12, 1938, National Capital Parks, File 1460, Section 1. The courts in Hagerstown and Washington approved the sale by September 22, 1938. T. S. Settle to Delano, September 22, 1938, George Washington Memorial Parkway Commission, File 500-10, Section 2; press release September 26, 1938, National Capital Parks, File 1460, Section 1.

[107] The National Resources Committee estimated it would cost $9,000,000 to restore the canal. Washington *Times*, February 5, 1937.

[108] See MS, National Capital Parks, File 1460, Sections 1 and 2, especially Finch to Finnan, February 21, 1939, Hartz to Demaray, July 2, 1940, Hartz to Ickes, September 14, 1940, Hartz to Demaray, January 14, 1941.

[109] MS, memorandum from Demaray to the Secretary of the Interior, January 27, 1939; Memorandum to Miss Ryan, February 24, 1939; *ibid.*, Section 1.

August, 1940.[110] As of old, the river rose to meet the challenge. In September it tested the scientifically reconstructed canal during a minor flood that caused some damage. The engineers, highly satisfied with the quality of their work, quickly made the necessary repairs. In 1942, the Potomac rose again and smashed the canal back into the wrecked condition in which the government had found it. Due to wartime conditions nothing has been done to restore the waterway since 1942. Park officials insist that ultimately it can and will be done. But older and wiser canal and river people sadly shake their heads.

[110] Press release, August 9, 1940, *ibid.*, Section 1.

Chapter XIII

THE HISTORICAL SIGNIFICANCE OF THE CANAL

The Chesapeake and Ohio Canal was the third and last effort to construct an all-water route to the West via the Potomac valley. The project for a permanent, artificial waterway to the Ohio was the direct outgrowth of the earlier attempts of the Ohio Company and the Potomac Company to utilize the river as a highway for the frontier trade. The canal company profited from the achievements and the errors of its predecessors and endeavored to carry their program of improvements to its logical culmination. Because of its role in the development of the central route between East and West, the Chesapeake and Ohio's chronicle forms an important chapter in the history of commerce and transportation in the eastern United States.

The project is also significant as a case study in the history of canal-building. Its experiences closely parallel those of the other major East-West canals in conception, construction, operation, and abandonment. The analysis of the reasons for the abandonment of the waterway is especially valuable as an indication of the causes for the general decline of canals in America. But the history of the waterway has a significance of its own, beyond that of its role as a case study. Throughout its existence the Chesapeake and Ohio stood in intimate relationship to great national movements and events. The course of canal fortunes thus reflects many aspects of the political and economic development of the nation. Finally, for almost a century the waterway was a major factor in the daily lives of the people and in the growth of the country through which it passed.

The origins, planning, and organization of the Chesapeake and Ohio Canal afford many clues as to the motives and support of the early proposals for western connections. The various projects for the improvement of the Potomac as a channel for trade originated in the rivalry between the merchants and capitalists of the Eastern seaports. Western merchants and farmers lent enthusiastic suport to the proposals on the whole, but the impetus and the capital came from Eastern sources. The canal as an object of capital investment by Eastern financiers reflects the contemporary faith of merchant capitalists in the profit-making potentialities of trade and of transportation agencies. Yet private support was insufficient for the realization of the projected improvement on the ambitious scale which characterized all such schemes in the early nineteenth century.[1] Hence public support was necessary. From the very beginning promoters of public works sought government capital and along with state and federal subscriptions went active participation in, and control of, the enterprise by the governments concerned. Thus there was a close relationship between the state and private enterprise engaged in internal improvements in this legendary age of laissez faire. Finally, the successful organization of this canal company in the years following the War of 1812 is but one example of the widespread interest in internal improvements and the Western trade which characterized the period.

The experiences of the Chesapeake and Ohio Canal during the early years of construction continued to reflect the general pattern of the history of other artificial waterways. The canal company formally inaugurated its project with the assistance of a nationally prominent personage, in this case the President of the United States, at the usual colorful ceremonies on the Fourth of July. It immediately plunged into the race for the western waters in competition with rival works in other states, and, contrary to the general pattern, in the same state. Its rapid progress was interrupted by a series of obstacles arising from the undertaking of so large a work in a thinly populated country with insufficient engineering knowledge. Unexpected

[1] The plans of the promoters of the Chesapeake and Ohio Canal were based on an intimate knowledge of European canals. Unfortunately, the circumstances were not always identical. The Old World waterways were usually state works, constructed and improved over a long period of time. On the other hand, the Chesapeake and Ohio, in common with most American canals, was a privately-constructed work (with public support, it is true) which was expected to produce a handsome profit within a reasonably short time. In terms of the differing circumstances, the proposals for a sixty to eighty foot width, almost 400 locks, four mile tunnel, perfect original construction, etc., was not only ambitious, but obviously unrealistic.

obstacles in excavation, the shortage of workers, widespread ill health in certain seasons of the year, disputes with local proprietors over land damages, troubles with contractors over rising costs, and the ever-present financial difficulties of the company itself delayed the progress and increased the cost of this project as they did others. The period of actual construction was thus characterized by cycles of optimism and pessimism similar to those on other public works.

The operation and early trade of the canal prior to 1850 also were typical of the experiences of the competing artificial waterways before their completion. Its trade was primarily agricultural in character, as it depended on the farmers of the valley for its early business. Lumber and stone in large quantities also sought the cheap route to market provided by the waterway. In its operation the canal continued in close association with the state which sponsored it, especially in matters of special privileges, control of policy, and political interference. It nourished the development of a colorful and leisurely life along the waterway. It exercised a marked influence on the social and economic development of its region through the local prosperity which its construction and operation brought. It also bore an important relationship to the growth and prosperity of the Eastern ports it served. And, of course, the waterway suffered the annoying interruptions to trade resulting from the occurrence of breaches, droughts, and floods. Although the Chesapeake and Ohio differed from its contemporaries in Pennsylvania and New York in that it never reached the western waters nor developed a through trade, it continued to mirror their experiences after 1850 in the fluctuations of the business cycle. Even its collapse as a business enterprise coincided with the general decline of canals in the face of railroad competition.

In many respects the canal was a failure, especially as a financial venture. It failed to achieve its goal of a short, cheap route to the Ohio. The company never paid any return on the original investment of capital. Its waterway did not become a major transportation agency. The canal was not able even to maintain itself under the combined assault of nature and competitors. It is today merely a magnificent wreck, a historic relic, a quaint reminder of less sophisticated times—preserved for public recreational purposes. But even in failure the Chesapeake and Ohio Canal illustrates the operation of the causes which led to the abandonment or state operation of other waterways.

It is not difficult to analyze the reasons for its failure. On the contrary, it is much more difficult to explain fully why the collapse did not occur sooner. The principal reason for its ultimate failure both as a financial undertaking and as a public transportation agency was its inability to reach the Ohio River and thereby to establish a large through trade. Because of this failure, other factors assumed greater influence in the ultimate abandonment of the waterway. In the first place, the company which was organized to construct the canal soon became grossly over-capitalized. Furthermore, it was hindered from the critical early years to the last hours of its independent existence by political interference. Thirdly, it failed to solve the basic problems of technological improvement, and consequently became obsolete. It was unable to survive the competition of other carriers, particularly the railroads. The heavy and increasing floods in the Potomac valley made its existence particularly expensive and eventually drove it into bankruptcy. Lastly, the Cumberland coal fields, the basis of its prosperity, declined in productivity—depriving the canal of its only reason for existence.

As a result of the unexpectedly heavy cost of construction, the canal company was capitalized at an amount far beyond the limits dictated by a reasonable expectation of return. It was over-capitalized in terms of the probable revenue from trade and, to a lesser extent, the real value of its physical properties and improvements. Its financial fate was sealed by its failure to reach the western waters. The Potomac valley itself was too poor in the beginning to warrant the large expenditure for the canal, and its potentialities were too doubtful to justify it. The canal did not produce in its two best years an annual profit equal to more than 2 per cent of the actual cost of construction (*c.* $14,000,000 excluding interest and repairs). Yet, had the additional funds necessary to complete the waterway to the Ohio been available, the company still would, in all probability have been over-capitalized because of the high cost of construction. The canal was not large enough, physically, to accommodate a volume of trade sufficient to pay a satisfactory return on the larger sum. In addition, there was little room for expansion in the valley, an undertaking which in any case would only increase the amount on which a profit would have to be earned. The final blow to canal finances was the coincidence of the period of its construction with an era of inflation in the thirties, and the period of its greatest indebtedness with an era of general deflation in the seventies and eighties. The only solution for its financial troubles would have been state maintenance and operation as a public highway, like its famous rival, the Erie Canal.

Although the state of Maryland, unlike New York and Pennsylvania, was reluctant to assume financial responsibility for the waterway (and soon stopped all aid), political parties within the state repeatedly intervened in canal affairs at every stage of its existence. This continuing interference of political influence was another factor in the ultimate failure of the waterway. In the beginning, the state intervened, in the interest of the city of Baltimore and the Baltimore and Ohio Railroad, over the question of the route to be adopted by the rival works. As a result of this intervention, work on the canal was restricted for three and one-half years. In the meantime, the rising costs of labor and materials made the construction of the waterway more expensive when the company was able to resume operations. By the compromise of 1833, dictated by Maryland, the canal agreed to adopt a more expensive and exposed channel between Point of Rocks and Harpers Ferry. Thus its costs were increased at the same time that its future stability was endangered.

Political parties and pressure groups working through the state continued to influence the conduct of canal affairs after Maryland took over the control and financing of the company. Two examples of this interference are the successive political revolutions in the direction of the company in 1839 and 1841, and the long dispute over the state waiver proposal from 1841 to 1845. Perhaps the most serious consequence of this exercise of political influence was that it helped prevent the completion of the waterway before the frontier had moved farther west and before the completion of rival transportation lines had cut into its probable share of the Ohio trade. The Chesapeake and Ohio had no head start, as did the Erie Canal, in which to establish its route, pay the cost of construction, and develop its own region of exploitation. As a result, the enterprise lost the confidence and support of private capitalists who began to doubt that the canal would ever be completed in the face of repeated state interference or that its productive capacity would be sufficient after completion to insure a return on the investment, in view of its competitors.

After the canal was finally opened as far as Cumberland, political parties in Maryland intensified their interference in the management and operation of the waterway. The application of the spoils system to the canal company during the turbulent fifties and sixties brought rapid turnover in personnel which was detrimental to the efficient operation of the work. The president and directors of the company were chosen from among local party leaders, and lesser positions on the waterway were awarded to the party faithful. During the post-Civil War years, the political direction of canal affairs was characterized by corruption and frauds indicative of the low moral tone then generally prevalent in the state and the nation. The rapid rotation of canal employees under the spoils system came to an end only when the regular Democratic party gained control of the state in 1870. Although the canal positions continued to be used for party purposes, the dominance of A. P. Gorman and his party in state affairs brought a degree of stability and influence to the Chesapeake and Ohio during the later years of its independent existence.

The failure to provide for technological improvements in order to reduce the cost of transportation and avoid obsolescence was a third factor in the collapse of the canal. The problem of the improvement of its service had faced the Ohio Company and the Potomac Company and had been one reason for the failure of these predecessors of the Chesapeake and Ohio. As unimproved river travel had been supplanted by the system of improvements instituted by the Potomac Company, so the latter had given way in turn to the all-artificial waterway built by the canal company. To avoid the same fate in the struggle with railroads, the Chesapeake and Ohio would have to improve its service and lower its charges. The successive canal administrations were aware of the problem, but were unable to do anything about solving it. Early boards were hampered by a lack of financial means and by a limited view of their own responsibility. On the other hand, local entrepreneurs seemed unwilling to take the necessary risks. Later boards were restricted in their efforts by the staggering burden of debt. The great efforts made in the seventies illustrate the acuteness of the problem by that time and the clarity of perception on the part of the company; but the program of improvements was adopted too late to prolong measurably the life of the old ditch. Declining canal revenues would not support the rapid execution of the extensive undertakings proposed. In the meantime, the winding lower river was filling up at the same time that the length and draft of river and coastal steamers were increasing. Thus the canal faced another threat to its continued profitable existence, one for which there seemed to be no satisfactory solution.

A fourth cause of the abandonment of the canal was the competition of other forms of transportation. In the turnpike and plank-road era water transportation had been less expensive than overland travel. The ratio of costs was estimated to be as high as 8 to 1 in favor of the former as late as 1822. The coming of the railroad, however, and the continual improvements in its services made the iron horse a serious threat to the flesh-and-blood canal mule. In the wide spaces of the United States, the saving of time in rail transportation often more than made up for the slightly lower over-all cost of canal and river transportation. In the case of the Chesapeake and Ohio, the rivalry was most intense with the Baltimore and Ohio Railroad. The canal was an old, established form of transportation, inheriting its rights from its predecessor, the Potomac Company. The railroad, on the other hand, was a novelty in America, almost a freak. It faced the necessity of building its road and winning its spurs in competition with a powerful vested interest, with only the political and financial support of Maryland behind it. As it happened, after the end of federal assistance to the canal, the aid of the state became a decisive factor in the immediate welfare of the rival works.

The railroad and the canal fought each other constantly and at every point. The struggle over the right of way in the Potomac valley was followed by another for the trade of the Shenandoah and upper Potomac at Harpers Ferry. Later it was the flour trade and, later still, the business of the coal mines over which they clashed. The improvements in railroad transportation and the stronger financial condition of the Baltimore and Ohio placed it in a more favorable position to endure the bitter rate wars of the late 1870's and the 1880's. Eventually the canal company was driven into bankruptcy by the combined effects of the rate war which reduced its revenues and the disastrous floods of 1877, 1886, and 1889, which greatly increased its expenses. The railroad company emerged as the victor over the canal, securing control of the waterway in the course of the bankruptcy proceedings in 1890. The victory was complete, for the canal was never again a serious competitor of the railroad.

The fifth reason for the collapse of the canal was the recurrence of great floods which repeatedly wrecked the waterway. In fact, the forces of nature were continually at work tearing down the physical perfection of the old ditch and interfering with its trade. In the summer months, the drought in the Potomac valley would lower the volume of water in the river until navigation in the canal became hampered or even suspended. In the spring and fall of the year, freshets would wash quantities of soil from the banks, undermine culverts, and cause breaches in the walls. A heavy rain or a small freshet at any time was likely to wash sand bars into the waterway, cause land or rock slides, and fill the vital Rock Creek basin. The canal company was never able to cope effectively with these natural occurrences. The most careful and expensive preparations would be undone in a few days by a freak storm, an abnormal rise in the river, or a weakness at an unexpected spot.

But the worst of all the destructive forces of nature were the periodic floods in the Potomac valley. As the area became deforested and more and more ground was cleared for cultivation, the run-off became greater and swifter. At the same time, the Potomac was filling up as a result of the deposits of silt in its bed; and the canal and the railroads were encroaching on the river channel at many points, particularly at the narrow passes of the stream. As a result of these developments, the major floods in the valley became increasingly ferocious and destructive. Repairs and improvements to the waterway based on the experience of earlier disasters proved insufficient to withstand the ever higher crests that swept down the river. On top of everything else, the floods were completely irregular and unpredictable.

The great floods of the seventies and eighties occurred at a most inopportune time. The canal company was hard pressed financially; it was meeting the most severe competition in its history from the railroads; and it faced the necessity of undertaking an extensive program of improvements. The floods struck the waterway a heavy blow on all three points. They reduced company income and increased expenses, rendered its transportation services highly irregular and unreliable, and forced the suspension of the program of improvements. The canal never recovered.

The final cause of the failure of the Chesapeake and Ohio Canal was the exhaustion of the western Maryland coal fields. There had never been a large amount of through commerce from east to west on the canal. Furthermore, the railroad had succeeded in winning the flour trade away, and the deforestation of the area threatened the ultimate decline of the lumber business. Thus the canal was left totally dependent upon the transportation of coal for a profitable existence. In the early years of the waterway, the Cumberland fields had been spoken of as inexhaustible, but after a century of exploitation, the fields had fallen in productivity until other mining regions could supply more coal at less expense. The western Maryland fields therefore began to give way to the newer areas, particularly in West Virginia. The canal, unable to follow the migration of the coal industry into the new fields, faced the threat of the loss of this business. In view of its dependence on the coal trade, this factor would have been decisive in the long run. As it was, however, it proved to be anti-climactic, for the most serious consequences of the decline of the Cumberland coal region were felt after the canal company had become bankrupt and after the waterway was no longer a major factor in the coal trade of that region.

In addition to its value as a case study in the history of artificial waterways, the chronicle of the Chesapeake and Ohio Canal has a national and local significance worthy of note. The relationship between the fortunes of the waterway and trends and events in the history of the nation was very close throughout its existence. In the earliest period, the concern of its promoters with the proposed connection with the western waters indicates that as late as 1828 there was still an opportunity to capture a large share of the Ohio trade. This was still a great national project after the completion of the Erie Canal, and there would have been far-reaching consequences in the economic development of the country and of the valley if the central route could have been opened at this early date.

The close relations of canal affairs to national movements was also demonstrated in the Jacksonian era. The early support of the project by the United States revived the old question of the proper policy for the federal government towards works of internal improvement. This in turn raised matters of the relations between the general government and private companies, the promotion of public utility monopolies by federal or state governments, and the creation of federally-sponsored powerful corporations in a field claimed by private enterprise. The Jacksonian Democrats solved all the problems by simply withdrawing aid and control from all companies in which the United States was interested or in which its assistance was sought.

Even after the canal was reduced to the position of a purely local transportation line, it continued to mirror in its history the general course of national development. The most obvious example of this close relationship between canal fortunes and national events was the role of the waterway in the vital border struggles of the Civil War. Its volume of trade also reflected the economic crises which followed major crop failures in the predominantly agricultural pre-Civil War epoch and the prosperity of the coal trade during the tremendous expansion of industry after the war. These instances are by no means exceptions to the general rule. The canal continued to experience the inflations and deflations, the wars and political revolutions, and the cycles of prosperity and depression which mark the development of the nation.

For most of its existence, however, the canal was primarily a regional transportation line. As such its principal significance is the influence it had on the life and prosperity of the valley. In general the waterway both deliberately and unconsciously promoted the economic development of the area. The directors sought to stimulate agriculture by providing a cheap means of transportation to the markets and by setting special low rates on manure and other fertilizers. The company encouraged the growth of small industries in the leading valley towns by the judicious disposal of water power from the river through the canal. It fostered the establishment and expansion of commercial centers as the focal points of local trade. Finally, the mere existence of the waterway gave ample opportunity for the creation of small businesses in related activities.

The greatest contribution of the canal to the economic progress of the Potomac valley is its share in the development of western Maryland and the commercial prosperity of Georgetown. Inasmuch as its influence on the growth of western Maryland and the rise of Georgetown was largely economic and social, many of the generalizations about its relation to the valley as a whole apply with particular force to these areas. The canal meant success and prestige to certain sections and certain persons within these centers. For the farmers it meant increased wealth through heavy land damages, and enhanced real-estate values. The waterway also provided the opportunity for the expansion of this wealth by affording cheap transportation to the local markets. To the mine owners and the large shippers the canal was important primarily as a trade channel. To the merchants and manufacturers of the District of Columbia it meant a cheap supply of raw materials, of food for their employees, and of power. The waterway was partly responsible for the growth of small towns along its banks in western Maryland, and for much of the local prosperity which its trade and boatmen brought to the town merchants. At some points, at Williamsport and Georgetown, for example, the company sponsored marked industrial activity.

Canal affairs exerted an important influence on the history of Maryland. Perhaps the most significant in the long run was the relationship between the canal and the growth of western Maryland. The canal also caused repercussions in state finances, for the major burden of the cost of construction fell upon Maryland. The expense of the construction and operation of the canal almost wrecked the state's credit, for the canal company never paid a direct return on most of the assistance granted by Maryland. Indirectly the canal became an influence in state politics. The financial position of Maryland became so acute in the thirties and forties that a candidate's stand on the question of state credit and the related question of the future of the canal often meant the difference between his success or failure. Eventually, the company began to take active part in state affairs in order to offset the influence of the Baltimore and Ohio Railroad. Finally, the canal itself became a political issue, dividing both the state and the parties.

After its completion the relationship between canal and the state became more intimate. The company, with its large number of employees, was incorporated into the state spoils system. Thereafter, its positions were filled by party followers as reward for their services. Its higher offices were used to train or to reward state political figures. The most famous product of the canal patronage was A. P. Gorman, state Democratic boss, United States Senator, and aspirant to the Democratic presidential nomination in 1892. All canal presidents after 1850 achieved prominence in state political circles, if only because of the large patronage they controlled.

Almost as important in the development of the region as the canal itself were its related activities. These provided a subsistence (and often a profitable one) for many more persons than those immediately connected with the waterway. The most important of these subsidiary occupations was boatbuilding and repair. Later, feed stores became a large and prosperous calling for other inhabitants. Merchants in the canal towns benefited from the trade of the boatmen and travelers as well as that of the canal employees. Owners of warehouses and wharf facilities shared richly in the prosperity created by the grain and coal trade. Countless others profited indirectly from the existence of the canal.

The picture, however, is yet incomplete. The canal meant still more to the local inhabitants. It had become a part of the everyday life of the valley. It was more than just a way to make a living, although that was important. For many of the valley folk it was the only means of communication with the outside world. Road networks were keyed to it, just as they were elsewhere to the turnpikes and the railroads. The canal provided companionship and rivalry for the farmers and canallers, performing to an even greater extent the function of the country road and crossroads store in rural America. It was the setting of all the drama associated with the workaday occurrences on the old ditch. It became, in fact, part of the folklore and legend of the valley, celebrated in song and story.

BIBLIOGRAPHICAL NOTE

Materials relevant to the history of the Chesapeake and Ohio Canal are quite numerous: the mere listing of known sources would require many pages. Fortunately there is neither the need nor the space for such a compilation here. A comprehensive review of the pertinent literature forms an appendix to my dissertation, manuscript copies of which are available in the University of Maryland Library and the Library of Congress. For those who wish to go beyond the references contained in the footnotes of this volume and in the pages to follow, the longer bibliography is recommended. The purpose of this note is to give the reader a description of the types of sources, the principal depositories for them, and an introduction to the nature of the materials.

There are five major categories of materials concerning the history of the canal. Perhaps the most important of these consists in the physical remains of the waterway and interviews with the few surviving canallers. A second group of primary sources includes the published and unpublished records of the canal company and other companies engaged in the early internal improvement projects. To supplement these there are two additional kinds of contemporary materials: official records and unofficial, or private, accounts. The former comprises federal, state, and local documents and legal papers, and the latter consists of personal archives, published speeches and letters, and newspaper reports. In the fifth category of sources are the secondary works: articles, monographs, and general histories.

The principal depositories of these materials are in the general neighborhood of the canal. The National Archives has the papers of the Potomac Company and the Chesapeake and Ohio Canal Company, as well as relevant governmental records. The Library of Congress possesses miscellaneous manuscript collections pertinent to the subject and the largest collection of printed materials on the history of the canal. The Department of the Interior has the official records concerning the history of the interest of the United States in the acquisition and restoration of the waterway. The Washington County Court House (Hagerstown, Maryland) has all the legal papers of the receivership period. Relevant newspaper files are scattered among the Library of Congress, the District of Columbia Public Library, the Enoch Pratt Free Library (Baltimore), the Burr Artz Library (Frederick), the Washington County Library (Hagerstown), and the Cumberland *Evening Times* office. Useful collections of printed materials can also be found in the libraries of the Bureau of Railway Statistics and the National University (Washington, D. C.), the University of Maryland (College Park), the Johns Hopkins University, the Maryland Historical Society, and the Peabody Institute (Baltimore). The Hall of Records, at Annapolis, contains pertinent state and county documents.

I. PHYSICAL SURVIVALS

The Canal

One of the most valuable sources of information for the history of the Chesapeake and Ohio Canal is the physical evidence which remains of the works undertaken by the several companies engaged in the construction of the waterway and related projects.

The canal itself is in a fair state of preservation for its entire length from Washington to Cumberland. Parts of it in the more exposed places such as Harpers Ferry have suffered heavy damage. For most of the distance, however, the trunk of the waterway is clearly discernible, though frequently bristling with saplings and shrubbery. The masonry is well preserved, a fact which is in itself a tribute to the care and excellence of its construction. The tunnel, aqueducts, culverts, and lock walls are in remarkably good condition, as are most of the stone lockhouses—some of which are still inhabited. Inevitably there has been extensive destruction from age, weather, and vandals. Wooden lockgates, frame lockhouses, and the boats themselves have decayed and crumbled. Temporary, makeshift repairs of the aqueducts, culverts, and other masonry works have not stood up so well. Some appurtenances of the canal have disappeared entirely. The basins at Rock Creek, on the waterway itself, and at Cumberland have been largely filled in by the action of natural and human agencies. The wharves and warehouses along the canal have long since vanished, although ruins, descriptions, and old pictures suffice to indicate the type, location, methods, and facilities then in use. All in all there remains ample evidence to study at first hand the engineering and building of the waterway, and to reconstruct some of the problems of construction and operation which the records mention so frequently. Above all, some of the physical background of the canal and the area it penetrated can readily be pictured from the evidence available. From Dam No. 1, at Little Falls, to Georgetown, the canal is still in operation as a mill race.

The works of the predecessor company, the Potomac Company, are unfortunately not in such a fine state of preservation. The best evidence still discernible is the canal and locks at Great Falls. There, the deep, narrow locks and the curious shute which was blasted from solid rock over one hundred feet thick bear witness to the magnitude of the task undertaken and the perseverance of its promoters. The trunk itself has been filled in and has produced a fine growth of trees and shrubs so as to be barely recognizable in places. Skeleton walls of two buildings, one of them reputedly the old jail, standing in the midst of a young forest are all that remain to indicate where the projected town of Mathildaville was planned, partially built, and then forgotten. Farther up the river the old government canal at Harpers Ferry is still in use as a mill race. Near the headwaters of the Potomac, in West Virginia, an old boat was discovered recently which is probably similar in style to the long, narrow craft which essayed to make the round trip on the Potomac. The rafts built for the trip downstream have, of course, long since disappeared.

Of the several branches from the Chesapeake and Ohio Canal but little evidence remains. The Washington branch vanished during the westward expansion of the city and the resultant encroachment on the river itself. The Washington Canal has been closed over, along with the Tiber and James Creeks, and is now a sewer, its course marked only by such names as "Canal Street." The Alexandria Canal was visible from the air until a short time ago. The piers of the old aqueduct bridge across the Potomac still stand in the river bed, and enough of the northern abutment remains to give an impression of the size and quality of the work. Of the projected western section, the best indication of its proposed course is the main line of the Baltimore and Ohio Railroad from Cumberland to Pittsburgh. According to the army engineers in 1874-1875 the railroad occupies the identical route surveyed for the canal, with the exception of the ambitious tunnel on the summit level.

The Canallers

In addition to the direct evidence supplied by viewing the physical remains of the waterway, there are a few former officials, employees, and boatmen still living in the valley. Interviews with these individuals provide a valuable insight into life on the canal in its declining years. Human memory is fallible, but the reminiscences of these people supply details and color which add a human touch to canal affairs and which cannot easily be obtained from other sources. The most profitable interview was that with Mr. George L. Nicholson, former superintendent of the canal, who supplied general information on the policies and administrative experiences of the company. Ex-canallers, valley citizens, and railroad employees added much incidental information, mostly concerning every-day life on the waterway.

II. COMPANY RECORDS

Unpublished Archives

The most important sources for the entire history of the canal and its predecessors are the private records of the canal company and the Potomac Company. These provide a continuous narrative of the project from the best informed and most reliable materials. Included in these archives are the minutes of the stockholders' and directors' meetings; the annual reports (to 1853); correspondence; manifests, ledgers, payrolls, and other financial documents; reports of engineers and superintendents; legal papers; and other miscellaneous materials. With a few exceptions the records are complete, and are deposited in the Department of Interior Archives of the National Archives. There are some papers of the canal company and the District cities deposited in the Manuscripts Division of the Library of Congress, along with several papers of the Alexandria Canal Company. The most serious gap in the collection occurs during the Gorman administration in the seventies. Many letters, ledgers, and a letter book for this period were taken from the Canal Office by Senator Gorman and reputedly destroyed by the fire which razed his home near Laurel, Maryland.

Published materials

To supplement these manuscript records there is a considerable body of published materials of all the internal improvement companies concerned. These include annual reports, special reports, published correspondence, and other pamphlets. They sometimes repeat, but frequently elaborate upon the information contained in the company archives. They proved to be an especially valuable source for the correspondence and views of the several railroad companies which are still active and which are reluctant to open their private archives to research on matters relating to the canal. Included in the list of companies whose published records contain information on the canal are the Alexandria Canal Company, the Baltimore and Ohio Railroad Company, the Chesapeake and Ohio Canal Company, the Washington Canal Company, the Western Maryland Railway Company, and the West Virginia Central and Pittsburgh Railroad Company.

III. OFFICIAL DOCUMENTS

Federal

There are two types of federal documents which proved to be valuable for the history of the canal: Congressional reports and departmental archives. The Congressional reports (almost a hundred of them) contain helpful summaries of certain episodes, provide valuable background material, and often contain in lengthy appendices many documents not available elsewhere. It is unnecessary to list the reports, for there is a fairly complete index in Ben Perley Poore, ed., *Descriptive Catalog of the Government Publications of the United States, 1774-1881* (Washington, 1885). The archives of the Treasury, War, Interior, and Commerce Departments all contain materials pertinent to the history of the canal. Of these the most important are the papers of the Engineer and Quartermaster Corps in the War Department, and the Rock Creek and Potomac Parkway Commission, the Park and Planning Commission, and the National Capital Parks records in the Interior Department. The latter pertain to the interest of the federal government in the acquisition of the canal during the years following the World War.

State and Local

State and local documents perform the same function in their fields that the Congressional reports do for the interest of the national government in the early progress of the canal project. The reports of the Maryland and Virginia legislative committees indicate and summarize the attitude of those states towards the Chesapeake and Ohio Canal and its many problems. Because of the dominant role of Maryland in canal affairs the papers of that state are particularly significant. Documents of the cities of Baltimore, Georgetown, Washington, and Alexandria make a similar contribution to the history of the canal on a local level. The proceedings of the various canal and internal improvement conventions in Washington, Baltimore, and Pittsburgh may also be included here as semi-official documents.

Legal

Court exhibits, sworn testimony, and judicial opinions and decisions form a third group of official documents. The canal company was involved in a multitude of cases in federal, District of Columbia, and state courts. The points in dispute covered the entire range of possibilities: land disputes, water power rights, financial claims, right-of-way disputes, and receivership controversies. These cases provide much the same type of materials that the government records do, that is, summaries of certain episodes, general information on the background of canal problems, and many documents not preserved elsewhere. The leading cases have already been cited in the footnotes; for references to the less important ones there are the standard indexes.

IV. CONTEMPORARY ACCOUNTS

Private Papers

The contribution of personal archives to the unfolding of canal history could have been invaluable. Unfortunately there are few collections of these papers in existence of any consequence in canal affairs. Not many of the men connected with the Potomac Company and the Chesapeake and Ohio Canal Company achieved a position of national prominence which might insure the preservation of their papers. The manuscripts of those who did have been largely lost or destroyed. George Washington's archives have been published in several editions, but most conveniently in John C. Fitzpatrick, ed., *The Writings of George Washington, from the Original Manuscript Sources* (37 vols., Washington, 1931-1944). The most promising of other collections, including Ohio Company papers, John Mason archives, and Charles F. Mercer documents, have been lost. It was last known to exist as a unit in Representative Mercer's home near Aldie, Virginia, on the eve of the Civil War. During the War the papers were dispersed or destroyed. Some of the Ohio Company records have since reappeared in Cleveland, Ohio. A fire which razed the home of A. P. Gorman near Laurel, Maryland, reputedly destroyed the most promising group of papers for the later years of the canal, along with some of the company archives. Less important for the history of the canal are the McFarland papers (now in the possession of Richard Wormser, New York), the Shriver papers (Maryland Historical Society Library), the Rush papers (many of which are in the Library of Congress), and others which may still exist in the Potomac valley.

Published Letters, Speeches, etc.

The place left unsatisfied by the paucity of private archives is partially filled by the existence of many personal papers which were published in pamphlet form during the early years of the nineteenth century. These materials serve much the same purpose for an earlier period that the interviews with living canallers did for the last years of the canal, that is, as the source of color, emphasis, opinion, and background. As in the case of the Congressional reports, there are too many pamphlets to mention individually, but in general they include: letters, speeches, statements, opinions, reports, journals, debates, and descriptions of the waterway by canal officials and promoters, state and local political and financial leaders, travellers, and engineers.

Newspapers

Local newspapers form a third contemporary source of information on the background and history of the canal project. The early papers proved to be of great value in setting the scene in which canal affairs took place. They were not so good for news of the waterway itself, however, for the standards of reporting were not too high. In general, editors relied upon local canal officials and letters from friends for their information and copied one another's reports. By the end of the nineteenth century a marked improvement in the quality of reporting had taken place, and by 1889 the papers supplied much more news about the canal itself. The most valuable periodical for the period up to 1849 was *Niles' Register.* The large metropolitan dailies in Baltimore and Washington were useful, particularly the Baltimore *American*, the Baltimore *Sun*, the Washington *National Intelligencer*, and the Washington *Evening Star*. Reports in local newspapers in Annapolis, Frederick, Hagerstown, Williamsport, Hancock, and Cumberland helped round out the story. A complete list of the papers and their principal depositories is contained in Winifred Gregory, ed., *American Newspapers, 1821-1936, A Union List of Files Available in the United States and Canada* (New York, 1937).

V. SECONDARY ACCOUNTS

Articles and Monographs

A few articles supplied information on certain incidents relating to canal history or contributed critical analyses of some aspects of it. In the main, however, this function was performed by the very able monographs on various phases of the history of the Potomac route. The latter aided the progress of this work by organizational and bibliographical leads which were of great help. Inasmuch as the principal studies have already been mentioned in the first chapter there is no need for repetition here. It is sufficient to add that although these earlier works have been considerably supplemented by other materials in this volume, this in no way denies the assistance which they provided in the early stages of research.

General Histories

Last in the long list of materials containing information on canal affairs are the more general accounts. These include histories of transportation, state and local chronicles, and miscellaneous works. They supplied the necessary background, a sense of continuity, and a brief summary of the significance of the canal in the long sweep of American history. Unfortunately, few of the more general volumes adequately fulfill their function.

Of the general histories of transportation which were useful for this study, Seymour Dunbar's *History of Travel in America* (4 vols. in 1,

New York, 1937), is the best and most interesting. Of the older works Henry S. Tanner, *A Description of the Canals and Rail Roads of the United States* (New York, 1840), and John L. Ringwalt, *Development of the Transportation Systems in the United States* (Philadelphia, 1888) are very good. Balthasar H. Meyer and Caroline MacGill, *History of Transportation in the United States Before 1860* (Washington, 1917) is amazingly confused and inaccurate in its account of the early history of the canal. Archer B. Hulbert, *Historic Highways of America* (16 vols., Cleveland, 1902-1905), especially volumes 13 and 14, *The Great American Canals*, and the very readable volume by Alvin F. Harlow, *Old Towpaths* (New York, 1927), are good in their fields.

There are few histories of the individual canals, and none at all of recent date. Noble E. Whitford's *History of the Canal System of the State of New York . . .* (2 vols., New York, 1906), and his *History of the Barge Canal of New York State* (Albany, 1922) are still the best on the Erie Canal. On the Pennsylvania Canal, T. B. Klein, *The Canals of Pennsylvania and the System of Internal Improvements* (Harrisburg, 1901) is about the only notable work. The history of the Chesapeake and Ohio Canal is covered by the monographs and by the more general accounts noted above. Some of the latter, for example, Meyer and MacGill's volume and Hungerford's *Story of the Baltimore and Ohio Railroad* (2 vols., New York, 1928) are inaccurate in their information and incorrect in the impression they give of the early history of the waterway.

The state and local histories which are pertinent to the account of the canal are of unequal value. Some were very helpful, but most were of little or no use for the study and therefore not worthy of mention here. John Thomas Scharf, *History of Maryland from the Earliest Period to the Present Day* (3 vols., Baltimore, 1879) is still the best as far as it goes. The most recent volume, Matthew Page Andrews, *History of Maryland: Province and State* (New York, 1929), contains little information to use for the history of the canal, and is disappointing as a source of background material. The volume emphasizes the colonial and political aspects of the history of Maryland and the rise of the city of Baltimore and tends to neglect economic and social developments and the role of sections, particularly western Maryland, in the history of the state. Local chronicles that were especially valuable for this study were: Wilhelmus B. Bryan, *A History of the National Capital* (2 vols., New York, 1916); John Thomas Scharf, *History of Western Maryland* (2 vols., Philadelphia, 1882); Thomas J. C. Williams, *History of Washington County, Maryland . . . .* (2 vols., Chambersburg [?] 1906); and Will H. Lowdermilk, *History of Cumberland . . .* (Washington, 1878).

APPENDIX

TABLE I

PRESIDENTS OF THE POTOMAC COMPANY

1785-1828

	Elected to Office
1. George Washington	May, 1785
2. Thomas Johns(t)on	August, 1789
3. John Fitzgerald	September, 1793
4. Tobias Lear	August, 1797
5. James Keith	August, 1798
6. Charles Simms (Simmes, Semmes)	August, 1807
7. Elie Williams	August, 1815
8. John Mason	August, 1817

Source: Proceedings of the Stockholders of the Potomac Company.

TABLE II

PRESIDENTS OF THE CHESAPEAKE AND OHIO CANAL COMPANY

1828-1890

	Elected to Office
1. Charles Fenton Mercer	June, 1828
2. John H. Eaton	June, 1833
3. George C. Washington	June, 1834
4. Francis Thomas, Jr.	June, 1839
5. Michael C. Sprigg	April, 1841
6. William Gibbs McNeill	December, 1842
7. James M. Coale	August, 1843
8. Samuel Sprigg	February, 1851
9. William Grason	June, 1852
10. Samuel Hambleton	June, 1854
11. William P. Maulsby	June, 1855
12. Lawrence J. Brengle	March, 1858
13. James Fitzpatrick	May, 1860
14. Alfred Spates	January, 1861
15. Jacob Snively	June, 1865
16. Alfred Spates	August, 1867
17. Josiah Gordon	June, 1869
18. James C. Clarke	June, 1870
19. Arthur P. Gorman	June, 1872
20. Lewis C. Smith	August, 1882
21. L. Victor Baughman	December, 1884
22. Stephen Gambrill	January, 1888

Source: Proceedings of the Stockholders of the Chesapeake and Ohio Canal Company.

TABLE III

Potomac Company Trade

1800–1828

Year	No. Boats	Tonnage	Bbls. Flour	Bbls. Whiskey	Hhds. Tobacco	Tons Iron	Value Other Produce	Value Return Goods	Total Estimated Value	Tolls
1800	296	1,643	16,584	84	25	.....	$ 2,950.00	$ 7,851.00	$129,414.00	$ 2,138.58
1801	413	2,993	28,219	619½	100	187½	14,060.00	6,180.00	328,445.32	4,210.19
1802	305	1,952	17,250	379	5	238½	27,232.50	....	163,916.00	3,479.69
1803	493	5,549	45,055	257	32	480½	3,936.00	10,386.00	345,472.82	9,353.93
1804	426	3,823	39,350	578	8	88	3,250.00	7,514.00	284,040.60	7,765.58
1805	405	3,208	28,507	436	11	137	32,975.18	7,486.00	340,334.18	5,213.24
1806	203	1,226	19,097	459	5	20½	3,553.40	4,998.00	86,790.40	2,123.69
1807	573	8,155	85,248	971	20	35	11,796.00	7,314.00	551,896.47	15,080.42
1808	508	5,994	48,463	1,535	3	13	10,532.37	7,613.00	337,007.47	9,924.27
1809	603	6,767	40,039	1,527	37	494	8,537.00	11,510.00	305,625.00	9,094.89
1810	568	5,374	40,757	1,080	13	191½	5,703.00	....	318,237.62	7,915.85
1811	1300	16,350	118,222	3,768	27	200	6,810.00	6,000.00	925,074.80	22,542.89
1812	613	9,214	55,829	3,143	6	360	1,694.00	7,319.75	515,525.75	11,471.37
1813	623	7,916	55,902	3,464	11	252	1,899.00	6,119.32	423,350.32	11,816.22
1814	596	5,987	38,769	2,684	18	361	675.60	5,314.12	312,093.72	9,109.82
1815	613	6,354	47,183	4,616	9	314	2,075.00	5,211.15	489,493.15	9,789.57
1816	550	6,132	35,918	1,774	29	419	9,291.65	6,371.35	357,661.00	7,501.52
1817	856	8,197	57,662	1,385	10	335	4,094.00	14,000.00	787,994.00	13,948.23
1818	745	9,778	58,226	3,126½	2	428¾	8,750.00	15,124.00	681,924.75	10,332.26
1819	775	7,550	66,542½	1,479	...	278½	9,988.00	15,521.00	565,010.62½	12,514.04
1820	917	16,506	75,272	1,215	14	227½	16,587.95	12,230.00	420,818.15	13,107.31½
1821	760	11,400	67,557	1,391	10	115	11,515.00	10,027.00	318,810.00	12,490.61
1822										11,103.50
1823										6,238.85
1824										9,851.14
1825										9,843.35
1826										11,505.33
1827										10,821.78
1828										11,895.24

Year: August 1–July 31.

Sources; 17th Cong,, 1st sess., House of Representatives, Report No. 111, Appendix B(a), p. 12: Special Report on the Completion of the Canal, Appendix G, p. 148.

TABLE IV

CHESAPEAKE AND OHIO CANAL TRADE

1828–1924

Year	Tonnage	Coal	Flour	Wheat	Lumber	Corn	Tolls
From June, 1828, to October 31, 1830—Potomac Company works							$ 33,281,26
From November 1, 1830, to December 31, 1830—Potomac Company works							142.61
1830 (November 1 to December 31)—Chesapeake and Ohio canal							2,044.36
1831							32,992.66
1832							24,976.02
1833							16,663.49
1834							20,131.62
1835							26,568.15
1836							28,769.33
1837							26,702.49
1838							34,958.55
1839							47,865.94
1840							43,808.02
1841							57,012.29
1842		111,293 bu.	151,966 bbls.	214,569 bu.	916,184 bd. ft.	59,199 bu.	56,005.80
1843		2,108 tons	156,242	142,785	500,000	167,326	44,540.51
1844		4,871	172,796	199,620	1,000,000	173,023	52,674.24
1845		2,376	170,464	299,607	508,083	126,799	51,810.70
1846	60,147	1,952	234,539	264,115	2,851,541	30,005	53,357.24
1847	60,440	2,170	176,789	235,212	1,583,600	238,216	52,440.35
1848	86,436	3,284	217,112	220,025	2,080,600	144,103	54,146.21
1849	102,041	5,224	236,620	240,073	1,560,956	244,281	61,823.17
1850	101,950	7,956	27,120 tons	5,318 tons	2,765 tons	1,726 tons	64,442.02

TABLE IV—CONTINUED

Year	Tonnage	Coal	Flour	Wheat	Lumber	Corn	Tolls
1851	203,893	82,690 tons	25,761 tons	6,861 tons	2,736 tons	5,783 tons	$ 110,504.43
1852	167,595	63,289	26,755	9,805	2,640	4,755	92,248.90
1853	270,705	151,959	25,602	9,966	3,606	8,327	145,100.54
1854	235,923	145,319	15,643	5,417	2,588	2,618	119,306.03
1855	283,252	188,029	14,240	6,986	3,051	628	138,675.84
1856	287,836	205,568	14,853	9,017	3,209	6,893	153,051.56
1857	196,525	123,536	10,967	3,750	1,847	5,592	94,802.37
1858		254,684					171,085.97
1859	359,716	300,743	12,106	5,531	4,931	2,810	189,134.57
1860	344,532	283,249	11,087	5,452	2,593	3,048	182,343.86
1861	144,814	119,893	7,067	4,286	1,994	1,941	70,566.99
1862	126,793	94,819	7,340	6,640	1,693	1,027	63,985.85
1863	265,847	229,416	8,566	9,014	1,403	1,789	154,928.26
1864	290,772	260,368	5,962	6,168	1,248	1,914	225,897.34
1865	372,335	340,736	5,383	5,700	1,216	775	346,165.47
1866	383,408	344,160	2,620	4,946	1,852	6,307	355,660.76
1867	521,402	458,009	3,058	9,510	3,051	10,794	374,932.75
1868	552,987	484,849	2,120	9,164	2,936	5,502	276,978.71
1869	723,938	661,828	2,220	15,147	1,097	2,339	368,483.42
1870	661,772	606,707	1,845	11,710	968	2,929	342,644..40
1871	968,827	848,199	2,025	14,369	2,410	5,005	485,019.65
1872	923,581	814,365	980	8,416	1,761	3,844	459,654.59
1873	880,630	796,717	1,794	8,569	1,582	3,285	482,528.27
1874	909,959	836,996	1,526	9,780	1,102	5,312	500,416.24
1875	973,805	904,898	1,000	8,894	1,270	3,553	458,534.66
1876	709,112	654.409	734	11,754	1,696	6,723	290,274.39
1877	627,913	603,096	519	10,048	353	5,382	187,756.66
1878	662,508	630,290	604	14,005	1,665	2,489	282,181 18

TABLE IV—CONTINUED

Year	Coal Tonnage	Tolls
1879	522,904	$234,976.52
1880	615,423	361,757.68
1881	521,189	284,435.59
1882	316,648	143,730.76
1883	707,468	284,234.00
1884	378,352	135,693.59
1885	398,012	106,940.39
1886	295,415	81,718.73
1887	277,688	110,667.83
1888	286,183	121,218.27
1889 (May 31)	57,079	24,579.48
1890	No trade on canal	
1891	50,533	} 135,979.89
1892	265,799	}
1893	336,295	130,923.35
1894*	....	117,622.29
1895	....	116,728.40
1896–1905	No statistics available on tolls received	
1906	....	59,840.01
1907	....	64,425.92
1908	....	62,094.16
1909	183,694	59,105.66
1910	170,444	52,965.37
1911	166,463	43,924.73
1912	172,556	41,644.24
1913	176,491	41,407.71
1914	171,062	42,236.97
1915	173,997	41,271.46
1916	158,036	38,956.77
1917	151,667	40,545.74
1918	138,087	71,404.43
1919	133,529	47,346.95
1920	127,871	62,102.38
1921	66,477	42,017.33
1922	....	3,435.18
1923	56,404	31,899.32
1924	....	1,215.60

*No figures on tonnage are available from 1894 to 1908. Tolls given are after deduction for rebates.

Sources: Annual Reports, Reports of Trustees, and Ledgers.

TABLE V

RECEIPTS AND EXPENDITURES
1845–1936

Year	Receipts (All Sources)	Expenditures (Excluding Interest on 1844 Bonds)	
1845	$ 76,767.74	$ 50,830.35	
1846	59,351.98	60,670.65	
1847	93,569.73	96,557.95	
1848	57,366.13	69,770.28	
1849	65,438.13	97,024.46	
1850	88,310.00	160,124.46	
1851	153,829.63	241,794.71	(includes $119,956.54 interest)
1852	176,770.86	323,659.28	(includes 132,133.01 interest)
1853	150,091.30	108,082.71	
1854	124,108.02	120,945.89	
1855	143,182.87	252,587.10	(includes 146,502.25 interest)
1856	158,233.48	231,716.73	(includes 140,520.87 interest)
1857	99,590.69	365,872.24	(includes 143,892.61 interest)
1858	. . . . .	. . . . .	
1859	198,328.43	242,689.88	
1860	191,890.20	329,620.15	(includes 153,760.68 interest)
1861	75,741.90	256,207.82	(includes 154,002.19 interest)
1862	72,624.95	231,711.68	(includes 154,349.57 interest)
1863	163,024.10	250,208.82	(includes 155,808.49 interest)
1864	234,699.30	257,732.09	(includes 144,973.00 interest)
1865	359,734.56	307,547.56	(includes 146,375.77 interest)
1866	366,846.86	222,288.56	(ordinary expenditures only)
1867	385,034.83	210,772.98	(ordinary expenditures only)
1868	287,563.99	275,263.60	
1869	388,694.10	263,170.94	
1870	357,349.52	24[illegible],749.19	
1871	495,554.03	212,006.96	
1872	478,273.62	222,855.13	
1873	507,660.52	277,015.38	(includes 56,814.76 improvements)
1874	517,412.22	227,204.63	
1875	473,218.40	256,370.04	(includes 37,326.86 improvements)
1876	304,121.20	236,976.80	(includes 42,357.90 improvements)
1877	201,303.27	279,484.81	
1878	289,013.17	395,722.87	
1879	233,567.57	296,808.39	(ordinary expenditures only)
1880	372,616.07	287,084.78	
1881	305,096.82	262,491.26	
1882	169,802.67	212,167.93	
1883	329,527.07	250,964.30	
1884	151,316.40	202,536.12	
1885	135,929.06	184,667.10	
1886	94,138.19	223,414.99	
1887	129,206.82	174,294.52	
1888	129,469.87	126,769.90	

TABLE V—CONTINUED

Year	Receipts (All Sources)	Expenditures (Excluding Interest on 1844 Bonds)
1889	$ 29,918.17	$ 73,562.28
1891–92	140,746.17	568,763.65
1893	147,414.51	124,949.21
1894	150,926.34	117,292.80
1895	138,602.29	112,085.65
1896	121,444.93	117,423.47
1897	81,565.43	124,703.54
1898	71,563.43	87,599.89
1899	63,619.39	94,235.84
1900	86,728.08	98,303.41
1901	97,973.60	97,680.92
1902	83,977.69	120,544.14
1903	97,110.19	124,041.23
1904	93,618.89	117,181.89
1905	87,435.95	104,208.92
1906	74,855.86	113,936.09
1907	80,661.42	100,166.53
1908	77,767.93	119,516.96
1909	76,359.24	107,613.22
1910	69,371.79	108,222.71
1911	59,161.59	108,422.73
1912	57,575.58	100,433.62
1913	57,787.36	101,853.49
1914	58,404.22	114,698.25
1915	57,334.54	104,447.03
1916	55,793.77	109,270.64
1917	58,125.10	104,219.35
1918	89,287.11	136,152.18
1919	66,087.42	156,797.57
1920	81,935.97	174,746.02
1921	63,924.52	162,843.03
1922	25,674.58	120,197.45
1923	60,604.08	132,372.23
1924	31,338.30	146,592.14
1925	30,814.95	39,361.40
1926	31,724.53	63,864.08
1927	34,033.46	42,991.33
1928	36,888.86	43,982.97
1929	33,891.21	51,538.11
1930	41,692.39	46,425.81
1931	37,190.44	37,845.10
1932	40,138.07	34,756.71
1933	42,559.26	31,042.49
1934	35,233.90	54,189.06
1935	24,977.71	28,333.83

Sources: Annual Reports and Reports of Trustees.

TABLE VI

POTOMAC COMPANY TOLLS

Article	Unit	Toll
		s. d.
Domestic spirits	Hogshead	1/6
Tobacco	Hogshead	1/0
Linseed oil	Cask	1/3
Wheat, peas, beans, flax seed	Bushel	0/½
Corn	Bushel	0/¼
Flour	Barrel	0/3
Beef	Barrel	0/4
Pork	Barrel	0/6
Hemp, flax, potash	Ton	2/6
Mfd. iron; copper, lead, etc. (ores)	Ton	2/0
Iron ores and stone	Ton	0/5
Lime	Bushel	1/3
Coal	Chaldron	0/5
Staves (hhds. and bbls.)	Hundred	0/2¼, 0/1½
Plank	Hundred feet	0/10
Timber	Hundred feet	0/5½
Packaged goods	Hundredweight	0/1½
Boats	Each (except empties returning)	2/6

These tolls were collected at three points on the river, the mouth of South Branch, Payne's Falls (above Harpers Ferry), and Great Falls. At the latter place, double tolls were collected. Hence the total charges for navigating the entire river were four times the above rates.

For the purposes of collecting tolls, the following values were assigned to coins circulating in the colonies, in terms of pounds sterling.

Coin	Weight	Value
		£ s. d.
Spanish pieces of eight, or dollars		4/6
Silver coins, per ounce		5/1¾
English or French crowns		5/0
Johannes, 18 pennyweight		3/12/0
Half-Johannes, 9 pennyweight		1/16/0
Moidores, 6 pennyweight		1/ 7/0
English guineas, 5 pennyweight, 6 grains		1/ 1/0
French guineas, 5 pennyweight, 5 grains		1/ 0/10
Doubloons, 17 pennyweight		3/ 6/0
Spanish pistoles, 4 pennyweight		16/6
French pistoles, 4 pennyweight, 4 grains		16/4
Arabian chequins, 2 pennyweight, 3 grains		8/6
Other gold coins (except German), per pennyweight		4/0

Sources: Act of Virginia, October, 1784: Act of Maryland, Nov. Sess., 1784. See *Documents Relating to Chesapeake and Ohio Canal*, July 11, 1840, pp. 80-81, 105-106.

TABLE VII

TOLL RATES ON THE CHESAPEAKE AND OHIO CANAL

October 30, 1830—Tolls on the newly opened canal, from Little Falls to Seneca, fixed at the same rates heretofore charged by the Potomac Company at Great Falls.

Rates Established:	1834		1835		1841*		1851		1860	
Articles	1	2	1	2	1	2	1	2	1	2
Tobacco	2	2	2	1½	2	2	2	1	1	1
Wheat, rye, barley	2	2	2	1½	2	2	2	1	1	1
Flour	2	2	2	1½	2	2	2	1	1	1
Corn, corn meal	2	2	2	1½	2	2	2	1	1**	1**
Corn (on the ear)	..	..	2	2	..	..	2	1	1	1
Flax and other seed	2	2	2	2	..	..	2	1	1	1
Mill offals	2	2	1½	1½	..	..	1	1	..	..
Oats	2	2	2	2	..	..	1	1	..	..
Potatoes, turnips	2	2	1½	1½	2	2	1	1	..	..
Apples, peaches	2	2	2	2	..	..	2	1	1	1
Dried apples, peaches	..	..	2	2	..	..	2	1	1	1
Hemp, flax	2	2	2	2	..	..	2	1	1	1
Hay, straw	2	1	2	1	2	2	1	1	..	..
Whiskey, domestic spirits	2	2	2	2	..	..	2**	1**	1	1
Cider, ale, beer	2	2	2	2	..	..	2	1	1	1
Wine, foreign spirits	2	2	2	2	..	..	2	1	1	1
Fresh meat	..	..	1½	1½	2	2	2**	1**	1	1
Salted beef, pork etc.	2	2	2	1½	2	2	2**	1**	1	1
Bacon	..	..	2	2	..	..	2**	1**	1	1
Livestock	2	2	2	2	..	..	2	1	1	1
Fish (shad, herring)	2	1	2	1	2	2	2**	1**	1**	1**
Oysters	..	..	2	1½	..	..	1	1	..	..
Salt	2	2	1½	1½	2	2	1**	¾**	1**	½**
Dry goods, groceries	..	..	2	2	..	..	2	1	1	1
Other goods	2	2	2	2	..	..	2	1	1	1
Horses and carriages	..	..	2	2	..	..	2	1	1	1
Firewood	2	½	1½	½	..	..	1	¼	..	..
Tanners' bark	3	1	2	¾	..	..	1	¼	..	..
Plank	2	1	2	1	..	..	1	1	1**	¼**
Timber	2	1	1	½	..	..	1	½	..	..
Shingles, laths	2	1	2	1	..	..	1	1	1**	¼**
Staves, headings	2	1	2	1	..	..	1	1	1**	¼**
Fence rails, posts	..	..	1	½	..	..	1	½	..	..
Hoop poles	..	..	2	1½	..	..	1	1	..	..
Glass	..	..	2	2	..	..	2	1	1	1
Fire brick	..	..	..	..	..	..	1**	½**	..	..
Bricks, tiles, slates	..	..	1	1	..	..	1	1	..	..
Rough stone	1	½	1	½	..	..	1	½	..	..
Wrought stone	2	2	2	2	..	..	2	1	1	1
Lime	2	1	½	½	1	1	1	½	..	..
Limestone	..	..	⅓	⅓	..	..	¼	¼	..	..
Plaster, fertilizers	2	1	1½	1	2	2	¼	¼	..	..
Charcoal	2	1	2	1	..	..	1	1	..	..

*The rates established in 1841 were repealed in 1843, and the charges listed under 1835 were "generally" restored.

**In 1851, charges were established on February 28, 1851; in the 1860 column, charges established January 8, 1857.

TABLE VII—CONTINUED

Rates Established:	1834		1835		1841*		1851		1860	
Articles	1	2	1	2	1	2	1	2	1	2
Coke	2	1	2	1	..	..	¼	¼	..	..
Coal	1	½	½	½	1	1	¼	¼	..	..
Iron, other ores	..	..	½	½	..	..	¼	¼	..	..
Pig, scrap iron	2	2	1	1	..	..	1	¼	..	..
Hammered, rolled iron	..	..	2	2	..	..	2	1	1	1
Steel, lead, other metals	..	..	2	2	..	..	2	1	1	1
Packet boats	10	8	8	4	..	..	8	4	..	..
Freight boats	5	3	4	2	..	..	4	2	..	..
French burrs	..	..	1½	1½	..	..	..	..	..	..
Bricks, ice	..	..	..	.	..	..	1**	¼**	..	..
Railroad iron, castings	..	..	..	..	..	..	1	½	..	..
Sand, gravel, earth, clay	..	..	..	..	..	..	¼**	¼**	..	..

*The rates established in 1841 were repealed in 1843, and the charges listed under 1835 were "generally" restored.

**In 1851, charges were established on February 28, 1851; in the 1860 column, charges established January 8, 1857.

NOTES TO TABLE VII

The dates of adoption of the general toll lists were: April 4, 1834; April 23, 1835; March 15, 1841; May 3, 1843; June 2, 1851; August 15, 1860.

The rates given are those per ton per mile. Where there is no rate given the existing charges remained in force. Articles not specifically enumerated paid the toll required for "other goods."

The rate on lumber products in rafts was double the charges listed above.

Columns 1 and 2 for 1834, 1835, and 1841 are for the first 15 miles and for any distance thereafter, respectively. For 1851 and 1860, they are for the first 20 miles and for any distance thereafter, respectively.

The unit of measurement is the ton or its equivalent in bushels, barrels, hogsheads, cubic feet. The exceptions were some types of lumber which were measured in cords, and stone, for which perches were the standard form of measure. Livestock was computed at 3 cattle, 15 hogs, or 30 sheep to the ton, and 2 carts, 1 wagon, 10 plows, 2 two-wheeled carriages or 1 four-wheeled carriage (with two horses) equaled a ton. Other values (subject to some variation) included.

Tobacco—2 or 2½ hhds; Salt—45 bu. fine, 32 bu. coarse; Lime—28 bu.; Flour—10 or 10½ bbls.; Charcoal—56 bu.; Glass—2800 feet; Oats—80 bu.; Wheat, barley, buckwheat, rye, corn, cornmeal, potatoes, turnips, flaxseed—40 bu.; Mill offals—100 bu.; Apples and peaches—40 to 45 bu.; Wine—tun, 250 gal.; Whiskey, cider, beer, ale—6 to 8 bbls.; Stone and limestone—15 to 25 cu.ft.; Fish—8 bbls. or 600 shad or 4000 herring; Oysters—28 bu. or 4000; Firewood and bark—128 cu. ft. (cord); Plank—1000 board feet; Timber—70 cu. ft.; 3000 shingles, 5000 laths, 1000 staves and heads (barrels), 500 staves and heads (hogsheads), 100 fence rails or posts, 750 or 1000 hoop poles.

On May 17, 1876, the toll on flour and grains was reduced to ¼ cent per ton per mile from points between Williamsport and Weverton to Washington.

After 1860, however, the important revisions were those in the toll on coal, the major article of trade. The rate of ¼ cent per ton per mile in 1851 was equal to about 46 cents for the 184½ miles from Cumberland to Rock Creek. Major revisions included:

	Per ton per mile
April	10, 1863—5/16¢
April	15, 1864—3/8¢
June	28, 1864—½¢
September	5, 1866—4 mills
March	26, 1868—¼¢

Per Ton Cumberland to Rock Creek

February	13, 1873—51¢	
†January	13, 1875—46¢	(plus 5¢ wharfage)
†April	18, 1876—41¢	(plus 5¢ wharfage)
†April	10, 1877—33¢	(plus 3¢ wharfage)
August	21, 1877—22¢	(plus 3¢ wharfage)
†April	10, 1878—36¢	(plus 4¢ wharfage)
†April	14, 1880—51¢	(plus 4¢ wharfage)
†June	13, 1883—36¢	(plus 4¢ wharfage)
April	10, 1884—33¢	(plus 3¢ wharfage)
February	6, 1885—22¢	(plus 4¢ wharfage)
††March	4, 1887—36¢	(plus 4¢ wharfage)
April	21, 1887—30¢	(plus 4¢ wharfage)
††February	14, 1888—40¢	(plus 4¢ wharfage)
††..........	, 1891—40¢	(plus 4¢ wharfage)

† Less rebate of from 5 to 10 cents per ton to large shippers.
†† Less rebate of 6 cents in 1887, and 10 cents in 1888 ff. on coal shipped coastwise from Georgetown.

Sources: Proceedings of Directors and 4th Report District of Columbia Receivers.

TABLE VIII

FINANCES OF THE POTOMAC COMPANY

Capital Stock:		
701 Shares @ £100 ($444.44) each		$311,555.55
220—Maryland		
120—Virginia		
361—Individuals		
Original subscription: 500 shares @ £100 each, 1784		
Second subscription: 100 shares @ £130 each, 1796		
Third subscription: 130 shares @ £130 each, 1798		
Indebtedness August 1, 1821		$174,390.12¼
To Banks in District of Columbia	$102,578.22	
To the State of Maryland	38,250.00	
To sundry persons near: Cumberland	7,904.31¼	
Antietam	16,372.86	
Shenandoah	4,508.89	
Monocacy	3,775.84	
To sundry individuals	1,000.00	
Indebtedness: May 16, 1825 (date of Potomac Company's assent to the charter of the Chesapeake and Ohio Canal Company)		$176,400.00

Sources: 17th Congress, 1st Session, House of Representatives, Report No. 111. Appendix B1 and B(b), pp. 11 and 13; Proceedings of Directors of Potomac Company, C, 126.

TABLE IX

Finances of the Chesapeake and Ohio Canal Company

Statement of Debts of the Company, December 31, 1889 (Excluding Interest)

Capital Stock		$3,857,593.67
United States of America	$2,490,000.00	
(Includes $990,000 by United States, $1,000,000 by Washington, $250,000 by Georgetown, $250,000 by Alexandria)		
State of Maryland	625,000.00	
State of Virginia	250,000.00	
City of Shepherdstown, Va.	20,000.00	
Baltimore and Ohio Railroad	266,000.00	
Individuals	206,593.67	
1834 Loan (State of Maryland)		2,000,000.00
Preferred Stock (State of Maryland)		4,375,000.00
Preferred Construction Bonds (1844 Act)		1,699,000.00
Repair Bonds of 1878		500,000.00
Potomac Company Claims and Interest		76,047.03
Claims	$ 56,896.48	
Interest	19,150.55	
Potomac Company—Unclaimed Dividend		216.45
Post Notes (Interest Bearing)		365,955.00
1834	$ 550.00	
1837	385.00	
1839	5,180.00	
1840	359,840.00	
Post Notes Reissued		6,644.00
Bonds Issued for the Payment of Post Notes		5,758.00
Bonds Issued to Contractors		303,745.60
Acceptances Issued to Contractors		122,139.52
Certificates for Repairs Prior to 1845		1,235.59
Certificates to Creditors of Hunter, Harris		94,450.82
Certificates for Funded Coupons and Interest		146,840.44
Certificates for Tolls, 1860		333.30
Balances Due Contractors, Prior to 1881		84,468.87
Registered Debt and Interest		321,160.87
Debts	$ 187,216.85	
Interest	133,944.02	
Pay Roll, 1883-1889		109,871.93
1883	$ 1,429.98	
1884	2,735.03	
1886	3,750.00	
1887	18,987.43	
1888	37,064.29	
1889	45,905.20	

The total debts of the company in 1938 were listed as "over $26,500,000" including interest. Of this total, the claims of Maryland, then held by the Baltimore and Ohio Railroad, amounted to $16,747,245.

Sources: 2nd Report of Receivers, filed June 9, 1890, *G. S. Brown et al.* vs. *Chesapeake and Ohio Canal Company;* Memorandum: Rupert A. Suirel to Herndon T. Morsell, 1938, National Capital Parks, File 1460 (Chesapeake and Ohio Canal).

WESTERN
Freeport
PITTSBURG
EASTERN SECTION

MIDDLE
PORTION
PENNSYLVANIA LINE
MAP
of the country between
refering to the contemplated
GENERAL ROUTE AND PROFILE
WASHINGTON

INDEX

LaVergne, TN USA
16 November 2009
164312LV00004B/31/A